The Economist's Handbook: A Research and Writing Guide

The Economist's Handbook
A Research and Writing Guide

Thomas L. Wyrick

WEST PUBLISHING COMPANY

Minneapolis/St. Paul   New York   Los Angeles

EST'S COMMITMENT TO THE ENVIRONMENT

1906, West Publishing Company began recycling materials left over from the production books. This began a tradition of efficient and responsible use of resources. Today, up to percent of our legal books and 70 percent of our college and school texts are printed on ycled, acid-free stock. West also recycles nearly 22 million pounds of scrap paper nually—the equivalent of 181,717 trees. Since the 1960s, West has devised ways to ture and recycle waste inks, solvents, oils, and vapors created in the printing process. also recycle plastics of all kinds, wood, glass, corrugated cardboard, and batteries, and ve eliminated the use of Styrofoam book packaging. We at West are proud of the gevity and the scope of our commitment to the environment.

duction, Prepress, Printing and Binding by West Publishing Company.

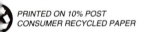

PRINTED ON 10% POST
CONSUMER RECYCLED PAPER

PYRIGHT © 1994   By WEST PUBLISHING COMPANY
610 Opperman Drive
P.O. Box 64526
St. Paul, MN 55164–0526

nted in the United States of America

00 99 98   8 7 6 5 4

rary of Congress Cataloging-in-Publication Data

rick, Thomas L.
The Economist's Handbook: A Research and Writing Guide / Thomas L. Wyrick.
    p.   cm.
Includes index.
ISBN 0-314-02803-X
1. Economics—Research.   I. Title.
74.5.W97   1994   94–200
'.072073—dc20   CIP

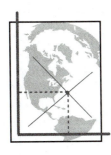

Table of Contents

Chapter 12   Reporting the Results of Economic Research   229

Appendices   A-1

Introduction to Economic Research

Tell me, I forget.
Show me, I remember.
Involve me, I understand.
—Ancient proverb

A combination of events has caused colleges and universities to develop research seminar courses in recent years. One is the increasingly career-oriented interests of students. A common complaint about the traditional economics degree has been that it is long on theory and short on practice. To satisfy the legitimate demands of their customers, economics departments now place greater emphasis on the application of economics than in the past. Second, the wide availability of computers has reduced the difficulty (lowered the cost) of writing and conducting quantitative research. Today most students have access to personal computers and software packages more advanced than were available to the best funded researchers a decade ago. Finally, budget pressures have caused officials in many states to adopt educational reforms that favor performance-based programs. Rather than fill students with as many new facts and theories as possible, universities have been making a greater effort to teach students how to engage in self-directed learning and study throughout their lives. This text is a guide for doing applied economic research. After reading the chapters and working through the end-of-chapter exercises you should be much better prepared for any career in which economics plays a significant role.

One model for the research seminar course was suggested by an essay written by W. Lee Hansen, a professor of economics at the University of Wisconsin.* In his essay, Hansen describes several skills, or "proficiencies," which he believes students—both undergraduate and graduate—should gain from their education. Hansen's list of desirable skills provides the outline for this text.

The *first proficiency* is the ability to gain access to existing knowledge. Suppose your employer asks you to prepare a brief report on inflation or interest rates during the past decade. Where would you begin? A

---

*W. Lee Hansen, "What Knowledge is Most Worth Knowing—For Economics Majors?" *American Economic Review* (May 1986), reprinted in Appendix 1 of this text.

practicing economist must be able to locate economic data and understand the methods used to compile them. In addition, one should be able to locate published research on a topic of interest. Researchers may already have done considerable work in the area you are investigating, so access to their work may answer your questions or point you in the right direction.

The *second proficiency* highlighted by Hansen is the ability to demonstrate command of existing knowledge. After locating published materials on some topic, one should be able to summarize that body of knowledge. How would you respond if asked to describe the current state of the economy, explain how economists use a key economic concept, or summarize a policy debate? Other than academics, few careers call for an economist to provide lengthy discussions of economic theories; many more jobs call for the economist to bring together and summarize what others have written.

The *third proficiency* is the ability to identify and discuss important economic concepts in academic journals and nontechnical publications. Whether you are reading a professional journal article or a weekly news magazine, you should be aware of key economic theories underlying the discussion. An article about water shortages in western states may not mention supply and demand or policies that depress water prices below their market-clearing level, but those issues should not escape the notice of a trained economist. In a professional journal article containing several economic concepts, you should be able to identify the one or two key concepts or theories that form the basis of the analysis. Having distinguished fundamental ideas from subsidiary concepts or facts, you should be prepared to explain their importance to the main argument.

The *fourth proficiency* is the ability to use existing knowledge to explore an issue of interest. Use background material, economic theories, and quantitative methods to conduct an in-depth study of some topic that you would like to know more about. This is not just a haphazard or random application of economic theory and statistical tools, but must follow certain conventions—our version of the scientific method—to increase the reliability and usefulness of the findings.

The following chapters contain numerous exercises, which will help you develop the skills identified by Professor Hansen. Only part of the material will be new to you—after all, the idea is to sharpen your ability to work with concepts, theories, and methods you are already familiar with. This text strives to help you develop independent research skills which you will be able to use in a variety of applications, so it is not enough to simply carry out each assignment in isolation. Along the way, consider how the techniques used to complete a particular exercise could be applied to another research project in the future.

Several appendices are included in this text, beginning on page A-1. In addition to research-oriented data and articles, some appendices also contain material of relevance to economists and the economics profession at large (e.g., information regarding careers in economics). The final appendix contains a glossary of terms that are frequently encountered by economists.

The quote on the following page suggests that economists approach issues from a perspective all their own. Successful economic research is not just a matter of including the required jargon and technical flourishes, although those are important, but it depends critically on the researcher's ability to "think like an economist." In addition to the four proficiencies discussed above, this text seeks to improve your ability to think like an economist.

The Goal of the Economics Major*

"Enabling students to develop a capacity to "think like an economist" is the overarching goal of the major. All other virtues follow. Thinking like an economist involves using chains of deductive reasoning in conjunction with simplified models (such as supply and demand, benefit-cost analysis, and comparative advantage) to illuminate economic phenomena. To some, economists tend to abstract too much from the richness of human behavior and reality; to many economists, the strength of our analysis is the provision of focus and clarity of thought; parsimonious models are a virtue, not a vice.

Thinking like an economist also involves identifying and evaluating tradeoffs in the context of constraints, distinguishing positive from normative analysis, and tracing behavioral implications of change while abstracting from aspects of reality. It, moreover, involves describing redistributive implications of change, amassing data to evaluate economic events, and testing hypotheses about how consumers and producers make choices and how the economy works. Finally, thinking like an economist involves examining many problems through a filter of efficiency—coping with limited resources.

Thinking like an economist requires creative skills, too. Identifying economic issues and problems, framing them in ways other people do not see, devising novel policy proposals for dealing with problems, analyzing both the intended and unintended effects of policies, and devising innovative methods to estimate the magnitude of these effects—all are as central to the discipline as is the development of logically coherent theories."

---

*John Siegfried et al., "The Goal of the Economics Major," *American Economic Review* (May 1991):21.

ACKNOWLEDGMENTS

During the preparation of this text I have benefited from the efforts and encouragement of many people. At West Educational Publishing, Clyde Perlee provided early support for the project and suggested the title that was ultimately chosen; Theresa O'Dell and Christine Henry coordinated the many different activities required to transform my unpolished manuscript into a readable textbook. Comments on an early draft of the manuscript were provided by Arthur Diamond (University of Nebraska, Omaha), Arlington Williams (Indiana University), Charles Becker (The Economics Institute, Colorado), David Cleeton (Oberlin College), Keith Rowley, and John Hoftyzer (Southwest Missouri State University). Many appendix items were contributed by John Hoftyzer and Larry Cox, colleagues of mine at Southwest Missouri State University. Permissions to reprint several items was provided by the publishers and authors, most notably, W. Lee Hansen. Finally, family members and close friends have provided moral support throughout the entire project. Their tolerance and encouragement have contributed much to the quality of the final product.

To the memory of
William Lee Atkins
(1953–1993)

PROFICIENCY **1**

The Ability to Gain Access to Existing Knowledge

The practicing economist should be able to gain access to existing knowledge—either data or published research. The economist should also understand some of the most commonly used methods of adjusting raw data to make it more meaningful. Chapters 1–3 develop these skills.

CHAPTER 1

Locating Economic Data

Published Data

The libraries of many colleges have a "government documents" section which contains a gold mine of economic data. Because of its taxing and regulating powers and economic stabilization responsibilities, governments have access to a wide range of economic data. Economists use much of this data in their research. Once a government agency collects a series of data it is not long until a document containing that data is acquired by your library. Accessing such documents has traditionally been done manually, but libraries have recently begun to add information about their book, periodical, and government document collections to computer database files. Such files, when combined with appropriate computer software, make it possible to conduct an exhaustive search of library resources in a few minutes. Even if your library does not use such equipment today, it probably will within the next few years.

Whether or not you have access to the latest generation of information technology, you should familiarize yourself with the resources available in your library. If you have not already had an official tour of the library —conducted by a library staff member rather than a fast walk-through with friends—then today would be a good time to take such a tour. Most librarians will appreciate the chance to show you around their library's research materials.

In general, the economic data in your library is contained in government documents, reference materials (such as almanacs and encyclopedias), current periodicals (newspapers and a few magazines), professional journals, and books. In practice, very little economic data are published in general-interest magazines, professional journals, or books. To economize on time, if you do not already know where to find a particular series of data it is wise to begin looking in your library's government documents or reference sections.

Before beginning your search for a specific data series, invest a minute or two in planning the search. The benefits of taking this "extra" step are best illustrated by considering a concrete example. *Suppose you are interested in learning the average person's income level.* Rather than immediately running to the library, consider a few issues that, if not addressed, can lead the inquiry astray. For example:

● What purpose is to be served by obtaining the information?

This is the first, and some would say the most important, question for an economic researcher to address. Many people begin a project with only a vague idea about what they intend to accomplish. The researcher who takes this approach may save a few minutes of planning time, but will waste time searching and be less likely to locate the desired information.

> Our plans miscarry because they have no aim. When a man does not know what harbor he is making for, no wind is the right wind.—*Seneca*

If the purpose of searching for average income data is to estimate the typical person's standard of living, then mean (average) income measures may not include all relevant information. Other factors that might influence the typical person's standard of living include transfer payments (gifts) received or personal property owned, such as a home or car. On the other hand, if you plan to use the income figure to estimate how much a typical person earns at work, then wage and salary income may be the relevant measure; other sources of income are not related to a worker's income-earning capacity. If the income figure is needed to compare the standard of living of a typical American to that of citizens of other countries, unadjusted income figures may not be of much practical use. Because goods can cost far more or far less in other countries than in the U.S., the researcher should use income figures that have been adjusted for differences in the cost of living in different countries. If the income figure will be used to compare the living standards of Americans today with those of earlier years, then both income levels should be adjusted for changes over time in the cost of living.

We could draw additional distinctions, but the idea is clear. The researcher has access to income figures that have been adjusted in many different ways, so one's purpose must be clearly defined before deciding which adjustment or which income measure is appropriate. A few of the most common adjustments ("transformations") made to economic data are discussed in Chapter 2.

A second part of your presearch planning is to identify imprecise terms in your research plan, then eliminate them. A lack of research experience or being in too much of a hurry may cause a researcher to spend time gathering information that ultimately proves not to be useful—or worse, misleading. To avoid these problems:

● Define the terms of your search.

What is meant by "the average person" whose income you want to know about? A simple average implies a per capita income measure, which is total income received by everyone divided by total population. Rather than a simple average, some researchers may prefer a *median* income measure, or the income of the person who is richer than half of the population and poorer than the other half. Since children spend far less than adults and because several people typically live together and share certain household expenses, perhaps the income of the average household would be a better measure of the typical person's standard of living.

Likewise, it is important to specify what you mean by the term "income." As noted earlier, the choice of an income definition should reflect one's purpose for collecting the data. If you are uncertain whether per capita GDP, national income, or personal income best suits your needs, leave all three on your list of possibilities. But you may be able to remove wage income, total compensation, median family income, and other income measures from your list. Research is partly an exercise in focusing on critical issues and ignoring less important ones. The more you can eliminate from consideration, the better.

Finally, it is easier to locate economic data if you look in the right place. Economic researchers sometimes stumble across useful data, but it is unwise to rely exclusively on serendipity (good luck) for one's data needs. Instead, ask yourself:

● What political jurisdiction, government agency, or private organization is most likely to collect the desired data?

If you are using data collected by someone else, then the figures you have access to will reflect the purposes of government agencies or private organizations that collect the data. Each agency has its special jurisdiction or area of interest, so by defining the domain over which the data applies it is much easier to identify particular organizations that might possess the information. For example, the president's economists mainly work with issues of national concern so the *Economic Report of the President* is likely to contain national economic data but not economic data for individual states and cities. The same logic suggests that the *Book of the States* will provide information for the fifty states but probably only limited information about cities, counties, or the nation as a whole. Following the same principle, crime statistics may be published by the FBI or the Justice Department and education statistics may be collected by the U.S. Department of Education. By searching in the right location, it is much easier to find what you are looking for.

A few agencies collect information on a wide range of topics. The U.S. Department of Commerce publishes one of the best reference guides available anywhere, the *Statistical Abstract of the U.S.* Published annually, the *Statistical Abstract* only contains data that has been published elsewhere. It is a collection of data from hundreds of different sources. Any time you are uncertain where to begin looking for information about a particular topic, turn to the *Statistical Abstract*. Even if it does not provide the specific figures you need, it will probably contain data on a closely related topic. Once you find a table of *related* data, the *footnote* for that table will provide a reference to the document or study from which the data were taken; the same document may contain the specific information you require. Even if it doesn't, the document will probably refer to additional articles or books that suit your purpose.

The more difficulty you have locating a given piece of information, the more you should appreciate writers who provide helpful footnotes and references. The more you appreciate such writers, the more you should follow their example in your own work by citing the data sources you rely on.

Another source of general information is the Commerce Department's monthly publication, the *Survey of Current Business*. The *Survey* is the official source of the detailed GDP/GNP accounts. In addition, the *Survey* carries various articles and statistics on the macroeconomy and an impressive collection of private statistics (on prices, employment, and production) for key industries. Exhibit 1–1 lists several sources of economic data that can be found in many college libraries.

Other Sources of Economic Data

One of the advantages of using the economic information in your college library is its cost—usually zero, not counting the value of your search time. Alternative sources of data exist, but often at significant cost. The costs of these alternatives must be weighed against the value of your time and the importance of the project.

On-line Databases

These are typically large databases loaded onto mainframe computers which can be accessed via a personal computer and modem (a device that computers use to send messages over telephone wires). One consumer-oriented database service with corporate information, financial data, and economic news is CompuServe®. In addition, the U.S. Commerce Department provides a broad range of economic data through its own database service. Third, Dialog Information Services combines hundreds of individual databases so the researcher can search for data, references to published research, and even full-text publications. Although relatively expensive, Dialog provides state-of-the-art service to corporate users and journalists. Depending on the size of your library, an experienced Dialog operator may be available to assist you. Information about on-line databases is provided in Appendix 4.

Experimental and Survey Data

Economic researchers usually rely on published information, but occasionally they go to the original source (individuals, households, companies) for some of their data. Because of the high costs of surveying large groups and the difficulty of avoiding biases, which reduce the reliability of one's findings, most economic researchers produce their own data only as a last resort. Psychologists, political scientists, and marketing specialists are more likely to conduct surveys or perform experiments than economists, so many of the reference materials on these methods were written by noneconomists. One subdiscipline of economics known as experimental economics tests the validity of economic theories by observing how participants in constructed "games" respond to incentives arranged by the economist-experimenter; some experiments are conducted with animals. In general, the experiments find that humans (and animals) do respond to incentives as predicted by economic theory.

Text Appendices

Finally, information regarding the development, release dates, and sources of economic data can be found in Appendices 2–4, 6, and 8 of this text. You may want to browse through the appendices just to be aware of some of the issues you may encounter when working with economic data.

EXHIBIT 1–1 Sources of economic data

General Information

Statistical Abstract of the United States
>Published annually by the U.S. Commerce Department. The most comprehensive data encyclopedia in publication. Consult table footnotes for citations to original data sources.

Survey of Current Business
>Published monthly by the U.S. Commerce Department. GDP accounts, reports on macroeconomic topics, production, commodity prices. See the "User's Guide to BEA Information" in the January issue for information on a broad range of economic data.

Historical Statistics of the United States
>Economic and social data for the U.S. for the period 1800–1970.

American Statistics Index
>Published annually. A guide for locating virtually all statistics appearing in print.

National Economic Statistics (U.S.)

Economic Report of the President
>Published annually by the President's Council of Economic Advisers. The first section examines economic policy proposals of the president; the second section contains U.S. economic data.

National Economic Trends
>Published monthly by the Federal Reserve Bank of St. Louis. National economic data.

CPI Detailed Report
>Published monthly by the U.S. Labor Department. Reports CPI data broken down by product categories and cities. A companion publication is *Producer Price Indexes*.

Business Statistics, 1963–1991
>Published in even-numbered years by the U.S. Commerce Department. Extensive data set for many variables in the *Survey of Current Business*.

Industry Data

"Gross Product by Industry, 1977–1990"
>*Survey of Current Business* (May 1993). Contribution to GDP by specific industries.

Census of Manufacturers
>Published by the U.S. Census Bureau. Data on the manufacturing sector of the economy.

U.S. Industrial Outlook
>Published annually by the U.S. Commerce Department. Reports and data for major industries.

(continued on next page)

EXHIBIT 1-1 (continued)

Fortune 500
> Summary data on nation's largest industrial corporations. The "Fortune 500" issue is published in *Fortune* magazine (late April). Other issues provide data for service corporations.

Value of New Construction Put in Place, Current Construction Reports (Series C-30)
> U.S. Census Bureau. Companion publications provide data on housing starts and home sales.

MVMA Motor Vehicle Facts & Figures
> Annual publication of the Motor Vehicle Manufacturers Association.

Petroleum Intelligence Weekly
> Information about world petroleum markets, including prices. Information about U.S. petroleum production and use is published by the U.S. Department of Energy.

Department of Agriculture Yearbook
> Annual publication of the U.S. Department of Agriculture. Data on the U.S. agricultural industry.

Money, Banking, and Financial Data

Federal Reserve Bulletin
> Published monthly by the Federal Reserve. Economic reports, Federal policy statements, industrial production statistics, banking and financial data.

Monetary Trends
> Published monthly by the Federal Reserve Bank of St. Louis. Money supply data.

Wall Street Journal
> Daily newspaper. Economic news. See "Tracking the Economy" column on Monday (p. A2).

Barron's
> Weekly financial newspaper. The last few pages of each issue contain economic data.

Banking and Monetary Statistics
> Published by the Federal Reserve. Money and banking data since 1914.

"Profitability of Insured Commercial Banks" (title varies)
> Annual article in the July issue of the *Federal Reserve Bulletin*. U.S. banking industry data.

City and State Data

1990 Census of Population: General Population Characteristics
> One of dozens of publications by the U.S. Bureau of Census. Reports contain economic, demographic, and other information about Americans. Data for cities and states.

"Comprehensive . . . Local Area Personal Income, 1969–90"
> *Survey of Current Business* (May 1993). Personal income for cities and counties.

(continued on next page)

EXHIBIT 1–1 (continued)

U.S. Census of Housing
>Published by the U.S. Census Bureau. Data relating to housing conditions in cities and states.

Book of the States
>Published biannually by the Council of State Governments. Economic and other data for the 50 states.

State Personal Income
>Published annually by the U.S. Commerce Department. Source of income for state residents.

County Business Patterns
>Published by the U.S. Commerce Department. County data; different volumes for each state.

State and Metropolitan Area Data Book
>Published by the U.S. Commerce Department. Data for states and several hundred cities.

Sales and Marketing Management
>S&MM is a private publication, available monthly. See the "Survey of Buying Power" issues. Income, population, spending by retail category, and other data for metro areas.

Almanac of American Politics
>Published biannually. Political and census data for each state and congressional district.

Places Rated Almanac
>Published periodically by Rand-McNally. Economic, demographic, and social data for cities.

Government Finances

The Budget of the U.S. Government
>The president's annual budget proposals. Information about spending programs and taxes.

Facts and Figures on Government Finance
>Reference book published biannually; contains data on government expenditures and taxes.

Labor Market Data

Handbook of Labor Statistics
>Published by the U.S. Department of Labor. Data on the national labor market.

Monthly Labor Review
>Published monthly by the U.S. Department of Labor. Reports and data on labor topics.

Area Wage Survey and *Occupational Compensation Survey*
>Published by the U.S. Department of Labor. Labor market conditions in most large cities.

Occupational Outlook Handbook and *Occupational Outlook Quarterly*
>Publications of the U.S. Department of Labor. Current data, trends, and reports for various occupations.

(continued on next page)

EXHIBIT 1–1 (continued)

Employment, Hours and Earnings, 1909–90
> Published by the U.S. Department of Labor. Historical labor
> market data by industry.

Money Income of Households, Families and Persons in the United States
> Published annually by the U.S. Census Bureau. Annual earnings
> of workers reported by age, education, race, and sex.

International Economic Data

International Economic Conditions
> Quarterly publication of the Federal Reserve Bank of St. Louis.
> Exchange rates and general economic information for major
> trading partners of the U.S.

"U.S. International Transactions, Fourth Quarter and Year 1992"
> *Survey of Current Business* (March 1993). Annual article with data
> on trade and international financial transactions by the U.S.

International Financial Statistics — Yearbook
> Published annually by the International Monetary Fund.
> Economic data for most nations.

Statistical Yearbook — 1993
> Published annually by the United Nations. Economic data for
> most nations.

World Bank World Tables 1993
> Published annually by the International Bank for Reconstruction
> and Development (World Bank). Economic data for most
> nations.

Main Economic Indicators
> Organization for Economic Cooperation and Development. Data
> for industrialized nations.

The Economist Book of Vital World Statistics
> From the publishers of *The Economist* magazine (1990). Economic
> data and charts.

World Quality of Life Indicators
> Text by Rose Schumacher (1989). Economic, health, social, and
> other data for most nations.

World Development Report 1992
> Annual World Bank report on economic development policies
> plus data for 180 nations.

Social Indicators of Development, 1990
> World Bank publication; includes a broad range of data for most
> nations.

Encyclopedia of the Third World
> Text by George Thomas Kurian (1992). Economic and other data
> for developing nations.

Summary

Economists rely on a wide range of data in performing their jobs or conducting economic research. This chapter introduced a number of data sources with which you should be familiar. It also suggested that when initiating a search for data you begin by explicitly stating the purpose of your search, focusing on key terms, and thinking about the most likely sources of the data you seek. Only after completing these preliminary steps should the actual search process begin. Investing a few minutes in these preliminary activities will greatly reduce the time cost of locating the data.

The exercises that follow are designed to familiarize you with data sources in your university library. Following the exercises you will find a brief discussion of other reference sources you might want to consult regarding issues discussed in this chapter. Finally, a page has been provided for you to jot down brief notes regarding things you learn from the text, from class discussion, or from completing the exercises. These notes will be useful later when you review what you learned here about locating economic data.

Exercises

Exercise 1: Go to your college library and locate the publications listed in Exhibit 1–1. Write their call numbers next to each title. Scan any publication whose title or contents you find interesting. Notice other publications on nearby shelves and jot down the titles of those you might want to refer to later. After completing this exercise you should be comfortable with the main sources of economic data and be able to locate them quickly.

Exercise 2: Suppose you seek information on the *national unemployment rate*. List three (3) publications from Exhibit 1–1 that probably contain this data.

1 _____ 2 _____ 3 _____

Exercise 3: Suppose you seek information on *corporate profits*. List three (3) publications from Exhibit 1–1 that probably contain this data.

1 _____ 2 _____ 3 _____

Exercise 4: Suppose you seek information on *personal income* for the past several years. List three publications from Exhibit 1–1 that probably contain this data.

1 _____ 2 _____ 3 _____

Exercise 5: Suppose you seek information on *mortgage interest rates*. List three publications from Exhibit 1–1 that probably contain this data.

1 _____ 2 _____ 3 _____

Exercise 6: Suppose you seek information on *U.S. auto production*. List three publications from Exhibit 1–1 that probably contain this data.

1 _____   2 _____   3 _____

Exercise 7: Complete this exercise in your college library.

- *Select* one (1) of the topics named in exercises 2–6:_____ . The following activities all relate to this one topic.
- *Collect* all available information on your topic from the three sources you identified in the exercise corresponding to your topic (above).
- *List* the titles of tables you find for your topic, the most recently reported figure in each table, and any terms used in the table to describe the data (e.g., millions of tons, seasonally adjusted, annual rates, per capita amounts). Space is provided below to list eight (8) tables. If you are unable to find at least two to four relevant tables for your topic, refer to other data sources in Exhibit 1–1.

1. Table title:_____

    Reported amount (most recent):_____

    Descriptive terms:_____

2. Table title:_____

    Reported amount (most recent):_____

    Descriptive terms:_____

3. Table title:_____

    Reported amount (most recent):_____

    Descriptive terms:_____

4. Table title:_____

    Reported amount (most recent):_____

    Descriptive terms:_____

5. Table title:_____

    Reported amount (most recent):_____

    Descriptive terms:_____

6. Table title:_____

    Reported amount (most recent):_____

    Descriptive terms:_____

7. Table title:_____

    Reported amount (most recent):_____

    Descriptive terms:_____

8. Table title:_____

    Reported amount (most recent):_____

    Descriptive terms:_____

Notes on Chapter 1

Use the space below to describe new concepts or methods that you learned in Chapter 1.

Bibliography

In practice, economists use data from a variety of different sources. Population figures are generally considered "demographic" information, but economists have used this data to investigate the relationship between migration patterns and wage differences between states and cities. Economists use crime statistics to explore the hypothesis that poverty influences people to commit economic crimes. They use data on highway deaths in studies of auto safety inspections. Because many aspects of human action are influenced by economic considerations, economists use many kinds of data that may not initially appear to have anything to do with economics.

This is a roundabout way of saying that it is impossible to give a comprehensive listing of sources for economic data. The best all-around source of data is the *Statistical Abstract of the United States*. The **national income accounts** (GNP, GDP, national income, investment spending, etc.) are published monthly in the *Survey of Current Business*. For an interesting account of methods used by the Commerce Department to estimate GNP see Hilary Stout, "Eagerly Awaited GNP Is a Product of Hours of Calls, Numbers Crunching," *Wall Street Journal* (January 26, 1990): A2. A discussion of the differences between GNP and GDP can be found in "Gross Domestic Product as a Measure of U.S. Production," *Survey of Current Business* (August 1991): 8. An alternative view of national income accounting is found in Robert Eisner, *The Total Incomes System of Accounts* (Chicago: University of Chicago Press, 1989) or Eisner's "Extended Accounts for National Income and Product," *Journal of Economic Literature* (December 1988): 1611–84. For international comparisons see Daniel J. Slottje et al., *Measuring the Quality of Life Across Countries* (Boulder, CO: Westview Press, 1991).

The *Survey of Current Business (SCB)* "yellow pages" includes information on **leading indicators,** which economists use to forecast business cycle recessions and expansions. Finally, the *SCB's* "blue pages" report prices and output levels for several hundred **commodities.** *Business Statistics* provides many of the data series contained in *SCB* for the past twenty-five to thirty years.

The *Federal Reserve Bulletin* is an important source of **financial market** data. Each monthly issue of the *Bulletin* contains data on the money supply, bank assets and liabilities, interest rates, and stock markets. A general discussion of these issues can be found in Keith M. Carlson, "The U.S. Balance Sheet: What Is It and What Does It Tell Us?" *Review,* Federal Reserve Bank of St. Louis (Sept./Oct. 1991).

Labor market data is reported in several publications from the U.S. Labor Department, including the *Monthly Labor Review.* Another Labor Department publication, the *CPI Detailed Report*, provides current and historical information on the **consumer price index.**

Industry information is found in the *U.S. Industrial Outlook*, published annually by the Commerce Department. Industry information is also found in detailed tables of the GDP reports *(Survey of Current Business).* The *Federal Reserve Bulletin* reports monthly on **industrial production** and **capacity utilization** by factories, mines, and utility companies. **Profit** reports for major industry groups are reported in the GNP accounts *(SCB).* The *Wall Street Journal* also carries a feature article on profits each quarter, about a month after the end of the quarter (e.g., the first week of February for the quarter ending December 31). Detailed information about individual firms can be found in *Value Line*, a publication to which many libraries subscribe. (Competing publications are available from Standard & Poor's Corporation and others.) A broad overview of profits in the private sector are published each year in the "Fortune 500" issue of *Fortune* magazine.

Locating economic data is just the first step. The **interpretation of economic data** is equally important. On this subject see David B. Johnson, *Finding & Using Economic Information* (Mountain View, CA: Mayfield Publishing Co., 1993); *Macroeconomic Data: A User's Guide* (Federal Reserve Bank of Richmond, 1991); Michael Boskin et al., "Economic Statistics: Measuring Economic Performance," in *Economic Report of the President, 1992* (Washington, D.C.: U.S. Government Printing Office, 1992): chapter 7; G. E. Clayton and M. G. Giesbrecht, *A Guide to Everyday Economic Statistics* (New York: McGraw-Hill, 1990); A. A. Hoel et al., *Economics Sourcebook of Government Statistics* (Lexington, MA: Lexington Books, 1983); Norman Frumkin, *Guide to Economic Indicators* (Armonk, NY: M. E. Sharpe, 1990); Murray F. Foss (ed.), *U.S. National Income and Product Accounts: Selected Topics* (Chicago: University of Chicago Press, 1983); "Notes on Current Labor Statistics" in each issue of the *Monthly Labor Review* (U.S. Department of Labor, monthly); the *BLS Handbook of Methods* (Washington: U.S. Department of Labor, 1988); and *Handbook of Cyclical Indicators* (Washington: U.S. Department of Commerce, 1984). The *Handbook of Cyclical Indicators* also contains detailed macroeconomic data going back to the 1940s.

Finally, economists learn from experience which data series to use to illustrate a certain point or theory. To learn more about the **practical application of economic data,** refer to: Fred C. Armstrong, *The Business of Economics* (St. Paul, MN: West Publishing Company, 1986); Albert T. Sommers, *The U.S. Economy Demystified* (Lexington, MA: Lexington Books, 1988); W. Stansbury Carnes et al., *The Atlas of Economic Indicators* (New York: Harper-Collins, 1992); and Geoffrey H. Moore, *Leading Indicators for the 1990s* (Homewood, IL: Dow Jones-Irwin, 1990).

CHAPTER 2

Transforming Economic Data

*Information is not knowledge. You can
mass-produce raw data and incredible
quantities of facts and figures. You cannot
mass-produce knowledge, which is created by
individual minds, drawing on individual
experience, separating the significant from the
irrelevant.*
—Theodore Roszak

Introduction

By the time economic data are published in official documents or reported
in the media they have almost always been adjusted in one way or
another by researchers whose job is to transform the raw data into
something more useful. When first collected, economic data may consist
of nothing more than a check mark beside the term "light manufacturing"
or the number "4" written next to "Number of employees." Only after a
large number of firms or households have been surveyed do meaningful
patterns appear in the data that find their way into documents that
describe employment conditions in a particular city or production trends
for the entire economy.

Economic survey responses are subjected to additional adjustments to
remove the effect of events or circumstances that have no bearing on
underlying economic relationships. Real income figures remove the
effects of rising wages and prices (inflation) from gross income. Seasonally
adjusted figures remove the effects of weather-related fluctuations in a

data series to show what presumably would have happened if the weather remained the same year round. Nonweather conditions can also impart a seasonal bias to economic data. For example, retail spending exhibits a seasonal pattern because of holidays, such as Christmas, and government spending may be affected by the timing of the federal government's fiscal year.

At first it might seem that having to adjust data for inflation, seasonal fluctuations, and other effects is a bothersome complication that most people would just as soon dispense with. But life is made up of trade-offs, and in this instance the trade-off is between simplicity and accuracy. If you decide to compare this year's nominal GDP to last year's without adjusting for inflation, then for many purposes your comparison will be of no use. Compared to the errors that otherwise would be committed, the cost of adjusting—or "transforming"—data into a more meaningful form is not great. The practicing economist should be aware of the most common adjustment procedures and take note when they are being applied. Less experienced researchers often become confused when two different tables provide different dollar values for the same economic phenomenon, only to realize later that figures in one table were adjusted for inflation while those in the other table are unadjusted.

It is not as difficult to interpret transformed economic data as one might imagine. A researcher who remains alert to titles, labels, and footnotes in tables or graphical exhibits will learn a lot about the modifications made to data. Second, one learns from experience. The more exposure one has to the adjustments made to economic data, the less confusing the adjustments will seem. Finally, *many of the transformations of economic data are suggested by intermediate economic analysis.* By reviewing that analysis the researcher can transform data in ways to better reveal underlying economic relationships.

For example, indifference curve–budget constraint analysis shows that the consumption of some good X depends on the consumer's real wealth and the slope of the budget constraint. If good X is graphed along the horizontal axis and good Y, a composite of all other goods, is graphed on the vertical axis, the slope of the consumer's budget constraint is $-P_x/P_y$, where the Ps refer to nominal (money) prices and subscripts refer to the two goods. In words, consumption of X is influenced by the price of X relative to the price of Y. Since Y is all other goods and P_y is the general price level, we conclude that economic theory suggests using the "real" inflation-adjusted price of X to explain the consumption of that good. Accordingly, researchers who forecast consumption patterns begin by adjusting price and income data for changes that occur over time in the overall price level. Failing to make this adjustment will bias estimates of the role played by relative prices in consumption decisions.

Transformation Methods and Procedures

With the foregoing comments in mind, it is useful to survey several commonly used transformations of economic data. The first few procedures may already be familiar to you, while others may be less familiar.

Percentage Change

You probably already know how to calculate percentage changes (%Δ) in economic data. A percentage change equals the change in a variable divided by the value of the variable, all multiplied by 100. When calculating elasticities, economists use the average value of the variable in the denominator, but in other cases it is more common to use the variable's original value (before its value changed).

Consider variable X. If X increases from 25 to 30, then X changes by 20%:

$$\%\Delta X = (\text{Change in } X \div \text{Original value of } X) \times 100$$
$$= (5 \div 25) \times 100 = 0.20 \times 100 = 20.0$$

In cases where the variable declines, the percentage change has a negative value.

In some instances, a researcher may prefer to speak in terms of changes in X rather than percentage changes. For example, if variable X is the average number of hours college students study per week, then one could report that in 1992 students devoted five more hours a week to study than they had the year before. This may be an easier statement for "consumers" of the information to understand than the equally correct statement that study time increased by 20% between 1991 and 1992.

In many cases however, knowing only how much a variable changes may not be enough to answer important questions. Suppose your father is promoted and receives a $10,000 pay increase. To a person whose annual income is $10,000, that may sound like a large pay increase. But if your father was already earning $200,000, the 5% increase may not be adequate to compensate him for the additional responsibilities of the new job. *A percentage change expresses a change in some variable relative to the size of the variable.* Once changes have been "normalized" in this way, they can be compared to other normalized changes. Working with percentage changes, one can compare fluctuations in the price of wheat to those in the price of soybeans, even though a bushel of soybeans is about twice as expensive as a bushel of wheat.

Per Capita Measures

The word "capita" means "head," so per capita figures refer to an amount of some item expressed on a per head or per person basis. In a three-person society where individuals have income levels of $5, $10, and $30, total income for the group equals $45 and per capita income equals $45 ÷ 3 = $15.

Many per capita figures are not useful because the group size included in the denominator of the calculation is not appropriate for the situation. For example, a newspaper report on population may remark that the birthrate in one state is 20 per 1,000 state residents while the birthrate in a nearby state is 25 per 1,000 residents. It appears that people in the second state have a greater desire to have children than those in the first. Men, young girls, and elderly women seldom give birth, however, so in this instance a per capita measure may provide a misleading impression about fertility rates in the two states. Population experts prefer to divide total births by the total number of females of childbearing age. Without this adjustment, birthrates are artificially depressed in states with a high ratio of males, children, or retirees to the total population.

Some economic measures are measured on a "per household" basis. For example, it may be reported that average household income is $20,000 in one city and $25,000 in another. Household measures are difficult to interpret because one cannot always be certain how many people live in the household, or how many household members hold jobs. *Ceteris paribus,* a household of two adults and no children will probably have a larger income than another household of one adult and two children. Census surveys show that the composition of households has changed a lot during the past generation, so it may not be meaningful to compare the typical household today with that of 1960.

In general, the researcher should be aware that *dividing a figure by the total population or by the total number of households implicitly assumes that it is valid to treat each member of the population like every other member.* For some purposes this is an acceptable assumption, but for others it is not—as in the example where the total number of births is divided by the overall population rather than the number of potential mothers. There is no general rule for deciding whether to use per capita figures or an alternative measure, so it is up to the researcher to remain aware of problems in interpretation and consider whether dividing by another denominator would be more appropriate.

Index Numbers

Index numbers are commonly used to compare two or more data series whose values are dissimilar. For example, financial newspapers often compare the price performance of two stocks since some arbitrary date such as the beginning of the calendar year. If both stocks begin the year at $50 and one rises to $55 while the other rises to $60, it is apparent that the second stock outperforms the first. Stocks usually do not begin the year at the same level, however, so it may be useful to use index numbers to compare their relative performance.

Suppose Company A's stock begins the year at $9.50 while Company B's stock is $123.25. These dollar amounts will be used as "base period" prices for each stock and subsequent price observations will be divided by these figures. The index number for a stock is calculated as:

$$\text{Index number} = (\text{Current price} \div \text{Base period price}) \times 100$$

On March 15, the price of A's stock is $12.75 and the price of B's stock is $141.375. It follows that:

$$\text{Index number for stock A} = (12.75 \div 9.50) \times 100 = 134.2$$
$$\text{Index number for stock B} = (141.375 \div 123.25) \times 100 = 114.7$$

These calculations make it apparent that A's stock price outperformed B's during the period under consideration. One way of interpreting these figures is to say that $100 worth of A's stock at the start of the year would now be worth \$134.20, while \$100 worth of B's stock would now be worth \$114.70.

Although it may seem like wasted effort to transform raw dollar amounts into index numbers for a simple problem like this one, the advantage of using index numbers is that it permits the researcher to compare the performance of the two stocks throughout the year, or to the performance of additional stocks not yet mentioned. In this situation, index numbers place all stock prices on an equal footing at the start of the comparison period and facilitate a comparison of their relative performance.

Exhibit 2–1 provides two comparisons between the price of Fidelity Magellan stock and the Dow Jones Industrial Average (DJIA). Magellan is a mutual fund company that uses the investments of its owners to purchase stocks of other corporations, while the DJIA is a composite measure of the prices of 30 large corporations including AT&T, IBM, and General Motors. Millions of investors own the stocks in the Dow average, so one may wish to compare Magellan's ability to select stocks to that of the millions of investors in the large "blue chip" stocks.

The left panel graphs end-of-month observations for each data series during the first half of 1990. The exhibit makes it clear that the DJIA began 1990 at a higher level than Magellan and ended at a higher level, but because values of the DJIA are 40–50 times as large as Magellan prices, it is difficult to compare the relative performance of the two indicators by

EXHIBIT 2–1 Stock market performance during the first half of 1990

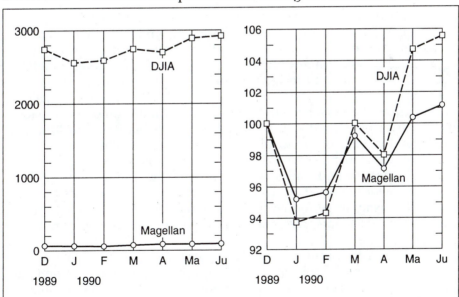

In the panel at left, the Dow Jones Industrial Average and the price of Fidelity Magellan stock are charted on the last Friday of each month, beginning in late December 1989. In the panel at right, index numbers are plotted for the DJIA and Magellan, where year-end 1989 is designated as the base period (index = 100 in base period).

referring to the chart. It appears that the Dow average fell and then rose somewhat more than Magellan, but changes in the DJIA will be 40 to 50 times as large as changes in Magellan even if the two change by equal percentage amounts.

The right panel graphs index numbers of the same raw data included in the left panel. Here, the end-of-1989 observation is indexed at 100 and subsequent changes in stock prices take the index numbers above or below that level. In the right panel one can easily see that Magellan did outperform the DJIA for the first two months of 1990, but underperformed the DJIA during March through June. The index numbers show that $100 worth of Magellan stock at the beginning of 1990 rose to about $101 by midyear, while $100 worth of the Dow stocks rose to over $105 during the same period. This chart clearly demonstrates that index numbers make it far easier to assess the relative performance of the two data series.

Index numbers can also be used to compare the relative sizes of economic data at a single point in time. For example, if one wishes to compare the relative incomes of people living in various states, an index number could be created for that purpose. Using per capita personal incomes as a basis of comparison, define a "base" for the index equal to average personal income for the entire nation. Next, divide per capita incomes in individual states by the base amount and multiply by 100. For example, if per capita income equals $12,000 nationally while in California it equals $14,000,

$$\text{Index number for California income} = (14{,}000 \div 12{,}000) \times 100 = 116.67$$

For $100 worth of income received in the "typical" state, people in California received $116.67. On this basis one could say that California residents have about 17% more income than people in the "typical" state.

As already noted, index numbers are useful for comparing dissimilar data collected at a point in time or for gauging changes over time. *The choice of a base for the index number determines how one's results will be interpreted.* In the stock price example, $100 worth of Company A's stock on January 1 grew to $134.20 by March 15; in the state personal income example, for $100 of personal income received in the typical state, California residents received $116.67. If these statements convey the essential idea behind one's analysis, then the index numbers are appropriate for the situation. However, if the researcher intends to focus on a relationship or performance measure that is not addressed by these interpretive statements, then the index numbers are not appropriate for the application.

Before actually calculating index numbers for a lengthy data series, write down a brief statement indicating how you would interpret the results. If your interpretative statement does not address issues contained in the economic analysis that accompanies your data or charts, then use a different index number instead, or do not use an index number at all.

Price Indexes

A price index is a special kind of index number frequently used by economists. A price index measures the price of a "basket" or collection of goods, and compares changes in the basket price over time. Price indexes are used to gauge the rate at which prices rise or fall on goods in the market basket and to transform nominal into real values.

A price index is constructed in a four-step procedure:

1. Specify a "basket" or collection of goods that is relevant for the purpose at hand. If one is interested in tracking the prices paid by consumers, begin by surveying consumers to find out what goods and services they purchase. Each component of the market basket will carry a "weight" that is proportional to the share of total spending going for the component. (Weights of all items in the basket sum to 100%.) The widely used consumer price index (CPI) is based on a collection of goods identified in Consumer Expenditure Surveys conducted in 1982–84. The contents of the basket are occasionally modified to keep pace with actual consumption patterns. There are actually two CPIs, each based on a slightly different market basket of goods. The CPI-U, where the "U" refers to urban consumers, is based on a market basket representative of that purchased by about 80% of the U.S. population.

2. Visit stores and other selling locations to determine the typical prices of goods in the basket. The Bureau of Labor Statistics, which compiles the CPI, sends representatives to thousands of outlets throughout the U.S. every month. Back in Washington, several price observations for each item are brought together to develop a nationwide average. Then all prices are added together to calculate the total cost of the market basket. The average price of each item is weighted according to its relative importance in total expenditures. (If an item absorbs 10% of total expenditures, its price will count twice as heavily as an item that absorbs 5% of outlays.)

3. Reprice the market basket periodically (e.g., monthly).

4. Calculate an index number by dividing the current price of the market basket by its price in the base period, then multiply by 100. (Index numbers are discussed immediately above.) Today the base period for the CPI-U is 1982–1984. This means that the current price of the market basket is divided by the average price of that basket in 36 monthly surveys conducted in 1982–84. In practice, there is no necessary connection between the base period for the index number and the period during which consumer expenditure surveys were conducted (step 1).

The fourth step is also carried out for individual components of the full market basket such as food, shelter, transportation, or medical services. Because of the huge volume of price information already collected to compute the CPI, little additional effort is required to create a price index for each component of the market basket. CPI information is available in various government publications including the *CPI Detailed Report*, distributed by the Bureau of Labor Statistics.

In addition, the Bureau of Labor Statistics follows the same procedures used to compute the national CPI to compute CPIs for several major cities. The CPI is used to estimate changes in the cost of the market basket over time rather than to compare the cost of living in one city relative to another one. If the CPI for New York is 155 while the CPI for St. Louis is 151, that does *not* mean that the cost of goods in New York is either higher or lower than goods in St. Louis. It means that the market basket in New York is 55% more expensive today than it was in the base period.

A price index that has been used to compare the cost of living between cities is compiled by the American Chamber of Commerce from price information collected by local chambers of commerce across the nation. The base for this price index is the average price of a market basket in all cities participating in the quarterly survey. A city whose price index is 110 has a market basket that is 10% more expensive than the average city; it requires $110 to buy goods that in the average city can be purchased for $100. Values for this index can be found in the *Statistical Abstract of The United States*.

Although the phrase is often used in conjunction with the CPI, the consumer price index does not really measure the "cost of living." The CPI reflects the cost of a broad basket of goods and services, but certain expenses people incur are not included in that basket, including certain taxes and outlays on illegal goods. One other problem with the CPI is that it does not adequately account for new goods or for improvements in the quality of goods that occurs over time. Many economists believe that quality improvements cause the price level to rise by 1% or more each year. In theory, price changes associated with quality improvements should be removed from the data before calculating a price index. Because this adjustment is not always made, contracts and government policies that link dollar payments to changes in the CPI unintentionally transfer wealth to those on the receiving end of the contracts or policies. In the case of Social Security alone, a 1% overpayment (for example) would represent about $4 billion per year.

Other price indexes include the producer price index (PPI), which measures the price of goods while they are still in intermediate stages of production, and the GDP fixed-weight price deflator, which is a price index for all final goods and services. Where the CPI and other fixed-weight indexes compare the price of a *constant* basket of goods over time, another approach is to compare the market value of the basket of goods *currently* purchased to the value of that (same) basket in base-year prices. Under this approach the market basket changes every time a new price index is calculated. The "price deflator" for GDP uses the second method, as do price deflators for major components of GDP (consumption, investment, government spending, etc.). Despite differences in computational methods, fixed-weight and changing-weight price indexes are interpreted in much the same way. Both types of indexes compare the current price of a basket of goods to the price of the same basket in the base period.

Converting Nominal to Real Values

Among other things, price indexes are used to express the current value of goods and services in terms of prices prevailing during the base year. The reason for doing this is to remove changes in valuation that reflect inflationary forces, which affect virtually all goods and services. The procedure yields an inflation-adjusted figure that reflects only the relative changes in the value of goods or services.

For example, suppose a worker's current income is $50,000 and the CPI equals 155. The CPI figure implies that a consumer needs $155 today to buy goods that could have been purchased for only $100 during the base year. Today's $50,000 can be transformed into *dollars of purchasing power during the base year* by *deflating* the current figure by the price index (after dividing the price index by 100).* This procedure suggests that $50,000 today would have purchased a little over $32,200 worth of goods in the base period:

Current income expressed in base year prices = $50,000 ÷ 1.55 = $32,258

After deflating values to base year prices the researcher can easily compare dollar values from different years. The calculation shows what would have happened if the overall price level had always remained at the level observed in the base year. If the overall price level did not change, changes in the values of specific goods and services would reflect fluctuations in *relative* demands, changes in *relative* production costs, or other circumstances that have nothing to do with the purchasing power of the dollar.

Values expressed in base year prices can be directly compared—indeed, the entire reason for converting values to their base year equivalents is to permit such comparisons. If a worker's income expressed in "constant" (inflation-adjusted) dollars declines, then the worker's real standard of living is depressed even if his or her nominal pay rate increases.

If you are confused by all of the terms thrown around in the past few paragraphs, it may help to know that there are only two different concepts to keep straight; economists use several terms to describe each, depending on the context of the situation. Dollar values that have not been adjusted to remove the effects of a changing general price level are *nominal* amounts or *current-dollar* figures. Dollar values that have been adjusted to eliminate the effects of a rising price level are referred to as *constant-dollar* figures, *real* amounts, or *inflation-adjusted* magnitudes.

Since a constant-dollar figure is calculated by dividing a current-dollar value by the price index, the process can be reversed. A constant-dollar value multiplied by the price index (divided by 100) equals a current-dollar amount. To continue the example used above, an income of $32,258 in the base year would have the same purchasing power as $50,000 today:

Base year income expressed in current prices = $32,258 × 1.55 = $50,000

Changing Base Years

Occasionally the researcher runs across a series of data that breaks over from one base year to another. For example, income figures in one document use 1967 as the base year while income figures in another document have a 1982–84 base period, as in the example in Exhibit 2–2.

Although both data sets are adjusted for inflation, the adjustments use different base years so the data are not comparable. Fortunately the researcher can adjust figures from one of the documents so that all data

---

*Step 4 in calculating price indexes called for multiplying the ratio of today's price to base year price by 100. Multiplying by 100 is done to scale the CPI and has no other functional purpose. Later calculations involving the CPI therefore often require the analyst to divide the CPI by 100 to remove the scaling factor.

EXHIBIT 2–2 Overlapping data, different base years

	Document A (1967 base year)	Document B (1982–84 base year)
1980 inflation-adjusted income	$10,000	$29,940
Memo: Ratio of 1982–84 price level to 1967 price level = 2.994		

Note: Income values from Documents A and B are hypothetical figures used for the purpose of illustration. In actual experience the income-adjusted figures are taken from two documents that contain data for overlapping years.

have the same base year. *The key to making this adjustment is to find an overlapping year contained in both documents.* It is usually not very difficult to find an overlapping year when one is needed—the disagreement between two values for the same year is often what brings the problem to light. Overlapping data usually occurs in years immediately preceding an official change in base periods.

In Exhibit 2–2 the same real income for 1980 is reported as $10,000 in one document and $29,940 in another. In this instance it is easy to see that prices in 1982–84 must have been about 2.994 times their 1967 level. Accordingly, to translate real income amounts in Document A into 1982–84 dollars, it is necessary to *multiply* Document A figures by 2.994. Alternatively, to adjust real income amounts in Document B to reflect a 1967 base year, *divide* all Document B amounts by 2.994. It is not necessary to carry out both sets of calculations: Once you decide which base year to use, transform only the data with the "wrong" base year.

Occasionally the researcher may wish to define an entirely new base year. Suppose that 1988 is a key year in a particular study the researcher is conducting, and for that reason he or she wishes to express all values with 1988 = 100. Now, *the new price index for any specific year equals the official price index number for that year divided by the official 1988 price index* (times 100). Then, convert dollar amounts for the specific year into 1988 dollars by dividing them by the new price index (after first dividing the index by 100).

To illustrate, suppose this year's price index is 155 (1982–84 = 100) and the 1988 price index was 120 (1982–84 = 100). This suggests that the current year's price index, with 1988 as the base year, equals (155 ÷ 120) × 100 = 129.2. According to this figure, the price level has risen by slightly more than 29% between 1988 and today. If income this year equals $50,000, it has the same purchasing power that $38,700 had in 1988. These calculations are shown in Exhibit 2–3.

For practice, consider what happens if income rises next year to $53,000 and the official price index increases to 162. Divide next year's published price index by the published index for 1988 to find that the new price level is 135.0 (when 1988 = 100). Then divide the new income figure ($53,000) by the new price level (divided by 100) to express the new income in 1988 dollars: $39,259. Comparing this figure to the bottom line

EXHIBIT 2–3 Transforming data to a new base year (1988 = 100)

Published data:	
Current price index (1982–84 = 100)	155.0
1988 price index (1982–84 = 100)	120.0
Transformation:	
Current price index (with 1988 = 100)	
= (Current published index ÷ 1988 published index) × 100	
= (155.0 ÷ 120.0) × 100	129.2
Application:	
Express purchasing power of today's $50,000 in terms of 1988 prices	
($50,000 ÷ 129.2) × 100	$38,700

Note: In actual experience a reference document provides official price index numbers for the current year and the newly designated base year (in this case 1988) and the nominal dollar figure is supplied by the analyst.

figure in Exhibit 2–2 shows a real income increase of $559, expressed in 1988 dollars. To put this increase in perspective, divide the real increase ($559) by the earlier real income figure ($38,700) and multiply by 100 to see that the $3000 increase in *nominal* income amounts to a 1.44% increase in *real* income. The incremental $3,000 actually amounts to only a small inflation-adjusted increase over the previous year.

Annualized Rates of Change

If all data were reported once a year, then the percentage change in any variable would also indicate its *annual* rate of change. Although some data are released annually, much of the data used by economists is reported weekly, monthly, or quarterly. In this setting, it is not meaningful to compare simple percentage changes. A 1% change in a variable certainly appears larger than a 0.5% change in a second variable. However, if the former variable is reported quarterly and the latter is reported monthly, then the second variable will actually exhibit greater growth over the course of an entire year. When economists need to compare the growth rates of different variables, it is common for them to express percentage changes as *annualized* rates.

When transforming data to annualized rates of change the researcher assumes that the most recent week's experience will be repeated in the following 51 weeks. If this assumption were met, what value would the variable have at the end of the year? For monthly data the researcher assumes that the most recent month's experience will be repeated in the following 11 months. For quarterly data the researcher assumes that the most recent quarter's experience will be repeated in the following three quarters. In each case the researcher projects the key variable's final value after a year of steady growth, then expresses the projected annual growth as a ratio to the variable's original value.

For example, variable Z equals $100 on January 1. By February 1, Z has risen to $104. This represents a 4% growth rate during January. If this growth rate continues throughout the year, by year's end Z's value will be _?_ .

The easy (but incorrect) answer is to say that if Z grows by 4% per month for 12 months, then it will grow by 48% during the year. Starting with Z = $100, this implies a year-end value of $148. The problem with this approach is that it does not consider the *compounding* that occurs when growth occurs over time. Four percent growth in February implies a gain of $4 on the original $100 *plus* 4% growth of January's four-dollar increase: $4 + (0.04 × $4) = $4.16. A 4% gain in March would equal $4 on the original $100 plus 4% of January's gain of $4 plus 4% of February's gain of $4.16.

To include the effects of compounding, the original value of variable Z should be multiplied by 1.04 for however many months that 4% growth is anticipated. This (1.04) is the decimal equivalent of 104%. At the end of any given month, the value of Z should equal 100% of its original value at the start of the previous month plus another 4% for that month's growth. By the end of the year, the value of Z will equal:

$$
\begin{aligned}
Z_{END} &= Z_{START} \times (1.04) \times (1.04) \times (1.04) \times (1.04) \times (1.04) \times (1.04) \\
&\quad\quad\quad \times (1.04) \times (1.04) \times (1.04) \times (1.04) \times (1.04) \times (1.04) \\
&= Z_{START} \times (1.04)^{12} \\
&= \$100 \times 1.601 \\
&= \$160.10
\end{aligned}
$$

Since Z would grow from $100 to $160 when it increases at a 4% *monthly* rate, the *annual* growth rate is about 60%.

The most difficult calculation in the example is raising 1.04 to the 12th power. Even the least complicated calculator can carry out this operation by multiplying 1.04 by 1.04, twelve times. More sophisticated calculators produce the same answer when you enter the two necessary numbers to perform the calculation (1.04 and 12) and touch a key to command the desired operation. Spreadsheet programs require the analyst to enter a formula such as: =1.04^12 [enter]. The cell will then reflect the value implied by the operation. All of these methods are comparatively easy to carry out. For weekly data, it is necessary to raise one plus the growth rate to the 52nd power. While even the least complicated calculators can perform this operation too, a large number of keystrokes is required so errors are more likely to occur. For such situations it is better to use one of the more sophisticated calculators or a computer spreadsheet.

The general formula for transforming a weekly, monthly, or quarterly rate to an annual rate of change (ARC) is:

$$ ARC = (Z_2 \div Z_1)^n - 1 $$

where Z_1 is the initial observation of variable Z, Z_2 is the next observation of that variable, and n is the number of compounding periods in a year (where a "period" is the duration of time separating the Z_1 and Z_2 observations). Using the earlier figures, the annual rate of change equals

ARC = ($104 ÷ $100)^{12} − 1 = (1.04)^{12} − 1 = 1.601 − 1 = 0.601 = 60.1%

For practice, suppose a variable begins the year with a value of $300 and then grows to $325 during the first *quarter*. The quarterly percentage change equals (25 ÷ 300) × 100 = 8.33% or 0.0833 in decimal form. To calculate an annual percentage change, ARC = (1.0833)^4 − 1 = 1.377 − 1 = 0.377 = 37.7%. This growth rate applied to the original $300 suggests that by the end of the year the variable will have grown by $113.21, and its new value would therefore equal $413.21.

Seasonal Adjustment

Another common transformation of economic data occurs because of *within-year* ("seasonal") *regularities* that speed up or slow down the pace of economic activity. The annual weather cycle is one cause of these within-year fluctuations in the economy, but so are widely observed holidays and financial conventions such as fiscal year accounting and annual tax payments. To avoid confusing economic fundamentals with effects caused by seasonal factors, economists use statistical procedures to isolate and remove regular seasonal patterns from the data. *A seasonally adjusted data series reflects what would have happened if seasonal effects had not intervened.*

Consider a hypothetical sales variable that is compiled and reported quarterly. To avoid complicating the analysis, assume that total sales of this particular product neither grow nor decline from one year to the next and show no irregular fluctuations caused by unexpected events, but that sales do fluctuate within the year because of seasonal factors.* Sales receipts during the past five years are provided in Exhibit 2–4.

Dollar sales figures reveal that sales tend to dip below normal during quarters 1 and 3, but perform about average during quarter 2 and are well above normal during quarter 4. Relative sales performance provides a seasonal index number for each quarter. In this example the seasonal index is the ratio of average sales during a given quarter to the quarterly average value throughout the "typical" year ($306). The index numbers are shown in the far right column of Exhibit 2–4. A seasonal index exceeding one implies that sales are stronger than average for that particular quarter, while an index below one implies sales weakness for the period.

Finally, the seasonal indexes in Exhibit 2–4 can be used to eliminate seasonal effects from newly reported sales figures. If this year's first-quarter sales report indicates that $190 worth of the product was sold, the analyst can *divide the reported figure by its seasonal index* (0.621) to discover that sales would have been $306 had no seasonal effects been present. The

---

*These assumptions eliminate several possibilities that in practice make seasonal adjustment a more difficult process than described here, to concentrate on the seasonality factor alone. In reality, economic time series data reflect trend, cyclical, seasonal, and irregular components. Statistical procedures can isolate each of these components and remove their effect from the data. Many introductory statistics textbooks provide a more detailed account of these procedures.

EXHIBIT 2–4 Average quarterly sales receipts for the past five years

Quarter	Sales receipts	Seasonal index*
1st	$ 190	0.621
2nd	310	1.013
3rd	240	0.784
4th	484	1.582
Annual total	$1,224	
Average, all quarters	$ 306	

*The seasonal index equals average quarterly sales divided by average sales in all quarters ($306).

seasonally adjusted figure is larger than the reported sales figure because first-quarter sales are depressed by negative seasonal factors, which seasonal adjustment removes from the data.

If the first-quarter sales report had been a different amount, say $195, this figure is again adjusted by dividing it by the corresponding seasonal index. Now, seasonally adjusted sales equal $314. This is an increase of $8 over typical first-quarter sales. The additional $8 in seasonally adjusted sales is attributed to something other than seasonal factors: trend, cyclical, or irregular effects. Similar procedures to those used to adjust for seasonal factors can also be used to remove trend and cyclical effects from the data; whatever fluctuations occur after these adjustments have been made are "irregular"—that is, the result of *micro*economic causes.

Measures of Market Concentration

Most of the transformation techniques discussed above relate to macroeconomic measures. One data transformation that microeconomists frequently encounter is the industry *concentration ratio*. The concentration ratio is the share of sales in the market for a specific good that is accounted for by the largest firms, and is usually interpreted as a measure of the market power (or "monopoly power") of sellers. A high concentration ratio suggests that an industry is under the "control" of fewer firms, so prices in that market may approximate those charged by a monopolist.

The concentration ratio is calculated by *adding the market shares (MS) of the four largest firms in the industry:*

$$\text{4-firm concentration ratio} = \sum_{i=1}^{4}(MS_i)$$

where the subscript i refers to the market shares of individual firms. A firm's market share equals its total sales revenue divided by total sales revenues of all firms in the industry. (That figure is then multiplied by 100 to convert decimals to percentages.) The concentration ratio can range from 0 to 100%, where 100% means that there are only four (or fewer) suppliers in the market. Occasionally eight-firm concentration ratios are calculated, but the four-firm ratio is the most commonly used.

An alternative measure of market concentration incorporates the market shares of all firms in the industry rather than just the largest four or eight. In recent years the *Herfindahl index* has received more attention from economists and policy makers than the concentration ratio. The Herfindahl index for an industry equals *the sum of squared market shares of all industry suppliers:*

$$\text{Herfindahl index} = \sum_{i=1}^{n} (\text{MS}_i)^2$$

where n is the number of firms in the industry.

For example, if the market is supplied by a single firm the Herfindahl index equals $100^2 = 10,000$; if the market is divided equally between four firms of equal size the index equals $4 \times (25^2) = 2,500$; if the market is divided equally between 100 firms of equal size the index equals $100 \times (1^2) = 100$.

The fact that market shares are squared causes the Herfindahl index to rise rapidly as a firm grows and attains dominant status in its industry. A merger between two firms with 10% market shares would cause the index to increase by 200 points, while a merger between two firms with 20% shares would cause the index to increase by 800 points. Although the firms being merged are only twice as large in the latter case, the Herfindahl index rises by four times as much as it did as a result of the former merger. Since 1982 the U.S. Justice Department has used the Herfindahl index (along with other factors) to evaluate the impact of mergers on market competition.*

An important problem with both measures of market concentration is their exclusive reliance on firm size as an indicator of market competition. Other factors may prevent firms from behaving as monopolists even if their market shares are substantial. For example, if new firms can enter an industry at low cost, then the threat of new competition may cause existing firms to charge near-competitive prices—even if the market is currently dominated by only a few firms. William Baumol and others have referred to such markets as "contestable markets."

Exchange Rate Conversions

Because most nations have their own currency and therefore their own "unit of account" in which market prices are expressed, the prices of goods and services in one country cannot be directly compared to

---

*Stephen A. Rhoades, "The Herfindahl-Hirschman Index," *Federal Reserve Bulletin* (March 1993), pp. 188–89.

prices in another country. Would you rather buy a Toyota for $7,500 or the identical car for £5,000? (The £ symbol represents the British pound.) The answer depends on the *exchange rate* between dollars and pounds.

If the pound-dollar exchange rate is £1 = $1.50, you would be indifferent between the two prices; if the pound-dollar exchange rate is £1 = $1.51 or higher, the car would be cheaper if purchased for $7,500 rather than £5,000; if the pound-dollar exchange rate is £1 = $1.49 or lower, the car would be cheaper if purchased for £5,000 rather than $7,500. Such comparisons as these are especially relevant in international trade, where export and import decisions reflect a desire to purchase a given product at the lowest possible price.

If £1 = $1.50, then divide each side of the equality by 1.50 to see that £0.667 = $1. In other words, there are two ways to express the exchange rate between currencies: the number of units of currency A that exchange for one unit of currency B, or the number of units of currency B that exchange for one unit of currency A. Each is the multiplicative inverse of the other. Because the dollar holds a special status in world trade and finance, it serves as a "reserve currency" for official transactions between nations and for other purposes. For this reason, *the standard way of expressing exchange rates is units of foreign currency that exchange for $1*, for example, 102 Japanese yen per dollar, 1.75 German marks per dollar, 3.11 Mexican pesos per dollar.*

To convert foreign prices into their dollar equivalents, divide the foreign price by the exchange rate. For example, if the ¥/$ exchange rate is 102 Japanese yen per dollar, then a ¥800,000 car can be purchased for $7,843:

Dollar price of good X = Foreign currency price of good X ÷ exchange rate
Dollar price of good X = ¥800,000 ÷ ¥102 per dollar
Dollar price of good X = $7,843.14

A Japanese buyer may consider purchasing an $8,000 American car. To the Japanese buyer the *yen price of the good equals its dollar price multiplied by the exchange rate:*

Yen price of good X = Dollar price of good X × exchange rate
Yen price of good X = $8,000 × ¥102 per dollar
Yen price of good X = ¥816,000

The same methods can be used for translating prices between the dollar and currencies other than the yen, or for translating prices between two other currencies. If £0.667 = $1 and ¥102 = $1, then transitive rules suggest that £0.667 = ¥102. Now, divide both sides of the equality by 0.667 to find the pound's value in yen: £1 = ¥102/0.667 = ¥152.92. Once the ¥/£ rate is known, divide the yen price of a Japanese car by this rate to find what it would cost a British purchaser: ¥800,000 ÷ ¥152.92 per pound = £5,231.49.

---

*Because the British pound served as the world's reserve currency before the dollar attained that status, the tradition is to express the pound-dollar exchange rate in the "old" way—so many dollars per pound. Consequently, one is more likely to see a quote of £1 = $1.50 than £0.667 = $1.

Finally, one can use exchange rates to translate incomes denominated in one currency into an alternative currency. If you hear that a typical Japanese worker earns 2 million yen annually, this is equivalent to about $19,600:

Dollar value of foreign earnings = Foreign earnings ÷ exchange rate
Dollar value of foreign earnings = ¥2,000,000 ÷ ¥102 per dollar
Dollar value of foreign earnings = $19,608

Such calculations make it easier to compare the earnings of workers in various nations. Unfortunately, these calculations do not take into account international differences in the prices of goods and services; with prices far higher in Japan than in the U.S., $19,608 has less purchasing power in Japan than in the U.S. Despite this particular shortcoming (which can be addressed by adjusting for differences in living costs), exchange-rate adjustments are increasingly necessary at a time of rapidly growing international trade and investment.

Summary

Economists use many procedures to transform raw data into a form that is more useful for assessing the economy's performance or for testing the validity of economic theories. Many of the data transformation procedures examined in this chapter can be used with only a little practice. That is not true in regard to constructing a price index or making seasonal adjustments, which involve procedures that are both more complicated and more controversial than the explanations provided above. In the latter two cases the explanations are useful for *interpreting* published economic data but not for transforming raw data. The bibliography for this chapter mentions technical sources of information for those who wish to learn more about either procedure.

On many occasions two or more data transformations are simultaneously applied—for example, you may run across a table that provides figures on the *seasonally adjusted annual percentage change of real per capita personal income.* Rather than throw up your hands and admit defeat, break the statement down into its constituent parts, come to grips with each adjustment, and understand how each helps translate the original data into a more useful form. Data are *seasonally adjusted* to remove the effects of holidays and other events, making it possible to see what would have happened if times were "normal." *Annual rates* are used to make a data series comparable to other series that are collected with greater or less frequency; the year is a standard unit of time just as a foot is a standard unit of length. *Changes* are used to measure improvement or deterioration in a data series, and *percentage* changes scale the actual increase or decrease to the size of the variable being measured. *Per capita* figures adjust for the size of the group affected by a particular data series. Finally, *real* figures remove the effects of general inflation from a data series to measure performance in relative terms.

Consider your own feelings about the following two statements. The first includes none of the adjustments mentioned above, while the second reflects all of them.

- U.S. personal income was $250 billion during January.
- If economic conditions remain as they were in January, the typical person's standard of living will rise by 3% this year.

For some uses the $250 billion figure is a useful one, but for many purposes it is not. The second statement, which incorporates several transformations of raw data, places the personal income report in perspective so that nonspecialists can understand how the personal income report relates to their own situation. No single adjustment or set of adjustments is right for every situation, so the analyst must have a purpose in mind before deciding how to transform a data series. By paying close attention to the *labels* and *footnotes* accompanying published data, you will have a much better understanding of what is being reported. Provide the same type of assistance to others by always describing data transformations in the tables and reports that you prepare.

Exercises

Exercise 1: Your income was $18,000 in 1993 and $22,400 in 1994. Using the percentage change formula, your income grew by _____ % in 1994.

Exercise 2: Gross domestic product was $5,463 billion in 1990 and the population was 252 million. During 1990, per capita GDP was $_____. (Hint: Be careful not to confuse units of measurement— millions and billions.)

Exercise 3: Gross domestic product was $2,732 billion in 1980 and $5,463 billion in 1990. Create an index number for 1990 GDP, with 1980 GDP as the "base period" for the index. According to your figures the 1990 GDP index was equal to _____ (1980 = 100). According to this index number, for every $100 worth of goods and services produced in 1980, $_____ worth of goods and services were produced in 1990.

Exercise 4: The consumer price index was 100 in 1982–84 and 130.7 in 1990. According to these figures, a typical basket of goods that in 1982–84 could be purchased for $100 would cost the consumer $_____ in 1990.

Exercise 5: The price index for GDP (the so-called implicit price deflator) was 106.4 in 1990 (compared to a base of 1982 = 100). Use this number and the 1990 GDP ($5,463 bil.) to calculate 1990 real GDP: $_____ bil. (1982–84 = 100).

Exercise 6: Suppose you are told that GDP this year is $6 trillion but that real GDP equals $5 trillion. The $6 trillion figure is *current/constant* dollar GDP; the $5 trillion figure is *current/constant* dollar GDP.

Exercise 7: Use the two GDP figures in Exercise 6 to calculate this year's GDP price index. The current GDP price deflator equals _____.

Exercise 8: Here is the price index for three years: 1980 index = 85.7, 1983 index = 100, 1990 index = 106.4. Use this information to answer the following questions:

- In this instance the *base year* for the price index is _____.
- Suppose you want to express the 1990 price level with 1980 as the base year. To do this, divide the 1990 price index by _____ and multiply by 100. With 1980 = 100 the 1990 price index is _____.

Exercise 9: Suppose GDP rises from $5,000 to $5,050 during the first quarter of the year. This represents a change of _____ % during the first quarter, and an annual rate of change (ARC) of _____%. If GNP grows at the same percentage rate for the next three quarters, by the start of next year GDP will equal $_____.

Exercise 10: Suppose sales equal $1,000 in the current month and the seasonal index for the month equals 1.035. Then seasonally adjusted sales for this month equal $_____.

Exercise 11: Consider an industry comprised of four firms with 15% market shares, four firms with 5% market shares, and ten firms with 2% market shares. In this industry the four-firm concentration ratio equals _____ %. The eight-firm concentration ratio equals_____ %. The Herfindahl index in this industry equals _____.

Exercise 12: Recall the market share figures in Exercise 11. If two of the largest firms in the industry merge (and create a single firm with a 30% market share), the new four-firm concentration ratio equals _____ %. The eight-firm concentration ratio equals _____ %. The Herfindahl index now equals _____.

Exercise 13: Suppose the yen/dollar exchange rate is ¥105 = $1 and you hear that an apartment in Tokyo rents for ¥225,000 per month. This rent is equivalent to $_____.

Exercise 14: Suppose the pound-dollar exchange rate is £0.75 = $1. Use this information and that in Exercise 13 to calculate the rent in pounds: £ _____.

Exercise 15: In Chapter 1, end-of-chapter exercise #7 asked you to list descriptive terms found in several tables of economic data. In the space provided below, list the descriptive terms you found in that exercise that correspond to the transformations discussed in *this* chapter.

1. Term: _____

2. Term: _____

3. Term: _____

4. Term: _____

5. Term: _____

6. Term: _____

7. Term: _____

8. Term: _____

Notes on Chapter 2

Use the space below to describe new concepts or methods that you learned in Chapter 2.

Bibliography

Several of the data transformations examined in this chapter are "common knowledge" among economists and are used far more often then they are discussed. Percentage changes, per capita measurements, and nominal-to-real transformations fall into this category.

Index Numbers. Early work on the theory of index numbers was done by Irving Fisher in his book, *The Making of Index Numbers* (1922). A more recent discussion is by Peter Hill, "Recent Developments in Index Number Theory and Practice," OECD Economic Studies #10 (1988). Several intermediate-level statistics textbooks contain material on the construction of index numbers.

Price Indexes. In addition to CPI-U, other price indexes are reported for different baskets of goods and services. One publication that provides a good overview of price indexes is by William Wallace and William Cullison, *Measuring Price Changes* (Richmond, VA: Federal Reserve Bank of Richmond, 1981). A similar but shorter essay is from Roy Webb and Rob Willemse, "Macroeconomic Price Indexes," *Economic Review* (Richmond, VA: Federal Reserve Bank of Richmond, July 1989). Another contribution in this area is by Philip Cagan and Geoffrey Moore, *The Consumer Price Index: Issues and Alternatives* (Washington, DC: American Enterprise Institute, 1981). The CPI and producer price index (PPI) are compiled by the Bureau of Labor Statistics, so the reader may want to refer to the *BLS Handbook of Methods* for a detailed description of procedures followed in constructing those indexes. Deflators for GNP are discussed in R. Dornbusch and S. Fisher, *Macroeconomics* (New York: McGraw-Hill, 1984).

Annual Rates of Change. The procedure for computing the annual rate of change discussed above illustrates how different methods can be used to express equivalent growth rates. In the example above, a 4% monthly rate of change was shown to be equivalent to a 60% annualized rate of change. The method used here to transform monthly or quarterly percentage changes into annual rates of change is discussed in the *Survey of Current Business* (January 1988):12–13; W. Stansbury Carnes and S. D. Slifer, *The Atlas of Economic Indicators* (New York: HarperCollins, 1992):39–40; and David B. Johnson, *Finding & Using Economic Information* (Mountain View, CA: Mayfield, 1993): 18–20.

Seasonal Adjustment. The seasonal adjustment of economic data is a complicated exercise that has been made easier in recent years by the widespread use of personal computers and statistical software packages. Several methods exist for making seasonal adjustments and no single one is widely recognized as superior. For a good introduction to seasonal adjustment see James Morsink, "Seasonal Adjustment," *Macroeconomic Data: A User's Guide* (Richmond, VA: Federal Reserve Bank of Richmond, 1991); "The BLS Seasonal Factor Method," *BLS Handbook of Methods* (U.S. Department of Labor, 1988); or F. A. den Butter and M. M. G. Fase, *Seasonal Adjustment as a Practical Problem* (Amsterdam: North Holland, 1991).

For additional readings, consult Appendix 8 in this text.

CHAPTER 3

Locating Published Research

Introduction

The economic researcher occasionally needs to locate published research on particular topics. Where you begin searching depends on what information you possess at the start of the search, the size of your library's economics collection, and the expense you are willing to incur. In information retrieval, a trade-off exists between time and money: faster identification and retrieval come at a higher cost.

Despite the availability of on-line (computerized) data services, most researchers continue to rely on local libraries for the majority of their information needs. For many projects the local library's collection is more than adequate. The library at a medium-size state university contains several thousand economics books, perhaps one to two hundred professional journals, and a few thousand economics-related government documents. Rather than finding a shortage of available information, a more common problem is that of navigating one's way through a morass of information whose organization was not optimized to suit your own needs. This chapter can be thought of as a kind of map to help you find your way to the information sources relevant to a particular topic.

First Things First

It is easier to locate published research if one has a well-defined topic before commencing the search. Rather than merely keeping a vague idea of the search topic in mind, write it down in a clearly worded sentence. To keep the investigation going in the proper direction, occasionally refer to that statement during your search of publications and indexes.

This is really only another way of saying that a researcher needs to have a clear sense of purpose before acting. Formally defining a topic in advance means that actual search time will be more focused, less random.

Once a particular topic is selected the researcher has also decided what topics are *not* of current interest. This can be important when reviewing published materials that are only indirectly related to the central issue under investigation. From such documents the researcher hopes to draw useful information, without being drawn into issues that are peripheral to the present research.

For example, suppose you are searching for published research on the factors that influence wages. A search of existing literature will turn up studies that mention labor productivity, working conditions, and discrimination against certain groups of workers. When actually reading articles about these issues you may become fascinated by the material on discrimination and, for personal reasons, read several articles on the subject. One grows intellectually by delving deeper into particular issues, so the additional reading may cause you to change the topic of the study to focus on wage discrimination as its central theme. But if you decide against doing that—for example, if the topic was assigned by someone else or selected by agreement among research partners—then you will need to guard against allowing your personal interest in wage discrimination from dominating your attention. Having already written down a specific description of the topic on which published research is needed (e.g., "factors that influence wages") you will be less likely to concentrate on discrimination, overlooking the role played by labor productivity, working conditions, and other critical factors.

The topic of a search does not have to be the same as the topic or theme of an entire research project. Within a given project, several smaller issues may arise that require a search for published materials. In the example above, you may decide to independently examine each of the factors that influence wages (productivity, working conditions, discrimination). Then, each of these factors become topics of their own, and you may conduct a literature search for each. As before, write down an explicit statement about the type of published research you are looking for in each area, then stick to the subject.

Writing down the topic of your literature search may only take a minute or two. If it takes much longer, that may be a sign that you are confused about your project's key issues. It is important to clear up any confusion at this stage rather than later, however, so spend whatever time is necessary to write down a clear statement of objective. Here are a few examples:

- Identify factors that influence wages.
- Locate articles that analyze the rising cost of health care.
- Find articles and books that discuss the causes of inflation.
- Compile a list of articles that discuss the link between local taxes and the location decisions of companies.
- Find articles that explain the theory of contestable markets.

To the Library!

What to do next depends on how much information you already possess about the research topic. Ideally, you will already have articles or books that contain numerous references to other research on the topic. (For example, check the footnotes in a textbook that discusses your topic.) In that case, one only needs call numbers for the materials to locate them in the library. That done, you can examine those materials for relevant information or use them to locate additional references. The researcher-as-detective may find an adequate number of references by combing the footnotes and bibliographies of each item.

The fact that some academic journals specialize in certain topics can also be useful for locating articles on a particular topic. To locate articles about the conduct of monetary policy, consult the *Federal Reserve Bulletin* and the monthly economic publications of individual Federal Reserve banks. For articles on the labor market, examine recent issues of the U.S. Labor Department's *Monthly Labor Review*. Articles that examine the role of legal institutions in the economy are included in the *Journal of Law and Economics*. Scan the table of contents in several issues to find articles related to your topic, then examine those for useful information and references to related books or articles. Appendix 10 at the back of this text lists economics journals grouped by area of specialization.

Many leading journals do not specialize in a particular subdiscipline of economics, but carry articles on numerous unrelated subjects. Included in this group are the *American Economic Review, Journal of Political Economy,* and *Economic Inquiry.* Rather than examine issues of these publications for articles on a particular topic, rely on specific citations from other research articles or from regular indexes.

One notable source of references is the *review articles* carried in each issue of the *Journal of Economic Literature (JEL),* published quarterly by the American Economics Association, a companion journal to the *American Economic Review. JEL* review articles are written by specialists to inform nonspecialists about the current state of knowledge in that area. Some of these articles have bibliographies that include well over a hundred entries. Exhibit 3–1 shows entries from the table of contents from an issue of the *JEL.* Key descriptive terms are in **boldface type** to suggest the general topic of each article.

EXHIBIT 3–1 Table of contents, *Journal of Economic Literature*

- March 1990 (vol. 28, no. 1)
  Masahiko Aoki, Toward an Economic Model of the **Japanese Firm**: 1–27.
  Zvi Bodie, **Pensions** as Retirement Income Insurance: 28–49.
  Agnar Sandmo, **Buchanan on Political Economy**: A Review Article: 50–65.

The first survey article in the *JEL* issue integrates certain aspects of Japanese management techniques, employment contracts, and cultural factors into the theory of the firm. The second article discusses issues relating to private pension plans—an important component of the nation's long-term savings. The third reviews the theoretical contributions of a recent Nobel Prize winner in economics. The first article contains 62 references to other published works, the second contains 51 references, and the third contains 21.

Table of contents entries from several years of *JEL* issues have been collected in Appendix 11 at the back of this book. That appendix provides a good starting point for researching many economic issues.

Unfortunately, the *JEL* has not carried review articles on every topic, particularly those of a practical (nontheoretical) nature. Most members of the American Economic Association are academicians rather than business economists, so *JEL* articles often appeal more to university faculty than to other researchers. To locate published research in areas not examined by the *JEL's* surveys, you may have to consult other reference sources.

To the Indexes!

The best-known index of library materials is the card catalog, or its electronic equivalent. Computerized library catalogs often make use of software programs that permit users to search the collection by author, subject, or title, just as one might search traditional card catalogs. In addition, the software may permit key word searches or Boolean commands that make it possible for the user to find information in ways that were never possible with cards. For example, one might request a listing of all records containing the words "economic" and "forecast" published since 1990. This technology greatly reduces the effort required to search through library materials.

With or without a computerized library catalog, a researcher should do some preliminary work before conducting an extensive search for publications on a particular topic. Develop a short list of *key words* that describe important elements of the search you plan to conduct. (The name of an author in whose research you are interested can also serve as a key word.) Some key words will be included in the statement of your search objective, discussed above. Some key words can be found in indexes and other reference materials, while closely related terms cannot. To avoid missing items due to terminological differences, ask yourself what synonyms might exist for the important terms in your statement of objective. Rather than "wages," researchers may have written about factors that influence worker compensation, pay, earnings, or salary. Economic theory can also be of use in compiling a list of key words. If you are aware of theories that explain why productivity and working conditions can be expected to influence worker pay, then place "productivity" and "working conditions" on your key word list.

Take the statement of your search objective and your key word list to the various indexes described below. Then, once you begin to locate specific publications of interest, examine their footnotes and bibliographies to identify other publications of interest.

JEL Indexes

In addition to major review articles, each issue of the *Journal of Economic Literature* also includes an *organized listing of virtually all newly published articles and books in economics.* Articles and books are grouped according to subject area (e.g., business economics, microeconomic theory, international economics). The subject classification system used by the *JEL* is provided in each issue. Many of the new articles and books are also reviewed or summarized.

Index information from the *JEL* is occasionally collected into a hardbound reference volume that many libraries have in their collections, the *Index of Economic Articles*. Articles and books in the *Index of Economic Articles* are also grouped according to subject area. Both the *JEL* and the *Index* have author indexes for locating the work of a particular economist who may publish articles in multiple subject areas.

Since the *JEL* is a quarterly publication, it contains up-to-date information about current economic research. Unfortunately, only one quarter of a year's articles and books are mentioned in any given *JEL* issue, so one has to look at several issues to survey the research output of the past few years. The *Index of Economic Articles* partially remedies this problem by bringing a year or more of information to one place, but the *Index* is not published until several (five or more) years have passed. Even if the *Index* were always current a researcher could not easily examine all of the publications pertaining to a single subject over a several-year period. For that reason, and to offer more powerful search techniques, an on-line version of the *Index* is available as the *Economic Literature Index*. More will be said about the *Economic Literature Index* later in this chapter.

Finally, each issue of the *JEL* reprints the tables of contents of many economics journals. In addition to academic journals the *JEL* includes the contents of journals of interest to practicing business economists. Titles of interest include the *Journal of Consumer Research, Business Economics,* and the *Survey of Current Business.*

Economic Dictionaries and Encyclopedias

A few companies publish economic dictionaries and encyclopedias that contain survey articles on important topics in economics. Many of these articles include a brief bibliography. *The New Palgrave* dictionary, published in 1987, is probably the best known of these reference books. It features articles by several important scholars. The *International Encyclopedia of the Social Sciences* also contains many useful summary articles written by economists. Other reference items are listed in Appendix 12.

On-line Databases

As noted earlier the *Economic Literature Index* is a bibliographic version of the *JEL* that can be accessed with a personal computer via a telecommunications link. The *Economic Literature Index* provides citations to publications that meet the description specified by the researcher. The researcher specifies an author's name, part of the title of a publication, descriptive terms regarding the subject of a publication, the year of publication, or other information. The key words that may be helpful to conduct a regular library search (see comments above) are absolutely necessary in on-line searches.

Suppose the researcher wants to locate publications on a particular subject such as auto safety regulations. After connecting to *Economic Literature Index* the researcher might specify the search with three descriptors: "auto" and "safety" and "regulation." By connecting the descriptors by the Boolean "and" command the search will only identify those items that contain all three phrases. Unless the researcher specifies differently, an article will be identified if it contains the three phrases anywhere in the item's record. After invoking a search command, *Economic Literature Index* will inform the researcher that (say) 22 items were located which contain all three descriptors. At that point one could ask for the 22 records (citations) to be displayed or search the set of 22 items according to some other descriptor, such as year of publication. Add a new descriptor, publication year of 1986 or later, and the index may report that only three articles satisfy that condition. This is a good point to ask for a display of records. Since time and per item charges are levied for the service, substantial savings may be realized by narrowing the scope of the search.

Some on-line databases provide full-text displays of articles and data, but the *Economic Literature Index* currently does not offer that service. Full-text information will eventually be available for major publications, once economies of scale lower the cost of articles to a level competitive with hard-copy subscriptions.

Occasional users of academic databases usually rely on professional search services rather than incur the fixed costs of learning to conduct their own searches. A search such as the one described above (on auto safety regulation) may cost about $10. Users should weigh these costs against the value of time required to search about 45 issues of the *JEL* for the same information.*

A commercial database that is easier to access and less expensive than the *Economic Literature Index*, though not intended primarily as a research tool, is *CompuServe®*. *CompuServe®* contains various consumer-oriented services including financial reports and stock prices, news sources, and a 33,000-article Grolier's *Academic American Encyclopedia*. To access the Grolier encyclopedia, first log onto *CompuServe®* and then type GO AAE. To search the encyclopedia, select on-screen menu items and respond to *CompuServe*'s prompts. The encyclopedia contains articles on current events, tables of data, and bibliographies on selected subjects. This service costs about 20 cents per minute.

One widely used database is *ABI Inform*, a bibliographic database for business periodicals, major newspapers, and other publications. As with the *Economic Literature Index*, a citation search begins by providing one or

---

*For more information on the Economic Literature Index see Drucilla Ekwurzel and Bernard Saffran, "Online Information Retrieval for Economists—The *Economic Literature Index*," *Journal of Economic Literature* (December 1985).

more descriptors for the topic being searched—key words, an author's name, part of a title. In most cases the citations provided by *ABI* are accompanied by a brief summary.

Finally, in recent years a number of on-line databases have become available at low (or no) charge. These are often accessible through *Internet*, a computer-based network using digital phone lines to link together many universities, research organizations, and others. Since *Internet* became available, users have been able to access the computerized library catalogs of major universities (e.g., Harvard, the University of Michigan), and several universities have developed their own specialized databases, which researchers elsewhere can use. For example, the University of Colorado's C.A.R.L. system contains several million article references in many disciplines that can be searched by title, author, and key word. For access to *Internet*, contact a favorite professor or your university's "computer services" department. Additional information about on-line databases can be found in Appendix 4.

Other Indexes

A variety of other indexes exist that may be useful from time to time. These other indexes either do not specialize in economic issues or provide a guide to locating nonprofessional items, such as articles from *Time* or *Newsweek*. A few of these indexes include: *Reader's Guide to Periodical Literature, Public Affairs Information Service Bulletin (P.A.I.S.), New York Times Index*, and *The Wall Street Journal Index*.

The *Social Science Citation Index* (Citation Index volume), published annually, provides a list of current articles that refer to articles published in earlier years. This index makes it possible to follow up on later publications stimulated by an original research paper. Citations in the *SSCI* are listed under the name of the original researcher. The *SSCI* is useful for investigating the impact of a given research project on later researchers, or for finding significant objections to the original article from other researchers in the area.

Summary

Before beginning a search for published research one should take the time to clearly define the search topic, to economize on time and minimize the probability of error. Many searches are no more complicated than locating references listed in articles and books already in the researcher's possession. Indexes of various kinds can also be used to locate relevant information. Before consulting an index the researcher should routinely prepare a short list of key words that may be used as descriptors in the index.

No single search strategy works best for all topics, so the researcher should consider which approach seems best for each project. The search strategies discussed in the present chapter are presented in graphical form in Exhibit 3–2.

EXHIBIT 3–2 Searching for published research

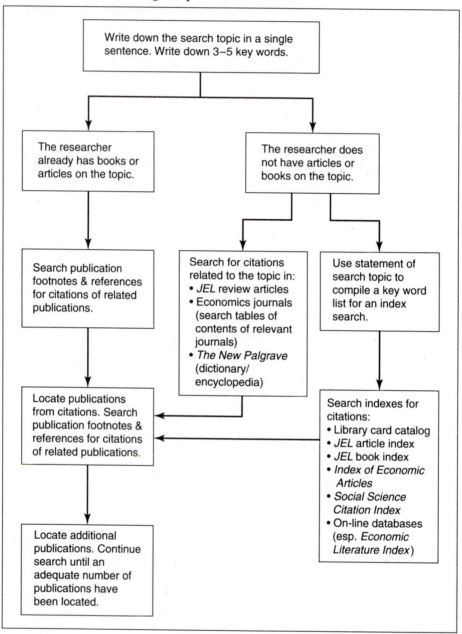

Exercises

Exercise 1: Go to your university library and locate the following materials. Indicate whether you find each item and write down the call number or library location of those you do locate.

Item/service	Call no./location
1. *Journal of Economic Literature*	
2. *Index of Economic Articles*	
3. *The New Palgrave* (dictionary)	
4. *Wall Street Journal Index*	
5. *Dialog* (on-line index)*	
6. *InfoTrac* (periodical index)	
7. *ABI/Inform* (business periodical index)	
8. *A Dictionary of Economic Quotations*	
9. *Social Science Citation Index*	
10. *Reader's Guide to Periodical Literature*	
11. *Statistical Abstract of the United States*	
12. *Federal Reserve Bulletin*	
13. *International Financial Statistics Yearbook*	
14. *Journal of Common Market Studies*	
15. *Economic Inquiry* (journal)	
16. *Monthly Labor Review*	

*It is unlikely that you will have direct access to this service, though one or two library staff members may conduct Dialog searches for library patrons.

17. *Survey of Current Business*   _____

18. *Review* of the Federal
     Reserve Bank of St. Louis   _____

19. United Nations *Statistical
     Yearbook*   _____

20. *Economic Report of the
     President*   _____

21. *Barron's* (weekly newspaper)   _____

22. *U.S. Industrial Outlook*   _____

23. *County Business Patterns*   _____

24. *CPI Detailed Report*   _____

25. *Asian Wall Street Journal*   _____

26. *The Economist* (magazine)   _____

27. *Book of the States*   _____

28. World Bank *World Tables*   _____

29. *Treasury Bulletin*   _____

30. *Who's Who in Economics*   _____

Exercise 2: Early in the chapter a few topics were listed for a hypothetical literature search (see the list below). Select *one* of the topics and conduct a thorough search. Write the citations you locate in the spaces provided on the following page.

Search Objectives (from text)

- Locate articles and books that identify factors that influence wages.
- Locate articles and books that analyze the rising cost of health care.
- Find articles and books that discuss the causes of inflation.
- Compile a list of articles and books that discuss the link between local taxes and the location decisions of companies.
- Find articles and books that explain the theory of contestable markets.

Journal citation format: Beneish, Messod D., "The Effect of Regulatory Changes in the Airline Industry on Shareholders' Wealth," *Journal of Law and Economics* (October 1991), 395–430.

Book citation format: Banfield, Edward, *The Unheavenly City: The Nature and Future of Our Urban Crisis* (Boston: Little, Brown and Company, 1970), chapter 7.

Article citation 1: _____

_____

Article citation 2: _____

_____

Book citation 1: _____

_____

Book citation 2: _____

_____

Exercise 3: Refer to the first article you cited in Exercise 2 (above). From the list of references contained in *that* article, select one article or book that appears to provide additional information relevant to your search topic.

Follow-up citation: _____

_____

Notes on Chapter 3

Use the space below to describe new concepts or methods that you learned in Chapter 3.

Bibliography

Many guides have been written on searching for published research. The real experts are reference librarians, who work constantly with the indexes discussed in this chapter. The topic is also discussed in textbooks on library science, which can be found in your college library.

Searching for published research in economics is discussed by David L. Weimer and Aidan R. Vining, *Policy Analysis* (Englewood Cliffs, N.J.: Prentice Hall, 1989): appendix 6A. Another discussion of literature searches is by Christine A. Hult, *Research and Writing Across the Curriculum* (Belmont, CA: Wadsworth, 1990).

One obvious place to start looking for published research on a particular topic is in the textbooks you have used in economics courses. Footnotes and end-of-chapter materials often refer to the work of others. You probably have a small collection of textbooks already, so this is an easy place to get started.

PROFICIENCY 2

The Ability to Demonstrate Command of Existing Knowledge

After locating data and published research on a given topic (proficiency 1) the practicing economist should be prepared to report on that information to a reader or listener. One may be asked to *write a short report* on some statistic or concept used by economists and to explain how it contributes to our understanding of human behavior or economic conditions. Many economic reports call for the *collection and summary of materials from several sources*. A third type of report is one that *presents competing sides of a policy debate*. Chapter 4 provides a general discussion of economic writing. Chapters 5–7 examine specific types of reports: a short report, a summary report, and a policy debate report. The methods presented in these chapters have been used by many writers, but are not intended as hard-and-fast rules that all writers must follow. After you have gained experience writing about economic issues you may decide to use a different approach if the assignment or the nature of the material itself calls for it.

CHAPTER 4

Writing Methods and Practices

What is written without effort is in general
read without pleasure.
—Samuel Johnson

Introduction

Having located economic data or research articles that bear on a topic you want to know more about, you may want to (or be required to) write a report on your findings. Many people consider writing a difficult task—including some accomplished authors who have written several books. It is interesting to speculate why so many people react this way to writing assignments. Were we intimidated in grammar school by teachers who took great delight in "correcting" (rejecting) what we wrote? Are we afraid that a reader will disagree with our ideas or maybe even ridicule them? Or are we intellectually lazy and unable to sit quietly for a few hours and write down our thoughts on some topic?

The fact that many successful authors find writing so difficult tells us that an author's reluctance to sit down and put pen to paper is not related to writing ability. It is a psychological barrier that you may be able to overcome without any formal training at all. We will return to this issue later in the chapter.

The second challenge you face is to write good economics. One can be a good writer in general without being able to fashion an argument that economists find convincing. This is a second issue discussed in the present chapter.

Finally, writers in all disciplines need to be aware of grammar, spelling, and other technical matters. Whatever skills you have in this area were probably developed in English composition classes. Although you may believe that the economic content of your essay is more important than sentence structure and related matters, your reader may not agree. In fact, your reader may conclude that anyone who is unable to write a simple declaratory sentence is also unable to have a single clear idea about economic matters. Consider this: A key reason American consumers have increased their purchases of Japanese cars in recent years is that carmakers in Japan produce products with fewer flaws—fewer rattles, fewer squeaks, and fewer loose screws and bolts. Now, rattles and squeaks do not have anything to do with a car's top speed or its ability to move passengers from point A to point B. But they are important to consumers. If you want to attract (rather than repel) readers, you have to pay as much attention to sentence structure and other "minor" issues as Japanese carmakers do to squeaks and rattles.

You may be thinking that you don't really care whether people are attracted to your writing or not. A lot of people feel that way, and the number who do seems to be growing every year. Another way of stating this is to say that the *supply* of people who think clearly and express themselves well is declining over time. The decreasing supply suggests that the wages of workers who have thinking and writing skills will tend to rise relative to the wages of people without those skills. Any effort you put into developing your writing skills is therefore an investment that is likely to pay future dividends. Because writing skills improve with practice, this form of human capital does not depreciate with use. The reward for whatever you learn now will tend to increase rather than diminish over time.

A General Overview

Later chapters will discuss the specific types of reports economists may be called on to write, so it is not necessary to go into great detail about that matter at this stage. The purpose of this chapter is to examine general guidelines that should be followed in just about any type of report.

Define the Theme

How does one get started? With the topic or *theme* of the report. What are you writing about? Some writers are so familiar with the theme of the paper they are writing that they launch immediately into issues of considerable complexity without telling the reader what their objective is. Many words can be interpreted in more than one way, and ideas can be connected to a number of other unrelated ideas. Consequently the person on the receiving end of any given communication can better understand the point you are driving at if he or she knows the *context* of your remarks. By clearly stating the theme of your report, you will have *focused* the mind of the other person on the issue you intend to address. Fewer words and ideas will be misinterpreted.

A second possibility is that the writer may be somewhat confused about what belongs in the report and what should be left out. This problem will diminish with experience, but can also be reduced by explicitly spelling out the theme of the report. A report on "wages" can go in many directions, but a report on "wage differences between workers in different occupations" is better focused and permits the writer to concentrate on issues that bear only on that topic. The previous paragraph argued that explicitly stating the theme of a report helps focus the mind of the reader; here we see that it also helps focus the mind of the writer.

Despite a few exceptions, here is the general rule: If you cannot state the point of a report in one or two carefully worded sentences, then you probably do not have a clear objective in mind for the report—and you are almost certain to confuse your reader as well. Inexperienced writers often write research papers as they might write a *mystery novel*—holding back the best for last as a reward to the reader to keep reading. In nearly everything but mystery novels, however, consumers like to be told up front what they are getting themselves into. Readers are no different. If they do not discover within a few sentences or paragraphs what you are trying to tell them about, it is unlikely that they will continue reading. You should experiment with the specific wording, but in the first or second paragraph of every report you should include a carefully crafted sentence that begins something like this:

The purpose of this report is to discuss [or analyze or investigate]____.

You may want to word your statement of purpose differently, but you should never fail to write such a sentence. Later, as you write the report, ask yourself whether your comments promote the defined objective, or whether your statement of purpose needs to be refined to make it clear to your reader what the report will accomplish. (Return to the opening paragraphs of the Preface to see if you can identify the statement of purpose for this text.)

Collect Information

After carefully defining the topic or theme of your report, you must collect information relevant to the issue you intend to write about. Chapters 1 and 3 discussed ways of locating economic data and published research. As you locate relevant information you should *collect notes and data* that will be used later in your report. Some researchers write the results of their research on 3-by-5 note cards, writing one important idea per card.

Writing only one idea on each note card may seem like a waste of cards, but cards are cheap compared to the value of your time. The information you find in your research is organized differently from the way it will be organized in the report you are writing, so eventually you will need to rearrange the information in a way that helps advance your own objectives. Researchers who collect key ideas on separate cards often use those cards at a later stage to *organize* the information according to a logical sequence. Some suggest sitting with your cards at a large table and laying the cards out in the sequence in which the ideas will appear in your report. You can move the cards around until you are satisfied with their order. This method should also make it easier to notice when something is missing from the discussion that logically should be included.

If you have a personal computer you can collect your notes in a word processing file and rearrange their order to reflect their placement in your report. If that doesn't work, print out key ideas on separate pages and arrange those as you would arrange note cards on a tabletop.

Organize/Structure the Information

Most reports begin with an *introductory section,* which describes the theme of the discussion that follows, explains what makes the subject matter interesting or important, and briefly discusses what other people have had to say about the issue. This material constitutes background information, which establishes a context for the remainder of the report. By setting the scene here, you prepare the reader for the more technical material that follows. If you are preparing a report about the impact of the computer on the U.S. economy, then your introductory remarks should probably mention the industry's total sales, the industry's impact on the producers of related goods like software and computer peripherals, and productivity gains by workers who use computers. Your subtle use of economic jargon (revenues, complementary goods, productivity) in the introductory discussion signals the reader what to expect later in the report and helps steer the discussion toward issues that you have been trained to address. Finally, this is a good time to define concepts that will be used throughout the report.

The *body* of the report will vary with the type of report you are working on. More will be said about this in later chapters. At this point it is enough to note that the body of most economic reports applies economic theory to the material discussed in the introductory section and may also apply empirical (statistical) methods to further investigate the issue. This material will be easier for the reader to comprehend if you used the introductory section to steer the discussion toward the few key issues emphasized in the body and if you make it clear what point you are attempting to demonstrate with your economic and statistical analysis.

The *concluding section* should provide a fast-paced summary of the main theme of the report. This summary should mention only the skeleton of your logic developed in the body and not get bogged down into a detailed explanation of various points. Use this section to point out the relevance of your findings to the reader. If your introduction was correctly written, you have already mentioned why the reader should be interested enough in your topic to read the report; now in the concluding section you can discuss the relevance of your remarks or findings to those issues of reader interest. Be careful to distinguish your findings from mere opinions so that you do not claim more than you actually delivered in the body of the paper. Finally, acknowledge the limits of your study so readers will be aware of the limits of what they have learned and what areas require further investigation.

Exhibit 4–1 illustrates this three-part division of the report described here.

Writing the Report

After you gain experience you will be able to start writing a report just about anywhere you want to start and experiment with different approaches to find which has the greatest impact on the reader.

EXHIBIT 4–1 Parts of the report

Introduction	Main body ——— Economic Empirical analysis evidence	Concluding section

Experience will help you recognize—instinctively—when you've done something wrong or left something out. Until you have had considerable experience writing economic reports, however, try sticking with the approach outlined above. *First, define the theme, then collect information, organize that information into a configuration implied by the theme (intro, body, close), then write the report.*

To avoid "writer's block," write the first draft of your report quickly and do not stop to correct errors in anything except factual detail or economic analysis. Everyone's first draft is imperfect and requires fixing later, but the key is to write as much as possible in a single sitting with your mind focused on the "story" your report will tell. By pouring out the story in a single setting, you will be more aware of gaps in your logic or missing evidence that would make the story complete. There will be time to fix spelling and grammatical errors later, so do not let such problems divert your mind from your task of putting words on paper (or on the computer screen). The sooner you complete the first draft of your report, the more time you have for perfecting it later on. Revisions should identify and fill in gaps in your discussion which might otherwise prevent the reader from arriving at the same conclusion you have drawn about the material.

Other than that, there is no single best way to write. Exercise imagination and show initiative, but do not depart from the approach described above (and in later chapters) unless you have a good reason for doing so. A report is not a melting pot of ideas, but an *organized* story that accomplishes a particular objective. Exhibit 4–2 illustrates the approach discussed above.

EXHIBIT 4–2 Economic report writing

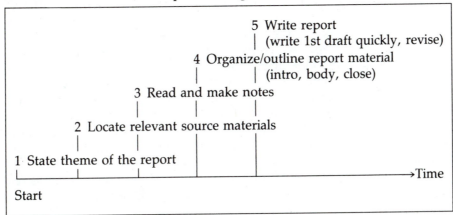

Good Economics

Just any "organized story that accomplishes a particular objective" does not automatically qualify as good economics, however. A good sociology report is also an organized story that accomplishes an objective. To write good economics you must be aware of things economists usually include in a report, or what they look for when reading one.

Economics is a science, and like other sciences has its own version of the scientific method. The scientific method is an approach to investigating issues that results in the greatest understanding both for the individual researcher and for the discipline as a whole. A very simple report may not contribute much to the discipline, but it should at least demonstrate that *you* are advancing—learning how to explore and write about the relationship between events, theories, and evidence in specific applications.

What events (phenomena, legislation, problems) are worth studying and reporting on? Many topics are interesting, but an economist's comparative advantage lies in those topics that can be analyzed with established economic theory. For example, suppose you want to write about slavery. This is a broad topic about which many books have been written. As you decide how to narrow the topic, leave it to sociologists to explain how slavery destroys the culture of those who have been enslaved—not because slavery does not have this effect, but because that is not your area of expertise. Leave it to political scientists to explain why the American political system was unable to find a peaceful way of abolishing slavery—not because you are satisfied with the efficiency of our political system, but because that is not your area of expertise. Instead, you might write about slave workers' absence of personal incentives to work hard since the entire value of their output belongs to their owner. Is there evidence to support this elementary economic proposition? If there is, then slavery could be described as an inefficient way of organizing production. In other words, workers could produce more as free men and women than as slaves.

The lesson here is that the greatest rewards come from focusing on the economic content of an issue. In such situations you can apply the concepts and theories you studied in economics courses. If you can't describe a situation with phrases like incentives, relative prices, aggregate demand, or similar ideas, then maybe you should write about a different issue.

The body of many of the reports and papers you write will include economic analysis. *Analysis* refers to breaking something down into its component parts and looking at those parts in order to better understand its nature and function. Slavery is many things, but it is partly a way of organizing the labor supply. Economics can be used to examine the impact of slavery on worker behavior, and thus contributes to our understanding of the institution. By breaking the whole into its constituent parts and looking at those, the analyst will have a better understanding of the overall subject.

Something else that economists often do in written reports is use real world observations to investigate (test) the credibility and usefulness of economic theory. Do cost and production data suggest that slaves are really less efficient workers than free men and women? *The scientific method requires us to subject the implications of our theorizing (the hypothesis) to empirical testing.* Although your own particular interest may be slavery, the economic profession's interest may be knowing more about the impact of personal incentives on worker behavior. Viewed from this wider perspective, we may use the findings of your study of slavery to predict what would happen if tax rates on workers are significantly increased. Empirical tests are performed to establish the reliability of a theory before attempting to apply it to other situations.

As economists test their theories over a wider range of human experience, their theories can be refined and made more useful. You can contribute to this effort by discussing in your introductory section the work done by other economists on closely related problems. In a study of slavery you might begin by discussing the impact of confiscatory taxes on the productivity and effort of other workers. Then in the concluding section of the slavery paper, discuss the implications of your findings about slavery to the tax issue. The economics profession advances as the domain of economic analysis is expanded, so each new contribution should be woven into the theoretical fabric to obtain the most complete coverage possible.

The logical development of your economic analysis and empirical test should be "transparent" so the reader can understand the conclusion you came to. Clearly spell out the assumptions you relied on to build your theory. Assumptions limit the domain over which your theoretical model can be applied and make it clear to other analysts where your work ends and where theirs should begin. Explain any transformations performed on your data so the reader is able to interpret your empirical findings. (Data transformations were discussed in Chapter 2.)

At first, you should do all of these things in a direct and obvious way. As you gain experience you will learn more subtle ways of building these features into your discussion. It is more important to touch all of the right bases than to be subtle, however, so the burden is on you to present a logical discussion and relevant evidence to make your conclusion convincing to the reader. Exhibit 4–3 provides a checklist of things (most) economic papers must include to be considered "good economics."

Grammar, Sentence Structure, Etc.

A text about economic research methods is not the ideal place to learn about grammar and sentence structure. However, it is a good place to mention that some writing habits obscure rather than clarify key ideas. Sometimes writers do things that annoy readers rather than invite them to continue reading. Rather than discuss the fundamentals of grammar and sentence structure, it is easier to list a few "rules" you should normally follow when writing economic reports. Those can be found in Exhibit 4–4. A more comprehensive list can be found in Donald McCloskey's book, *The Writing of Economics* (New York: Macmillan, 1987).

Like other rules of thumb, these guidelines are not carved in stone. If your better judgment tells you to break one of them in a particular case,

EXHIBIT 4–3 Economic content checklist

- Does your topic have economic content? What economic terms and concepts can you use to describe the topic? _____ (If the topic has little or no economic content, then consider selecting a different topic.)

- What economic theory is most applicable to the topic you are examining? _____ (If your topic can be broken down into distinct parts, perhaps each part should be analyzed with a different theoretical model.)

- What does economic theory say about your topic? _____

- The predictions (implications) from economic analysis can often be stated as "testable hypotheses" which can be compared to actual experience. State one or more of the implications of your economic analysis in the form of a testable hypothesis. (E.g., "The analysis predicts that slavery reduces the incentive to work.") _____

- What evidence could be used to test the hypothesis? _____ (If a test has been performed, what are the findings?)

- List one or two related issues that can be better understood with this new insight: _____ .

you are free to do so. The rules are provided so that you are on guard to not violate the guidelines *unthinkingly*. Regardless of the rules laid down by others or rules that you define for yourself, writing is successful only to the extent you actually *communicate* with the reader. A good rule to keep in mind is:

> "The reader is always right: no matter how brilliantly you write, if the reader cannot understand what you've written, then you have failed to get the point across. Don't argue about whether or not something is unclear; find out why it's unclear" *and fix it.* [Francis Dane, *Research Methods*, p. 71]

Economics as Rhetoric

No comprehensive list can tell you all of the things to do to become a good writer of economic reports. As the quote above from Francis Dane suggests, report writing is successful if it communicates the writer's message.

Donald McCloskey, a University of Iowa economist, has argued persuasively that economic writing should follow common-sense rules of rhetoric—rules of argument and persuasion.* McCloskey believes that many types of theorizing and evidence can be used to examine economic questions, not just the "standard" methods used in most published

---

The Rhetoric of Economics (U. of Wisconsin Press, 1985).

EXHIBIT 4–4 Top 10 rules of economical writing*

- Write simple, direct sentences whenever possible. Absolutely no one is impressed by a sentence they cannot understand. The quality of your economic logic is what counts, not big words or complicated sentences.

- Rewrite/edit your first draft—and your second one, too. The quote cited at the beginning of this chapter is apt: Easy writing makes difficult reading. Revise your words if you want others to read them.

- If it is possible to cut out a word (or sentence), cut it out. Cut material no matter how brilliant you consider it, if it does not advance the topic of your paper.

- Make sure that every sentence has the three required parts: subject, verb, and object. When possible, place the main idea (emphasis) of each sentence at its end.

- Avoid excessive introduction and summary, overelaboration, or restatement of well-known ideas. Once you have stated in direct terms what you intend to do in your paper, do it. Many of the things that people write do not move the discussion along to its ultimate objective, but merely take up space.

- Use active verbs rather than passive ones to add life to your writing. Donald McCloskey suggests deleting the word "is" whenever possible and rewriting the sentence using an active verb.

- Be concrete—give examples rather than discussing things in vague terms. Discuss the supply and demand for gasoline, rather than the supply and demand for good X.

- Do not use a lot of different words to express the same idea just for the sake of variety. It is far better to repeat a word than to use synonyms and confuse your reader. Repetition of important terms adds cohesion to your writing.

- Minimize use of doublets. Doublets are two words that mean essentially the same thing, used alongside each other in a sentence. Using the same *ideas or phrases* when a *single or solitary* one would do is a *certain and sure-fire* way of writing an *unreadable and confusing* report. Pick the best word and use it; do not say everything twice.

- Avoid excessive use of This, That, These and Those. In most cases "the" will do nicely. Instead of saying "this," try repeating the word it represents instead.

---

*Adapted from Donald McCloskey, "Economical Writing," *Economic Inquiry* (April 1985).

research articles. By presenting specific examples from respected books and articles he demonstrates that successful economists make use of many rhetorical methods. These writers frequently *appeal to authority* by citing the results of previous research, *draw analogies* to similar problems, *state simplifying assumptions*, and apply other techniques of argumentation. By becoming conscious of others' use of rhetorical devices, one can learn to use them more skillfully. McCloskey hopes to persuade economists to take a broader view of what constitutes a good economics discussion. He believes that good economics is whatever literary or statistical technique economists find persuasive in a given situation. No particular method of developing an argument or of investigating a question is best in all cases.

McCloskey's message aims more at practicing economists than at students with minimal research experience of their own. When reading economic articles and books you should learn to identify the methods (rhetorical devices) that writers use to make their arguments more persuasive. These devices may have the power to persuade even when the idea they are promoting is flawed.

As you gain experience in spotting the rhetorical techniques used by accomplished writers, you may want to experiment with rhetorical methods in your own work. *Whether or not your efforts are successful will depend on the strength of the logical argument you present in support of your findings or conclusion.* Don't forget that theories and empirical evidence are also rhetorical devices—in fact, they are the rhetorical devices that scientists and other specialists usually find most convincing. As a reader you should notice and learn to appreciate the techniques used by other writers to make their presentation more effective; these are the methods you should strive to emulate when writing your own reports.

Exercise

Exercise: Prepare an outline of Chapter 4. Use the space below to subdivide the chapter into major parts (which you should denote by Roman numerals I, II, III, etc.). For each major part, write down key words and ideas discussed there, and include a brief explanation to clarify ambiguous terms.

_____

_____

_____

_____

_____

_____

_____

_____

_____

_____

_____

_____

_____

_____

_____

_____

_____

_____

_____

_____

Notes on Chapter 4

Use the space below to describe new concepts or methods that you learned in Chapter 4.

Bibliography

Many people have written about the issues discussed in this chapter. For an excellent discussion of research reports see Sylvester Carter, *Writing for Your Peers* (New York: Praeger, 1987). Research paper design is also discussed by Judith Richlin-Klonsky and Ellen Strenski (eds.), *A Guide to Writing Sociology Papers* (New York: St. Martin's Press, 1991): chapter 9. Chapter 7 of *A Guide to Writing Sociology Papers* also explains the advantages of collecting key ideas on 3-by-5 notecards; Conal Furay and Michael J. Salevouris, *The Methods and Skills of History* (Arlington Heights, IL: Harlan Davidson, 1988), recommend larger 4-by-6 or 5-by-8 cards. Other issues regarding paper writing are discussed by Christine A. Hult, *Researching and Writing Across the Curriculum* (Belmont, CA: Wadsworth, 1990) and Joan H. Garrett-Goodyear et al, *Writing Papers: A Handbook for Students at Smith College* (Littleton, MA: Sundance, 1986).

Donald McCloskey's recent articles and books provide pointers on sentence construction and economic rhetoric. See McCloskey's *The Rhetoric of Economics* (1985) and "Economical Writing," *Economic Inquiry* (April 1985): 187–222. A good survey of economic methodology that endorses McCloskey's views on economic rhetoric is by Daniel M. Hausman, "Economic Methodology in a Nutshell," *Journal of Economic Perspectives* (Spring 1989): 115–27.

General tips on writing can be found in English composition textbooks, available in most college libraries and bookstores.

CHAPTER 5

Writing a Short Descriptive Report

*I keep six honest serving men, (they taught me
all I knew), their names are What, and Why,
and When, and How, and Where, and Who.*
—Rudyard Kipling
(Just So Stories)

Introduction

If a news report states that the inflation rate is 3%, how do you interpret
that figure? When an analyst predicts that the dollar's value is likely to
decline in currency markets, how do you expect that to affect employment
in the manufacturing sector? Speaking to each other, economists use
jargon like "inflation" and "exchange rates" all the time—so often that
we take it for granted that other people know instinctively what these
terms mean.

Well, they don't. Economists are frequently called on to explain the
meaning of economic ideas to people who have little or no formal
economic training. Often, one is asked to explain the meaning of
economic terms ("inflation" or "exchange rate") or to explain some
phenomenon (What causes inflation? What causes the dollar's value to
decline?). These questions may come up in conversation or may be the
subject of a short report you are asked to write or deliver orally. Either
way, as an economist you should be able to summarize ideas for
interested nonspecialists. The present chapter develops that skill. *The
objective is to organize ideas so they will be of greatest use to your audience.*

Preliminary Work on the Descriptive Report

Short descriptive reports are used to introduce ideas and provide essential information about them. They are not lengthy essays that provide the final word on a subject, nor do they examine all of the refinements or implications of some theory. (We examine the organization of longer reports in later chapters.) In most instances a short explanation will run about 100–400 words. This is about one or two pages of writing or about one to three minutes of talking.

Before writing the report, first *write down the essential point or theme* that you want to emphasize. This point is the *focus* of the report, and will play a key role in determining what you say and just how you say it. It may take several minutes to sort through and refine your thoughts to define a point of emphasis, but this is an essential step. If you do not know much about the subject, you may have to do some *preliminary reading* (say, selections from two or three books or articles you find in the library) to decide what message you want the report to convey. If you do not have a specific theme in mind, it is unlikely that you will convey any clear message to the reader.

Whether you already know a lot about the subject that you plan to write about or have to do some preliminary research, *jot down several key concepts or ideas* that you are considering including in the report. If you do not already have a main theme, seeing these key concepts on paper may suggest a direction for the report.

The final step before beginning to write is to *identify relationships between the key concepts* you plan to discuss in the report. Establishing logical relationships between concepts simplifies the writer's task of *organizing* the material and simplifies the reader's task of understanding it as a logical whole, rather than many unrelated parts. If the reader is unfamiliar with the topic, he or she will greatly benefit from your insights about cause-and-effect relationships. Next, we examine one method of organizing material into a short descriptive report.

A Framework for Short Descriptive Reports

One approach used by many newspaper reporters to organize information into a short discussion is the **Who-What-Where-When-Why-How** framework. Often, a reporter will carefully craft a single sentence that contains all of these components of a story. Then a person who reads only the opening sentence of the news item will be reasonably well informed about the thrust of the entire story. Depth and detail can be found in later paragraphs. For example, consider this opening sentence from a recent *Wall Street Journal* news item:

> OTTAWA (Sept. 4, 1992)—Canadian Prime Minister Brian Mulroney called for a national vote Oct. 26 on a constitutional agreement designed to keep Quebec within Canada.

Who? Brian Mulroney. *What?* A national vote. *Where?* The vote will be held nationwide. *When?* October 26. *Why?* To keep Quebec within Canada. *How?* The following two sentences, which are not printed here, explain that the vote is the first national referendum (a referendum is an issue decided directly by voters) since 1942, and that the issue voters are being asked to accept is an agreement regarding the relationship between the central government and local governments negotiated by national, provincial, and other Canadian leaders.

The remainder of the article does little more than elaborate on each of these issues—details of the agreement, information about the controversy that caused the vote to be held, and the likelihood that the agreement will be approved by voters.

The Who-What-Where-When-Why-How framework has two major advantages over other methods of organizing a brief discussion. First, stories that fail to include all of these components usually fail to answer the reader's basic questions about the subject. Because the purpose of a descriptive report is to inform, this means that the report has failed to perform its basic function. Second, readers are usually busy people who do not always want to read lengthy essays on some subject. These readers benefit when you get to the point quickly and provide them with essential information so they will be reasonably well informed after only a few sentences. Newspaper reporters and editors use this method to make their product more appealing to customers, and that is a good habit for all writers to develop.

Suppose someone asks you to explain something mentioned on the evening news—say, the marginal tax rate. How do you respond? "The marginal tax rate is the percentage share of an incremental dollar of income taken by government in taxes." Since you have not defined incremental income the listener may still be a little confused, so you quickly add: "By incremental income I mean an additional dollar of income, over and above current income." Finish with an example: "If a person earns one more dollar of income and the marginal tax rate is 30%, the worker keeps 70¢ of the incremental dollar after taxes."

A good beginning, but this leaves many questions unanswered. *How* does the marginal tax rate differ from other tax rates (such as the effective tax rate)? *Who* is subject to the tax? *Why* do economists care about the marginal tax rate (other than the need to calculate their own tax bills)? *What* income is the tax levied against? *When* was the tax established at its current rate? *How* is the total tax levy calculated once the tax rate is known?

Economic writers have the same objectives as journalists: first, to inform the reader or listener about essential facts relating to a subject; second, to get to the point quickly so that readers or listeners can learn a maximum amount in the minimum amount of time. This suggests that the Who-What-Where . . . framework may frequently be useful in organizing short economic reports. The nature of these questions is summarized in Exhibit 5–1.

The reports prepared by economists typically have a different tone and content from news articles. Economists place more emphasis on theoretical issues than reporters and pay less attention to personalities and local issues. Within the Who-What-Where framework, this says that *economists are more likely to emphasize the Why and How questions* and to play down the Who and Where questions. Although economists and journalists both have to address What questions, economists are more likely to answer

EXHIBIT 5–1 Questions to address in a short descriptive report

---

What? What concept or theory are you discussing? Define the concept or specify the theoretical issue you intend to discuss.

Why? Why is the concept of interest? Why do private individuals behave in the way predicted by the relevant economic theory? Describe the relationship between human behavior (or market outcomes, etc.) and "variables" (concepts) that are most closely linked to it.

How? How is the concept applied in practice? How is the theory associated with real-world circumstances or problems? Provide a numerical or verbal example.

Who? Who is the person or group whose behavior is most closely linked to the concept or theory you are discussing? Specifically name the individual or group and discuss the issues that concern them.

Where? Is the concept or theory more relevant to some geographic areas than others? Do American policy makers take a different approach from their foreign counterparts?

When? What is the relevant time frame for the concept or theory? When was it first discussed by economists? What historical observations should be pointed out—changes over time in theory, in policy, or in practice?

---

them with formal definitions while journalists are more likely to provide a less precise definition and place more emphasis on an illustrative example or personal experience.

To summarize, it may be useful to *begin* a short descriptive report with a strong introductory sentence that provides brief answers to as many of the Who-What-Where-When-Why-How questions as possible. *Later sentences and paragraphs* should elaborate on points raised in the introductory question, giving particular attention to What, Why, and How issues. Matters relating to Who, Where, and When should be raised only as circumstances require it. If possible, *conclude* the discussion with a statement about a continuing problem that will eventually have to be addressed or prospects for future change. These remarks should draw on issues already raised in the body of the report.

An Example

Suppose you are assigned the task of writing a short report on the marginal tax rate. After reading and compiling notes from a few articles and textbooks, you may decide to mention the following points in your discussion:

- **What?** A definition. The marginal tax rate is the percentage share of an additional dollar of income that is absorbed by taxes.

- **When?** The marginal tax rate has changed over time. The top federal income tax rate was 91% during the early 1960s. In 1964 the top rate was lowered to 70%. In 1981 legislation lowered the top rate to 50%. In 1986 the top rate was lowered to 33%, but those with the highest incomes paid only 28%. In 1990 the top rate was reduced to 31%, and in 1993 it was increased to 39.6% for people with incomes above $250,000.
- **Who?** The marginal tax rate varies among different groups of taxpayers. For individuals with low earnings, the marginal tax rate is 0%. For those with moderate incomes the marginal tax rate is 14%. For those with the highest incomes the marginal tax rate is 39.6%.
- **Why?** The marginal tax rate is important in economic analysis. Economists believe the marginal tax rate is more important than the average tax rate for creating or destroying incentives to work and invest. Workers and investors receive 100% of wages and profits minus the incremental share going to taxes. When the top tax rate was 91%, an additional dollar's worth of income was worth as little as 9¢ in take-home income; when the top rate fell to 31%, the same dollar of earnings yielded 69¢ worth of take-home income—more than seven times as much as during the early 1960s. The change in after-tax rewards is predicted to increase the supply of labor and capital.
- **How?** Application of the tax. The first few thousand dollars of income a person earns is exempt from tax —nontaxable income. Anyone with taxable income pays an income tax. Additional income is taxed, but can be "converted" into nontaxable income by spending the income in certain ways—open an IRA account, pay interest on a home mortgage, make charitable contributions, incur medical expenses. Higher marginal tax rates provide a stronger incentive to convert taxable income into nontaxable income. The tax rules that permit this are informally called "loopholes," but in more technical discussions are called "deductions" from income.
- **Where?** State tax rates. State income taxes vary greatly. Some states have no income tax; others charge a marginal rate as high as 12%.

Finally, write a brief essay around the key ideas above. The essay does not have to address the Who-What-Where questions in any particular order; mention the comments in whatever order is most effective for communicating the theme of your marginal tax rate report. In addition to providing general remarks on taxes, you might also discuss the influence of the marginal tax rate on work and investment decisions. This approach highlights the role of taxes in shaping incentives. One of the distinguishing features of economics as a discipline, of course, is the emphasis it places on incentives in decision making. This analytical material on marginal taxes addresses the "Why" question.

Report: The Marginal Income Tax Rate

Major changes in the federal tax code during the 1980s significantly lowered marginal income tax rates, thereby increasing the fraction of each dollar of earnings retained after taxes and providing major new incentives to workers and investors. Those with the highest incomes paid a marginal rate of 70% in 1980 but as little as 28% under the new code adopted in 1986; other taxpayers experienced significant but somewhat smaller reductions. Changes in the tax code in 1993 raised the rate on those with the highest incomes to 39.6%. Additional taxes are levied by most states at rates as high as 12%.

The marginal tax rate is the share of an incremental dollar of income collected by government. To calculate a person's tax bill, multiply each dollar of taxable income by the appropriate marginal tax rate, and sum the tax liability over all dollars of income. An incremental dollar of income is taxed at the appropriate marginal rate, rather than at a tax rate averaged over all income. For example, an extra day of work increases income at the margin so the worker's tax bill increases by the marginal tax rate multiplied by the daily wage rate. This charge tends to discourage the extra work. For this reason, economists consider the marginal tax rate the best measure of the disincentive effects of taxes. Even after the 1980s tax cuts, combined federal, state, and local marginal tax rates can absorb about 50% of incremental earnings—leaving only about half for the worker or investor who earned the income.

Everyone whose earnings rise above a certain level is subject to the income tax, but the tax code permits a deduction from gross income of dollars spent on certain goods or services—including interest on a home mortgage or charitable donations. When marginal tax rates are highest, economists predict that workers and investors will modify their spending and investment decisions in order to lower their tax burdens, such as acquiring larger mortgages or investing in state and local bonds, which earn tax-free interest.

A generation ago the marginal tax rate was as high as 91% for individuals with the highest incomes. At that rate, another dollar of income would only leave 9 cents for the income earner. At today's 39.6% rate, the income earner would retain 60.4 cents of the same dollar. Thus for high-income individuals the incentive to earn additional income is several times greater today than a generation ago. Their incentive to convert taxable income into nontaxable income is less today than in 1963.

Despite the reduction in marginal tax rates in the 1980s, troubling budget deficits have caused legislators to increase taxes in the 1990s. As a result incentives to work and invest have been eroded and the incentive to hold tax-free securities has increased in recent years.

This short essay begins with two sentences that touch briefly on all of the Who-What-Where-When-Why-How questions. Later paragraphs expand on several of the most significant points raised in the opening sentences, particularly those relating to the Why and How questions. Notice that *the Why comments tend to be theoretical in nature and are usually the most difficult for an audience of noneconomists to understand.* They also contribute the ideas that are most highly valued by other economists. Finally, the last paragraph concludes that recent increases in tax rates have lowered the incentive to earn income and have increased the incentive to hold tax-free municipal securities. These conclusions amount to predictions about the performance of the economy and financial markets.

Until you have gained experience writing short reports, it is wise to check which of the Who-What-Where-When-Why-How questions each key point of your report addresses. This will highlight patterns in your writing and thinking and will help you discover whether you have inadvertently omitted essential parts of the discussion.

Summary: An 8-Step Procedure

The procedure discussed in this chapter is summarized graphically in Exhibit 5–2. A writer who is already knowledgeable about the topic may

EXHIBIT 5–2 Eight steps in preparing a short descriptive report

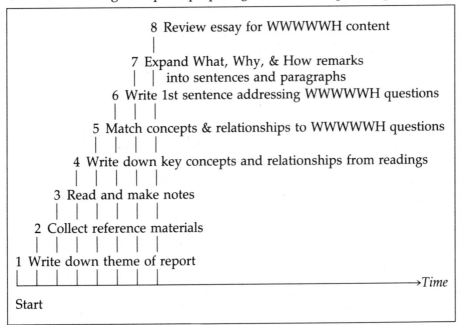

be able to write the report without expending much effort on steps 1–3. Match key concepts and relationships identified in reference materials to the Who-What-Where-When-Why-How framework discussed above and write the report around those ideas. Once you have formulated sentences or paragraphs to address the WWWWWH questions, you may need to rearrange their order to achieve the desired effect. This is easily done with the "cut and paste" features of word processing software.

Exercises

Exercise 1: Select one of the following topics and write a short descriptive report (about 300 words) about it. Address Who-What-Where-When-Why-How issues in your report, as those were defined and discussed in Exhibit 5–1 above. To accompany your report, collect data and prepare a hand-drawn or computer-generated chart showing observations of the variable over the past 10 years. Your chart should identify units of measurement and any transformations of the data (seasonal adjustment, growth rates, etc.).

1. Balance of trade
2. Business cycle
3. Capacity utilization rate
4. Civilian labor force and total employment
5. Consumer confidence and consumer sentiment indexes
6. Durable goods orders
7. Economic growth
8. Exchange rate (dollar-yen rate plus one rate of your own selection)
9. Federal budget (outlays, receipts, and deficit)
10. Federal debt
11. Gross domestic product (GDP)
12. Gross private domestic investment
13. Gross state product
14. Index of coincident indicators
15. Index of industrial production
16. Index of leading indicators
17. Interest rates (real and nominal)
18. Inventories, inventory/sales ratio
19. Labor force participation rate
20. Money supply (M1, M2, M3)
21. Off-budget federal spending
22. Phillips curve (entire population, males, females, teens)
23. Price indexes (CPI, PPI, GNP deflator)
24. Unemployment rate (in the U.S. and in the state where you live)
25. Yield curve

Exercise 2: Prepare a 2–3 minute oral report on one of the topics listed above. To accompany your report, collect data and prepare a hand-drawn or computer-generated chart showing movement of the variable over the past 10 years. Your chart should identify units of measurement and any transformations of the data (seasonal adjustment, growth rates, etc.). *Suggestions for preparing an oral report can be found in Appendix 18.*

Notes on Chapter 5

Use the space below to describe new concepts or methods that you learned in Chapter 5.

Bibliography

The Who-What-Where-When-Why-How approach to writing a descriptive research report is discussed in Willam G. Zikmund's *Business Research Methods* (Chicago: Dryden Press, 1988): 10–11; and Francis C. Dane discusses the Who-What-Where-When-Why-How approach in more than one context. For a discussion most closely linked to the one in this chapter, see Dane's *Research Methods* (Belmont, CA: Wadsworth, 1990): chapter 9. The Who-What-Where-When-Why-How approach has also been discussed by writers of journalism textbooks, but not for the application discussed here.

CHAPTER 6

Writing a Summary Report

*While information may be infinite, the ways
of structuring it are not.*
—Richard Saul Wurman

Introduction

By arranging a jumbled collection of facts in the right way a writer can convert them into useful information—knowledge. The economist is sometimes called on to collect material from a variety of sources, decide what is important for the reader to know and what the reader is not really interested in, then write a summary report of three to five pages which includes the former and omits the latter. The most important skill for preparing a summary report is the ability to organize relevant information into a meaningful structure. *A good summary report should do more than bring information together in a single location. By clarifying the relationship between individual pieces of information, the summary report should be of greater value to the reader than sum of its individual parts.*

A 7-Step Procedure

Each project is unique, but the planning and writing of a summary report follows a certain pattern which is repeated in other summary reports. Allowing for some variation, the researcher may undertake most or all of the following tasks when preparing a summary report. Exhibit 6–1 provides a graphical representation of the procedure.

EXHIBIT 6–1 Seven steps in preparing a summary report

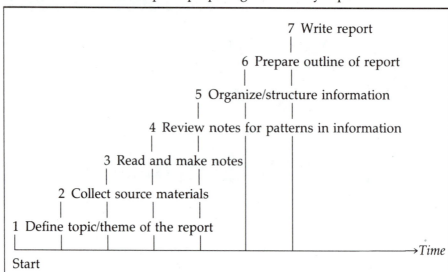

- First, *write down the essential point or theme* that you want to emphasize. This point is the focus of the report and will play a large role in determining what you say and how you say it. It may take several minutes to sort through and refine your thoughts enough to define a point of emphasis, but this is an essential step. If you do not know much about the subject, you may have to do some preliminary reading (say, selections from two or three books or articles you find in the library) to decide what you feel is important enough to write your report about. As noted earlier, unless you have a specific theme in mind, it is doubtful that you will convey any clear message to the reader.
- Second, *collect books, articles, and other information* related to the theme of the report. (Collecting data and published research was discussed in Chapters 1 and 3.) Since collecting information is still preliminary to preparing a final report, you may not have a well-defined sense of what information is worth collecting. A clear statement of purpose (step 1 above) and research experience will reduce the amount of wasted effort at this stage of the project.
- Third, read the materials you have collected and *compile brief notes about key concepts and ideas* they contain. These notes should be extensive enough to identify important ideas, but not so extensive that an inordinate amount of time is spent putting them together. Collect notes on index cards (one card per key idea), on a page of paper (no more than one article or book per page), or in a computer file. The computer file provides greater flexibility (since items can be "cut and pasted" into any desired order), but this approach may not be feasible for a researcher without continuous access to a computer. Include source information (titles, authors, page numbers) with your notes so you can return to the original when necessary.
- Fourth, *review the notes* collected in step 3. During this review you should *identify patterns and relationships between key concepts.* Such

patterns may suggest the best way of organizing the summary material. An important part of writing the final report is explaining these mental relationships to the reader in a meaningful way. Second, your review of the notes also helps you identify areas in which additional information is needed.

- Fifth, use notes from the readings to *organize the summary information* that will comprise the main section (body) of the report. The material should be organized around the concepts and relationships identified above (in steps 3 and 4) and focus on the theme of the report. More will be said about structuring the report later in the chapter (see "Organizing Summary Information," below). This step may go quickly or require considerable thought, but it is critical to developing a useful summary.
- Sixth, use notes from the readings and other relevant ideas of your own to help you to *prepare an outline of the report*. The outline is a "map" of the summary report that shows the logical connection between its various components. The main parts or sections of a summary report are discussed below (see "Elements of the Final Report"). The outline-map should arrange key points of the report into an introduction, body, and conclusion.
- Seventh, *write the summary report*. As you write, reconsider the organization of key ideas in the body of the report to decide whether some other arrangement might provide a more effective message, or whether additional explanation is required to establish the logical connection between key concepts included in the report.

If anything, this seven-step procedure makes it appear that the process of putting together a summary report is more precise than it actually is. In practice, a considerable amount of rewriting and fine-tuning is required to organize the report into a structure that does the best job of informing readers. The use of a personal computer simplifies the process by keeping all notes in a single place and permitting key points to be reordered and modified until the material is arranged in its most useful configuration.

Elements of the Final Report

The list of procedures (above) calls for the researcher to prepare an outline of the summary report, then to write the final report. Like other essays and reports the summary report should open with introductory remarks and close with concluding comments. The summary of information collected from other sources constitutes the *main body* of the report. The body may be divided into two main sections if the researcher wishes to include his or her own analysis of the summary material.

Part 1. Introduction

A report whose purpose is to summarize the state of existing knowledge about some subject should begin with introductory remarks that provide perspective for the rest of the report. The introduction should *always* state the purpose or objective of the report. If the report arrives at some conclusion, the report's objective may be to provide the reader with the logic and supporting information that leads to that conclusion. In many cases it is wise to state the purpose of the report in the first sentence. A strong opening statement will help the reader focus on important issues in the report. Consider this opening statement: "The purpose of this report is to examine recent developments in the national economy and discuss their likely impact on the automobile industry."

Apart from its effect on the reader, a strong statement of purpose also helps focus the mind of the author. If you cannot write a direct statement about your report like the one concerning the auto industry (above), perhaps your report does not have a clear objective. Without a clear objective the report may include material that has no direct bearing on the original assignment, or may fail to include information that is absolutely critical to the assignment. To avoid these problems, write down a one-sentence statement of your objective and make certain that everything that goes into the report contributes to the objective.

Some writers know their objective, but decide not to "let the cat out of the bag" too early, i.e., before the final sentence of the report. This is a perfectly acceptable technique for writing a mystery novel, but will quickly kill reader interest in an economic report. In no case should the economic writer take more than a few sentences to offer a clear and direct statement of purpose.

A second requirement of the introduction is to explain to readers why they should want to know more about the subject. This requires your knowing who the likely reader is, and something about his or her interests. For example, suppose your report will summarize current developments in the national economy. If the reader is a member of the general public, you might briefly explain the connection between GDP and the prosperity of the average American. If the reader is a business manager the report might explain the connection between GDP and the prosperity of the industry in which the manager is employed. In addition the report could mention other groups that are most affected by the subject of the report. In a report about the current state of the macroeconomy, you might note that the construction industry and manufacturers of durable goods suffer disproportionately during periods of recession and enjoy disproportionate benefits during periods of recovery. Many people will not read a report on any economic topic unless they have a good reason for doing so. The first couple of paragraphs is the place to provide that reason.

Third, the introductory section may include one or more definitions of key concepts or terms. This is especially important if the reader is a nonspecialist who may be confused by terms like "gross domestic product" or "consumer price index." Many writers take it for granted that readers are already informed about an issue and do not need simple definitions. Clear writing requires the opposite attitude. Readers should not be expected to translate professional jargon into ordinary language, so if there is any doubt about the reader's technical background, provide the necessary (but brief) definition.

For example, after stating that gross domestic product has risen during the past two years, include a sentence like this one: "Gross domestic product, or GDP, is the dollar value of all goods and services produced in the nation during the year." Or after stating that real GDP declined during the first quarter the next sentence might be: "Real GDP reflects the value of national production during the year, assuming that the overall price level remains unchanged." After commenting that the economy may now be in a recession, note that, "Some analysts define a recession as a two-quarter decline in real GDP." Include similar definitional statements after introducing terms that might otherwise distract the reader. (A glossary of economic terms is provided in Appendix 20 of this text.)

Finally, the introductory part of a report is a good place to provide historical perspective or background information. How long have government economists been compiling GDP? How long has it been since the last recession? How long do recessions typically last, considering the experience of the past five or ten business cycles?

To summarize, the introductory section of a summary report should include the following key elements:

- Statement of the objective of the report.
- Explanation of the importance of the topic to the reader.
- Definitions of important concepts and terms.
- Historical perspective or other background information.

The particular order in which these points are addressed will depend on the author's own preferences and the nature of the material being discussed.

Part 2. Summary of Published Materials

The main body of a summary report is the actual summary of information collected from various sources. The ability to *organize* diverse information is a critical skill at this juncture. Because of its importance, the discussion of how one goes about organizing and structuring information for a summary report is discussed at greater length later in this chapter. (See "Organizing Summary Material," below.)

Part 3. Economic Analysis of Summary Material

This is an optional part of the summary report. The economist-writer may decide to use economic theory to analyze the summary material introduced in part 2, either by blending theoretical remarks with the summary material or by providing a separate theory discussion. A theoretical discussion may be particularly valuable if the concepts and relationships highlighted in the summary material have a high degree of economic content or if the summary discussion indicates that other writers employ faulty economic reasoning. The purpose for which the report is intended may also indicate whether a separate section of economic analysis would be appropriate.

Economic analysis can be used to assist readers who are confused by conflicting explanations of the same phenomena. When source materials arrive at different conclusions about some phenomenon, many readers are unable to decide which claim has greater merit, even if economists consider the matter an open-and-shut case. If nothing else the economist should point out conflicting opinions between the "experts" and mention the principles or criteria that provide a basis for choosing between them. In this setting the economist-writer is presenting his or her *evaluation* of the material summarized in part 2. If evidence exists to throw light on the controversy, this is a good place to briefly summarize that material.

Part 4. Concluding Remarks

The concluding section of the report should remind the reader in a sentence or two of the problem or question that originally stimulated preparation of the summary report. Second, mention the two or three most important ideas that emerged from the summary (in part 2). Only those ideas that bear a close relationship to the the report's original purpose or theme should be mentioned. To keep the narrative moving, key points should be only briefly touched on, without most of the details provided in parts 2 and 3. Finally, the concluding section should mention any unanswered questions or remaining problems that the reader is likely to encounter again in the future.

This four-part outline, or any other "formula" for writing a summary report, is only a suggested approach. In specific cases the writer may decide that a different format is superior to this one. Until he or she is more experienced, the researcher should follow the recommended outline. It is also a good idea to *explicitly* divide a report into parts 1–4 (or 1–3 in reports without economic analysis) to minimize the likelihood of omitting key parts of the discussion.

Organizing Summary Material in Part 2

Part 2 is the body of the summary report. In part 2, information collected from published sources should be brought together and organized in a way that makes it more useful to the reader. The author's logical arrangement of information imposes a "vision" that reflects insights he or she has gained while studying and reflecting on it. The information is structured so that each main point is related in some way to the others. *By showing the relationship between them, the collection of ideas has a greater value than the individual pieces of information that comprise it.*

According to information specialist Richard Wurman, "The ways of organizing information are finite. It can only be organized by (1) category, (2) time, (3) location, (4) alphabet, or (5) continuum. . . . Each way will will permit a different understanding of the information."* When initially organizing summary material, the researcher can begin by asking which of the structural forms is best suited to accomplishing the objectives of the present report. The following comments about alternative organization schemes may help answer that question.

1. Category. Things are organized by category in many walks of life. Wal-Mart stores are divided into "Automotive," "Electronics," "Toys,"

*Richard Saul Wurman, *Information Anxiety*, p. 59.

and other departments, where goods are organized by category. Like-wise, an economist who is reporting on significant trends in the macroeconomy can divide the subject into logical components and discuss each in turn. The designation of categories is not random; Wal-Mart does not define its departments by the color or weight of goods, but according to customer interests. In the same way the economist should define categories according to the theme of the report. It is often appropriate to organize a discussion into categories when the subjects to be included are of approximately equal importance. The present discussion about ways to organize summary material is divided into five categories, for example.

Dividing information into categories can be compared to drawing a pie chart. A pie chart divides a total into its component parts and provides information about each. In a pie chart, the separate components must add up to 100% of the total. As an example, a discussion of gross domestic product could be divided into four expenditure categories: consumption expenditures, investment outlays, government purchases, and net exports. It may not always be meaningful to conceive of a discussion in terms of percentage contributions by various categories, but the idea of dividing a phenomenon into its main components and discussing each in turn is a valid one.

2. Time. According to Wurman, "Time works best as an organizing principle for events that happen over fixed durations. . . . [It] is an easily understandable framework from which changes can be observed and comparisons made" (Wurman, p. 60). Percentage changes over time are commonly used to assess economic performance. In addition, historical summaries may classify information along a time dimension. Business cycle discussions span several-year periods and typically examine the sequence of events leading up to recessions and recoveries. Discussions of cause-and-effect relationships may also be conceived as falling along a time dimension.

3. Location. Economic information is organized by location when the object of the discussion is to compare information from different states, nations, or regions.

4. Alphabet. Occasionally it is useful to organize information according to the alphabetical (lexicographic) order of key words. This method is often used to organize large bodies of information, such as names in a phone book, but is not often used in economic reports. (However, economic data for nations, states, and localities are often ordered alphabetically.)

5. Continuum. Information is organized along a continuum when it can be measured or ranked, and compared to other information. For example, a report on the banking industry might be divided into three parts: large money center banks, medium-size regional banks, and small community banks. A report on a particular company might divide the company into its major divisions, then discuss them in order of their contribution to total revenues.

Once it is decided to organize a report into important categories, along a continuum or some other way, *further subdivision* of the information within each category can be carried out according to one of the other criteria. For example, after grouping states into various geographic regions the researcher may then order states within each region according to per capita income levels (continuum). Wurman warns against attempting to mix the different methods of organization at a given level of specificity. Some people run into difficulties when they try to describe something "simultaneously in terms of size, geography, and category without a clear understanding that these are all *valid but separate* means of structuring information" (Wurman, p. 65). The rules for organizing information are useful to researchers who need to prepare a report on some subject, but are even more useful to readers who can extract greater value from reports once they understand the structure of the information before them. As a general rule, the summary material that comprises the body of the report should be divided into 3–5 major sections.

More on Structure

If you are still uncertain how to structure a report after collecting reference materials and locating relevant data, return to the published materials for hints. How are the published works organized? What ideas do they emphasize? Do different authors focus on the same few issues?

Second, economic theory may help you decide how a report should be broken down into its major components. For example, every economist is familiar with the supply and demand model, so a report about factors that affect a good's price could arrange information into supply and demand categories.

Finally, if certain information definitely belongs in a report but you are uncertain how to arrange or categorize it, write a one-sentence description of each important piece of summary information, then select one or two key terms that figure prominently in each. Collect key words from all of the items and consider how they are related. Whatever relationships you identify may be useful for structuring the report.

Summary

A report designed to summarize published materials and other information should have a clearly defined objective that the intended reader will find interesting or informative. The main body of the report should organize materials collected from various sources into a structure that increases the reader's understanding of key issues and relationships. The information should be divided into major sections according to one or more of the following organizing principles: category, time, location, alphabet, or continuum. In the (optional) third part of the report the economist may use economic analysis to examine controversies or other problems identified in the summary. The concluding section of the report should repeat for emphasis the key ideas identified in the summary and relate them to the questions or problems that first caused the researcher to prepare the summary report. Exhibit 6–2 provides an outline for a typical summary report. In practice it is often necessary to depart from this outline, so it should be considered a starting point instead of a strict formula.

EXHIBIT 6–2 Summary report outline

Part 1. Introduction

- State the objective of the report (or findings of the report)
- Explain the importance of the topic to the reader
- Define important terms
- Provide background information

Part 2. Summary of published materials

- Organize information into a structure based on one of these criteria:
  - Category
  - Time
  - Location
  - Alphabet
  - Continuum
- Information contained *within* major divisions of the summary can also be organized by category, time, location, alphabet, or continuum.

Part 3. Economic analysis of summarized materials (optional)

- Use economic theory to analyze cases where:
  - Economic analysis can help clarify key issues
  - Summary material is controversial
  - Summary material conflicts with economic theory
  - Published materials conflict with each another

Part 4. Concluding remarks

- State question/problem that stimulated preparation of the report
- Summarize key points from the summary material
- Relate key points to the question/problem that stimulated the report
- Identify unresolved issues or anticipated future problems

This chapter provides a guide for writing summary reports, but most economists read more summary reports than they will ever write. By paying attention to the way other writers structure summary material, you can gain the most from reading their reports. Words tell only part of the story; the way the words are organized can be equally important.

Exercises

Exercise 1: A summary report on "Business Cycle Theories" is reprinted here. Read the report and then answer the following questions:

a. Summarize the theme of the summary report in one sentence.

b. If we conceive of the report as having three parts—introduction, body, and concluding remarks—where does the body of the report begin? (Describe the beginning of the body and logically justify your decision.)

c. How does the author define a business cycle? Does he provide adequate facts and information to make it clear to the reader what economists mean by a business cycle? Write down the author's definition plus additional descriptive terms included in the essay.

d. This chapter discusses various criteria for organizing/structuring summary material for a report (see Exhibit 6–2, Part 2). What criteria would you say is used to organize the material in the body of "Business Cycle Theories"? Explain your answer.

e. Have the major divisions of material that make up the body of "Business Cycle Theories" been further subdivided and discussed in a systematic way? If your answer is "yes," label and describe the subdivisions. Are all three major divisions subdivided according to the same criteria?

f. Do you believe it was appropriate for the author to blend economic analysis with other summary material in the body of the report, or do you believe it would have been more effective if the author had only described explanations for the business cycle in part 2 and then provided a separate theoretical discussion (part 3) that would have illustrated all three types of theories in a single place? Explain which approach is most effective from the reader's perspective.

g. How do you rate the various graphical figures and boxes in the report? Are they clear? Do they illustrate key points of the discussion? Would the report be just as effective if some of these were omitted? (Explain your answer.) Place a check mark next to each paragraph in the body that is illustrated/summarized by one of the exhibits.

Business Cycle Theories

Craig Carlock, "Business Cycle Theories," *Cross Sections,* Federal Reserve Bank of Richmond (Winter 1990/91):6–9.

Much attention is being focused on the current slowdown of the U.S. economy. This article sketches three of the more prominent explanations for such changes in the economy's performance. The discussion may provide some insight into the reasons for the present downturn and the expansion that will follow.

Background: The Business Cycle

The pattern of ups and downs in economic activity is termed the *business cycle.* Business cycles are usually measured from successive peaks or troughs in economic activity. If measured from trough to trough, the business cycle is characterized by a phase of expanding economic activity followed by a phase of contracting economic activity (Figure 1).

The National Bureau of Economic Research (NBER), the official arbiter of the business cycle, uses a complex formula to measure aggregate economic activity. This formula allows the NBER to determine the month in which expansions and contractions begin. Others frequently use the *Real Gross National Product (RGNP)* to determine which phase of the business cycle the economy is in. RGNP, defined as the economy's total production of goods and services adjusted for inflation, is a simple and reliable proxy for the NBER method.

Each business cycle is unique. The length of expansions and contractions varies from cycle to cycle, and the expansion generally lasts longer than the contraction. The amplitude of each cycle is also different. Some contractions, such as the Great Depression, are extended and result in substantial unemployment; other contractions are less painful and may last only six months. Terminology has changed through the years, but currently a severe

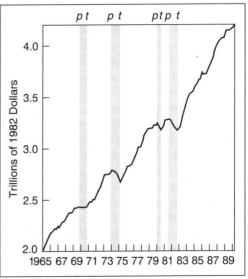

FIGURE 1 Real Gross National Product

Source: U.S. Department of Commerce.

contraction is termed a depression, a mild one a recession.

Despite its cyclical nature, the U.S. economy has generally grown over time. That is, despite occasional decreases, output of goods and services has tended to increase, not merely oscillate. Peaks in the business cycle are likely to be consecutively higher, as are troughs (Figure 1).

Attempts to understand the business cycle can be traced to the nineteenth century and are still under way today. Despite the effort that economists and others have devoted to studying business cycles, disagreement on the central cause or causes of business fluctuations persists. Three explanations generally considered plausible are outlined below.

Keynes and *The General Theory*

British economist John Maynard Keynes, writing during the Great Depression, offered an explanation for economic instability in *The General Theory of Employment, Interest and Money*. He sought to explain the high unemployment of the Depression, and he also suggested the appropriate government policy to induce expansion. Those who have adopted Keynes' major tenets are referred to as Keynesians, and the ideas they expound are termed "Keynesian."

Keynesian explanations for the business cycle focus on *aggregate demand*, or the economy's total demand for goods and services. Recession and involuntary unemployment, Keynesians believe, result primarily from insufficient aggregate demand (Figure 2, point 1). Demand may be deficient for several reasons. For example, business confidence might decline, causing firms to decrease their investment in plant and equipment. Or, consumers might curtail their spending because they are uncertain about future economic prospects.

In an economy with a dominant private sector, as in the United States, insufficient aggregate demand means that the demand for the goods and services produced by private businesses is weak. As firms realize that there is weak demand for their products, they respond by decreasing employment and output. In such circumstances, one might expect unemployed workers to lower their wage demands enough that businesses would hire them and full employment would result. But Keynesians argue that money wages do not fall quickly because of labor contracts and other factors. For example, an unemployed factory worker may not be able to work for less than the going wage because his factory is a union shop. Thus, say the Keynesians, wages remain too high for all workers to be employed, and involuntary unemployment persists.

Keynesian prescriptions for rectifying economic downturns aim to increase aggregate demand through discretionary government fiscal and monetary policies. In

FIGURE 2 The Keynesian View

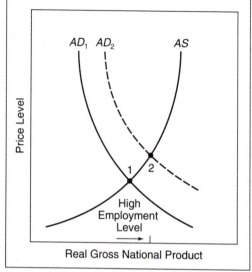

AD   (Aggregate Demand) The total quantity of goods and services demanded by businesses and consumers at each price level. All else constant, as the price level falls, the quantity of goods and services demanded increases.

AS   (Aggregate Supply) The quantity of goods and services that firms are willing and able to supply at each price. All else constant, as the price level rises, firms are willing to supply more goods.

Point 1   Aggregate demand is weak; unemployment exists.

Point 2   As the government stimulates aggregate demand through active policies, output and employment increase.

particular, Keynesians believe that the federal government's fiscal policy ought to be countercyclical. That is, when economic growth falters, the federal government should cut taxes and increase spending. Lower taxes, according to the Keynesians, would stimulate consumer spending; increased government purchases would spur employment and income growth in those industries that sell goods to, or provide services for, the government. As those who benefit from government purchases spend their additional income, other areas of the economy would be invigorated (Figure 2, point 2).

Although Keynes questioned the ability of easier monetary policy to boost the economy during the Depression, today's Keynesians suggest that the central bank take action to reduce interest rates in times of economic weakness. Lower interest rates, they say, would stimulate investment and increase aggregate demand. Keynesians stress, however, that the boost to the economy from an expansionary monetary policy is much less than the boost from an expansionary fiscal policy.

Keynesian detractors argue that expansionary fiscal and monetary policies may not produce their intended effects. For instance, these skeptics explain that as the government borrows (sells Treasury securities) to spend, it must raise interest rates to entice investors to purchase its securities. As interest rates rise, less investment in factories, equipment, housing, and other durable goods occurs. In other words, investment that would have taken place in the absence of greater government borrowing and spending is *crowded out* by higher interest rates. These skeptics conclude that the stimulus created by an expansionary fiscal policy is offset by the contractionary effects of decreased investment.

The Monetary Paradigm

In the late 1960s, Milton Friedman and Anna Schwartz offered another explanation for the business cycle in their book, *A Monetary History of the United States, 1867–1960*. Economists who have adopted their views are considered advocates of *monetarism*. Monetarists theorize that changes in the growth rate of the money supply—accelerations and decelerations—lead to changes in economic activity (Figure 3) and ultimately to changes in the price level.

As support for their theory, monetarists cite periods of declining money supply growth that coincided with recessions. For instance, monetarists point to the 1969 credit crunch and ensuing recession and to

FIGURE 3 Growth Rates of M2 and RGNP

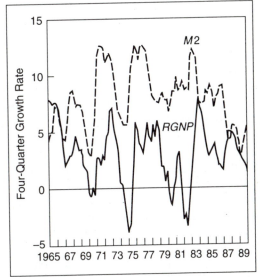

Sources: Board of Governors of the Federal Reserve System and U.S. Department of Commerce. Note: Growth rates are the four-quarter differences of the logs of M2 and RGNP.

the erratic money behavior of the late 1970s and the 1980 and 1981–82 recessions.

Although monetarists attribute cyclical variations in economic activity to changes in the money supply, they argue against trying to fine-tune the economy with monetary policy. Monetarists believe that the effects of policy on the subsequent behavior of the economy occur with long and variable lags. They stress that it takes a lag, or some time, for a change in the growth rate of the money supply to affect RGNP. Additionally, the lag time is variable—it differs from business cycle to business cycle. Empirical estimates of the lag between changes in money growth and changes in economic growth range from six months to two years.

For these reasons and because the monetarists believe that erratic money growth hinders the economy's performance, they propose that policymakers adopt a *monetary rule*. They suggest that the central bank increase the money supply at a constant rate each year (they suggest a 4 percent growth rate). Such a rule would guarantee predictable and stable money growth and would remove much uncertainty about monetary policy from the decisions facing economic agents.

Monetarists offer several explanations for how money influences the economy; one account focuses on how money affects interest rates. Like the Keynesians, the monetarists believe that increases or decreases in the money supply lead to changes in interest rates. Monetarists, however, argue that changes in the money supply affect interest rates to a much greater degree than the Keynesians contend. Monetarists submit that because the money supply can substantially alter interest rates, changes in the money supply can significantly influence economic activity.

Economists who subscribe to monetary theories explain that a sharp reduction in money growth raises interest rates. High interest rates deter aggregate business expenditures and investment; similarly, consumers become less willing to purchase items that must be financed. Firms in interest-sensitive industries thus face weak demand and respond by decreasing production and laying off workers. Laid-off workers curtail their spending, which further reduces demand for goods and services.

The monetary theorists posit that weaker demand induces producers of goods and services to restrain price increases, which slows the inflation rate. Employees' wages, however, may continue to increase due to contracts. A lower inflation rate coupled with unchanged growth in nominal wages raises *real wages* (nominal wages/price level). Firms respond by further cutting employment.

Monetarists advocate a limited response from policymakers to economic contractions. In the case of a recession that is apparently not the result of slow money growth, the central bank ought only to ensure that the money supply increases at its desired rate. In the case of a recession

evidently resulting from slow money growth, the central bank should return the growth rate of the money supply to its appropriate rate (determined by the rule). A resumption of desired money growth will, they assert, eventually lower interest rates and induce individuals to increase interest-sensitive consumption and businesses to expand investment. Once the recovery is under way, monetarists stress the importance of maintaining a constant growth rate in the money supply.

In addition to addressing the business cycle, monetarists also comment on the causes of inflation. They believe that, over time, increases in the price level result directly from increases in the money supply. They recognize that disturbances, such as an oil shock, can raise prices in the short run. They argue, however, that over a period of several years, the quantity of money determines the price level.

Real Business Cycle Theory

Although GNP movements and money supply movements appear to be correlated as the monetarists contend, real wages have not behaved as the monetarists predict. The empirical evidence demonstrates that, contrary to monetary—and Keynesian—theory, real wages fall during recessions. This discrepancy, coupled with the monetarists' inability to account for the 1974–75 recession, led to the formulation of the real business cycle theory.

Real business cycle (RBC) theory posits that both positive and negative movements in economic activity can be traced to random *real*—as opposed to *monetary*—shocks. Oil embargoes, strikes, changes in the tax code, and technological improvements are all real shocks. Supply and demand shocks such as these, the theory argues, can set in motion a chain of events capable of generating aggregate economic fluctuations.

For example, suppose one sector of the economy experiences a negative productivity shock such as a labor strike. The income of the individuals employed in this sector falls, and many of these individuals respond by decreasing their consumption of goods and services. This decrease in consumer expenditure adversely affects some businesses which then restrict their investment. If the troubled economic sector is sufficiently large, then its decrease in consumption and business investment can reduce aggregate demand and induce recession.

As the economy weakens and unemployment rises, individuals in other economic sectors lower their wage demands to maintain their jobs. Note that the downward adjustment of real wages contradicts the Keynesian and monetarist theories and better conforms to the empirical evidence.

Real business cycle theory is compatible with the positive correlation between money supply growth and GNP growth. RBC theorists contend that businesses demand money for transactions purposes because money is an inexpensive method of payment for goods and services. As output expands (contracts), the volume of transactions grows (shrinks), and the demand for money increases (decreases). Thus, the demand for money and money growth will increase or decrease along with GNP. The coincident movement of GNP and money growth is, RBC theorists purport, an *effect* of the business cycle and not a *cause* as monetarists contend.

Policy prescriptions from real business cycle theory differ markedly from the suggestions of the Keynesian or monetary paradigms. For instance, RBC theory suggests that recessions often result *not* from policy mistakes, but from unforeseeable demand or supply shocks. Real business cycle theorists are unlikely to advocate government attempts to stimulate a weak economy. Instead, they are likely to support predictable fiscal and monetary policies with the belief that in an environment with as little uncertainty as possible economic growth will return.

FIGURE 4 The Real Business Cycle Theory

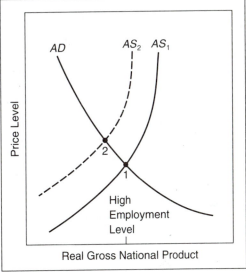

Point 1   Output is near capacity; unemployment is minimal.

Point 2   A supply shock—such as an oil embargo—hits the economy. Businesses incur higher costs and respond by reducing output and employment. Prices rise.

Postscript

The Keynesian, monetary, and real business cycle theories have greatly enhanced our understanding of business cycles. Although each theory offers a different principal cause for the business cycle, there is common ground. That is, a Keynesian would likely admit that a severe supply shock could cause a recession, and a real business cycle theorist probably would agree that erratic money growth is disruptive.

In addition to providing a better grasp of the causes of economic fluctuations, these theories also shed light on the capabilities and limitations of government policy. Although no "cure" for the business cycle appears imminent, this research provides hope that someday it may be possible to lengthen expansions and shorten contractions.

(continued)

A QUICK RUNDOWN ON BUSINESS CONTRACTIONS

Cause	Solution
Keynesians: Insufficient aggregate demand, inability of labor market to adjust because wages are rigid.	**Keynesians:** Increased government spending, decreased taxes, looser monetary policy.
Monetarists: Erratic or slow money growth, disruptive changes in banking regulations.	**Monetarists:** Constant and stable money growth, through a minority suggest short-term money injection.
RBC Theorists: Random demand and supply shocks such as an oil embargo or a labor strike.	**RBC Theorists:** Stable fiscal and monetary policies, no overt action called for.

Exercise 2: A summary report titled "U.S. Cars Grow Old" by Marla Kessler, an economist at the Federal Reserve Bank of Richmond, begins on the following page. Read the report and then answer the following questions:

a. Summarize the theme of the summary report in one sentence.

b. If we conceive of the report as having three parts—introduction, body, and concluding remarks—where does the body of the report begin and end? (Describe the beginning and end of the body and logically justify your decision.)

c. This chapter of the text discusses various criteria for organizing/ structuring material which comprises the body of a summary report (see Exhibit 6–2, Part 2). What criteria would you say is used to organize the material in the body of "U.S. Cars Grow Old"? Explain your answer.

d. 1) List the major divisions of material in the body of the report.
2) Do these divisions/components of the body follow any apparent theme, or do they have any identifiable relationship to each other? What is it?

e. Draw an economic diagram (e.g., a production function, cost curve, demand curve, etc.) to illustrate each economic relationship discussed in the body of the report. If the discussion suggests a shift or movement along a curve, include that in your diagram.

f. How many different sources of data and other outside information is incorporated in this report? List the various sources and describe their location in the report.

g. Do the theoretical arguments and empirical evidence in the article suggest that the average age of autos will continue to increase during the 1990s, or that the trend is likely to turn around? Explain and justify your answer.

U.S. Cars Grow Old

Marla Kessler, "U.S. Cars Grow Old," *Cross Sections*, Federal Reserve Bank of Richmond (Fall 1991): 4–5, 7.

The U.S. automobile stock is getting older. In 1990, the average age of the 100 million cars driven in the United States was 7.8 years, the oldest in forty years (Chart 1).

The U.S. car stock ages when fewer new cars are bought and fewer old cars are scrapped. During World War II, for example, no new cars were produced, so people kept using their older models. As a result, the average age of U.S. cars rose to a peak of 9.0 years, then fell sharply as new car production resumed after the War.

In the years since 1969, the average age of cars on the road has increased primarily because of a decline in the rate of purchase of new cars. The new car purchase rate and the scrappage rate tend to move together, but while the scrappage rate has fluctuated around 8 percent for many years, the new car purchase rate has trended downward (Chart 2). The difference between these two rates is the growth rate of the U.S. car stock.

New car supplies have not been limited since World War II, except temporarily by occasional work stoppages, so new car sales have depended on new car demand. The factors that contributed to the depressed demand for new cars in recent years included the improved quality of older cars, the lower real income of new car buyers, and the higher prices of new cars.

Quality

The quality of cars—both foreign and domestic—has improved considerably over time. Improvements in features such as comfort, safety, and gasoline economy make new cars more attractive than ever to consumers. But older cars also last longer and have fewer problems and better fea-

CHART 1 Average Age of Automobiles Annually, 1946–90

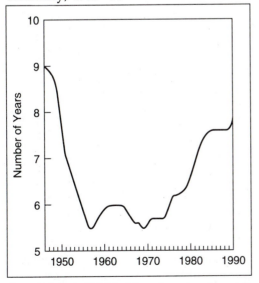

Source: Motor Vehicle Manufacturers Association. *Facts and Figures.*

CHART 2 Annual Growth, Scrappage and New Car Purchase Rates Percent of the U.S. Car Stock

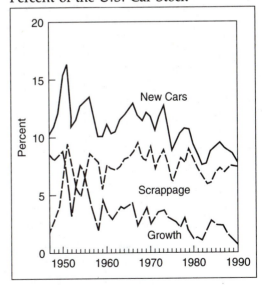

Source: *Ward's Automotive Yearbook.*

tures than in previous years, which makes it easier to postpone their replacement.

For many years, Consumers Union has surveyed car owners and reported frequency-of-repair experiences in the magazine *Consumer Reports*. These survey results document the continued improvement in car quality over the years. In 1990, for example, 5-year-old cars as well as new cars spent less time in the shop than in 1980 (Chart 3).

Many analysts agree that heightened competition from foreign cars has been largely responsible for the quality improvement in American cars. As foreign manufacturers captured a larger share of new car sales, domestic manufacturers improved the quality of their cars, and, according to *Consumer Reports*, the "quality gap" narrowed.

Consumers generally prefer new cars to older cars, other things equal. However, other things did not stay equal. In particular, the ability of consumers to buy new cars declined because their incomes did not keep pace with either inflation or new car prices.

Income

The average real earnings of U.S. workers trended downward from 1972 to 1990 (Chart 4), interrupted only by brief increases following recessions. Some analysts attribute this decline to the rapid increase in the labor force during this period and to the changes in its composition as more women entered the workforce. A recent *Business Week* profile of average workers' earnings revealed that average wages for women are only about 65 percent of those for men. Meanwhile, the industrial makeup of jobs has shifted from higher paying jobs in manufacturing to lower paying ones in the service-producing sectors.

To be sure, the increased number of workers intensified the demand for cars, as demonstrated by the decline in the number of drivers per car, which went from 1.42 in 1960 to 1.15 in 1989. However, the decline in average real earnings tended to decrease the demand for new cars. Consequently, the average age of cars on the road rose.

CHART 3 Average Annual Problems Per 100 Cars

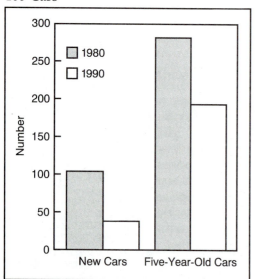

Source: *Consumer Reports*.

CHART 4 Real Annual Income of Average U.S. Worker

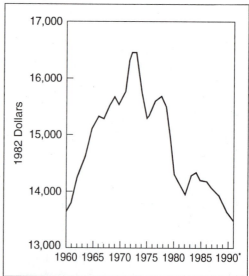

*Estimated for 1991.
Source: Bureau of Labor Statistics.

The recent recession also contributed to the aging of the U.S. automobile stock. The business cycle affects the demand for new cars because income and employment rise and fall with business conditions. During the recessions of 1970, 1973–75, and the early 1980s, for example, the average age of cars on the road rose rapidly. This past year, as the economy slowed, the average age of cars rose again for the first time in six years.

Price

The average price of a new car in 1990 was almost six times greater than the average new car price thirty years earlier, but over half of the increase was due to quality improvements. In fact, the price of today's new car, adjusted for quality improvements to make it comparable to one available years ago, has not risen as much as the general price level (Chart 5). That is, if a 1957 Chevrolet were being manufactured and sold today, its price would not have risen as much as the general level of prices.

But today, there are no "new" 1957 Chevrolets. Instead, there are new cars that are simply better in many ways than those of years ago, and these quality improvements are reflected in the price.

During the 1980s, however, the price of the average new car, including all of the quality improvements as well as options, transportation costs, and sales taxes, and allowing for rebates, rose faster than the income of the average American worker (Chart 6), and sales of new cars suffered. In the late 1970s, about 11 million new cars were sold each year. In 1990, about 9 million were sold.

A measure of new car affordability tells the story best. The ratio of an average worker's before-tax income to the average price of a new car was 1.86 in the mid 1970s. By 1990, however, new car affordability as measured by this ratio had fallen to 1.21 (Chart 7). But there is some good news. According to a 1991 survey by *Autoweek*, new car affordability increased recently as new car prices eased somewhat.

CHART 5 Price Indexes New Cars and All Consumer Items

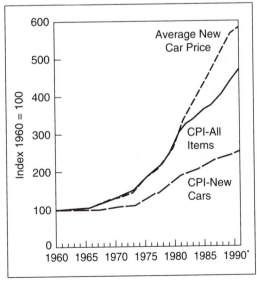

*Estimated for 1991.
Source: Bureau of Economic Analysis.

CHART 6 Change in Income and New Car Prices, 1961–91

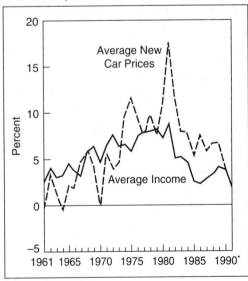

*Estimated for 1991.
Source: Bureau of Economic Analysis and Bureau of Labor Statistics.

CHART 7 New Car Affordability Ratio: Average Worker's Annual Income to Average New Car Price

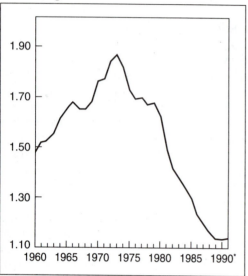

*Estimated for 1991.
Source: Bureau of Economic Analysis and Bureau of Labor Statistics.

CHART 8 New Car Sales and Loan Interest Rates, 1971–90

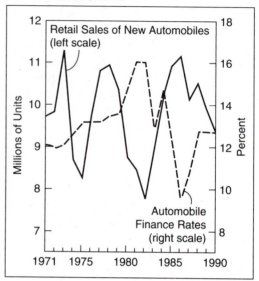

Source: Motor Vehicle Manufacturers Association. *Facts and Figures* and the Board of Governors of the Federal Reserve System.

The affordability of new cars also depends on automobile financing costs because these costs are, in effect, part of the price (or cost of owning) a car. Higher interest rates mean higher monthly payments. Chart 8 shows that new car sales have moved opposite to the interest rates charged for new car financing.

Used cars are a substitute for new cars, so higher prices for new cars tend to increase the demand for the limited supply of used cars and push up their prices. The data show that the prices of used cars tend to rise when the demand for new cars is depressed.

Conclusion

The average age of the U.S. auto stock rose in recent years as new car prices rose more rapidly than incomes and as the reliability of older cars improved along with that of the newer ones. As the economy recovers from the recent recession and if new car prices do not discourage buyers, new car sales should revive somewhat, especially since the aging stock of cars on the road will require more replacements. Also, as the nation moves toward price stability, interest rates should fall, reducing the effective cost of car ownership.

Exercise 3: Write a 1,000-word summary report about an industry that you are interested in. Gather background information on the industry from *U.S. Industrial Outlook* (Washington, DC: U.S. Department of Commerce, annual) and the *Wall Street Journal* (refer to the *WSJ Index* for related articles and to the *WSJ*'s quarterly profits reports that appear in February, May, August, and November).

Exercise 4: Locate a recent copy of *Time* magazine or *The Economist* (most college libraries subscribe to these publications) and identify one "summary report" article that follows the approach described in this chapter. The article should focus on an economic issue or problem.

a.   Identify the main theme of the article-report.
b.   What method does the article use to grab the reader's attention within the first few sentences? (Describe the anecdote or quotes that attract reader interest.)
c.   Point out major subdivisions of material in the main body of the article-report. (Write down titles of the subdivisions if those are provided; if they aren't, write down your own descriptive terms.)
d.   Describe the relationship between the subdivisions of material. Are they arranged into categories, along a continuum, or chronologically? How does the first subdivision relate to the second and third (etc.)?
e.   Does the article present concepts or relationships that you have studied in economics courses? (List them.)
f.   Does the final paragraph mention an unresolved problem or controversy that the reader is likely to encounter in the future? (Describe it.)

Notes on Chapter 6

Use the space below to describe new concepts or methods that you learned in Chapter 6.

Bibliography

Much can be learned about the most effective methods for putting together summary reports by reading a few summary reports. Many *magazine articles* are little more than summaries that bring together information from a wide variety of sources. The first few paragraphs of such articles typically contain introductory material, including an anecdote (story) or quote that grabs the reader's attention and helps place the topic of the article in perspective (part 1). The next several paragraphs typically discuss important considerations that one should know about before forming a final opinion—events, policies, or research findings. This part of the discussion is usually broken into three or four smaller discussions identified by boldface captions to signal readers that a new point is being emphasized. Collectively, these smaller discussions comprise the body of the report (part 2). Depending on the publication, some analysis may be blended into the summary material or identified in a separate section with its own boldface caption near the end

of the article (part 3). Finally, the article might conclude by drawing together key points from earlier parts of the article and providing some kind of statement (prediction or social commentary) that invites the reader to give the matter further thought (part 4).

Richard Saul Wurman, whose work was cited earlier in this chapter, is an information specialist whose business is packaging information to make it more valuable to users. The material in this chapter is most closely related to chapter 2 of Wurman's *Information Anxiety* (New York: Bantam Books, 1989).

Some of the ideas developed in this chapter are also discussed in Conal Furay and Michael J. Salevouris, *The Methods and Skills of History* (Arlington Heights, IL: Harlan Davidson, 1988): chapter 5; Judith Richlin-Klonsky and Ellen Strenski (eds.), *A Guide to Writing Sociology Papers* (New York: St. Martin's Press, 1991): chapter 6; and Francis C. Dane, *Research Methods* (Belmont, CA: Wadsworth, 1990): chapter 9.

CHAPTER 7

Summarizing a Policy Debate

An educated person is tolerant of the views of others and welcomes them into the marketplace of ideas. . . . The public philosophy of this country is such that what Judge Learned Hand called a "fair field and an honest race to all ideas" is promised. Failure to reach a compromise is not fatal.
—*Barbara Jordan*

Introduction

Economists are occasionally asked to explain or summarize a policy debate. Should the minimum wage be increased, or not? Should the Federal Reserve stimulate the economy by increasing the money supply, or not? Will a free trade agreement between the U.S. and Latin American countries contribute to the prosperity of all those nations, or not? All policy debates include two (or more) opinions about some policy question. An essay that summarizes the debate should provide a fair statement of both views; an essay that presents only one point of view is an editorial.

That does not mean you are not entitled to a personal opinion about a policy debate, or even to express that opinion at the appropriate time. But the appropriate time is late in the report, after the contending views have been fairly presented and explained. Economic analysis may suggest that one or both sides of the debate are mistaken about key issues. The economist's opinion should follow, and be based on, an analysis of the views of the parties involved in the debate.

A 6-Step Procedure

As for other reports, the economic writer must carry out several distinct tasks to summarize a policy debate. The tasks themselves are fairly standard, but each writer may carry them out in a different order or spend more or less time on each. With this in mind, review Exhibit 7–1 and the following comments regarding the process of putting together a summary report on a policy debate.

EXHIBIT 7–1 Six steps in preparing a policy debate report

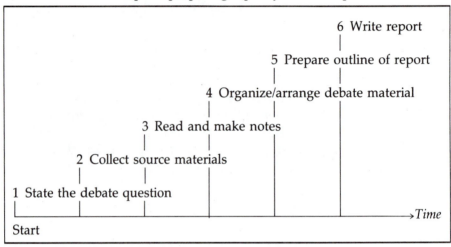

- First, *define the question or issue* being debated. Write this down in a simple, unadorned statement that a nonexpert could understand. Refer frequently to this statement to ensure that your background research and writing do not stray from the topic. If you later discover that the statement is inaccurate or can be stated more clearly, rewrite it.
- Second, *collect information* related to the debate. In most instances this will require a trip to the library, the use of indexes, and other activities discussed in Chapter 3, "Locating Published Research." (These activities were illustrated graphically in Exhibit 3–2.) Policy debates are typically reported in the general news media rather than in specialized economics publications, so it may be useful to refer to the *Reader's Guide to Periodical Literature, InfoTrac* and other general-purpose indexes. One of the best sources of unbiased information about pending legislation and other policy proposals is the *Congressional Quarterly Weekly Report*. The *CQ* index, published every six months, provides a guide to *CQ* articles.
- Third, *read the materials* you have collected *and compile brief notes* about issues relevant to the debate, either background information you uncover or points raised by the debaters themselves. Many researchers

use note cards for writing their research notes and only include one main idea per card. Another approach is to write all of your notes from a single book or article on a sheet of paper, then return to this sheet when it is necessary to locate a certain piece of information. A third approach is to collect notes in a file (or document) on a personal computer. This permits notes to be collected in a single group during the reading stage, then moved into an outline at the appropriate time (as index cards might be). Regardless of the approach you take, make notes on each main claim or rebuttal made by the parties engaged in debate. Include page numbers and other reference information with your notes so you can easily return to the original document when necessary.

- Fourth, use notes from your readings to decide how to *organize the debate material* that will comprise the main section (body) of the report. As noted in Chapter 4, note cards can be laid out on a table to arrange information in the actual order it will appear in the report. One method of organizing this material is to present a strong statement or claim from one side of the debate, follow it with critical remarks from the other side, then present rebuttals and additional critical remarks. Another method is to thoroughly summarize one side's point of view, do the same for the other side, then discuss disagreement between the two sides. More attention will be given to structuring the report later in this chapter. (See "Organizing the Debate," below.)

- Fifth, use notes from the readings and other ideas you might have to *prepare an outline of the complete report*. The outline provides a *map* of the debate and related information. This map should show how various components of the report are connected to the other parts and establish the flow of the report from beginning to end. The main elements of a debate summary are discussed below (see "Outlining the Debate Report"). The outline-map should include the key points you plan to mention in the introduction, body, and conclusion of the report.

- Sixth, *write a summary of the debate*. As you write, reconsider the organization of key ideas in the debate to decide whether some other arrangement might provide a more logical presentation.

Outlining the Debate Report

The final two steps in preparing the debate report (Exhibit 7-1) indicate that the researcher should outline and then write the report. As in other types of reports, a good place to begin is with *introductory remarks* that provide a context for the rest of the discussion; a good place to close is with *summary comments* that reiterate key points raised earlier in the report. The debate material itself constitutes the *main body* of the report. If you decide to include an economic analysis of issues raised in the debate, that part of the report should follow the debate material. To reduce the odds of leaving important material out of the report, explicitly divide it into four major functional parts, identified below. Adjust titles to reflect the specific content of each part of your report.

Part 1. Introduction

A report whose purpose is to summarize a policy debate should explain the origin of the debate (usually a perceived problem), outline the general position of each party to the debate, and provide additional material that would help readers understand the nature of the debate. The introduction should *always* state the question or issue being debated in a direct statement that no reader will fail to grasp. Consider a statement of this nature: "The purpose of this report is to describe the debate between proponents and opponents of a free trade agreement between the U.S. and Mexico." It is the author's responsibility to make sure that any material included in the final report contributes to the stated objective. Information that does not help the reader understand the policy debate should be omitted from the report.

The introductory section should also contain brief definitions of key terms when they are first mentioned. Key terms are those that figure prominently in the debate. This will introduce the reader to terms (and jargon) used by specialists in the area. Specialists often use short phrases to describe a complex policy proposal ("education voucher") or to summarize a theoretical analysis ("moral hazard problem"); the nonspecialist reader requires additional explanation to comprehend such phrases.

To summarize, the introductory section of a summary report should include the following key elements:

- Statement of debate question or issue.
- Discussion of problems that led to the policy proposals being debated.
- List of parties engaged in the debate and the positions they take.
- Definition of key terms.

The particular order in which these points are addressed will depend on the author's own preferences and the nature of the material being discussed.

Part 2. The Debate

The main body of a debate report is the actual summary of positions taken by the participants in the debate, as well as their responses to the other's claims. This is the most important part of the report, so it is examined in greater detail later in the chapter. (See "Organizing the Debate," below.)

Part 3. Economic Analysis of Debate Material

This is an optional part of a policy debate report, but many economists decide to include it. In this part of the report the writer examines claims or assumptions by debate participants that conflict with the principles of economic theory, e.g., the failure to recognize that price ceilings cause shortages or the implicit assumption that individuals are not self-interested. It is not always possible to settle a disagreement by demonstrating flaws in the argument of one side or the other, but recognizing such flaws may allow one to identify problems that are likely to arise if a given policy is adopted. For example, those who promote rent controls may not mention that a shortage of apartments is likely to develop. The economist can make this point, and may also want to mention specific communities in which rent controls have led to housing shortages.

Economic analysis refers to the act of dividing some position or policy into its component parts and examining those components with the use of economic theory. Any generalizations you draw from the analysis should stick to specific issues you have examined. It is not helpful to make sweeping statements like, "This proposal is foolish and the people who support it are hopelessly confused." If that is true, then you should be able to demonstrate what is wrong with the proposal by analyzing each of its component parts. Readers like to be provided with *reasons* so they can draw their own conclusions about who is confused and which proposals are totally without merit. The person or group advocating a particular proposal has a reason for supporting it; your job is to understand that reason, fairly present it to your readers, and use economic theory to demonstrate its likely effects, both on proponents and on others in society. Because everything desirable comes at a cost, an economist should be able to identify and discuss those costs.

Part 4. Concluding Remarks

The concluding section of a policy debate should reflect one's purpose for writing the report. If the report has no other purpose than to draw together information about opposing points of view, it may be acceptable to restate the proposal and summarize in one or two sentences the main contention or claim of those on each side of the debate. If the purpose of the report is to *convince* the reader that one position is more meritorious than the other, the concluding section is a good place to explain why one advantage or problem is so important that it should outweigh considerations presented by the other side. A third approach is to emphasize the arguments that seem most persuasive to policy makers, in order to *predict* which policy ultimately will be adopted. This may also be a good time to predict whether the policy is likely—because of some conflict with economic principles—to cause even greater problems than those it was designed to solve.

Your influence over readers at this stage—your ability to convince them to accept your conclusion—depends on the quality of your economic analysis (part 3) and on whether or not you were evenhanded toward both points of view earlier in the report. The people you most hope to influence initially hold the opposing point of view, and to change their minds you must understand their perspective and answer their objections. Nothing significant is gained by setting up a "straw man" argument and then knocking it down, since those on the other side of the issue will not consider the "defeat" meaningful. (A straw man argument is a foolish and easy-to-defeat version of an argument that is created by opponents; its only purpose is to permit the opponent to claim victory in a debate.) To repeat the point made a moment ago, the only lasting victory in a debate is one that identifies and addresses the concerns of those on the other side of the issue.

Organizing the Debate in Part 2

Economic policy debates are about policies and the people who support or oppose them. This suggests two methods of presenting a policy debate (in part 2 of the report). In the first approach the debate summary is organized around the specific *features* of a policy or according to *claims made* for the policy's effectiveness. This method is frequently used by economists, whose methods are suited to analyzing the effects of policies. The second approach is to organize the debate summary around the *individuals or groups* whose views are in opposition. To be adopted, most policies have to gain the support of powerful interest groups or members of Congress. A political scientist may divide the discussion between supporters and opponents, to better see which side has the politically stronger argument and is most likely to prevail. Journalists may also prefer this approach, since readers are more likely to read stories about competitive events where the outcome is in doubt. Exhibit 7–2 summarizes these two methods of organizing a policy debate.

EXHIBIT 7–2 Policy debate outlines

1. Arranged by features or effects of the proposal	2. Arranged by contending sides in the debate
Point 1 • Feature or claim • Critique • Rebuttal	**Proponents** • Feature/claim 1 • Feature/claim 2 • Feature/claim 3
Point 2 • Feature or claim • Critique • Rebuttal	**Opponents** • Critique 1 • Critique 2 • Critique 3
Point 3 • Feature or claim • Critique • Rebuttal	**Rebuttal** • Answer and reaction 1 • Counterclaim and reaction 2

The left half of the exhibit shows how the debate might be structured around major features or claims made for the policy proposal. With this approach, the body of the report begins by presenting the strongest reason proponents have for supporting a policy. Opponents either disagree with the objectives of the proposal or with the analysis that supporters use to justify their views, so the opposing point of view is given at this time. This point-counterpoint presentation is followed by one or two remarks from each side, to rebut comments made by the other. The same approach is used to present a second and third major point of contention.

In the right half of Exhibit 7–2, the same debate could be organized around the positions taken by proponents and opponents of the proposed policy. In this scheme the views of policy advocates are stated at length. Next, the critical views of their opponents are stated, so that each claim or policy suggestion from proponents is questioned. Finally, answers and counterclaims are given for the most significant areas of disagreement. This permits each side to further refine their argument by fine-tuning it to answer specific objections.

An Example

The two approaches can be illustrated by focusing on a hypothetical policy debate. In this instance the debate is over the desirability of relying more on earmarked taxes and user charges to finance government services, and less on other taxes. An earmarked tax is a tax whose revenues are dedicated to providing specific services rather than going into the government's general budget. For example, the federal gasoline tax is earmarked for highway construction. User charges are the government's version of market prices; consumers pay a fee for the service they receive and nonconsumers pay nothing. For example, campers pay a fee to stay overnight at certain national parks.

Proponents of earmarking and user charges claim that they require program beneficiaries to pay for the services they receive, and prevent government from taking income from the general public in order to provide benefits to favored groups. They believe that putting each program on a self-financing basis will make the agency or bureau that administers the program more responsible to their immediate customers rather than their political bosses. And they note that when user charges are levied an increase in demand for some service will automatically generate the funds needed to provide additional services. When services are financed out of the general revenue fund, special legislation would be required—but may not be forthcoming—to channel money to the area where consumer demand is increasing.

Opponents of earmarked taxes and user charges feel that such rules place too many constraints on policy makers. By "locking up" certain parts of government revenue these rules prevent officials from responding to increasing demand for other (nonearmarked) services. The fact that an earmarked fee is being collected for the provision of some service does not mean that actual tax receipts bear a close relationship to the number of dollars needed to provide the service. If the amount falls short, then it must be supplemented from the government's general revenue funds. If earmarked revenues exceed the government's cost of providing necessary services, excess dollars may be spent on low-priority items. Finally, opponents claim that user charges discourage citizens from making full use of desirable public services. By eliminating charges for these services, everyone has access to roads, libraries, and parks.

Exhibits 7–3 and 7–4 are just reorganized versions of the two paragraphs of remarks above. In each instance, a *structured argument* is created from a series of comments, observations, and opinions. Either outline could be used to write a summary report of the tax debate.

EXHIBIT 7–3 Tax debate organized by proponent/opponent groups*

Proponents

- Beneficiaries should pay for services, not the general public.
- User fees provide an automatic mechanism to channel more funds to services where consumer demands are increasing (and reduce funds to services where consumer demands are decreasing).
- Agencies are more responsive to customer needs when they receive their funding from customers.

Opponents

- Some consumers will be prevented from receiving public services when charges are imposed.
- Revenues collected under earmarked taxes and user charges are unlikely to match the amount needed to fund each particular program or service.
- Earmarking funds to certain services prevents officials from using those funds in other (unrelated) areas that are underfunded when citizen demands increase.

Rebuttal

- *Answer* (proponents): User fees *do* prevent people from consuming what they do not pay for, but that is the way it *should* be. *Reaction* (opponents): What about health care? What about schools? Should the poor do without these services? *Answer* (proponents): Many of the people who receive these services free of charge are not poor. To deal with poverty, provide money transfers to the poor; to provide a particular service to the poor, give them "vouchers" they can use to purchase the service. Other consumers should pay for their own benefits.
- *Counterclaim* (opponents): A major problem with the proposal is the waste that results when certain government revenues are placed off limits for other uses. If there is an excess of dollars in the highway trust fund (collected from earmarked taxes on gasoline), then we will not be able to use those dollars where they are most needed. We may build highways that are low on the priority list rather than hospitals that are more urgently needed. *Reaction* (proponents): That is a problem that can be solved by adjusting the fees and tax rates—an administrative detail. Hire a consultant from the private sector to learn what price would recover the government agency's cost of production.

---

*The point being debated is whether states and cities should place greater reliance on user charges and earmarked taxes (rather than income, sales, and other taxes) to finance government services.

EXHIBIT 7–4 Tax debate organized by features of the proposal*

Feature 1

- *Claim:* Specific beneficiaries of a service should pay the cost of providing it, not the general public.
- *Critique:* When we impose charges, some consumers will be prevented from receiving important public services.
- *Rebuttal:* Proponents—that is the way it *should* be. Opponents— Should the poor do without essential health care and schools? Proponents—Giving free services to rich and poor alike does not solve poverty. Provide the poor with money income or vouchers, then let them purchase their own services. Other consumers should pay the cost of providing the benefits they receive.

Feature 2

- *Claim:* User fees provide a mechanism to channel more funds to government agencies that provide services in greatest demand by consumers, and vice versa.
- *Critique:* Funds collected under earmarked taxes and user charges are unlikely to match the cost of providing every particular program or service.
- *Rebuttal:* Opponents—When taxes and fees generate more revenue than needed to supply some service, the additional dollars should be used by other government agencies. Earmarked taxes do not permit this. Proponents—Any mismatch between revenues and expenses only means that fees should be adjusted, not that we should do without fees. Private companies make these types of pricing decisions every day.

Feature 3

- *Claim:* Agencies are more responsive to consumer needs when they receive their funding directly from customers.
- *Critique:* Earmarking funds for certain government activities prevent officials from using funds in other areas that are underfunded. In effect, earmarking funds makes it impossible to satisfy *other* consumer needs. That cannot be efficient.
- *Rebuttal:* Proponents—Perhaps those other services need to have their own earmarked charges. Opponents—Or perhaps we should refrain from earmarking any revenues so policy makers will be able to react to changing circumstances.

*The point being debated is whether states and cities should place greater reliance on user charges and earmarked taxes (rather than income, sales, and other taxes) to finance government services.

Additional supporting material could be added to support any of the ideas mentioned in the outline. For example, government revenue amounts might be included to illustrate some point, or explicit value judgments (of proponents or opponents) could be discussed if it is claimed that one group or the other is promoting ideas that conflict with cherished beliefs. Policy makers, especially those elected to office, take values and beliefs into account, so it is important to be aware of the role played by normative issues in a policy debate.

Summary

Experts, government officials, and interest groups often disagree about policy issues. The economic writer may want to organize the opinions of various groups into a debate format, so that each idea is balanced against a competing idea. The competition of ideas increases the likelihood that the best ideas will be recognized and adopted, while the worst are exposed and rejected. The writer's role is to bring competing ideas together and arrange them so that the reader can understand the position of each side and arrive at an informed opinion. The writer is not personally responsible for answering the questions raised by either side, and is not required to judge which argument is most convincing.

In the present discussion it was suggested that actual debate material be arranged by either of two organizing principles. Key components or features of the proposal can be discussed one at a time, or the views and objections of opposing advocacy groups can be discussed one at a time. It was suggested that economists may prefer the former approach, while political scientists and journalists may prefer the latter.

Exhibit 7–5 provides a sample outline for a policy debate summary. In addition to the body of the report (part 2) the report should contain introductory comments, economic analysis, and concluding remarks.

EXHIBIT 7–5 Policy debate outline

Part 1. Introduction

- State the policy question being debated
- Discuss problems that caused the policy to be proposed
- Name parties involved in the debate and state their position on the proposal

Part 2. Organizing the debate summary (select one approach)

- Organize debate material by major *features or claims made* for the proposal or results claimed
  - Positive comment about some aspect of the proposal, a critique, then rebuttal
  - Positive comment 2, critique, rebuttal
  - Positive comment 3, critique, rebuttal

  or

EXHIBIT 7–5   (continued)

- Organize material by *proponent* and *opponent* views of the policy proposal
  - Comments of policy advocates regarding the desirability of the policy
  - Critical remarks by policy opponents
  - Answer-reaction-counterclaim on key points

Part 3. Economic analysis of the debate

- Identify the assumptions and examine the claims made by both sides
- Use economic principles to point out inconsistencies between assumptions and claims made by either group
- Predict the likely effects of the proposal, if it is adopted (or of the status quo, if it is not adopted)

Part 4. Concluding remarks

- Restate the policy proposal and summarize major views of both sides
- Mention any overriding considerations or major flaws on either side
- Offer predictions for the future (if appropriate)

Exercises

Exercise 1: The North American Free Trade Agreement (NAFTA) between the U.S., Mexico, and Canada was negotiated and signed by President Bush in 1992 and endorsed by candidate (later President) Clinton during the 1992 election campaign. Nevertheless, NAFTA has a number of opponents who have argued that the treaty should be either renegotiated or rejected outright. The U.S. continues to face vexing trade problems, and many of the arguments made for and against NAFTA are also raised in regard to other trade issues.

Read several articles on NAFTA and prepare a 1,200-word essay summarizing the policy debate that raged at the time. Your debate paper should be organized in the manner suggested in Exhibit 7–5. It should be easy to locate articles in newspapers and magazines regarding NAFTA, but to get you started, here is a short list of items you may want to consult:

Patrice Rhoades-Baum, "Trade Pact Would Remove Barriers in North America," *The Margin* (Spring 1993): 66–67.

Bill Clinton, "Clinton Urges Passage of Free-Trade Pact," *Congressional Quarterly Weekly Report* (September 18, 1993): 2501–02.

Bob Davis, "Free Trade Pact Spurs a Diverse Coalition of Grass-Roots Foes," *Wall Street Journal* (December 23, 1992): A1.

David S. Cloud, "Sound and Fury Over NAFTA Overshadows the Debate," *Congressional Quarterly Weekly Report* (October 16, 1993): 2791–96.

Exercise 2: During 1991–93 the money supply (M2) expanded far less rapidly than the Fed's targets, causing many to complain that Fed policy slowed recovery from the recent recession. An opposing view is that restrictive monetary policies are necessary to wring inflation out of the economy, and that alternative measures of money growth indicate that monetary policy has not been as restrictive as commonly believed.

   Read several articles on this issue and prepare a 1,200-word essay summarizing the policy debate that raged at the time. Your debate paper should be organized in the manner suggested in Exhibit 7–5. A number of articles regarding monetary policy appeared during 1992, but to get you started, here is a short list of items you may want to consult:

Timothy Tregarthen, "M2 Growth Remains Weak: Does it Matter?" *The Margin* (Spring 1993): 20–21.

Federal Open Market Committee, "Record of Policy Actions of the Federal Open Market Committee," *Federal Reserve Bulletin* (October 1992): 755–63, esp. 759–60.

Alan Greenspan, "Statement Before the Committee on Banking, Housing and Urban Affairs of the U.S. Senate," *Federal Reserve Bulletin* (September 1992): 673–78, esp. 676–77.

Exercise 3: Locate, read, and make notes on recent articles on *one* of the following topics, then prepare a 1,200-word essay summarizing the policy debate surrounding it. Your debate paper should be organized in the manner suggested in Exhibit 7–5.

a. Fixed exchange rates/European Monetary System—Should major European nations adopt a single currency or fix the value of their currency in terms of other currencies (rather than permitting exchange rates to fluctuate in currency markets)?

b. Federal budget deficit—Should the federal deficit be reduced by increasing taxes or by reducing government spending?

c. Vouchers in education—Should parents be given vouchers or some other option that permits them greater choice in selecting an elementary or secondary school for their children?

d. Body organ sales—Should it be legal for close relatives to sell body organs of deceased people for money, as a means of eliminating the shortage of organs for transplanting?

e. Profiteering during emergencies—Should lumberyards and other merchants be permitted to increase product prices to increase their profits following a natural disaster (such as Hurricane Hugo in 1989 or Hurricane Andrew in 1992)?

f. Executive salaries—Should a federally mandated ceiling be established for salaries of business executives?

g. Drug war—Would decriminalization of recreational drugs eliminate the profits of drug suppliers and reduce the incidence of violent crime?

h. Additional policy debates in the news are discussed in various newspapers (especially *USA Today*) and news magazines. One publication that focuses on policy debates is *Congressional Quarterly Weekly Report;* a comprehensive index to *CQ* articles is published every six months.

Notes on Chapter 7

Use the space below to describe new concepts or methods that you learned in Chapter 7.

Bibliography

A summary of a policy debate is a special case of a summary report, discussed in the previous chapter. In a debate summary, material in the body of the report is organized by categories related to the issues being debated or the groups carrying on the debate. For additional bibliographic material, see sources cited at the end of Chapter 6. The graphical representation of a debate in Exhibit 7–2 was suggested by a discussion in Judith Richlin-Klonsky and Ellen Strenski (eds.), *A Guide to Writing Sociology Papers* (New York: St. Martin's Press, 1991): 60. Background information on most major policy debates is provided by articles in *Congressional Quarterly Weekly Report*. See the *CQ* index to locate articles on specific issues.

The Ability to Identify and Discuss Economic Concepts in Published Materials

When you read articles in newspapers or news magazines, do you notice the economic content of stories even when economics is not directly mentioned? Anyone who reads such publications can understand the individual words written on the page, but that does not mean everyone can understand the full content of the story— the unseen economic forces that drive events toward the outcome that is reported.

This section of the text will exercise your ability to identify the economic content of articles contained in popular and professional publications. If your experience is typical, most of what you have read about economics has been published in textbooks. Textbooks are great for teaching theoretical models, but in doing so they exclude most of the real-world detail that practicing economists confront every day. In fact, most textbooks don't make you search for anything at all; they announce in bold letters that THIS IS IMPORTANT and you had better study it for an upcoming test. Theoretical concepts like supply and demand are powerful, but in actual career situations you must know when to apply such models and learn to recognize events that have theoretical implications.

Chapter 8 develops your ability to identify and discuss economic concepts contained in the popular media and, indirectly, those contained in the issues you confront in everyday experiences. Chapter 9 provides similar opportunities to examine professional journal articles. Recognizing the economic content of what others write is an important prerequisite for those who hope to write significant reports of their own.

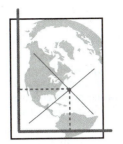

CHAPTER 8

The Economic Content of News Stories

By the conscious questioning of what you see,
hear and read, you can make material release
information it might ordinarily conceal.
—Richard Saul Wurman

Introduction

Pick up your city's newspaper or read an issue of *Time* magazine and you may run across several articles that focus on economic phenomena. Consider this sample of issues and the economic analysis they bring to mind:

Issue: Many new companies have started manufacturing computers in recent years.

Analysis: Entry increases competition and lowers the price of the industry's product. This will depress the profits of computer manufacturers.

Issue: Higher taxes have been proposed in your city to provide new public services.

Analysis: If the new taxes exceed the incremental value of services, there is less incentive for people to move into your community than before. This is tantamount to a decrease in demand for homes, which will reduce home prices and other real property values in the community.

Issue: The federal budget deficit is large and is not expected to decrease anytime soon.

Analysis: The demand for credit due to government borrowing causes interest rates to increase. Higher interest rates raise the cost of business investment and new home construction, and thereby lower the stock of private capital goods.

Issue: F.D.I.C. insurance of bank deposits reduces risk to depositors.

Analysis: Deposit insurance removes the incentive to avoid depositing funds in risky and poorly run banks. As a result, deposit insurance helps channel funds toward such banks and ultimately contributes to the instability of the banking system.

Issue: Policies that prohibit the sale of illicit drugs reduce their availability.

Analysis: Because demand for drugs is inelastic, the supply restriction caused by prohibition causes dramatic increases in drug prices. The price increases cause drug dealers to fight among themselves for market share, to bribe public officials not to arrest them, and to develop smaller, more potent drugs that are less easily detected during shipment.

Additional Examples

The foregoing examples show that much of the analysis used by economists is pretty simple. *The practice, as distinguished from the study, of economics has less to do with developing new theoretical skills than with learning to apply a given body of thought to ordinary human experience.*

Economics has been applied to many issues that you may not have considered. Masanori Hashimoto has suggested that increases in the minimum wage, which cause low-skilled workers to become unemployed, may also contribute to a higher crime rate.[*] Unemployed workers continue to incur living expenses for food, clothing, and shelter; so if the minimum wage prevents them from earning dollars from legal employment, they may turn to illegal employment to earn their living instead. Hashimoto's investigation finds empirical support for this hypothesis by examining the incidence of several property-related crimes.

Another study by Richard McKenzie and John Warner investigated the impact of government regulation of airline fares in the 1960s and 1970s. It is well known that government regulations reduced entry by competing airlines during that era, which resulted in higher fares than would have prevailed in a competitive marketplace. The higher air fares reduced air travel and caused more people to travel by automobile. What you may not have considered is this: The death rate per million miles of travel is far greater in cars than in commercial airlines, so the substitution of one form of travel for another will affect the incidence of travel-related deaths. McKenzie and Warner's study of airline regulation suggests that up to 1,700 more travelers were killed in cars each year than would have been killed if competitive air fares had prevailed.[†]

More complex than the examples in the introduction to this chapter, even these cases do not require much more economics than a good understanding of supply and demand or of substitute goods. After reading about Hashimoto's findings on the minimum wage, would you be surprised to learn that occupational licensing—government-sponsored rules that limit the number of people working in particular occupations—

---

[*]Masanori Hashimoto, "The Minimum Wage Law and Youth Crimes: Time Series Evidence," *Journal of Law and Economics* (October 1987). pps. 443–464.

[†]Tim Tregarthen, "Do Cheaper Skies Save Lives?" *The Margin* (January 1988), p. 9.

also contributes to unemployment and higher crime rates? After reading about McKenzie and Warner's study of air fares, would you be surprised to learn that a tax on gasoline would stimulate greater air travel and thereby lower the number of travelers killed every year?

The Economic Domain

Stop! you're probably thinking by now. Is there an economic explanation for absolutely everything? Some people think so, but others disagree. Because the purpose of this chapter is to develop your ability to recognize the economic content of everyday news items, it is useful to consider a few issues concerning the use and limitations of economics.

Economic Subjects

What is economics? Economics has been described in many ways: the study of the allocation of resources to satisfy human wants, the study of self-interested human behavior, the study of market transactions, the study of scarcity. In fact, economists have worked in areas that would justify all of these definitions. The *functional* definition is that economics is whatever economists do. If a news item brings to mind an issue that you studied in class or read about in an economic textbook, that is an indication that the item probably has economic content. Product prices, unemployment, inflation, externalities, taxes, deficits, exchange rates, economic growth, worker productivity—these subjects and others lie within the domain of economics.

Influence, Not Determinism

One does not have to believe that every human endeavor is dominated by economic considerations to believe that *at the margin*, economic factors do influence human behavior. The study of air fares and highway deaths mentioned earlier does not argue that there is an economic explanation for *all* highway deaths. It states that to the extent some people change their travel plans in response to higher air fares, then an *increase* in the number of highway deaths is predictable.

For years critics have charged that economists try to explain absolutely everything with economic theory. But believing that economic incentives and conditions can *influence* events is not the same as believing that they *determine* events. To take another example, price is not the only thing that influences consumer purchases, but who would deny that a significant price increase would drive some customers away from an item? Focusing on the economic content of a news item is not the same as claiming that the issue lacks other dimensions. Given your training, the law of comparative advantage suggests that your time is more effectively applied by focusing your attention on news stories with a high degree of economic content.

Positive or Normative?

You probably learned the difference between positive and normative economic statements in your first economics course, so it is not necessary at this stage to explain the distinction between scientific, value-free economic analysis and personal preferences applied to economic issues. Some writers do not try to conceal their normative views. For example, a writer might say something like, "Government policies are needed to protect the well-being of minority groups." Other writers do not say what they are promoting but do indicate what they are against; these too are normative discussions. You have also probably encountered people who use carefully worded statements to provide the appearance of positive economic analysis, while they actually intend to promote normative goals. This is not using logic to get to the bottom of an issue, but to justify a particular (desirable) conclusion.

Whether the analysis is normative or positive, the quality of an economic discussion can be judged by examining the accuracy of *facts* cited in a particular case or deciding if other relevant facts have been omitted that, if considered, would change the conclusions of the discussion; by asking whether the *assumptions* about motivations and relationships contained within the discussion are reasonable; and by asking whether the *theoretical analysis* is correctly done or whether it fails to account for certain phenomena. Normative discussions do not always apply economic theory incorrectly or rely on misleading information. But writers with a personal interest may place different emphasis on some details than a disinterested analyst. Identifying the normative components of a particular story can help you decide whether a writer's conclusions follow from some fact or logical assumption, or reflect only the writer's version of the way things "ought to be."

In summary the issues examined here are on a different plane from the technical analysis discussed in classes and contained in textbooks. To be a successful practicing economist, you must be able to recognize the subtleties of economic discourse. This will help you distinguish the important phenomena and relationships in news stories from less significant details, and will also help you develop a stronger writing style. Some of the questions to ask yourself when reading about economic issues can be found in Exhibit 8–1. These questions are implied by the issues discussed earlier in the chapter.

Economics in the News

As mentioned earlier, an economic story is any story that contains concepts which economists commonly discuss. Few people are expert in every area of economics, but any well-trained student should at least be informed about core issues in microeconomics, macroeconomics, and one or two economic subdisciplines—say, public finance and international economics. You can see below the author's lists of the "Top Ten" issues from microeconomics and macroeconomics that you might expect to encounter in news stories with an economic slant. *Because news stories are written for a general audience rather than for economists, the economic terms listed below may not be explicitly mentioned in the story. You have to rely on your own experience and insight to realize when the article is alluding to an economic issue, but under a different name than what you are accustomed to.*

EXHIBIT 8-1 Reading between the lines

As you read a news story containing an economic issue, ask yourself these questions. (If you are reading your own magazine or newspaper, write your comments about these matters in the margin of the article.)

- What makes this an *economic subject?* What conditions or observations in this article remind you of something you learned about in an economics class you have previously taken (e.g., externalities or price changes)? List economic concepts explicitly contained in the news item or implied by the discussion.
- What *explanation* does the writer offer for the economic phenomenon under consideration? Is this an "economic" explanation, which uses such concepts as scarcity, profit maximization, or the Phillips curve? Are noneconomic explanations also offered for the phenomenon?
- Is the analysis a *positive* or a *normative* one? (Does the author advocate or harshly criticize a certain point of view?) To promote a normative objective a writer may have to rely on a fundamentally weak logical model—weak not by design, but because nothing else may be available to support a predetermined conclusion.
- What are the writer's *assumptions* about human motives (utility maximizers, altruists)? What are the author's assumptions about the relationships between people (arms-length traders, close relatives, master and slave)? Do these assumptions ring true in the current situation? Are they consistent with those used in standard economic analysis?
- Does the writer describe the *conditions* that influence economic decisions or fail to describe relevant conditions which, if their effects were considered, would change the conclusions reached in the article? List the key conditions described by the article.
- Is the author's *logic* (economic theory) correctly developed? If the logic seems correct but arrives at unexpected conclusions, how do you explain this result?

The issues mentioned on these lists are by no means original. You can see the same topics mentioned in most principles and intermediate-level economics textbooks. Many other concepts mentioned in your textbooks—indifference curves, rational expectations, kinked demand curves—are seldom if ever mentioned in newspapers and magazines. Experience in reading popular news publications helps narrow down the full list of economic concepts to the few encountered in everyday experience.

There is no advantage to labeling the highlights of news stories if that is where it ends. "Hey—that sounds like they're talking about a price ceiling." Yes, and what else? Describe the policy that created the price ceiling. Explain how the policy is enforced. What is the stated purpose of the policy? Is the result of the price ceiling a shortage of the product (as

TOP TEN MICRO ISSUES	TOP TEN MACRO ISSUES
1. monopoly, cartels, entry	1. CPI, inflation, and indexing
2. technological change (lower costs)	2. unemployment and employment
3. supply, demand, and price	3. monetary policy and tools
4. health care economics	4. fiscal policy/budget deficit
5. costs of economic regulation	5. economic growth
6. price ceilings and floors	6. aggregate supply and demand
7. taxes and subsidies on specific goods	7. business cycles
8. wages: productivity vs. discrimination	8. Phillips curves
9. externalities	9. GDP (or GNP)
10. ownership (rights to sell, modify, or use)	10. interest rates

economic theory would predict)? How do buyers and sellers react to the shortage? (Do they passively accept it, or do they react in a way not anticipated by policy makers?)

In short, after you attach the appropriate economic labels to key features of a story, then it is time to call on your economic training to break the story down into smaller segments and apply economic analysis to each. If you can identify even two or three economic elements of a news story, then you may understand far more about the issue than most other readers, who only read the words as they are written on the page.

Summary

This chapter has discussed activities that would help a practicing economist identify the economic content of news stories. Apart from learning to recognize familiar theories and concepts in unfamiliar (non-textbook) circumstances, the economist must remain aware of certain methodological issues that lie below the surface. These were summarized in Exhibit 8–1. With experience, it becomes almost second nature to focus on these elements of a news report to evaluate the "reasonableness" or credibility of the picture it paints. In this setting the economist serves as a (constructive) *critic* of the news media. Over the long run this role is an important one that helps shape official and public perception of policy issues.

Exercises

Exercise 1: Select one economics subdiscipline (international economics, public finance, labor economics, money and banking, etc.) and list the top ten ideas or concepts in the field that you are most likely to confront in ordinary news stories. (Your list should be similar to those above, labeled "Top Ten Micro Issues" and "Top Ten Macro Issues.") Write a brief descriptive phrase to accompany each concept so that its meaning is apparent.

Exercise 2: Locate three recently published news stories in newspapers and magazines that discuss economic concepts. Write margin notes that point out economic concepts and discuss the economic theory most closely associated with them.

Exercise 3: As you may know, collectors of baseball trading cards during the 1950s and 1960s were eventually able to sell those cards at large profits in the 1980s and 1990s. (The *Wall Street Journal* has carried several articles about baseball trading cards during the past few years, and guides are now published to track prices in the trading card market.)

How do you predict these profits will affect the desire to collect (the demand for) baseball cards in the 1990s? How do you predict this change in demand will affect the number of trading card collections in the 1990s? Do you expect today's collectors will earn large profits when they sell their cards 10–30 years from today? Draw supply and demand diagrams to illustrate your ideas.

Exercise 4: Two recent studies and an editorial published in the *New England Journal of Medicine* have attacked the practice of doctors who refer patients to medical facilities in which they own a stake. Typically, such facilities provide physical rehabilitation services, X-rays, cancer therapy, or mental health care.*

What impact do you expect *self-referrals* have on the decisions made by doctors to recommend that patients obtain treatment at outside medical facilities? What does your analysis assume about the motives of doctors? Assuming that your analysis is correct, what impact do you predict self-referrals have on the total costs of medical care? Illustrate your analysis by drawing a diagram showing the supply and demand for medical services, with and without self-referrals.

Exercise 5: Highway funding bills, proposals for mass transit projects, and local street construction are nearly always justified by pointing to traffic jams and other conditions that reflect a shortage of transportation facilities in populated areas during "prime" travel hours. Yet the roads are not so crowded at other times.

---

*Michael Waldholz, "Doctor Practice of Self-Referrals Draws Harsh Criticism from Medical Journal," *Wall Street Journal* (November 19, 1992). p. B1.

How do economists explain the existence of shortages during certain times of the day and surpluses at others? Discuss this situation in the context of street and highway space and draw a diagram to illustrate your ideas. How could the shortage of road space be eliminated without constructing new roadways?

Exercise 6: Exercise 2 called for you to collect news stories and point out their economic content. Select one of those stories and discuss it from the perspective suggested in Exhibit 8–1. (What makes this an economic subject? What explanation does the writer provide for the phenomena under consideration? Is the analysis positive or normative? What are the writer's assumptions about human motives? Identify key conditions that influence economic decisions. Is the writer's logic correctly developed?)

Notes on Chapter 8

Use the space below to describe new concepts or methods that you learned in Chapter 8.

Bibliography

Economic analysis is applied to well-known issues and problems in "economic issues" textbooks, including those by Ansel Sharp, *Economics of Social Issues* (Homewood, IL: Irwin, 1991); Herbert Stein and Murray F. Foss, *An Illustrated Guide to the American Economy* (Washington, D.C.: AEI Press, 1992); Robert B. Carson, *Economic Issues Today: Alternative Approaches* (New York: St. Martin's Press, 1990); Richard McKenzie, *Economic Issues in Public Policy* (New York: McGraw-Hill, 1979); Saul Pleeter, *Economics in the News* (Reading, MA: Addison-Wesley, 1992); Julian LeGrand and Ray Robinson, *Economics of Social Problems* (Orlando, FL: HBJ, 1980). Contemporary economic issues are also discussed in *The Margin*, a magazine published for economics students. (A one-semester subscription is $5.95 from *The Margin*, University of Colorado, P.O. Box 7150, Colorado Springs, CO 80933-7150.)

CHAPTER 9

The Economic Content of Published Research

*Regardless of the form of publication, all
research reports have similar content.*
—*Jacqueline Fawcett and Florence S. Downs*

Introduction

If you are assigned an article to read from a leading economics journal,
you may have any number of reactions: this is an exciting piece of research, this article bores me to tears (or to sleep), this article confuses me
and I hope I don't have to explain what it says to the professor who
assigned it. What you may not be aware of is that most empirical research
articles in economics follow well-established patterns that you will learn to
recognize if you read enough of them. That point is emphasized in the
quote from Fawcett and Downs above. From the writer's point of view,
there is a kind of "recipe" for writing a research article, and unless one
follows the recipe it is just as difficult to produce an acceptable research
report as it is to bake a good cake without a recipe. This chapter examines
the pattern used by many economists who write empirical research
reports.

This discussion has two practical benefits that you will appreciate
throughout your economics career. First, by learning the framework
discussed here you have a far better chance of developing into a good
economic researcher. If most good economists do research in a particular
way, then you will probably have to adopt many of the same methods to
produce work they consider acceptable. Second, once you learn to

identify the pattern followed by research articles, you will become a more efficient reader of such reports. Remarks that are not entirely clear when taken out of context are easier to interpret once you know the recipe the researcher is following. Likewise, it is much easier to recognize when a researcher leaves out an essential ingredient if you are already aware of the recipe he or she is working from. ("Hey," you might think, "you shouldn't go on and discuss these other issues until you state the hypothesis you propose to test.") Finally, when you have prior knowledge of the structure of a research report it is possible to read the article in far less time—just as it is quicker to drive from city A to city B after you've traveled the same route a dozen times than when you first made the trip.

Key Elements of an Empirical Research Study

Some economic researchers work on purely theoretical subjects, for example, exploring the logical implications of assuming that firms attempt to maximize revenues rather than profits. Although theoretical economists make important contributions to the discipline, in this chapter (and in this text) we are more interested in focusing on the process of doing *applied* economic work, including empirically estimating the impact of one economic variable on another and testing a hypothesis against real-world experience. Many economists do empirical research of the kind discussed here, and if you continue to practice economics it is far more likely that you will do empirical research than work on purely theoretical issues.

Empirical studies in economics are carried out according to a method that many economists believe contributes most to economic understanding. Economics is a science, and for the discipline to advance over time it is helpful if certain conventions are followed. Empirical studies in economics nearly always contain the following elements:

1. *A definition of the topic,* including a description of the *distinctive aspects of the topic* that will be analyzed with economic theory. Rather than state that you are studying the effects of the minimum wage, say that you intend to examine the effect of the minimum wage on teenage unemployment. The more *specific* you can be, the better. By carefully defining the problem you intend to address, you simplify the task of deciding which economic theory is the best one for the task at hand. Make sure your readers know in advance what you intend to accomplish (and what you do not intend to address) in the study.

2. *A review of the work of other researchers* who have examined the same topic, or whose work on other subjects is relevant to your own investigation. This review will provide information about data and techniques that can be used in your study. Reviewing related literature will inform readers about evidence contrary to your findings or show them that your findings reinforce with those of other specialists. Readers need this information to place your findings in perspective and to decide how useful your conclusions are.

3. *An application of economic theory to the issue* under consideration. To avoid confusion, it is best if the theory is explicitly named: supply and demand, the marginal productivity theory of wages, the quantity theory of money, and so on.

4. *A statement of the implications or predictions of economic analysis* in the form of a *hypothesis* that could be tested against actual experience.

5. *A test of the hypothesis,* which combines data or other evidence and a statistical testing or estimating method. (Regression analysis is the most commonly used statistical technique among economists.)

6. *A discussion of the results of the statistical exercise.* Are they consistent with or contrary to the hypothesis being tested? Provide insights to help the reader interpret your findings, and integrate the findings with those of other researchers. If you "discover" something that other economists have never observed before—e.g., an upward-sloping demand curve— then explain to the reader what assumption has been violated or what peculiarities in the sample you examined probably account for the discovery. If your findings agree with those of other researchers, discuss the implications of your findings.

In combination, these comprise one version of the scientific method in economics. Each step logically follows the one that preceded it, and at the end of the project the researcher knows whether knowledge has been advanced and how that knowledge can be used elsewhere. (Before reading further, review the six steps above. Do you see how "each step logically follows the one that precedes it"? Could you describe the logical progression if asked to do so?)

You may be deeply interested in the problem or policy you are investigating, but *the interest of the economics profession at large is to learn how economic theories perform in various real-world applications and to improve those theories to extend the domain of economics.* For the profession to derive these benefits it is necessary for each researcher to explain the details of an investigation in the clearest possible terms and to follow procedures that others can have confidence in. There is no place for sloppiness or deceit in this enterprise; depending on circumstances, one researcher's mistake may cause others to spend hundreds of hours attempting to verify or extend results that never should have been reported in the first instance.

An Outline of the Empirical Report (or Article)

The best structure for a research *report* is the one that most effectively communicates knowledge gained from a research *study.* (Here we are distinguishing between the elements of an *original study* or investigation, discussed above, and the written *report of the study* and its results.) Research reports are not merely 300 well-written sentences arranged to suit the personality of the researcher or the composition requirements of an English professor. Experience shows that empirical research reports in economics are often most effective when they are conceptually divided into *four main parts* that touch on each of the key elements of a research study highlighted above:

1. Introduction—Introduce and define the subject, including a discussion of what other researchers have contributed in this area and a brief statement about the findings of the present study.

2. Economic analysis—Conduct an economic analysis of the problem and state the hypothesis suggested by economic theorizing.

3. Empirical evidence—Discuss how the hypothesis could be tested, test the hypothesis, and discuss the results of the test.

4. Concluding remarks—Summarize the study's findings and explain how the study contributes to economic understanding.

This four-part outline is slightly different from the three-part report outline discussed in Chapter 4 (Introduction, Body, Conclusion), but is similar in general form. What was called the *body* of the report in Chapter 4 has now been divided into two parts: *economic analysis* and *empirical evidence*. Economic research demands a higher level of economic analysis and empirical evidence than the summary-type studies discussed in earlier chapters; consequently the report of economic research has a more sophisticated structure than the summary-type reports examined in Chapters 5–7.

As you read unpublished research reports and published research articles, learn to *consciously examine the structure of the report* to gain the most from reading it. Most reports or articles may be conceived as having four parts, some of which may be further subdivided. Try to determine where the introductory remarks of a report end and the economic theory begins, where the theory ends and the presentation of empirical evidence begins, where the empirical discussion ends and the concluding comments begin.

Reading an Empirical Research Article

On the following few pages an empirical study taken from a leading economics journal is reprinted. The article, "An Economic Analysis of the Demand for Abortions," by Marshall Medoff, is arranged according to the four-part report outline presented above: introduction, economic analysis, empirical test, concluding discussion. In addition, *margin notes* have been added to point out the six elements of an empirical study.

This particular article was selected for a couple of reasons. First, it is interesting to see how an economist addresses an issue (abortion) that is not usually considered to be economic in nature. Second, the economic theory contained in Medoff's part II is comparatively easy to understand and will not keep your mind so occupied that you do not notice the author's technique for *organizing* the report. In addition, the two-stage regression in part III illustrates a clever method sometimes used by researchers to overcome a common problem in empirical economics—simultaneity. That is, price changes influence consumer demand decisions, but the position of the demand curve simultaneously influences price. To address this difficulty, in footnote 12 the author estimates a price series that reflects fluctuations in both supply and demand; then he uses this (equilibrium) price series to estimate the demand function in his regression equation (2). Some of the most frequently used statistical techniques are discussed at greater length in Chapter 11.

Whether you have any particular interest in an economic analysis of abortion demand or not, it is recommended that you read and reread the

Medoff article two or three times. At this stage the most important thing to focus on is the structure imposed by Medoff on his report to logically examine the impact of key variables on one type of consumer decision. In principle, the same general approach could be used to investigate the demand for any other good.

After you are thoroughly familiar with the article, ask yourself whether Medoff's economic analysis seems correct and if his empirical methods are convincing. Can you think of other issues that should have been addressed to better estimate the demand function? Do you see why each of the six elements of the study (identified in the margin) are essential to the success of the overall investigation? (How would you have felt if, for example, footnote 9 had not mentioned the source of data used in the empirical estimates? How would you have felt if no definition had been provided for variables in the demand function, such as M and LFP? Is it clear to you that the 50 states are the units of observation for which data are available?)

As you read the Medoff article, *write your own comments in the margin that point out why the author decided to include various remarks and the logical role they play* in the story he has to tell. By observing methods used by experienced researchers you can learn to conduct research of your own.

Summary

Because of the variety of topics examined by economists and the different writing styles of researchers, readers often fail to notice the similar structure of most empirical research reports. This makes the task of reading economic research reports more difficult than it need be and prevents the reader from extracting the maximum amount of information from a given investigation. Just as important, the economist who is unaware of the essential elements of a research report is not likely to be a productive researcher. Later chapters develop your ability to conduct an empirical investigation, so it is important that you have a good understanding of issues in this chapter before proceeding.

An Economic Analysis of the Demand for Abortions

MARSHALL H. MEDOFF*

Marshall Medoff, "An Economic Analysis of the Demand for Abortions," *Economic Inquiry*, April 1988, 353–59.

This study uses an economic model of fertility control to estimate the demand for abortions. The results show that the fundamental law of demand holds for abortions, with the price elasticity of demand equal to −.81. Abortions are a normal good with an income elasticity of demand equal to .79. The demand for abortions is also positively related to the labor force participation of women and to being unmarried. Catholic religion, education and the poverty status of women were found to have no statistically significant impact on the demand for abortions.

I. Introduction

Background → information

On 22 January 1973, the United States Supreme Court ruled in *Roe v. Wade* that states could not prohibit a woman from having an abortion, as long as it was done in the first three months of pregnancy. States could regulate, but not prohibit, second-trimester abortions and could prohibit abortions during the third trimester only.[1]

Previous → research.

The focus on abortions since the Supreme Court's decision has been primarily on moral and ethical issues. Research on the issue consists principally of numerical tabulations according to selected demographic characteristics (age, race, weeks of gestation, etc.) of the women obtaining abortions.[2] Absent are socioeconomic considerations explaining the demand for abortions.

Topic/pur- → pose of study.

This study empirically estimates the demand for abortions using the economic model of fertility control developed by Michael [1973]. The effect of many of the socioeconomic factors discussed by Michael should also be relevant in explaining the demand for abortions. Section II outlines the abortion demand model in terms of the general theory of fertility control. The third section examines the empirical results and the last section discusses the policy implications of the results.

*Professor, Department of Economics, California State University, Long Beach. I would like to thank Stanley K. Henshaw, Deputy Director of Research of the Alan Guttmacher Institute, for providing me data from the 1981–82 Abortion Provider Survey. Funding for this research was provided by California State University, Long Beach through the Scholarly and Creative Activity Committee Assigned Time Program.

1.   During the second trimester many states required all abortions to be performed in a hospital. In June 1983, the U.S. Supreme Court ruled that such state regulations did not advance maternal health and, therefore, were illegal.

Previous → research.

2.   Two exceptions are Deyak and Smith [1976] who estimated the benefits for women seeking abortions as a result of the 1973 Supreme Court ruling, and Coelen and McIntyre [1978] who analyzed the pronatalist and abortion policies in Hungary.

II. Abortion Demand Model

Michael [1973, S132] argues that fertility control behavior can be explained within a household choice-theoretic framework in terms of a household production model. Michael's model suggests that a household's fertility control decision is based on a comparison of the costs and benefits associated with an additional child over time. The net cost simply represents a household's effective excess demand for children given prices, income level, level of production of complements and substitutes, etc. If the net cost is positive, a woman will engage in fertility control by purchasing and using goods and time inputs to reduce the probability of conception. One such good reducing the probability of conception to zero is abortion. ← Previous research.

← Economic analysis.

Household choices on abortions thus arise from the interaction of income, prices, and preferences. Abortion is a posterior decision—the decision by a woman who is pregnant not to have the child. Since abortion can be considered a method of contraception, the demand for abortions is modeled in terms of the explicit and opportunity costs at the time of the abortion decision[Coelen and McIntyre 1978].

The abortion demand equation to be estimated is[3]

$$A_i = b_0 + b_1 P_i + b_2 Y_i + b_3 SNGL_i + b_4 LFP_i \\ + b_5 CATH_i + b_6 W + b_7 M. \quad (1)$$

← Hypothesized demand function.

The dependent variable is the abortion rate (the number of abortions per thousand pregnancies) of women of childbearing age fifteen to forty-four in state i during the 1980 calendar year.[4]

The price of abortions (P) is the average cost of an abortion using a local anesthesia in nonhospital facilities performed the first twelve weeks in each state.[5] Since abortions are not fundamentally different from other conventional goods and services one would expect the fundamental law of demand to hold.[6] Income Y is the average income of women fifteen to forty-four years old and reflects the budget constraint. ← Hypothesis (price).

---

3. The linear specification is preferable to the log-linear form since the linear form is a first-order approximation of an arbitrary demand function and it allows the elasticities of demand to vary along the demand curve rather than restricting them to a constant value. Equation (1) was estimated using the log-linear specification and the empirical results, which are available upon request, were qualitatively the same as those reported.

4. About 3 percent of all women of childbearing age obtained an abortion in 1980 [Alan Guttmacher Institute 1985].

5. Ninety-two percent of all abortions are done in the first trimester and 78 percent of all abortions are performed in a nonhospital facility [Alan Guttmacher Institute 1985].

6. Abortion rates and prices were obtained from the Alan Guttmacher Institute [1985], which is a research foundation affiliated with Planned Parenthood. Each year the Guttmacher Institute does a national survey of abortion providers and the services they offer. The survey produces the most complete available information about abortions in the U.S. and in each state, and the results are summarized by the U.S. Department of Commerce in the *Statistical Abstract of the United States*.

Analysis and →
hypothesis
(marital
status).
Also relevant in an abortion decision is a woman's marital status. Unmarried women may have a greater demand for abortions since their outlays for an additional child are higher than married women.[7] Married women (spouse present) are more likely to have lower outlays for child-bearing and childrearing (due to shared household responsibilities, and because of economies of scale, as well as greater productivity of time and information with additional children) than unmarried women.[7] The variable *SNGL* is the percentage of women fifteen to forty-four who are unmarried and its predicted effect is positive.

Analysis and →
hypothesis
(labor force
participation)
Women in the labor force, regardless of marital status, have a greater opportunity cost of an additional child than women not in the labor force and should have a greater demand for abortions. This may reflect, in part, a greater aspiration for material goods or longer time horizon (i.e., a greater weight attached to a future unwanted outcome) as well as a greater value of time. The predicted effect of *LFP*, the labor force participation rate of women fifteen to forty-four, is positive.[8]

Analysis and →
hypothesis
(religion).
An additional determinant of the demand for abortions is demographic differences in tastes or preferences. One such taste factor is religion. Religious faith and affiliation are powerful forces in influencing household choices. The Roman Catholic Church strongly disapproves of abortion and imposes severe psychological sanctions against women having an abortion. The Church's disapproval likely increases the subjective costs of abortions for Catholics and lowers their demand for them. The variable *CATH* is the percentage of Catholic population in each state.[9]

Analysis
and →
hypothesis
(region).
Most fertility studies typically assume constant cross-section tastes across groups or populations. While it is likely that tastes change slowly over time, such an assumption appears doubtful when cross-section differences across women in different states are of particular interest. Hamermesh and Soss [1974] argue that the degree of social stability, social ties, and social norms of states in the far West is substantially different from that in other regions. Some anomie in western states might foster a greater tendency by households to have abortions. To control for the possibility of differential tastes, a dummy variable equal to one for states in the far West (California, Oregon, Washington, Nevada, Arizona and Hawaii) is included.

---

7. In 1980, 50.5 percent of all married women (spouse present) had at least one child, versus 14.2 percent for unmarried women [U.S. Bureau of the Census 1983].

8. The variables in equation (1) are restricted to women since the production of children is done exclusively by women and, as noted by De Tray [1973], methods of fertility regulation are generally controlled by women. One might argue that the independent variables should be the characteristics of pregnant women, not all fertile women. Since abortion is a quasi-method of contraception there is no bias in the estimated coefficients; the explicit and opportunity costs at the time of the abortion decision are the same for fertile and for pregnant women.

9. The data on all economic variables were obtained from the U.S. Bureau of the Census, State Reports, Detailed Characteristics [1983]. The data on Catholic membership by state are from Churches and Church Membership in the United States, a census commissioned by the National Council of Churches [Johnson, Picard and Quinn 1974].

Source of
data for →
testing
hypotheses.

...nds to provide abortions for indigent ...ram was severely restricted. However, ...vide Medicaid abortions at their own ...ould expect the demand for abortions to ...t is not a consideration in the utilization ...M is a dummy variable equal to one for ...l Medicaid funding.[10]

← Analysis and hypothesis (subsidy).

...determined simultaneously with the ...imated using two-stage least squares.[11] ...ion (1) are the average hospital cost per ...er of abortion clinics and number of ...n in each state.[12] The two-stage least-...tion (1) (absolute value of t-statistics in

← Statistical test (method).

$$.031Y + 4.194SNGL + 4.456LFP$$
$$(3.31) \qquad (1.74) \qquad (2.57)$$
$$\ldots TH + 43.775M, \qquad R^2 = .77. \qquad (2)$$
$$(2.12)$$

← Estimated demand function.

...ubstantial support for the a priori expec-...odel.[13] The price of abortions is negative ...ero at the .05 level of significance. The ...etween the price of abortions and the

← Discuss estimates.

...rgia, Hawaii, Maryland, Michigan, New Jersey, ...ennsylvania, Washington, and West Virginia. ...t the residual variance decreased with the size ...feld-Quandt [1965] procedure was utilized on ...e calculated F-value did not exceed the critical ...and hence the null hypothesis of homoscedas-

...l in the two-stage least-squares estimates of the ...tatistics in parentheses):

← Estimated supply price. Use $\hat{p}$ to estimate Equation (2).

$$+ .475COST - .164HOSP$$
$$(4.19) \qquad (1.85)$$
$$.776PHY - 58.403W + 9.465M.$$
$$(2.24) \qquad (2.69) \qquad (.64)$$

...with the number of abortions per thousand live ...thousand women of childbearing age fifteen to ...qualitatively the same as those reported in the ...nwhite women fifteen to forty-four to equation ...race was not significantly different from zero ...ther variables in equation (1) remained virtually ...he complete empirical results are available upon abortion rate confirms that the fundamental law of demand is applicable to abortions. Income is positive and statistically significantly different from zero at the .01 level of significance, which suggests that abortions are normal goods with respect to income.[14] Both *SNGL* and *LFP* are significantly positive which is consistent with the hypothesis that women in the labor force and unmarried women, due to the greater explicit and implicit cost of childbearing, have a greater demand for abortions. Women have eighteen more abortions per thousand pregnancies in western states and forty-four more abortions per thousand pregnancies in Medicaid states.

A somewhat surprising result is that the percentage of a state's Catholic population does not have a statistically significant influence on the demand for abortions. One possible explanation is that Catholic women do not uniformly support the official position of the Catholic Church against abortions. The Harris and Gallup Opinion polls in 1979 found that 74 percent of those surveyed believe that a woman who is no more than three months pregnant should have the right to decide whether or not she wants to have an abortion [Alan Guttmacher Institute 1985]. Assuming these surveys are representative, the results suggest that Catholic women do not necessarily view abortion as an unacceptable means of fertility control merely because of the Catholic Church's opposition.

Theory and → estimate of education's impact on abortion demand.

Michael [1973, S137–41] argues that education operating through several different channels may have an influence on a household's fertility control decision. Education may reduce the demand for abortions by increasing the knowledge about effective contraceptive techniques. On the other hand, education may also increase the demand for abortions since it raises the opportunity cost of a household's time and, if children are time-intensive relative to other goods purchased, increases the relative price of an additional child [Becker 1965; Willis 1973]. To provide additional evidence on the effect of education, equation (1) was re-estimated with the percentage of women in each state aged fifteen to forty-four who have completed twelve years of school added to equation (1). The effect of education was negative but not statistically significantly different from zero. The estimated coefficients of all the other variables remained virtually identical to the previous estimates reported.[15]

Theory and → estimate of AFDC's impact on abortion demand.

Bernstam and Swan [1986] contend that the Aid to Families with Dependent Children (AFDC) subsidy is an incentive for poor women to have children. If their contention is correct then the estimated coefficient of income in equation (1) would be biased upwards since the AFDC subsidy is income related. Poor women are subsidized relative to rich women, which increases the number of abortions of high income women relative to low income women. In order to test for this possibility equation (1) was re-estimated with the percentage of women in each state aged fifteen to forty-four in poverty added to equation (1). The empirical results

---

14.   These latter results are consistent with Deyak and Smith [1976] who found that the abortion rate was inversely related to travel costs (a proxy for the price of abortion services) and the percentage of women with incomes under $3000. They also found neither age or education had a statistically significant effect on the abortion rate.

15.   The complete empirical results are available upon request.

showed that the percentage of women in poverty was not statistically significantly different from zero. The estimated coefficients of all the other variables remained virtually identical to the previous estimates presented.[16] Thus the empirical results remain robust with respect to the adjustment for education and for the presence of women in poverty.

An important practical question to economists is how sensitive the demand for abortions is to changes in any of the economic variables in the demand function. The estimated elasticities are computed at the sample mean.[17] The price elasticity of demand for abortions is −.81, which is consistent with other studies that have found that the price elasticity of demand for health services is inelastic [Klarman 1965]. The positive elasticity with respect to income is .79 and shows that abortion is a normal good.[18] The labor force elasticity of demand is 1.10, while the unmarried women elasticity of demand is .57.

← Estimates of price and income elasticities.

IV. Policy Implications

Many opponents of abortion have attempted, through the political process, to limit or prohibit legal abortions. The estimated demand equation provides the likely impact of such actions.

One policy proposal has been to prohibit all Medicaid-financed abortions. The results suggest that forbidding all Medicaid-financed abortions would, everything else constant, have resulted in a reduction of forty-four abortions per thousand pregnancies or equivalently a 17.5 percent drop in the 1980 abortion rate. In 1980 there were approximately 1.5 million abortions performed. This would imply that prohibiting all Medicaid financed abortions would result in 262,500 less abortions being consumed.

← Policy implications of estimates.

A second proposal is to prohibit all abortions constitutionally. This would not eliminate all abortions since a possible alternative to a legal abortion is an illegally obtained abortion. Making abortions illegal, however, would raise the total price. Assuming that the illegal price was 50 percent higher than the prevailing 1980 market price and using the estimated price elasticity of demand of −.81 suggests that, ceteris paribus, the abortion rate would decrease by 40.5 percent. Applying this latter figure to the 1980 total of 1.5 million abortions performed implies that making abortions illegal would have reduced the number of abortions consumed by 607,500. If the illegal price were 75 percent higher than the 1980 market price, the reduction in the number of abortions consumed would be 911,250; if the illegal price were 100 percent higher, the drop in the number of abortions consumed would be 1,215,500.

---

16. The complete empirical results are available upon request.

17. The mean and standard deviation (in parentheses) for the dependent variable and explanatory variables in equation (1) are A: 250.898 (87.847); P: 213.64 (43.15); Y: 6407.3 (936.338); $SNGL$: 34.158 (3.956); LFP: 61.99 (4.602); $CATH$: 20.022 (13.806); W: .12 (.3249); M: .28 (.0448).

18. These results cannot be compared with those of Deyak and Smith [1976] or Coelen and McIntyre [1978] since neither study provided sample means for their price or income variables.

Estimates →
help
predict
future
abortion
demand.

Future trends in the abortion rate will be determined by changes in many factors not discussed in this study, such as sexual behavior patterns, availability of contraceptive services, and the perceived risks of contraceptive methods. However, the projected secular increase in the income and labor force participation of women combined with a decline in marriage rates and increase in divorce rates suggests, based on the empirical results, an increase in abortion rates in the United States. The annual increases in the abortion rate are likely to be small but persistent.

References

Alan Guttmacher Institute. *Abortion Services in the United States, Each State and Metropolitan Area, 1981–1982*. New York: The Alan Guttmacher Institute, 1985.

Becker, Gary S. "A Theory of the Allocation of Time." *Economic Journal*, September 1965, 493–517.

Bernstam, Mikhail and Peter Swan. "In Production of Children as Claims on the State: A Comprehensive Labor Market Approach to Illegitimacy in the United States, 1960–1980." Hoover Institution, 1986.

Coelen, Stephen P. and Robert J. McIntyre. "An Econometric Model of Pronatalist and Abortion Policies." *Journal of Political Economy*, December 1978, 1077–1101.

De Tray, Dennis. "Child Quality and the Demand for Children." *Journal of Political Economy*, March/April 1973, S70–95.

Deyak, Timothy A. and V. Kerry Smith. "The Economic Value of Statute Reform: The Case of Liberalized Abortion." *Journal of Political Economy*, February 1976, 83–99.

Goldfeld, Steven M. and Richard E. Quandt. "Some Tests for Homoscedasticity." *Journal of the American Statistical Association*, September 1965, 539–47.

Hamermesh, Daniel S. and Neal M. Soss. "An Economic Theory of Suicide." *Journal of Political Economy*, January/February 1974, 83–98.

Johnson, Douglas W., Paul R. Picard, and Bernard Quinn. *Churches and Church Membership in the United States*. Washington, D.C.: Glenmary Research Center, 1974.

Klarman, Herbert E. *The Economics of Health*. New York: Columbia University Press, 1965.

Michael, Robert T. "Education and the Derived Demand for Children." *Journal of Political Economy*, March/April 1973, S128–64.

U.S. Bureau of the Census. *State Reports, Detailed Characteristics: 1980*. Washington, D.C.: Government Printing Office, 1983.

Willis, Robert J. "A New Approach to the Economic Theory of Fertility Behavior." *Journal of Political Economy*, March/April 1973, S14–64.

Exercises

Exercise 1: Use margin notes that accompany the Medoff article, "An Economic Analysis of the Demand for Abortions" (above), plus any others that you might have written to **prepare a summary report of the article.** By carefully considering the methods other economists use to structure research reports, insights will occur to you about how to write a report of your own.

Your summary report should be shorter than Medoff's, while still incorporating all of the essential elements of his study. Your report should be about four typewritten pages long and be *explicitly divided into four parts:*

1.   Introduction (about ½ page). Briefly describe the general public's views on abortion as well as the Supreme Court's position. Explain the view that abortion services are an economic good and the demand for those services can be investigated using the same methods as for other goods. Summarize in one sentence the findings of the Medoff study.

2.   Economic theory (about 1½ pages). Summarize the economic theory of consumer demand for goods in general, then focus the theory on the demand for abortion services in particular. When stating that condition X can be expected to affect consumer purchases of good Y, explain the logical connection between condition X and the predicted behavior. Summarize this discussion by stating a hypothesis about abortion purchases that one could potentially test against actual experience.

3.   Empirical evidence (about 1½ pages). What regression equation does Medoff estimate? What connection exists between this equation and the hypothesis being tested? Write down the estimated demand function and interpret: (a) the signs on the coefficients, (b) the coefficient values, and (c) the statistical significance of each explanatory variable in the model. Do these findings corroborate (support) or refute (undermine) the analysis that produced the hypothesis?

4.   Concluding remarks (about ½ page). According to the empirical evidence presented by Medoff, what impact would various policies have on the number of abortions "purchased" annually? What other economic, social, and demographic conditions are likely to affect the annual number of abortions?

The reason for *explicitly dividing your summary into four parts* is to ensure that each key element of the report is addressed. If your report is written as a continuous essay with no clear breaks between the logical sections of the report, there is a greater chance that you will omit important material.

Exercises 2–4: E. W. Eckard's article that follows examines the effect of automobile dealer entry regulations on the selling prices of cars. It is a more complex piece of work than the Medoff article on abortion (above). Read the Eckard article and make margin notes regarding its structure and key elements, similar to those provided with the Medoff article on abortion. You should also have a good understanding of the economic theory and statistical exercise described in the report.

The exercises following the article include a series of questions to test your comprehension and an assignment to provide a written summary of the article. You may want to quickly look over those questions before reading Eckard's article so you will read it with a specific purpose in mind.

The Effects of State Automobile Dealer Entry Regulation on New Car Prices

E. W. ECKARD, JR.*

E. W. Eckard, Jr., "The Effects of State Automobile Dealer Entry Regulation on New Car Prices," *Economic Inquiry*, April 1985, 223–42.

This paper examines the impact of state regulations restricting entry into new car retailing. The central hypothesis is that these regulations create artificial scarcity rents for existing dealers, which are collected through higher car prices. A reduced form multiple regression model is specified with retail price as the dependent variable. The model is estimated using transactions price data for a sample of over 5,000 Chevrolet dealers and seven car lines in 1978. The results confirm the hypothesis that entry restrictions cause higher car prices.

In the United States, virtually all new cars are sold through independent franchised dealerships, rather than (say) manufacturer owned and operated outlets. Dealers purchase cars "wholesale" from manufacturers, and then sell them to consumers at a negotiated price.[1] In connection with their new car sales, dealers invest in certain physical assets such as showrooms, inventories (along with necessary vehicle storage space), and facilities for preparing the car for final delivery to the consumer. In addition, dealers hire sales and other support personnel, engage in local advertising, maintain demonstration vehicles, and provide point-of-sale promotional material in various forms (*e.g.*, brochures). Finally, new car dealers provide auto repair service, specializing in the makes they sell. This is important to the sales activity since consumers thereby are assured of parts and service availability.

State regulations applying specifically to various aspects of auto retailing have existed since the mid-1930's.[2] These regulations have resulted from concerted political action by dealers who maintain they need state protection from alleged economic abuses by manufacturers. Accordingly, the focus of the relevant statutes has been on the franchise agreement which forms the legal basis of the dealer-manufacturer relationship. By 1966, at least twenty states had laws affecting some aspect of this relationship.[3] However, direct state regulation of new dealer entry is a relatively recent phenomenon.[4] Prior to 1970, only one state (Colorado) regulated entry, a situation

---

*College of Business, University of Colorado at Denver. This research was conducted while the author was employed on the Economics Staff of General Motors Corporation. All opinions and conclusions stated herein are the sole responsibility of the author.

1. Roughly twenty-five percent of new cars are built to a retail customer's order by the manufacturer, rather than purchased from dealer stock. However, the purchase price is still negotiated between the buyer and the dealer, and the manufacturer still charges the dealer the wholesale price.

2. Kessler (1957, p. 1169) reports that the first such law was passed by Mississippi in 1934. For summaries of the development and spread of these laws during various periods, see Palamountain (1955, pp. 107–158), Macauley (1966), and Brown (1980).

3. See Macauley (1966, p. 34). Brown (1980, p. 399) reports that by 1980 all but five of the fifty states had laws applying directly to new car franchising. For an analysis of the aggregated effects of these other types of auto dealer regulation, see R. L. Smith. For an earlier, but less rigorous attempt, see Macauley (1966, pp. 180–188).

4. Many states have for some time required that dealers be licensed. However, these stipulations have not proved to be significant entry barriers.

which has changed drastically over the last decade. Currently over thirty states have such laws. It is this relatively new type of regulation which is the focus of the present study.

In the following, auto dealer entry regulations are viewed from the perspective of the well-known "capture" theory of regulation.[5] It is assumed that dealers have been able to use the political process to obtain some degree of protection from the economic consequences of new entry into the auto retailing business. In this regard, the effects of new car dealer entry regulations are similar to those of other laws regulating entry into various industries or occupations.[6] Specifically, restricted entry means reduced competition and ultimately higher product prices. This hypothesis is tested using car sales data for Chevrolet dealers in 1978. The results of a multiple regression analysis indicate that auto dealer entry regulation does, in fact, produce higher car prices.

The remainder of the study is organized as follows. First, the state laws regulating dealer entry are described. Second, the economic effects of these laws are analyzed on an *a priori* basis. Next, the data are discussed and presented in summary form. The empirical model of the effect of the entry laws on car prices is specified in Part IV and estimated in Part V. The last section presents a summary and some concluding remarks.

I. The Regulatory Laws

State regulation of the establishment of new auto franchises, or the relocation of existing ones, generally operates as follows. First, a manufacturer is required to make known its intention of establishing a new dealership. In most states this means direct written notification of dealers eligible to protest. In the remainder, it means informing the appropriate board or agency, which then contacts affected dealers.

Next, one or more eligible extant dealers must file a written protest. The entry of a dealer of a given make can be protested only by established dealers of the same make, *i.e.*, a Chevy dealer cannot protest a proposed Pontiac or Toyota dealership. Also, only dealers in the same "relevant market area" (RMA) may file protests. This area can be defined by existing political boundaries (*i.e.*, county or "community") or by a specified radial distance (*e.g.*, 10 miles) from the proposed new site. In some states it is determined *ad hoc* by the appropriate agency or board. In many states, the RMA is the area of dealer sales responsibility as stipulated in the franchise agreement. As a practical matter, however, RMA's coincide roughly with metropolitan areas, and even relatively small metropolitan areas usually have at least one existing dealer representing each major car make.

Finally, a dealer protest initiates a formal proceeding which ultimately may lead to a denial by the relevant authority of permission to establish the new dealership, and in any event can produce significant delays. In some states the proceeding may involve a hearing before a state agency or official, often supported by a special advisory board. Other states rely entirely on special hearing boards appointed by the state. In still others, the "protest" consists of bringing a case in equity before a state court. It is significant that the advisory boards or full hearing boards often are mandated by law to contain a certain number of dealers. For example, in Texas the hearing board must consist of five dealers and four "consumer representatives." In fact, dealers usually constitute a substantial portion, if not a majority, of

5. For example, see Stigler (1971), Posner (1974), and Peltzman (1976).

6. For example, see Eckert and Hilton (1972), Frew (1981), Jarrell (1978), MacAvoy and Snow (1977), and Paul (1982).

TABLE 1
States with Entry Regulation as of
January 1, 1978

Year Effective	State
1963	Colorado
1970	Iowa
1971	Nebraska, Ohio, South Dakota
1972	Vermont
1973	New Hampshire, New Mexico, North Carolina
1974	Arizona, California, Rhode Island
1975	Minnesota
1976	Florida, Louisiana, West Virginia
1977	Massachusetts, Montana, Nevada, Tennessee, Texas, Virginia

board membership.[7] In most states, dealer entry regulation is administered through the same institutional arrangements as are other types of auto franchise regulation which generally pre-date entry regulation.

All entry regulation laws stipulate that the decision made by the relevant authority be based on certain criteria which are similar across states. In general, a showing of "good cause" (or its absence) for the entry of a new dealer is required, as is some consideration by the relevant authority of the public "interest," "welfare," or "convenience and necessity." These in turn usually depend on analyses of past, present, and expected future performance of extant dealers from the point of view of both manufacturers and consumers.[8] It is significant that many of these laws require explicitly that the decision maker consider the effect of a proposed new dealership on the investments of extant dealers. Thus the possibility of reduced profitability among existing dealers may be part of the rationale for preventing new entry.

States having laws containing entry restriction provisions as of January 1, 1978, are listed in table 1, along with the year the provisions became effective. Note that of the 22 states listed, only one had an entry restriction law prior to 1970, and nine did not have laws in effect as recently as 1975. As discussed below, 1978 data are used in the statistical analysis of the effects of these laws, and so information on states enacting laws during or after 1978 is irrelevant for this study.

II. Economic Effects

From an economic perspective, auto dealer entry regulation raises entry barriers which may block the flow of resources into new car retailing. The result may be fewer resources devoted to this activity than would occur otherwise in an open market environment. As noted in the introduction, the central hypothesis of this study is that the net effect of entry regulation is to increase new car prices. However, since this regulation does not apply directly to the price or quantity of new cars sold, it is

---

7. For a summary of board membership composition, see Brown (1980, p. 420 and pp. 403–405). He argues that boards containing dealers represent an unconstitutional violation of due process.

8. It is, of course, not at all clear that the interests of manufacturers and consumers diverge. From the manufacturer's perspective, distribution costs are equivalent to a tax with regard to their effect on demand at the wholesale level. Therefore, the manufacturer has the same interest in minimizing distribution costs as do consumers.

worthwhile to trace the theoretical linkage between dealer entry regulation and car prices.

An important part of the "good" purchased by a new car buyer consists of services supplied by the dealer.[9] In effect, this good may be conceptually partitioned into two components jointly demanded (and paid for) by consumers. The first is the "car" supplied by the manufacturer. The second consists of various ancillary sales services provided by the dealer, including adequate showrooms, sales personnel, information (*e.g.*, local advertising), and a selection (*i.e.*, an inventory) of new cars.[10] These services are made artificially scarce by the restrictive laws. The resulting monopoly rents then are collected by the dealer through higher car prices.

Consider the effects of the regulation on a typical metropolitan area. Assume at the time of enactment of the relevant law an optimum number of new car dealers exist, *i.e.*, resources allocated to providing sales services are earning a normal return and consumer purchase costs are minimized. Assume next that as time passes the demand for new cars in this area increases, implying an increase in the derived demand for ancillary sales services. Quasirents therefore appear for resources currently allocated to supplying these services. Absent the law, these short-run effects would attract entry (*i.e.*, a new dealer) and the quasi-rents would thereby be dissipated. However, if extant dealers

are successful in using the law to block entry, then the rents become permanent. In sum, given an outward shift of the (downward sloping) demand curve for sales services, competition among consumers causes the price of these services to be bid up which in turn, leads directly to an increase in the new car transaction price. With new entry barred, these price increases become permanent.

This process is illustrated in figure 1. The horizontal axis of this figure represents the quantity of sales services available in some metropolitan area, while the vertical axis represents the corresponding (implicit) price.[11] An initial equilibrium occurs at the point (P_s^o, Q_N^o) where the derived demand curve for these services (D_o) intersects the supply curve (S_N). This supply curve is the horizontal sum of the rising marginal cost curves of the N existing dealers.

Now suppose that due to (say) population growth the demand curve shifts outward to D_1 without an increase in the number of dealers. The output of sales services expands along S_N until a new equilibrium is established at (P_s', Q_N'), where $P_s' > P_s^o$. Existing dealers are now earning rents and, absent barriers, new entry would occur, *i.e.*, the new equilibrium at (P_s', Q_N') would be temporary. The effect of new entry is illustrated by an outward shift in the supply curve to S_{N+1}, which results in a "final" equilibrium at (P_s^o, Q_{N+1}'). Output increases from Q_N' to Q_{N+1}' and prices fall from P_s' to P_s^o, eliminating dealer rents.

However, if entry is barred, the equilibrium at (P_s', Q_N') becomes permanent. Prices remain higher, dealer rents are not dissipated, and output is at a lower level

---

9. Based on 1978 Chevrolet data, the value added by the dealer is roughly ten percent of the retail price of a new car.

10. Dealers, of course, also supply after-sales service, including warranty work and specialized repair, and provide an assurance of parts availability. The knowledge that such post-sales services are easily obtained enhances significantly the value of a car to a consumer. The increased scarcity of these services caused by dealer entry regulation is an additional increased cost to consumers.

---

11. Since the good purchased by a new car buyer can be partitioned into two complementary components, so too can the price: $P = P_w + P_s$, where P is the retail price of the car, P_w is the wholesale price paid by the dealer, and P_s is the implicit price paid by consumers for dealer services.

FIGURE 1
The Effect of Entry Barriers on the Market for Dealer Services

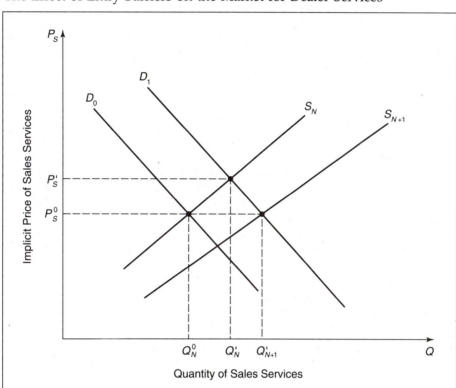

than would occur if entry were open. The dealers collect these higher "prices" for their artificially scarce services through higher new car prices.

Another way in which entry regulation affects car prices is by its adverse impact on consumer search costs. The market for a costly multi-attribute good such as an automobile is characterized by a relatively high demand for information relevant to the purchase decision. A substantial portion of this information is "self-supplied" by consumers through their own search efforts, *i.e.*, an implicit supply schedule exists depicting the marginal costs of generating various levels of information. As first noted by Stigler, the amount of search undertaken by a prospective buyer depends on the relationship of associated marginal costs and benefits. If

entry regulation results in fewer dealers than would exist otherwise, then the marginal costs of obtaining various levels of information are greater, *i.e.*, the supply curve shifts up. Therefore less search is undertaken. The impact on total search costs depends on the elasticity of the information demand curve. However, since one principal benefit of additional search is the possibility of locating selling prices lower than previously encountered, reduced search implies higher transaction prices on average.[12]

12. See Stigler, (1961, pp. 171–178), for further discussion of this point. It is worth noting here that actual transaction prices and the well-known "sticker prices" can differ significantly. For example, see Crafton and Hoffer (1981), and references cited therein.

Two final points should be emphasized with regard to the effects of these laws. First, actual blockage need not occur in order to cause higher prices. Significant delays caused by the hearing process, which typically takes a minimum of nine to fourteen months, can have the same effect. Furthermore, the prospect of a costly time-consuming hearing process, accompanied by the possibility of failure, can significantly alter a manufacturer's calculus regarding the entry decision in the first place. In particular, the decision to proceed in establishing a new dealer will likely be postponed, since as time passes, the "need" for an additional dealer in general becomes more obvious, thereby (presumably) increasing the probability that the hearing process will result in success. This could lead to a chronic "shortage" of dealers in states with entry restrictions, as the supply of dealers systematically lags behind the demand.

The second point concerns the effect of the protest eligibility criterion common to these laws, *i.e.*, a protest may be filed only by dealers of the same make. This does not mean that only the blocking dealer, or others of the same make, benefit. New cars of different makes are substitutes. Therefore, all dealers in an area benefit to a greater or lesser extent if one dealer in that area can prevent new entry in his particular make.

III. The Data

The principal data used in this study are obtained from detailed car sales reports submitted monthly by individual dealers to General Motors Corporation under the terms of the franchise agreement.[13] Separate data are submitted for each car line. Included are units sold, total sales revenue,

---

13. Care has been taken to avoid disclosure problems in assembling and presenting the data, and in performing the analysis.

and the total wholesale cost of purchasing the cars from GM. From these data, average retail and wholesale price by car line are computed for each dealer in the sample. These average prices are then used in the statistical analysis of part V. A more detailed discussion of these data is presented in the Appendix.

The sample used in this study consists of 5,717 Chevrolet dealers in business during 1978. The year 1978 was selected on the grounds that it was the most recent "normal" year for the auto industry prior to the shocks initiated by the 1979 Iranian oil crisis. Chevrolet was selected to obtain maximum coverage and to minimize data and analytical costs. Chevrolet dealers constitute more than fifty percent of all GM franchises, and separate data are available for seven major Chevy passenger car lines.

Table 2 presents summary statistics for these data on a national basis for each of the seven top selling Chevy car lines in 1978. The first column shows the number of dealers in the sample for each car line after screening for suspect data (see Appendix for discussion of sample selection), while the second indicates the total number of units sold by the dealers. There are over 5,000 dealers in the sample for each car line. The last two columns show the average retail price (P) and wholesale price (P_w). The Chevette is the lowest priced line, with an average P and P_w of \$4,107, and \$3,720 respectively. The B-cars have the highest P (\$6,449) and P_w (\$5,928).

Also of interest is the variation in these data across states. Only B-car data are discussed for ease of exposition. Since the number of included dealers and state averages for P and P_w are highly correlated among car lines, the variation in B-car data is representative. State average retail prices for B-cars vary from \$7,152 (California) to \$6,063 (Michigan). The mean of state averages is \$6502, with a standard

TABLE 2
Summary Statistics—Major Car Lines

Car Line	Nameplate	Number of Dealers	Units Sold	Average Price	
				Retail	Wholesale
A	Malibu	5634	272,003	$5694	$5216
Asp[1]	Monte Carlo	5643	284,665	6265	5760
B	Bel Air/ Impala/ Caprice	5705	444,579	6449	5928
F	Camaro	5496	220,531	6369	5783
Hsp[1]	Monza	5214	142,634	4680	4279
T	Chevette	5549	203,991	4107	3720
X	Nova	5602	195,500	4948	4525

1. "sp" is an abbreviation for "special."

deviation of $245. State average wholesale prices vary from $6,464 (California) to $5,515 (Maine). The mean of state averages is $5960, with a standard deviation of $213.[14] The number of dealers by state varies from 11 in Nevada, to 374 in Texas, with a mean of 119 (median = 92.5).

One additional piece of information is available from the dealer financial data which plays an important role in the following analysis. It is the "population code," which indicates whether a dealer is located in an area with a population greater or less than 200,000 persons. These areas are defined according to internal GM criteria and are roughly equivalent to metropolitan areas. However, they do not correspond exactly to the Standard Metropolitan Statistical Areas as defined by the Bureau of Census. According to this code, there are 809 dealers located in areas with populations greater than 200,000, leaving 4,908 dealers in other areas. On average, the "urban"

dealers are about four times larger in terms of unit sales than "rural" dealers. The relevance of this information is explained later.

IV. Model Specification

In this section the multiple regression model is developed which is used subsequently to estimate the effects of auto dealer entry regulation on new car prices. A linear reduced form price equation is specified in which the transactions price (P) is stated as a function of wholesale price (P_w) and certain other variables. The effects of the entry regulation are then measured by means of dummy variables.

These effects are measured in terms of car price rather than overall dealership profitability partly because of the usual problems associated with measuring economic profits from accounting data. Such problems are particularly acute in relatively small, closely held businesses, such as auto dealerships. However, more importantly, while the laws can be expected to produce higher car prices, there are *a priori* grounds for expecting no significant effect on dealer profitability. First, these laws do not restrain competition among existing dealers. Therefore, rents could be dissipated by competitive (but wasteful) attempts by each dealer to attract customers away from

---

14. As noted below, eighty percent of the variance in retail price is accounted for by corresponding variance in wholesale price. This variance is, in turn, due primarily to destination charges and other factors such as different option mixes selected by consumers. Additional variance in the retail price is introduced by differences among dealers in costs of operation.

other dealers.[15] Second, the protection afforded by the regulation affects each dealer's work-leisure trade-off. In particular, a lower probability of entry reduces the cost of leisure at the margin, and therefore more will be consumed.[16] It implies that some rents may also be dissipated through higher costs caused by reduced management efficiency. Third, the sale price of dealerships purchased after the passage of an entry restricting law would reflect the capitalized value of the anticipated monopoly rent stream. Thus, even correctly measured profits for such dealers would show only normal returns.

It also is assumed that monopoly rents accruing to dealers as a result of entry restrictions will be manifested primarily in higher prices for new cars, as opposed to the other goods and services sold by dealers.[17] New cars are sold only by franchised dealers. Therefore, the entry regulation applies to all potential new car sellers.

However, this is not the case with regard to sellers of used cars or repair services, the two other principal sources of dealer income. With regard to the supply of these goods, reduced entry of new car dealers may be offset by increased entry of other sellers. Consequently, the prices of these goods should be affected to a significantly lesser degree than the prices of new cars.[18]

The first variable included in the multiple regression model is P_w, which alone accounts for about 80 percent of the variance in average P among the Chevy dealers in the sample. In fact, *ceteris paribus*, at long run equilibrium, it might be expected that differences in P_w among dealers on average would be reflected dollar for dollar in differences in P; *i.e.*, as an initial hypothesis, the coefficient of P_w can be expected to be unity.[19] As noted earlier, P_w represents the cost of a car to the dealer, including destination charges, and is available by car line and dealer from the data discussed in section III.

The second major factor accounted for is labor costs, the major component of dealer costs aside from wholesale car purchases. Differences in nominal wages among states may be responsible in part for variations in P among dealers in different states. The proxy used for nominal labor cost is state average weekly earnings of franchised new car dealer employees (WAGE), as reported by the National Automobile Dealers Asso-

---

15. Price competition among existing dealers drives price to marginal cost (P'_s in figure 1). Rents exist because this price is above average cost, and can be dissipated by such *average* cost increasing expenditures as additional advertising or more attractive showrooms. This is similar to the rent dissipating process described by Posner (1975, p. 352) in the case of the regulated airline industry.

16. See, *e.g.*, Alchian and Kessel (1962) and Jensen and Meckling (1976). This theory implies that such a behavior change is less likely when ownership and "control" are separated, *i.e.*, owners can fire managers who attempt to increase their consumption of leisure. New car dealerships are generally owned and operated by the same individual. Note that this implies nothing about the relative efficiency *levels* of the two alternative arrangements. The existence of agency costs implies that regulated dealer-owners could still be more efficient than employee-managers.

17. About sixty percent of a typical dealership's total sales comes from its new car department, with the remainder divided more or less evenly between the service and the used car departments. *e.g.*, see National Automobile Dealer Association (1981, p 4).

18. One exception here would be certain specialized non-warranty repair work. This category of repair and maintenance is becoming increasingly important as cars become more technologically sophisticated.

19. This is based on the proposition that the retail car price equals average cost under long run competitive equilibrium (*i.e.*, absent entry restrictions). Assuming that the long run supply curve for dealer services is flat (see figure 1), a coefficient on P_w other than unity implies that economic profits or losses exist for dealers, *or* that the supply costs underlying P_w and P_s are correlated (see below).

ciation (NADA).[20] This procedure implicitly assumes that each dealer within a state confronts identical, or at least comparable, labor markets, an unlikely circumstance. However, the problem is attenuated to some extent by partitioning the data into urban and rural sets, as discussed in the next section. Labor costs are likely to be more similar within each set than between sets, with urban dealers on average confronting higher costs.

Scale economies may also affect unit costs, and therefore retail prices. To the extent that such economies exist, larger dealers operate at lower costs per unit sold, and may therefore sell at lower gross margins. Because the dependent variable in the analysis is unit price, it must be assumed that it is an adequate proxy for average cost. The proxy for dealer size is the total number of new units sold by the dealer in 1978 (SIZE), including non-Chevy units. For Chevy dealers also selling other car makes (*i.e.*, "duals"), scale economies are probably more closely related to total units, rather than just Chevy units.[21] This variable is available from the data set discussed in section III.

The next variable in the model is population growth between 1970 and 1980 (GRTH), a proxy for auto demand growth. Expectations regarding auto demand growth are an important consideration in a manufacturer's decision to create a new dealership. Unexpected growth can produce disequilibrium situations, as described previously, characterized by the existence of quasi-rents for dealers and higher car prices. It is assumed that states experiencing more rapid growth are more-likely to have dealer "shortages" of this

type. The inclusion of a population growth variable avoids a possible confounding of growth effects and regulation effects. Dealers are more likely to expend resources to obtain entry regulation the greater the expected returns to such investment. These returns are proportional to entry prospects, which in turn are related to population growth, suggesting that entry regulation might be correlated with growth.[22] If this is so, and if higher growth is associated with higher prices, then the failure to include a growth variable might falsely attribute growth effects to regulation. Separate data are available for urban and rural population growth in each state.

The last variables in the model are dummy variables designed to measure the effects of the entry restriction laws. It is assumed that a law is more likely to produce a measurable effect after some period of time has passed since its enactment. Consequently, two dummy variables are used. The first (RNEW) has a value of unity if a given dealer's state has a relatively "new" law, and is zero otherwise. The second (ROLD) has a value of unity if a given dealer's state has a relatively "old" law, and is zero otherwise. As indicated in table 1, nine of the twenty-two states regulating entry as of January 1978 had laws in effect for only one or two years (*i.e.*, since 1976 or 1977). These states, plus Minnesota (1975), comprise the "new" law group, while the remainder, *i.e.*, states with laws in effect as of 1974 or earlier, comprise the "old" law group. The coefficients of RNEW and ROLD variables, as estimated in the next section, represent the per unit increase in car prices hypothesized to result from the entry restriction laws.

20. State average weekly earnings in 1978 varied from $226 (Maine) to $338 (California), with a national mean of $278. See National Automobile Dealers Association (1981, p. 10).
21. In fact, there is little difference between the two in terms of their empirical relationship to car prices.

22. The twenty-two states with laws in effect in 1978 had a mean population growth of 10.7 percent from 1970 to 1978. The remaining states during the same period had a mean growth of 7.6 percent. The difference between these means is significant at the ten percent level.

This age-of-law distinction accounts for some of the variance in the effects of the entry regulation among dealers. However, other important sources of variance remain. For example, due to limited local demand prospects, there may be some areas in regulated states where no manufacturer has even contemplated locating a new dealership since the relevant law was enacted, and so no effects could be expected on existing dealers. Also, depending on local circumstances, many Chevy dealers, even in urban areas, may not have confronted a potential new Chevy entrant. While, as noted earlier, a Chevy dealer may still benefit if a potential dealership of another make is blocked, the benefits would tend to be lower, depending on how close a substitute the blocked dealer's cars are for Chevrolets. Furthermore, there may be significant differences in the laws which influence their effectiveness. These differences might be due to variations among states in the criteria on which the relevant authority's decision under the law is based, different placement of the burden of proof, or differences in the enforcement mechanism. Finally, there may be differences among dealers in their abilities to use the laws to their advantage.

The model may now be summarized as follows, keeping in mind that the unit of observation is the individual dealer:

$$(1)\ P = b_0 + b_1 RNEW + b_2 ROLD + b_3 P_w$$
$$+ b_4 WAGE + b_5 SIZE + b_6 GRTH + e;$$

where RNEW and ROLD are dummy variables indicating the presence, respectively, of "new" or "old" laws, P_w is the average new car wholesale price, WAGE is the statewide average weekly earnings of new car dealer employees, SIZE is total new car units sold (including non-Chevy units), GRTH is average population growth between 1970 and 1980, and e is a random error term. Expectations regarding dummy variable coefficients are $b_1 > 0$, $b_2 > 0$, and $b_2 > b_1$. For the remaining variables, expectations are that $b_3 = 1$, $b_4 > 0$, $b_5 < 0$, and $b_6 > 0$.

V. Empirical Results

In this section, the multiple regression model summarized in equation (1) is estimated using ordinary least squares and the data discussed in section III. The data are partitioned into two sets according to whether or not a given dealer is located in a major urban area. Separate estimates are then made of the effects of the laws on each of the two data sets. This approach is used because (1) the effects of the laws on car prices are expected to differ between the two groups and (2) other factors affecting dealer operating costs, and therefore retail prices, are expected to differ between the two groups.

The criterion for the data partition is the "population code" for each dealer, as discussed in Part II, which indicates whether that dealer is located in a city with a population of greater or less than 200,000. The rationale is that the effect of the entry restriction laws should be more noticeable in larger cities. These laws allow a dealer to restrict the entry of another dealer of the same make only; *i.e.*, a Chevrolet dealer cannot block a new Ford franchise. Thus, conflicts under these laws can only arise in a location where a manufacturer is interested in establishing a new dealership of the same make as an existing dealer. The probability of this occurring is higher in urban areas. The urban/rural partition also accounts to some extent for differences among dealers in the cost of operations. For example, land rental costs are likely higher in big cities. The same may also be true for certain types of taxes and labor costs. However, it should be kept in mind that this is at best a crude way of accounting for such differences.

For each data set, separate equations are estimated for each of the seven major Chevrolet car lines sold in 1978. The principal advantage of this approach is that a significantly stronger test of the basic hypothesis can be performed by examining the data "disaggregated" by car line. There is no reason to expect, on *a priori* grounds, major differences in the effects of the laws among car lines; and inconsistencies in results among car lines could be masked by analyzing price data averaged across all car lines. A second advantage of this approach is that a major source of price variance is avoided, *i.e.*, that created by basic cost differences among car lines. Prices are generally more similar among cars within a given car line than between lines.

Regression results are presented in table 3 for urban dealers by car line.[23] Looking first at the non-dummy variables, P_w is a highly significant explanatory variable in all equations.[24] As expected, the coefficients are close to unity, although they are in fact slightly greater than unity in six of the seven equations, with this difference being statistically significant in five equations. The variable WAGE also performs as expected, and is statistically significant to a high degree in six of the seven equations. The variable SIZE, the proxy for scale economies, also has the expected sign and is statistically significant, although small in magnitude, in all seven equations. For example, the SIZE coefficient for the A cars indicates that on average P is lower by $2.50 for each additional 100 cars sold. The last non-dummy variable, GRTH, is signif-

icant in three of the seven equations, and its sign is positive as expected.

Recall that the coefficients of the dummy variables RNEW and ROLD measure the effect of the restrictive laws on car prices in states with "new" and "old" laws, respectively, relative to unregulated states.[25] The coefficient of ROLD ranges from $15.1 (T) to $71.9 (F), and is statistically significant to a high degree in all equations. Its average value, weighted by unit sales for each car line, is $56.3. These results support the hypothesis being tested. The differences among car lines may be accounted for in part by price differences, *i.e.*, higher priced cars have higher absolute price effects (compare table 2). They may also reflect differences in relative demand—1978 was a relatively strong year for the larger cars (*A, Asp, B,* and *F*). The coefficients of RNEW indicate that "new" laws have little effect, a result consistent with expectations. The coefficients range from $−9.6 to $14.0 and are statistically indistinguishable from zero.

Table 4 presents the regression results for equation (1) for rural Chevy dealers by car line. P_w is again a highly significant explanatory variable.[26] As in Table 3, six of the seven P_w coefficients are greater than unity (although again by very small amounts), and in three equations this difference is statistically significant. These results taken together suggest that increases in P_w may be associated with increases in P on slightly more than a dollar for dollar basis, which may reflect complementarity between automobiles and dealer

---

23. It should be noted that, according to the Chevrolet criteria, fifteen states have no urban dealers. Nine of these states had no entry regulation in 1978 (*i.e.,* RNEW = ROLD = 0). Three had "new" laws (RNEW = 1) and three had "old" laws (ROLD = 1).

24. The *t*-statistics reported for P_w in table 3 are for the null hypothesis $P_w = 1.00$. For the null hypothesis $P_w = 0$, the lowest *t*-statistic among the seven equations is 58.8.

25. Table 3 indicates that there were about 809 urban dealers in 1978. Of these, 141 were in states with laws in effect after 1974 (RNEW = 1) and 202 were in states with laws in effect during or before 1974 (ROLD = 1). The remaining 466 urban dealers were in states with no laws as of 1978.

26. The *t*-statistics reported for P_w in table 4 are for the null hypothesis $P_w = 1.00$. For the null hypothesis $P_w = 0$, the lowest *t*-statistic among the seven equations is 147.8.

TABLE 3
Regression Results for Urban Dealers

Car Line[2]	Intercept	RNEW	ROLD	P_w	SIZE	WAGE	GRTH	R	N
A	89.3	−3.9	61.4	1.035	−.025	.94	5.02	.94	810
	(1.18)	(.40)	(7.57)***	(2.80)**	(5.65)***	(5.71)***	(1.47)		
Asp	60.8	−2.5	71.8	1.029	−.020	1.27	3.11	.93	810
	(.72)	(.24)	(8.22)***	(2.30)*	(4.32)***	(7.05)***	(.89)		
B	164.4	−9.6	71.1	1.010	−.032	1.26	11.30	.94	809
	(1.89)	(.84)	(7.34)***	(.78)	(5.97)***	(6.47)***	(2.79)**		
F	195.2	−1.3	71.9	1.063	−.013	.31	26.91	.92	810
	(1.97)*	(.10)	(7.06)***	(4.10)***	(2.33)*	(1.49)	(6.19)***		
Hsp	64.2	−4.8	29.2	1.033	−.016	.95	5.32	.94	809
	(1.10)	(.53)	(3.89)***	(2.98)***	(3.73)***	(6.09)***	(1.72)		
T	450.0	14.0	15.1	.965	−.017	.46	6.57	.87	807
	(6.24)***	(1.70)	(2.22)*	(2.14)*	(4.58)***	(3.32)***	(2.34)*		
X	194.6	−.9	41.5	1.006	−.022	.95	4.49	.94	809
	(3.00)**	(.095)	(5.55)***	(.48)	(5.28)***	(6.19)***	(1.38)		

1. For the variable P_w, the null hypothesis for the t-test is $P_w = 1.00$.
   For the remaining variables, the null hypothesis is that the variable in question equals zero.
2. See Table 2 for car line nameplates.

*Significant at the 95% level
**Significant at the 99% level
***Significant at the 99.9% level

TABLE 4
Regression Results for Rural Dealers

Car Line[2]	Intercept	RNEW	ROLD	P_w	SIZE	WAGE	GRTH	R	N
A	325.4	−0.8	34.7	.997	.009	.54	18.19	.87	4826
	(7.79)***	(.15)	(6.37)***	(.55)	(1.30)	(5.69)***	(8.45)***		
Asp	266.0	−5.0	33.8	1.007	.011	.64	19.72	.83	4835
	(5.38)***	(.81)	(5.44)***	(.99)	(1.39)	(5.98)***	(8.05)***		
B	326.5	−2.3	37.3	1.007	−.019	.50	19.52	.84	4898
	(6.59)***	(.36)	(5.72)***	(1.00)	(2.28)*	(4.48)***	(7.49)***		
F	71.6	13.1	25.6	1.065	.098	.26	22.00	.91	4688
	(1.75)	(2.19)*	(4.25)***	(13.11)***	(12.87)***	(2.46)*	(9.35)***		
Hsp	250.6	−3.5	9.5	1.011	.028	.26	15.71	.91	4407
	(7.51)***	(.66)	(1.80)	(2.23)*	(4.31)***	(2.82)**	(7.60)***		
T	200.8	7.6	11.4	1.014	.044	.39	13.46	.88	4744
	(6.75)***	(1.81)	(2.71)**	(2.41)*	(8.23)***	(5.30)***	(8.17)***		
X	275.2	−0.7	23.6	1.005	0.014	.38	12.31	.90	4795
	(8.10)***	(.15)	(4.99)***	(1.02)	(2.31)*	(4.57)***	(6.58)***		

1. For the variable P_w, the null hypothesis for the t-test is $P_w = 1.00$.
   For the remaining variables, the null hypothesis is that the variable in question equals zero.
2. See Table 2 for car line nameplates.

*Significant at the 95% level
**Significant at the 99% level
***Significant at the 99.9% level

services. Those who demand more expensive (*i.e.*, higher quality) cars may also demand more expensive (*i.e.*, higher quality) levels of sales service.

WAGE and GRTH have the expected signs and are statistically significant in all seven equations. However, SIZE has the "wrong" (*i.e.*, positive) sign for six of the seven car lines and is statistically significant, although low in magnitude, in four of these six lines. When coupled with the weak negative correlations reported in table 3 for SIZE, these results are ambiguous regarding auto dealer scale economies, to the extent they can be measured by size-price correlations.[27] The ambiguity may arise from the fact that average cost is a more suitable measure of the effects of scale economies than is product price. In fact, it might be expected that competition would produce similar prices among firms, even if average cost differences are not insignificant.

The effects of the entry restriction laws are again represented by the dummy variables RNEW and ROLD. The coefficient of ROLD is positive and statistically significant in six of the seven equations, ranging from about $9 to about $37. Its average value, weighted by unit sales, is $27.8. As with the urban sample, the higher absolute price effects occur for the higher priced cars. Also, RNEW is insignificant in all but one of the equations of table 4, indicating no discernible effect due to "new" laws.

The results of the regressions presented in tables 3 and 4 can now be summarized. The consistently positive and significant coefficients for ROLD provide solid support for the hypothesis that new car dealer entry restriction laws produce higher car prices. ROLD is positive and statistically

significant for all seven car lines in the urban data set and for six car lines in the rural data set. The general insignificance of the coefficients of RNEW in both the urban and rural data sets is consistent with the expectation that at least some time must pass after enactment before the laws produce measurable effects. Finally, a comparison by car line of the coefficients of ROLD between the two data sets indicates that, as expected, the effects of the laws are greater in urban areas. The average (sales weighted) effect for urban dealers is about $56.3, almost exactly twice the $27.8 effect for rural dealers. Thus, the overall pattern of coefficients of both dummy variables reinforces the conclusion reached by examining the coefficients of ROLD for each car line separately, *i.e.*, state regulation of new car dealer entry produces higher car prices.[28]

These results can be used to estimate the cost to consumers (*i.e.*, ignoring deadweight welfare losses) associated with the

---

27. Pashigian (1961, p. 211), in an earlier study of the dealership size-profitability relationship, found "weak support for the contention that there are economies of scale in automobile retailing."

28. As noted earlier, dealer services and the car supplied by the manufacturer are complements. A regulation-induced rise in the price of the former causes a fall in demand for the latter. If the vehicle supply curve in the relevant range is rising (falling), this inward demand shift could be reflected partly in a reduction (increase) in P_w, in addition to a fall in output. To the extent this is true, the change in P_s (see footnote 11) would differ from the coefficient values of the dummy variables, *i.e.*, these coefficients represent the *net* impact on retail price of an increase in P_s and (perhaps) a change in P_w.

To measure these separate effects all 14 regression equations reported in tables 3 and 4 were reestimated with dealer gross margin ($P_s = P - P_w$) as the dependent variable, and P_w removed from the right-hand side. The coefficients of the ROLD variables were higher in 12 of the 14 equations, but only slightly so. The results for the other independent variables were essentially unchanged. This implies that the drop in demand as seen by the manufacturer occurs primarily through a decrease in output, with little impact on P_w. The increase in P therefore reflects an increase in P_s'.

entry restriction laws. In the twelve states with laws in effect prior to 1975 (*i.e.*, ROLD = 1), unit sales for the seven major 1978 Chevy car lines in urban and rural areas were, respectively, 180,897 and 188,887. Given the $56.3 and $27.8 average price effects noted above, the implied costs in urban and rural areas were, respectively, $10.2 million and $5.3 million. Thus, the total cost to consumers from higher prices caused by these laws in 1978 was about $15.7 million.

The effects of entry regulation on all new car buyers may be estimated by assuming that the per car price effects for Chevrolet apply to all other car makes. In the twelve "old law" states, all new car sales in 1978, including Chevrolet, totaled about 2.6 million units. Assuming urban sales were the same proportion of total sales for all makes as for Chevrolet, the costs to consumers associated with sales in urban and rural areas can be calculated as $71.6 million and $36.9 million, respectively. Accordingly, the total income transfer in 1978 for all car makes, including Chevrolet, is estimated to have been $108.5 million.

VI. Summary and Concluding Remarks

The results of the statistical analysis in Section V confirm the principal hypothesis under examination in this study that state regulation of new car dealer entry produces higher new car prices, as predicted by economic theory. The magnitude of the effect depends on dealer location within the state and the length of time the law has been in effect. For Chevys sold in 1978, the average price effect was about $56 per car for cars sold by dealers located in major urban areas in states where the regulation had been in effect for from four to eight years. For cars sold in these same states by dealers in rural areas, the average per car price effect was about $28. On this basis,

the total cost of these laws to new car buyers of all makes in 1978 is estimated to have been about $109 million.

It is worth adding that this cost may be expected to have grown (in constant dollar terms) since 1978 for two reasons. First, several states have enacted new auto dealer entry restriction laws since 1978. Second, as time passes, the effect of existing laws can be expected to increase, *e.g.*, as additional states move from the "RNEW" to "ROLD" category. Thus, the above figures are low if used as estimates of the current effects of these laws (in 1978 dollars).[29]

As noted in the introduction, entry regulation is but one aspect of state regulation of new car dealers. Smith has recently estimated the aggregate effect on car prices of all other types of auto dealer regulations. He found an average "pure price effect" across all states and car makes of about $134 in 1972 dollars, or $209 in 1978 dollars.[30] This result is consistent with the unit price effects for entry regulation alone found in the present study.

The qualitative aspects of these results will probably surprise few economists. So-called "economic regulation" in general has been a popular topic for economic research during the past decade, with the bulk of such research indicating that this

---

29. Furthermore, these cost estimates exclude the increase in consumer search costs resulting from these laws, and any cost increase in non-sales services provided by the dealer.

30. See Smith (1982, p. 153). Smith estimates the costs of franchise regulation using 1954 and 1972 data. Only five states had entry regulations prior to 1972 (see table 1), and only one at that time had such regulation in effect for more than two years. Therefore, Smith's estimates include very little, if any, of the impact of entry regulations. The impacts of these regulations reported in the present paper are in addition to the impacts measured by Smith for other types of auto franchise regulation.

type of regulation is costly to consumers. This knowledge apparently has filtered into the public policy arena at the federal level, as evidenced by widespread bipartisan support for "deregulation" of industries subject to such regulation. Furthermore, there has been an increasing public awareness of the likely consequences of legal entry restrictions in particular. Open entry was a major objective underlying recent federal moves to deregulate the airline and trucking industries. Nevertheless, concurrent to these developments state laws regulating new automobile dealer entry have proliferated. This study suggests that consumers would benefit if the various state capitals undertook deregulation programs similar to those currently under way in Washington.

Appendix

This appendix describes in more detail the sample selection process and the data used in calculating wholesale and retail prices. The variables used in estimating these prices are the dealer's total new car sales revenue and the total wholesale cost to the dealer of purchasing the cars from GM (*i.e.,* "dealer cost").

Sample Selection   In 1978 there were a total of 6,100 Chevy-contact dealers. However, not all these dealers are included in the data set. First, dealers not reporting year-end totals were eliminated, leaving a total of 5,726. Next, the nine Chevy-contact dealers located in Alaska and the District of Columbia were dropped, leaving a total of 5,717. (Hawaii dealerships are not included among the original 6,100.) Finally, an attempt was made to discard data which appeared clearly erroneous, *i.e.,* a calculated unit retail and/or wholesale price which was unrealistic. For example, according to reported data, a dealer in North Dakota sold two Monte Carlos for $140

each. Also, a dealer in Texas, again according to reported data, sold eleven Monte Carlos for an average price of $109,000. This "weeding out" process was accomplished by arbitrarily discarding data for a car line if the calculated unit price or cost was greater or less than the national average by more than fifty percent. Since the criteria were by car line rather than dealer, this process did not affect the total number of dealers in the data set. However, it did further reduce to some extent the number of dealers representing each car line, although there remained over 5,000 dealer "observations" for each of the seven major car lines (see table 2 for the number of remaining dealers).

Variable Description   Total new car sales revenue is the sum of the actual selling prices of cars sold in each car line, including destination charges. Destination charges represent an attempt to recover three cost factors associated with production of the motor vehicle that arise from the decentralization of manufacturing and assembly operations. These factors are: (1) the movement of finished products from assembly plants to dealers; (2) the excess freight cost associated with the movement of parts and components to remote assembly locations *versus* the cost of shipping to home plant assembly locations; and (3) related costs, such as packaging components for shipping to outlying assembly plants, and for vehicle protective shipping devices. While destination charges are paid as separate line items by consumers, they are (implicitly) treated as liabilities incurred by the dealer to GM upon receipt of each vehicle. Thus, although destination charges are included in the sales revenue data, they "wash" with regard to calculating dealer gross margins.

Trade-in allowances are not subtracted from revenue data. These allowances are, in effect, the prices paid by dealers for used cars "traded-in" by new car purchasers. If trade-in allowances were subtracted out, then new car retail price could not be calculated directly from the sales revenue data.

Dealer cost is primarily the sum of the prices paid by the dealer to GM for each car sold in each car line; *i.e.,* on a per unit basis, it is (primarily) the wholesale price of a car. In addition, dealer cost includes destination charges (see above) and any dealer "add-ons." Dealer add-ons refer to extras purchased by the consumer which are added by the dealer rather than the manufacturer, and are therefore not included in the wholesale price paid by the dealer to GM. Common examples are radios and undercoating. Dealer cost includes the cost to the dealer of adding these extras, but excludes any related profit. No precise data are available regarding the relative magnitude of dealer add-ons. However, such costs probably average less than five percent of wholesale price for cars purchased from dealer inventory, and significantly less than that for cars built to customer order.

References

Alchian, A. A., and R. A. Kessel, "Competition, Monopoly, and the Pursuit of Money," *Aspects of Labor Economics*, Princeton, N.J.: Princeton University Press, 1962, 157–75.

Brown, G. M., "State Motor Vehicle Franchise Legislation: A Survey and Due Process Challenge to Board Composition," *Vanderbilt Law Review*, 1980, 33, 385–440.

Crafton, S. M., and G. E. Hoffer, "Estimating a Transactions Price for New Automobiles," *The Journal of Business*, October 1981, 611–621.

Eckert, R. D., and G. W. Hilton, "The Jitneys," *The Journal of Law and Economics*, 1972, 2, 293–326.

Frew, James R., "The Existence of Monopoly Profits in the Motor Carrier Industry," *The Journal of Law and Economics*, 1981, 2.

Jarrell, Gregg A., "The Demand for State Regulation of the Electric Utility Industry," *The Journal of Law and Economics*, 1978, 2, 269–296.

Jensen, M. C., and W. H. Meckling, "Theory of the Firm: Managerial Behavior, Agency Costs, and Ownership Structure," *Journal of Financial Economics*, 1976, 3, 305–360.

Kessler, F., "Automobile Dealer Franchise: Vertical Integration by Contract," *The Yale Law Journal*, July 1957, 1135–1190.

Macauley, S., *Law and the Balance of Power: The Automobile Manufacturers and Their Dealers*, New York: Russel Sage Foundation 1966.

MacAvoy, P. W., and J. W. Snow, eds., *Regulation of Passenger Fares and Competition Among the Airlines*, American Enterprise Institute for Public Policy Research, Washington, D.C., 1977.

National Automobile Dealers Association, "NADA Data for 1981: Economic Impact of American New Car and Truck Dealers," NADA Research Division, 8400 Westpark Drive, McLean, Virginia 22102.

Palamountain, J. C., Jr., *The Politics of Distribution*, Cambridge: Harvard University Press, 1955, 107–158.

Pashigian, B. P., *The Distribution of Automobiles, An Economic Analysis of the Franchise System*, Englewood Cliffs, N.J.: Prentice-Hall, Inc., 1961.

Paul, Chris W. II, "Competition in the Medical Profession: An Application of the Economic Theory of Regulation," *Southern Economic Journal*, 1982, 3, 559–569.

Peltzman, S., "Toward a More General Theory of Regulation," *Journal of Law and Economics*, 1976, 14, 109–148.

Posner, R., "Theories of Economic Regulation," *Bell Journal of Economics and Management Science*, 1974, 5, 335–358.

Smith, R. L., "Franchise Regulation: An Economic Analysis of State Restrictions on Automobile Distribution," *Journal of Law and Economics*, 1982, 25, 125–157.

Stigler, G. J., "The Economics of Information," *Journal of Political Economy*, 1961, 69, 213–225.

Stigler, G. J., "The Theory of Economic Regulation," *Bell Journal of Economics and Management Science*, 1971, 1, 3–21.

Exercise 2: Determine whether the Eckard article contains the *six major elements* of an empirical study, which you presumably identified in margin notes while reading the article. Write brief (3–5 sentence) responses to each of the following questions.

1.   How does Eckard **define his topic?** Where does he specifically say what the article will accomplish? (Write down one or two sentences from the opening few paragraphs that state his intentions.)

What **distinctive aspect** of the auto dealer market is he examining? What economic theory is most closely related to this issue? (Write down one or two sentences from the opening few paragraphs that state the condition or policy that gives rise to the study, and requires economic analysis to understand.)

2.   How does Eckard use **the work of other researchers** who have examined auto dealer entry regulations or related subjects? (Write down the names of three other researchers in the area and describe the information Eckard derives from their work.)

3.   What **economic theory** does Eckard use to analyze the effects of auto dealer entry regulations? The theory may be verbal, graphical, or mathematical. (Label the theory in a few words—do not give a full explanation of it.) What theories of regulation does Eckard use to explain why states regulate entry by auto dealers? (List the two theories of regulation he discusses. Hint: Examine the 3rd and 8th paragraphs of the article.)

4.   What **hypothesis** emerges from the theoretical analysis? (What does the author predict will be the effect of dealer entry regulations?)

5.   Where does Eckard find the **data** he uses to test the hypothesis? Does this appear to be a substantial data set that is capable of providing insight into the effects of dealer entry rules? (Describe the source of Eckard's data and explain why you do or do not have confidence in its usefulness.) What is the unit of observation in the data set (consumers, dealers, states, etc.)?

What **statistical method** does Eckard propose to test the hypothesis? Does he explain why he has confidence in this method to measure the independent impact of the regulation on car prices? (Write down the name Eckard gives the statistical method, and explain whether or not you feel the author has adequately justified using this method.)

6. Does the author **discuss the results** of his investigation? Does he discuss his findings for each of the variables he uses to explain car prices? Does he give proper emphasis to the question of rejecting or not rejecting the hypothesis of the study? Does he explain the implications of his findings as they relate to the regulation of other industries? (Write down the estimated impact of entry rules on car prices and explain whether this finding is consistent with the economic analysis presented earlier in the article. Briefly indicate what these findings suggest about regulating entry into other professions and industries.)

Exercise 3: In a later exercise you will be asked to write a summary of the Eckard article. Before getting to that assignment, the following quiz will discover whether you have read the article carefully enough. Answer each of the following questions.

1. In 1978 (when data for the study were collected) _____ states had laws restricting entry by new car dealerships.
    a. 0 **b.** 50 **c.** 22 **d.** 28 **e.** 35 **f.** 11 **g.** 41

2. In states with dealer entry regulations _____ are permitted to file protests against new dealers and initiate a regulatory hearing process.
    a. county officials
    b. state officials
    c. car manufacturers
    d. existing dealers (of the same car make) in the market area
    e. existing dealers (any car make) in the market area
    f. companies located within a few blocks of the proposed dealership

3. The "capture theory" of regulation suggests that entry regulations _____ product prices for the benefit of _____.
    a. increase, sellers   **d.** decrease, buyers
    b. decrease, sellers   **e.** do not affect, regulators and state
    c. increase, buyers   residents

4. According to the article _____ are made artificially scarce by auto dealer entry restrictions.
    a. new cars   **c.** gasoline service stations   **e.** used cars
    b. dealer services   **d.** car washes

5. Based on 1978 Chevrolet data, the value added by dealers is roughly _____ % of the retail price of new cars. (Hint: Read the footnotes.)
    a. 2%   **c.** 10%   **e.** 33%   **g.** 50%
    b. 5%   **d.** 20%   **f.** 40%

6. The economic model in figure 1 gives the supply and demand curves for what good or service?
    a. ancillary dealer services   **c.** gasoline   **e.** car accessories
    b. new cars   **d.** car dealerships **f.** used cars

7. According to the definition given in the article, the wholesale price of Chevys is defined as _____ .
    a. the price paid by ordinary buyers for cars from dealers
    b. the price dealers pay Chevrolet for new cars
    c. the price paid by large-volume buyers (e.g., large companies)
    d. the price paid at new car auctions for Chevys
    e. Chevrolet's cost of producing new cars

8. The "population code" used in the study identifies areas with a population of _____ or greater.

    a. 50,000   **c.** 200,000   **e.** 500,000

    b. 100,000   **d.** 400,000   **f.** 1 million

9. In the regressions estimated by Eckard, the dependent variable is:

    a. new car price   **d.** quantity of cars sold

    b. wholesale price of cars (paid by dealers)   **e.** used car prices

        f. gas mileage

    c. price of dealer services

10. The coefficient on ROLD averages about $ _____ for all (urban) car lines.

    a. $12   **b.** $25   **c.** $32   **d.** $56   **e.** $72   **f.** $99

11. According to statistical estimates, the effects of entry laws are greater in _____ areas.

    a. urban   **b.** rural

12. The coefficients on RNEW suggest that auto prices generally _____ higher in states with *new* entry regulations than in other states (with no entry rules).

    a. are   **b.** are not

Exercise 4: Prepare a summary report of the Eckard article on entry regulations. This report should shorten Eckard's discussion, but convey all of the essential elements of his study. Your report should be about six typewritten pages long *and explicitly divided into four main parts:*

1. Introduction. Describe entry regulations and explain in no more than one or two sentences the predicted impact of entry regulations on car prices. Indicate to the reader whether Eckard's study supports or rejects this basic prediction.

2. Economic analysis. Identify the specific good or service that auto dealer entry regulation has the greatest impact on, then carry out the economic analysis of entry rules for that good. Draw a graph to illustrate this case. Briefly discuss *other variables* besides entry regulations that can logically be expected to influence the level of car prices. When the analysis is complete, formally state the prediction of the economic analysis in the form of a hypothesis.

3. Empirical evidence. Explain the regression method used by Eckard to test the hypothesis, describe the source of his data, state how many different regressions he estimates (and describe the coverage of these), then write down one of his regression equations and explain how to interpret each of the coefficients. Discuss the sign, size, and significance of the coefficient on ROLD. Does the study provide support for or tend to reject the hypothesis about entry regulations?

4. Concluding remarks. Are Eckard's findings consistent with or contrary to the capture theory of regulation? What do Eckard's findings imply about government regulations of entry in general?

In general, part 1 might be about one page, parts 2 and 3 should be about two pages each, and part 4 should be one page. Because you only have about six pages to touch on all of these points, you will have to address each of the relevant issues directly and not spend a lot of time elaborating on less important points. Write the first draft of your summary relatively quickly and do not worry too much about space constraints (pay more attention to the outline above). Then in your second draft, omit unnecessary material and add key ideas that were left out of the first draft. In a third draft, drop additional unnecessary comments and add other ideas that should be included in the summary.

Your final draft should clearly summarize the article so that any well informed person—not just a professional economist— could understand the basics of Eckard's research project by reading your essay. Use economic jargon sparingly. Any ideas that are difficult to explain deserve your special attention: these are the same ideas that your reader will probably have difficulty understanding.

To assist you on this assignment, begin by writing short answers to each of the following questions; once you have completed your answers, *expand each into one of the main parts of your paper.*

1.   In one sentence, what is the *specific issue* examined in the article? Try this beginning: "The author is interested in establishing whether . . . " Work hard to make this one sentence precise and informative.

2a.   What *economic analysis* (or theory) is explicit or implicit in the reading? Be sure to emphasize the economic analysis that is associated with the main topic of your paper. (Your statement might read something like this: "The author uses a model of supply and demand to show why wheat prices are expected to rise during years of low rainfall.") Then go on to explain why economic theory suggests this result. Draw a graph to help illustrate your point. If other conditions also contribute to the phenomena you are investigating, provide a brief theoretical discussion of those too. (E.g., "In addition to annual rainfall, wheat prices are also expected to reflect the level of consumer income and the prices of substitute products such as rice." Then discuss why economic theory suggests these effects.)

2b.   According to Eckard's economic analysis of the situation, what is the *exact prediction* to be verified by actual experience? (Craft a carefully worded, direct statement that makes the issue clear to the reader.)

3a.   How does Eckard justify/explain his use of regression analysis to test the main hypothesis? (In particular, read the section on "model specification." If you are not satisfied with Eckard's discussion of regression analysis, add one or two sentences of your own.)

3b.   What *regression equation* is estimated? Write down the regression equation for *one* car line.

3c.   Write down the value of the regression equation's "constant" term and explain its meaning.

3d.   Write down the regression equation's single most important variable (related to the study's main theme).

3e.   Write down the value of the coefficient estimate for the variable identified in 3d.

3f.   Interpret the meaning of the coefficient above. A one-unit change in the independent variable will cause the dependent variable to change by _____ units.

3g.   Is the variable you identified as important a statistically "significant" one? How do you know?

3h. Illustrate the article's statistical findings by a supply and demand diagram that illustrates the effects of dealer entry restrictions. Show the price change that occurs for a *specific* car line of your choice.

3i. Explain why several *other* independent variables are also included in the regression. Interpret their coefficients.

4. Overall, what *conclusions* can be drawn from the study, either about dealer entry rules or similar policies? (Explain how your conclusion is based on the statistical results presented in part 3 above.)

Notes on Chapter 9

Use the space below to describe new concepts or methods that you learned in Chapter 9.

Bibliography

The structure of research reports is most carefully and clearly discussed by Sylvester Carter, *Writing for Your Peers* (New York: Praeger, 1987). Another good discussion of research reports can be found in William G. Zikmund, *Business Research Methods* (Chicago: Dryden, 1988): chapter 23.

PROFICIENCY 4

The Ability to Use Existing Knowledge to Explore an Issue

Previous chapters have discussed methods that can be used to locate published data or research, to present debates and report on issues already in the public forum, and to summarize investigations conducted by other researchers. It is important for the practicing economist to be able to perform all of these tasks, but in a larger sense these activities are inputs into the production of new research—a skill you will develop in the following three chapters. By the time you finish reading these chapters and working the exercises that accompany them, you should be able to use familiar economic theories and statistical procedures to explore issues that interest you. Such investigations are routinely conducted by business economists and by academicians in economics and other disciplines.

CHAPTER 10

Theory in Economic Research

*The primary purpose of any theory is to clarify
concepts and ideas which have become, as it
were, confused and entangled.*
—*Carl von Clausewitz*

Introduction

This is an ambitious chapter that covers a lot of ground. It begins with a
discussion of the scientific method in economics and an examination of
methodological issues in economic research. It would be far simpler to
skip over these preliminary matters and get on with the main subject of
the chapter—theoretical aspects of an economic research project—but it
is necessary to have a deeper understanding of the process if one aspires
to be a good economist. Researchers follow certain ground rules that
transcend a specific project, yet these issues are rarely mentioned in
research articles so it may not be clear to an inexperienced researcher what
those ground rules are.

The final part of the chapter concentrates on the organization of the
theoretical section of a research report. As you gain experience writing
research reports you may have insights that allow you to modify the
approach suggested here to suit the particulars of a given project. Until
you have that experience, however, you should concentrate on providing
those elements of a research report that experienced readers expect from
a scientific investigation.

Scientific Methodology in Economic Research

Economists do research for many reasons: to satisfy the requirements of their jobs, to earn consulting fees, or merely to gain the satisfaction of conducting research. Regardless of motivation, good economics must satisfy the requirements of good science if the exercise is to be worthwhile. Bad science may escape the notice of others for a while, but it would be foolish to believe that it can escape notice forever. In academia, economists conduct research to gain promotion and tenure at the universities that employ them. For them flawed research will almost certainly be detected by peers who specialize in the same subject area and review (or "referee") research papers before they can be published. In the private sector, if an employer requests an economic study of some issue in order to decide whether or not to make a capital investment, bad science will become apparent when the investment fails. If an economic consultant conducts substandard research, other consultants are likely to identify poorly done work. Once this happens, the consultant will be discredited in the eyes of clients (customers) and will be replaced by other economists whose reputations are intact. The economist who conducts research as a pleasurable "hobby" will disappoint only himself by cutting corners and failing to comply with professional standards, but such disappointments are profound and eliminate the pleasure which was the original motive for doing research.

These observations suggest that there is a "survivor principle" at work in economics: Poor research either attracts harsh criticism or does not generate the personal motivation required to continue with additional projects in the future. This seems to suggest that over time the quantity of low-quality economic research will decline, since poor researchers will ultimately give up doing research and find other ways to spend their afternoons and evenings: fishing or gardening, for example. But in fact there will always be a large volume of low-quality research, if only because of the continuing flow of new economists into the profession.

There is another group of economists worth mentioning here—*those who want and hope to do good research but do not know how to get started or what is expected of them.* It is for this third group that the present text was written. For those who do not consider themselves "natural born" researchers, it is important to become informed about the methods used by successful researchers, and then practice those methods. Following the "wrong" approach may prevent a current project from being successfully completed, and may also reinforce bad habits that work against the successful completion of future projects.

The Scientific Method

When people hear the term "science," they may think of physics, chemistry, and biology. However, those fields became sciences by making use of certain methods of inquiry and investigation. Most of us learned a little about Greek and Roman mythology at some point in our education. The Greek and Roman myths often provided appealing explanations for natural phenomena which people of the day did not understand, such as the changing of the seasons. Those myths attempted to answer many of the same questions as modern-day physics, chemistry, and biology, but they certainly do not qualify as science as we understand that term today.

Science refers to the systematic search for knowledge based on observation, study, and experimentation. *The scientific method is generally understood to include the formulation of testable propositions using established theories, and the testing of those propositions against actual experience.* If real-world experience is contrary to the predictions of the theory, then that is taken as a sign that the theory should either be modified or rejected in favor of a superior one. One philosopher of science, Karl Popper, has argued that for a line of inquiry to qualify as a science it must produce "falsifiable" statements, that is, predictions that can be compared to real-world experience to test the power of the theory. Popper's approach is summarized in Exhibit 10–1.

Scientists do not usually reject a theory on the first occasion that it fails to stand up to experimental evidence or real-world observations. In a typical case they might first reexamine the logical process by which they developed the testable proposition to discover whether error might have led them to predict something that the theory does not in fact imply. Assuming that no logical error was committed, they might reexamine the data used in the test to discover whether it might have been "contaminated" by bias, measurement error, or some other difficulty. If no problems are found with the data, they might then inquire what problems with the theory itself might account for the incorrect prediction. It is at this stage that consideration would be given to amending the original theory to improve its performance. Failing that, perhaps the theory will be rejected entirely in favor of another one that can explain all of the phenomena explained by the first theory, plus the new phenomena that the first theory has failed explain.

As such, science is revolutionary. The scientific method's very purpose is to systematically compare the performance of even the best-known and most respected theories against actual experience, and to reject those theories when substantial evidence suggests that alternative theories can answer questions that they cannot. The systematic way that scientists search for new knowledge and their willingness to replace respected but inferior ideas with new but superior ones is responsible for many of the advantages of modern life (medicines, foods, air travel). In economics, the search for knowledge has greatly reduced the likelihood of experiencing another economic collapse like the one of the 1930s, has identified conditions that promote long-run economic growth, and has reduced the likelihood that laws will be passed that provide small benefits at a high cost to society.

Nearly everyone has heard the story about the apple that fell on Isaac Newton's head and triggered new insights about the nature of gravity. In fact, only a small proportion of the work done by scientists in economics and other disciplines represents a major breakthrough of this kind. Instead, most scientific research consists of testing an existing theory against a new data set or making minor modifications to established theories to extend their usefulness to new phenomena. Though less dramatic, small gains of knowledge have a large cumulative effect on the profession's understanding of real-world phenomena.

EXHIBIT 10–1 Karl Popper's Methodology of Science*

1.   Science presents us with the clearest case of the systematic growth of knowledge. In order to examine the growth of scientific knowledge, we must be able to distinguish science from nonscience; we need a *demarcation criterion.*

2.   Popper's criterion of demarcation is *falsifiability.* A statement or theory "has the status of belonging to the empirical sciences if and only if it is falsifiable." Some statements are potentially falsifiable but currently untestable, however.

3.   Popper considered a scientific explanation one in which an "explanandum" can be deduced from an "explanans." In other words, a scientific explanation is one where *a condition being explained can be deduced from initial conditions and at least one universal law.* In economics the universal law is usually the rationality, or maximizing, principle.

4.   If a statement (theory) has been tested, then there are two possibilities:

   a.   If a test result is positive, the theory is *corroborated.* Scientists often accept a theory that has been corroborated as *provisionally true,* but this does not mean proven true. All knowledge is conjectural.

   b.   If a test result is negative, the theory is *refuted* or falsified. Just as corroboration does not prove a theory true, refutation does not prove it false. Final rejection of a theory is a separate matter.

5.   Refutations are always more interesting than corroborations, for they force scientists to reexamine the theory to determine what went wrong. Such critical reexamination offers the best hope that false theories will be eliminated from science. During reexamination, *Popper's approach prohibits what he called immunizing stratagems, or ad hoc theory adjustments whose sole purpose is to protect a theory from being refuted.*

6.   Even in situations where clean tests are difficult, scientists should *specify in advance what sort of empirical observations would lead them to abandon their theories.* Scientists should adopt a critical attitude in which they attempt to seek refutations rather than confirmations, even of their own theories.

*Adapted from Bruce J. Caldwell, "Clarifying Popper," *Journal of Economic Literature* (March 1991): 2–4.

The nature of scientific research can be illustrated graphically. Phenomena that people do not currently understand are represented in Exhibit 10–2 as a *forest of ignorance* and misunderstanding, and scientists are responsible for clearing away the forest using whatever means (theories) they can devise. One scientist may believe that theory *A* is a superior theory, while others may have confidence in theories *B* and *C*. As each scientist applies his or her respective theory, the forest gradually gives way. The scientists observe that no single theory is most effective at

EXHIBIT 10–2 Pushing Back the Frontiers of Ignorance

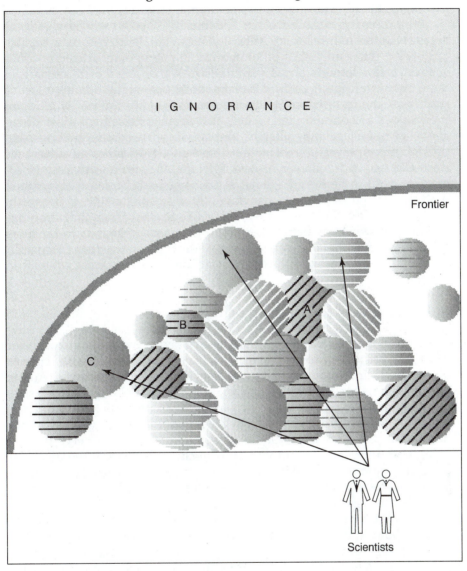

removing all kinds of trees, and they also learn from the successes of competing theories that their own theory must be modified or rejected in favor of a more successful one. And so they go, pushing back the frontiers of ignorance, sometimes by small increments and sometimes by large ones. Even minor applications of a theory that do not push back the frontiers of ignorance are useful in this enterprise, since lessons may be learned which may ultimately contribute significantly to the overall effort. In general, researchers in the physical and natural sciences (physics, chemistry, biology, etc.) tend to conduct a large number of "small" experiments to test the usefulness and limits of each theory, while economists and other social scientists conduct relatively few larger-scale studies that overlap each other less. Some observers believe that the social sciences could make greater progress against the forest of ignorance by moving in the direction taken by the natural sciences.*

The "forest of ignorance" in Exhibit 10–2 is merely one way of illustrating the nature of scientific advancement, and you may be able to develop other analogies of your own. The foregoing discussion does suggest a few lessons about scientific work that are worth keeping in mind, however. First, each of us can contribute to the overall effort to push back the frontiers of ignorance even when we are not working at the frontier. Second, some theories that seem promising—even dominant—at one stage may later be displaced by alternative theories that provide more powerful explanations of reality. As science advances, we learn that no theory is ever proved right for all times and places. Third, theories need to be tested against actual experience to learn about their practical usefulness and to convince other scientists that it is worthwhile to modify their own theories. Anyone can claim that "my axe will chop down trees better than any other axe," but we are far more convinced after having seen it chop down a few trees. Empirical methods used in economic research are discussed in greater detail in Chapter 11.

Inductive and Deductive Logic

Scientists in most fields employ inductive or deductive logic to explain the relationships that interest them. *Inductive logic* begins with specific observations and builds to a general conclusion. As described by Adrian Darnell and Lynne Evans, "Induction is a general label which emphasizes the role of data as a major vehicle by which to accumulate knowledge and the inductive method seeks to draw general conclusions based on a finite number of particular observations."[†] For example, you observe the sun rising each morning for a month and conclude that it will therefore rise tomorrow morning. Inductive reasoning was commonly used by scientists in the nineteenth century, but it is used less often today.

Deductive logic employs general propositions about reality—often, theories that have been successful in previous tests—and factual information about a given situation to derive conclusions (testable hypotheses) about specific phenomena. For example, you might accept the general proposition that demand curves are downward sloping. Now if circumstances cause lumber prices to rise, *ceteris paribus*, you predict that people will react by building fewer homes than otherwise.

For the most part, economists employ deductive logic in their research projects. Theoretical discussions typically contain a general proposition about economic behavior that serves as a starting point for the analysis. Other premises or assumptions are also invoked, such as the condition above that the price of lumber rose while other determinants of demand remained unchanged. Finally, a testable hypothesis or conclusion is "deduced" from the proposition and premises. As Fawcett and Downs put it, "The transitive rule of relationships is used to deduce" a conclusion

---

*See Theodore Morgan, "Theory versus Empiricism in Academic Economics: Update and Comparisons," *Journal of Economic Perspectives*, Fall 1988: 159–64.
[†]Adrian C. Darnell and J. Lynne Evans, *The Limits of Econometrics*, 1990, p. 26.

from previously stated propositions and premises.* If X affects Y and Y affects Z, then a change in X will cause the value of Z to change. As you read the theoretical sections of research papers, you can benefit by identifying the general propositions and assumptions that were used to deduce the main hypothesis of the study. Or when you write a research paper, be sure to include these components of a theoretical argument. Don't leave it up to the reader to guess about the specific chain of reasoning that you applied to a problem.

In practice, modern science is advanced by a combination of inductive and deductive logic. Deductive logic is used to derive statements (hypotheses) that can be tested against actual experience. Occasionally however, scientists observe phenomena that have not been explained with existing theories and offer explanations based on experience and observation which, after successful testing, may ultimately be accepted by other scientists.

Assumptions

Critics sometimes charge that economic science is of limited usefulness because of the excessive number of assumptions that economists make when developing their theories. (There is a joke about a physicist, a chemist, and an economist stranded on a remote island with only one can of beans to eat. After the physicist and chemist fail to open the can using the best methods their disciplines have to offer, the economist offers to try. He begins with: "Assume we've got a can opener . . .") But theories in every line of inquiry make use of assumptions. The pure laws of gravity assume a vacuum, and therefore no wind resistance, when objects fall. Without the assumption of a vacuum, a dropped ball and feather no longer reach the ground at the same time.

The absence of a vacuum (and the presence of wind resistance) in real-world applications means that physicists eventually had to modify their predictions to explain earthly experiences. Viewing this process over time, the first scientist used the assumption of a vacuum to create a simplified environment within which a "pure" theory of gravity could be developed. After developing the simplest version of the theory, additional complexities could be built into the model—by eliminating some of the simplifying assumptions.

This extended discussion of assumptions and gravity has implications for economics. No economist believes that corporations are managed solely for the purpose of maximizing profit; no economist believes that markets are always in equilibrium; no economist believes that utility functions are everywhere "continuous and differentiable." We assume these things to simplify the development of our theories. Later, if circumstances or mere curiosity require it, one can go back and reformulate the theory by modifying some of its assumptions. Theories are by their very nature simplified statements about reality. Scientists in all fields assume away "irrelevant" conditions to concentrate on the influence of only a few relevant ones. The assumed conditions retained in

---

*Jacqueline Fawcett and Florence S. Downs, *The Relationship of Theory and Research* (1986), p. 35.

a theoretical model establish the *domain* over which a theory can be expected to apply. If other conditions actually prevail, then in practice a theoretical model may not be very useful; but if those other conditions are not in fact very important, then even a highly simplified theory that ignores the effect of these conditions may be a powerful tool of analysis.*

One assumption that strikes some noneconomists as extreme is the assumption that decision makers are utility maximizers. Certainly the existence of charity suggests that people are not always narrowly self-interested. Does our observation of voluntary charity mean that actual market outcomes will differ significantly from those predicted by supply and demand analysis? After all, that model is based on the twin assumptions of utility- and profit-maximization. The existence of charity appears to violate these assumptions.

The problem is more apparent than real, however. Supply and demand analysis does not require that everyone maximize utility and profits on every occasion. These assumptions are only relevant in situations involving market transactions examined by the analysis. Even the most charitable person may strive to buy for the lowest price and sell for the highest price, however—if only to gain wealth that can be contributed to those in need. Because charity can exist without extending into every transaction, the domain of economics covers the majority of transactions that are undertaken for personal gain.

Explanations or Predictions?

Economists sometimes use their theories to explain economic phenomena, sometimes to predict economic phenomena. So far, so good. A problem arises when they (we) try to blend prediction and explanation within a single discussion.

To *predict*, economists typically state a set of assumptions about prevailing conditions, about individual motivations, and about various relationships, then ask, "If conditions A, B, and C prevail, what outcome can be expected?" To *explain*, economists begin with an observed outcome and look backward: "This outcome we observe is the result of economic conditions A and B, relationship C, and the attempt by decision makers to maximize utility."

In other words, *prediction* requires the economist to work with a fixed set of assumptions while *explanation* requires the economist to describe a set of assumptions (assumed conditions) that are consistent with an observed outcome. In the first instance we begin with assumptions while in the second we search for them. Either exercise is valid, but it is not legitimate to treat assumptions from both perspectives within a single discussion.

---

*In the 1940s, a controversy arose over the practice of incorporating the assumption of profit maximization into theories of the firm. The defender of profit maximizing theories (Fritz Machlup) considered this a valid simplifying assumption for constructing a theoretical model of the firm, while the critic (Richard Lester) disagreed and called for more "realism" in the models. For more on this controversy see the Lester-Machlup exchange in four articles appearing in the *American Economic Review* between March 1946 and March 1947.

A concrete example illustrates the nature of the problem. Suppose you are asked to predict what will happen if the minimum wage is increased by $1 per hour above its current level. You might begin by assuming that the current wage for unskilled labor is initially at or above its market-clearing level, that employers are profit maximizers, and that employers are free to alter the mix of labor and capital they employ. The result? You predict that the minimum wage increase will cause employers to substitute capital inputs and skilled labor for unskilled labor and that a greater number of unskilled workers will be unemployed than before.

Following your prediction, suppose we observe just the opposite—the unemployment rate among unskilled workers declines rather than increases during subsequent months. *What do you have to say about that?*

Well, you might say, the minimum wage increase *would have* created unemployment but a simultaneous increase in aggregate demand helped create new jobs; or perhaps an even larger increase in the cost of capital also occurred, which caused employers to substitute labor for capital.

Maybe all true, but we are not questioning your ability to *explain* events after the fact. *Predictions* are based on the set of assumptions the forecaster selects before the fact, and the ones you selected in this particular instance—constant aggregate demand and capital costs—were not adequate for the task at hand. Period. You are justified in reviewing past events to see what prevented your prediction from being validated, but coming up with an explanation now is an entirely different exercise from the one to which you originally committed yourself.

> Properly extended, economic theory can . . . explain everything, but this is . . . equivalent to saying that it predicts nothing. [James M. Buchanan, *What Should Economists Do?* (Indianapolis: Liberty Press, 1979), pp. 78–79]

All of this may seem painfully obvious, but in the heat of debate or to extricate oneself from an embarrassing forecast it is easy—*too easy*—to slip from prediction to explanation so subtly that the transition goes unnoticed by all. The trained economist has a responsibility not only to notice but to avoid committing this offense. Predict or explain, but do not attempt to combine both in the same exercise.

In a larger research investigation, the economist plays different roles so it is appropriate to both explain and predict—though at different points in the project. As an observer of past events and earlier research, the economist might use economic analysis to *explain* past phenomena or lessons that have emerged from past research investigations. The explanation is offered to gain insights that can be incorporated into the present research investigation. For the most part, this discussion is included in the literature review and general analysis that is undertaken at the beginning of a research report.

At another point, the researcher combines concepts, assumptions about economic and other conditions, and previously identified relationships to produce a hypothesis—a *prediction*—about the specific outcome we are most likely to observe. The economist plays this role when developing the theoretical analysis of a research investigation. The remainder of Chapter 10 focuses on the economist's role as a predictor and producer of testable hypotheses.

In summary, at its best, economics provides an integrated approach for explaining, predicting, and understanding many types of human behavior. Economic theories gain credence when their implications are tested and found consistent with observations drawn from actual experience. The rejection of theories that are inconsistent with experience and their replacement by superior theories provides the mechanism by which economics improves with each passing year.

Theory Development in the Research Paper

Research projects in the sciences represent attempts to expand knowledge about a phenomenon or to discover whether established theories can be successfully applied to that phenomenon. In either instance it is necessary to devote a significant part of the final research report providing a logical argument in terms acceptable to scientists in the discipline. This logical analysis is often referred to as the "theory section" of a research report.

Theoretical discussions *abstract from reality*, that is, they do not incorporate every detail about a situation to explain a phenomenon. To better understand the process of theory development, it is useful to consider the increasing levels of abstraction. *Concepts* are terms that correspond to real-world phenomena which generalize about their nature, such as "productivity" and "capital goods." In economics, such concepts are often referred to as "variables." The analyst hopes to explain variations in one concept by referring to variations in another set of concepts. Concepts are the basic building blocks of theories, and the scientist's job is to assemble those blocks into a unified structure that offers a plausible explanation of the conclusion reached by the analysis. Along with the concepts themselves the analyst should provide definitions of concepts when their meaning is not readily apparent to readers, and may also assume certain things about them to avoid unnecessarily complicating the discussion. In applied research, concepts must correspond to an *operational variable* that can be empirically observed and measured. For example, "human capital" is an *abstract concept* that can't be observed directly, while "years of education" is an operationally defined concept that could be used in empirical analysis. Depending on the nature and purpose of the research, years of education may or may not be a useful empirical counterpart to (proxy for) human capital. The researcher should discuss the adequacy of operational variables to anticipate problems that could arise in the analysis and also to answer questions a reader might have.

At a higher level of abstraction, declarative statements about concepts or about relationships between concepts are known as *propositions*. Ideally, some of the propositions describe *causal relationships that are already familiar to economists*. For example, one proposition is that labor productivity is positively related to the quantity of capital available to workers. A proposition may specify the direction of the relationship between variables (direct, inverse), the shape of the relationship (linear, diminishing, U-shaped), the strength of the relationship (two-to-one, proportional) and so forth. In most instances, economic analysis suggests the direction and (occasionally) the shape of relationships between variables. *Definitions* of concepts and *assumptions* about concepts—e.g., X is assumed to change by 10 units—are two more propositions. The theoretical analysis is strengthened if some of the relationships it incorporates have been identified and documented by previous researchers.

The highest level of abstraction occurs when propositions are used in combination with other propositions to *deduce* a conclusion. (Later the empirical adequacy of the conclusion is tested against actual experience.) Typically, the scientist combines propositions according to *transitive rules of logic,* which follow the general form: If X is related to Y and Y is related to Z, then X is related to Z. In this discussion X, Y, and Z are concepts, the statements about the relationships between X and Y, and Y and Z are propositions, and deductive logic is used to reach the testable proposition (conclusion) that X is related to Z. Researchers often refer to a *testable proposition* as a *hypothesis.*

A theory combines all of these elements: concepts, propositions (concept definitions, assumptions, and relationships), logical manipulation of concepts and propositions, and a hypothesis that can be tested against actual experience.

Continuing the earlier example, consider what happens when the proposition that labor productivity is a positive function of the quantity of capital is combined with another proposition (assumption) that in the short run the quantity of capital employed by the firm is fixed. From these two propositions the conclusion can be deduced that hiring additional workers will cause less-than-proportional increases in the quantity of output—a phenomenon normally referred to as diminishing returns. When operational definitions are applied to capital, labor, and output, the conclusion can be stated as a testable hypothesis.

In actual practice, most theoretical discussions in economics examine far more complex problems containing many concepts and propositions. Moreover, *they may not explicitly state concepts and propositions that are already well known to readers.* For example, all economists know that demand curves slope downward so it is not necessary to remind them of that relationship every time the idea is utilized. Discussing such matters adds nothing to the analysis, but risks *boring* readers and causing them to stop reading. The author's peers prefer that these parts of the argument be omitted, but nonspecialist readers may not realize that certain concepts and propositions have been omitted, in which case they may become *confused* and stop reading. You should keep this trade-off in mind when deciding how much detail to provide in the theoretical passage, and write at a level that is geared toward the intended reader.

These remarks about theory development can be illustrated by a passage drawn from an actual research article. According to Geoffrey Tootell, the "law of one price" explains why a given product will tend to have the same price in different geographic markets. This conclusion is derived by the logical process of combining concepts into propositions, then combining propositions to derive a testable hypothesis:

> If a BMW costs $20,000 in Germany and $40,000 net of transportation costs in the United States, some entrepreneur will start buying BMWs in Germany and sending them to this country. . . . [T]he entrepreneur will reap huge gains. [Due to the relative shift in supply, BMW prices will increase in Germany and decrease in the United States. After all such profitable exchanges have been carried out,] the price of the same good in different regions should be equivalent. [Geoffrey M. B. Tootell, "Purchasing Power Parity Within the United States," *New England Economic Review* (Federal Reserve Bank of Boston), July/August 1992: p. 15]

In this passage several concepts are introduced: BMW, German price ("cost"), United States price ("net of transportation cost"), entrepreneur, buy, sell, profit ("gains"), shift in supply. The first three concepts—BMW, German price, and U.S. price—describe the setting to be examined. In that setting, a price difference exists between what BMWs sell for in Germany and in the U.S.

From these concepts the proposition can be derived that a price differential between different locations provides profitable trading opportunities. In fact, this proposition is not stated explicitly, but is implied by the sentence describing the "huge gains" that can be reaped by those who trade goods between markets. If readers were less aware of economic analysis, the author could have explicitly stated in the first sentence (following the comma) that "an entrepreneur could receive the $20,000 price differential by buying a BMW in Germany and selling it in the U.S. at the higher price."

Another proposition is implicit in the discussion, namely that entrepreneurs are motivated to act on profitable trading opportunities: "some entrepreneur will start buying BMWs in Germany and sending them to this country." This second proposition could have been stated as a testable hypothesis regarding the behavior of entrepreneurs, but its validity has been established elsewhere so its status here is that of a supporting proposition used to develop a testable hypothesis about some other event.

The profit-seeking behavior just discussed suggests additional propositions: an increased supply of BMWs can be expected to lower BMW prices in the U.S. market; a reduced supply in Germany can be expected to increase prices in that market. These propositions could also be tested against actual experience to determine whether or not markets "behave" as expected. Instead, they are used in the development of another testable hypothesis.

Finally, Tootell combines the various propositions regarding the behavior of entrepreneurs and the performance of markets to derive the testable hypothesis that after markets reach equilibrium, "the price of the same good in different regions [is predicted to] be equivalent." This is the hypothesis Tootell later tests in his study.

The presentation of concepts and propositions, and logically manipulating them to arrive at a testable hypothesis can be done formally, using mathematical symbols, or informally, by describing the chain of reasoning employed by the researcher. It is also common in economic research reports to provide graphical representations of important relationships between concepts.

Research reports usually present the elements of a theoretical discussion in the order described here: concepts, propositions, logical combination and manipulation of propositions, then a testable hypothesis. These are illustrated in Exhibit 10–3. Arrows indicate the flow of the theoretical

EXHIBIT 10–3 A Map of Theory Development*

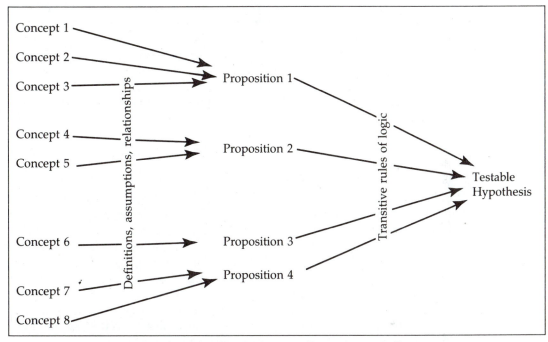

*The theory may be developed graphically, mathematically, and/or verbally.

argument. According to Fawcett and Downs, "The hypothesis is the final step in the deductive process, and so the other propositions are arranged in the order that leads to this end point" (Fawcett and Downs, p. 38). Once the theoretical part of a research paper is written, Artinian suggests diagramming the components of the argument.* An inventory of concepts, propositions, logical manipulation, and hypothesis should reveal whether essential links in the logical chain have been omitted.

Writing the Theory Passage

The theory section of a research report is where the author provides the logical foundation on which the findings of the study are based. We have seen that

*B. M. Artinian, "Conceptual Mapping: Development of the Strategy," *West Journal of Nursing Research,* vol. 4 (1982): 379–93.

theory development advances through various stages of abstraction, from concepts, to propositions, to a testable hypothesis. The present discussion examines issues relating to organizing and writing the theoretical section of a research report. *The researcher's most important responsibility in this section is to provide the reader with the clearest possible statement of the logical structure upon which the findings of the study rest.* The following section of the research report will provide empirical backing for the claims, but at this stage the researcher hopes to convince the reader that the findings of the study rest on a strong logical foundation.

To make the most effective presentation, *begin the theoretical section by stating what you intend to demonstrate in your analysis.* When the reader knows where the argument is headed, he or she is less likely to be led astray by a poorly worded sentence or other distraction.

After stating what you intend to accomplish, it is time to *present the theoretical argument* in the manner suggested in the section above. Discuss the real-world problem or issue you intend to examine, then if possible divide the larger problem into smaller parts. For each part, identify relevant concepts (variables) corresponding to real-world phenomena, provide definitions, make assumptions, and discuss relationships among the concepts. This exercise will produce a series of propositions, which you will eventually combine to produce a testable hypothesis—presumably the same hypothesis you specified at the outset of the discussion. As noted earlier, the theoretical discussion may consist largely of mathematical manipulations, written explanations, or graphical exhibits, or some combination of the three. Provide concrete examples to illustrate abstract ideas. Particularly effective is the "running example," or a single example that you return to at various points in the discussion to illustrate how additional features of the argument fit into the larger picture. For example, a running example regarding labor productivity and diminishing returns was used earlier in this chapter to illustrate the relationships between concepts, propositions, and testable hypotheses.

It is useful to emphasize a suggestion made in the previous paragraph: For all but the least complex discussions, *divide the argument into smaller parts*—say, one part for each main proposition—and give each your full attention. Large tasks are more easily attacked when divided into smaller parts, and dividing a discussion into parts also reduces the risk of blending together issues that really do not belong together. Moreover, the very act of dividing the theoretical discussion into parts forces the writer to develop a "grand strategy" of the argument being presented. At the revision stage it may be necessary to remove duplicate material when two or more parts overlap, or to add transitional remarks to tie the parts of the discussion together.

In a larger study, two or more testable hypotheses may emerge from the theoretical analysis. In such cases, it is essential to treat each hypothesis as a separate topic that requires its own supporting foundation of concepts, propositions, and logical manipulation.

As you write, it will occasionally be necessary to *provide additional information* to contribute to the overall effectiveness of the argument. If assumptions were made about some variable, explain why they are (a) necessary and (b) logically consistent with the conclusions of the theoretical model. Provide a definition when introducing a new term whose meaning is not apparent to the reader. If mathematical symbols are used, explain the notation. If you are aware of some subtle fact that is relevant to the discussion which the reader is unlikely to know, mention that fact at the appropriate point in the discussion. Without this background information, theoretical discussions may lack the cohesion and substance which clear communication requires.

To avoid confusion, *the style of writing in this section should be simple and direct.* Use declarative sentences with few subordinate clauses and adjectives. Such sentences will typically be somewhat shorter than those you normally use. Complex sentences are more likely to confuse the reader, and it is particularly important in this section of the paper to avoid all forms of confusion. It is also wise to omit unnecessary sentences, parenthetical remarks, and footnotes that do not bear on the argument being presented. This is known as a *terse* writing style—no fat, only muscle.

Other Explanations of the Phenomenon

In economic research the economist often wants to investigate the relationship between two variables $X1$ and Y, although Y is also thought to be influenced by other variables, $X2$ and $X3$, that are of no direct interest to the present study. For example, suppose Y is the quantity of output produced per worker, $X1$ is a "work ethic index" which incorporates cultural factors thought to contribute to work effort, $X2$ is the quantity of physical capital available to the average worker, and $X3$ is the quantity of human capital possessed by the typical worker. In combination, these variables suggest the production function:

$$Y = f(X1, X2, X3) \tag{1}$$

Despite the impression that one might get from listening to a debate between experts, one can argue that a particular variable is "important" without denying the possible significance of other variables. In terms of the example, one can believe that the work ethic contributes to production without denying the simultaneous contribution of capital or other factors. In this instance the economist might say that his or her study attempts to isolate the impact of the work ethic on production *at the margin*, that is, given a fixed quantity of physical and human capital available to the worker.

Although the stated purpose of a study might be to investigate the relationship between production and the work ethic (Y and $X1$), the implied deeper purpose is to achieve a more complete understanding of the factors that influence labor productivity. That explains why the theoretical section of a report on the influence of the work ethic on productivity should include a production function written as equation (1) rather than a simply modeling Y as a function of $X1$ alone: $Y = f(X1)$.

When writing the theoretical section of the research paper, the writer should find an appropriate place to briefly discuss the other variables ($X2$ and $X3$) that are also believed to affect production. One approach is to begin the theory section by stating the conventional view that output (Y) is a function of the quantity of physical and human capital used by workers, then discuss at greater length the possibility that the work ethic can also contribute to production. Alternatively, one could begin the theory section with a lengthy discussion of the work ethic, and conclude the section by mentioning other factors which researchers believe also contribute to production.

A third approach would be to discuss the impact of the variables examined by other researchers in a separate "review of the literature" contained in the introductory section of the report, then only briefly mention those findings again in the theory section when writing down the production function in equation (1)—which contains not only the "new" variable ($X1$) but the variables identified by other researchers as well. Finally, one could designate a special section of the report to examine the additional variables. This approach might be followed when several of these additional variables require a lengthy discussion and there is a risk of confusing the reader about the distinction between existing knowledge and new insights provided by the present study. This approach has the advantage of locating the additional explanatory variables as near as possible to the empirical part of the report, which always follows the theoretical passage.

In general, the approach suggested here is to include a discussion of the additional explanatory variables in the theory section. This discussion may be brief if it repeats information already provided in the introductory section's literature review. Including all explanatory variables in the theory discussion reduces the likelihood that the reader will disagree with the present contribution on the grounds that it overlooks the influence of other important variables. Since the researcher is claiming that the work ethic has an impact at the margin, it only confuses matters to write the production function in a form suggesting that the work ethic is the *only* variable that explains productivity.

Regardless of the ultimate decision on where to discuss additional explanatory variables, they must also be included in the empirical investigation. The statistical procedure most often used by economists to estimate the impact of one variable on another is regression analysis. Regression analysis requires that observations of all relevant explanatory variables be included to generate an unbiased estimate of the influence of the variable of interest. For this reason, the researcher who fails to consider variables identified by others will be unable to conduct a reliable statistical test of his or her own hypothesis.

Summary

The theoretical section of a research report is intended to provide a logical explanation for the findings of a research project. To do good *research*, the economist must have a thorough understanding of the immediate problem or issue being examined as well as a clear sense of the scientific method. To write a good research *report*, the economist must provide readers with a clear explanation of the logical underpinnings of the project's findings. An outline and checklist for the theory section of a research report is provided in Exhibit 10–4. If you write a research paper that departs significantly from this outline, it is likely that you will have omitted an essential part of the argument and run the risk that readers will

EXHIBIT 10–4 Content and Style of the Theory Section

Purpose: *The theory section should convince the reader that the findings of the study rest on a strong logical foundation.*

- *State what you intend to demonstrate* in your analysis.
- *Discuss the problem* or issue that you intend to examine, and if necessary divide it into smaller parts that you can analyze one by one.
- Develop the theoretical argument by identifying and defining *concepts,* then by developing *propositions,* which are statements about concepts or relationships between them. When writing the theory section, concentrate on a single proposition at a time. After the appropriate propositions have been stated, combine several propositions to develop a testable *hypothesis.*
- The theory passage may contain written explanations, mathematical expressions, and graphical demonstrations of the concepts and propositions you are examining. Elementary concepts and propositions that the reader already knows about can be omitted when preparing the final draft of the report, but probably should be included in early drafts so the author is aware of every step required to demonstrate the logic of the conclusions.
- Provide additional *background information* (definitions, mathematical notation, relevant facts not known to the reader, concrete examples) to make the argument more convincing to the reader.
- Use a *terse writing style* containing declarative sentences with few subordinate clauses and phrases. Omit unnecessary remarks to minimize the possibility of confusing the reader.
- If other researchers have examined the same general phenomenon you are studying, mention the *additional variables and relationships* they suggest are important. (Represent your own insights as having an impact at the margin, without denying the influence of other factors that may also belong in a larger theory of the phenomenon.)

---

not agree with or understand the logical background for the conclusions of your report.

Inexperienced researchers often believe that complex arguments are the most convincing ones, and that simple arguments will be dismissed as unsophisticated. As a result, they may unnecessarily complicate their message and confuse even themselves about what they are attempting to demonstrate.

The view advanced here is that an uncomplicated writing style combined with clear thinking makes for an elegant theoretical argument that is a pleasure to read, is easy to remember, and is effective for advancing knowledge. In practice it is often very difficult to develop an elegant theoretical argument. The first draft of the theoretical section may be a lengthy discussion containing side issues of no direct relevance to the present study, unnecessary remarks about issues the reader already understands, and implicit assumptions that need to be made explicit.

Substantial editing is necessary to pare down even a good first draft into a finished product, but that effort will mean the difference between a successful research report and an unsuccessful one.

Exercises

Reread the second (theoretical) section of Marshall Medoff's article, "An Economic Analysis of the Demand for Abortions" (Chapter 9, p. 136). Then complete the following exercises.

Exercise 1: List the concepts, propositions, and the hypothesis contained in Michael's model of "effective excess demand for children," contained in the first two paragraphs of part II of the Medoff article.

Exercise 2: What variables (concepts) does Medoff say increase the cost of having a child? What variables (concepts) does he imply influence the benefits of having a child? Explain how each variable affects costs and/or benefits of having a child in Medoff's discussion.

Exercise 3: In Exercise 2 above, how are the costs and benefits of having a child linked to the decision to have an abortion? What is Medoff's testable hypothesis?

Exercise 4: Develop a drawing (map) linking concepts, propositions and the testable hypothesis in the Medoff article. The drawing should look something like Exhibit 10–3.

Exercise 5: Write a one-page essay that evaluates Medoff's theoretical discussion according to criteria provided in Exhibit 10–4.

Reread the second (theoretical) section of E. W. Eckard's article, "The Effects of State Automobile Dealer Entry Regulation on New Car Prices" (Chapter 9, p. 145). Then complete the following exercises.

Exercise 6: List the concepts, propositions, and the hypothesis contained in Eckard's third paragraph of part II relating to the impact of an increase in demand on the price of cars when entry by new dealers is *not* blocked by government regulations.

Exercise 7: Repeat Exercise 6, but now assume that entry by new dealers *is* blocked by government regulations. What is Eckard's testable hypothesis regarding the effect of auto dealer entry regulation on the price of cars?

Exercise 8: What additional variables (beside entry regulations) does Eckard say might affect the price of cars? Explain their relationship to car prices by discussing familiar economic propositions.

Exercise 9: Write a one-page essay that evaluates Eckard's theoretical discussion according to criteria provided in Exhibit 10–4.

Notes on Chapter 10

Use the space below to describe new concepts or methods that you learned in Chapter 10.

Bibliography

This chapter draws on discussions of theory development from several books. My favorites include Sylvester Carter, *Writing for Your Peers* (New York: Praeger, 1987): chapter 3; and Jacqueline Fawcett and Florence S. Downs, *The Relationship of Theory and Research* (Norwalk, CT: Appleton-Century-Crofts, 1986): chapter 2. Carter's book is less technical, but discusses the nature of the theoretical section and emphasizes the need for clarity and simplicity in the written report. Fawcett and Downs provide a detailed examination of the components of the theoretical passage. In appendices, they examine specific research reports to identify components of the theoretical discussion—concepts, propositions, hypotheses, etc.

Three other books that discuss many of the topics examined in this chapter include Chava Frankfort-Nachmias and David Nachmias, *Research Methods in the Social Sciences* (New York: St. Martin's, 1992): chapters 1–2; William G. Zikmund, *Business Research Methods* (Chicago: Dryden, 1988): chapter 2; and Peter W. House and Roger D. Shull, *Managing Research on Demand* (Lanham, MD: University Press of America, 1985): 35–38.

An excellent summary of Karl Popper's views on science, including not only falsificationism but views he developed later (situational analysis and critical rationalism), can be found in Bruce J. Caldwell, "Clarifying Popper," *Journal of Economic Literature* (March 1991): 1–33.

CHAPTER 11

Empirical Methods in Economic Research

We do not, strictly speaking, have knowledge.
What we have are theories about the real world
which have so far resisted refutation. . . .
[O]ur theories at the moment are not
truthfully knowledge. They are conjectures.
—Gordon Tullock

Introduction

Chapter 10 discussed the scientific method as it applies to economic research. Economic thought is often advanced by comparing predictions developed through logical analysis against observations drawn from actual experience. If experience conflicts with theoretical predictions, that may be taken as a sign that the theoretical model is flawed and requires revision, that its usefulness is limited to a different domain (or range of experience) than the one currently examined, or that the theory is without merit and should be rejected in favor of a superior one—which may or may not yet have been formulated.

In economics, theoretical conclusions are commonly tested by comparing them to personal observations or to statistical measures of data obtained from government agencies or others. No testing method is superior in every instance. The researcher learns, through intuition and experience, which method to rely on for testing a particular hypothesis. Occasionally data limitations may prevent testing the hypothesis by one statistical method, so circumstances require that another be used instead.

Regardless of the specific method employed to test a hypothesis, an observed consistency between actual experience and the predictions derived from a theoretical model does not "prove" the validity of the theory. According to the scientific method, no theory ever attains the status of ultimate truth; every theory remains in jeopardy of failing to predict accurately in the next application, or failing to predict as accurately as a competing theory. The assumption held by most scientists, however, is that a theory which has successfully passed several tests is more reliable than theories that have tested successfully only once or twice. A theory is also considered more reliable, the more varied the statistical procedures used to test it.

This chapter discusses several issues related to the testing of hypotheses. After briefly discussing several less sophisticated tests, the remainder of the chapter examines regression analysis. Regression analysis is the statistical method most often used by economists to test their theoretical hypotheses.

This chapter is largely a *review* of methods you should already be familiar with. Many students remain uncomfortable with statistical methods even after completing courses on the subject, however, so it is hoped that a less technical and more intuitive examination of the issues will reduce that discomfort. In addition, the chapter emphasizes statistical procedures that actually find their way into research reports and pays less attention to their technical underpinnings. The fourth proficiency developed in this text is the ability to conduct independent research investigations, so our interest in statistical methods is based purely on the role they play in economic research.

A Sampling of Empirical Methods

As noted above, there is no single best way to test all hypotheses. Many methods are available, so the choice often comes down to questions concerning the availability of data, computation costs, or the ability of a particular test to provide information needed by the researcher. The following methods have all been used by economists at one time or another.

Introspection

Introspection refers to relying on one's personal feelings, first, to develop a hypothesis about human behavior, or second, to "test" whether a particular hypothesis about human behavior rings true. For example, a test of diminishing marginal utility may be conducted by contemplating your own feelings and impressions as a consumer. Because utility cannot be measured, statistical methods that depend on explicit measurement cannot be used to test whether marginal utility declines as consumption levels increase. Austrian economists, who often emphasize subjective (utility-based) measures of cost and the role of uncertainty in decision making, rely more often on introspection than most other groups (schools) of economists.*

---

*Subjective cost theory is discussed in James M. Buchanan, *Cost and Choice* (Chicago: University of Chicago Press, 1978).

One problem with introspection as a technique for hypothesis testing results from the fact that it is unwise to generalize from a small sample. *You* may have experienced the feeling we call diminishing marginal utility, but how do you know that *others* have? A related problem occurs when the theoretician has not personally had an experience whose interpretation is critical for understanding a given issue, such as discrimination.

These difficulties aside, most economists rely on introspection at least occasionally to do a preliminary check of the reasonableness of a proposition. The advantage of introspection is that it is quick and requires no extensive search for data or access to a computer.

Personal Observation ("Casual Empiricism")

Some people rely on personal—unplanned and unanalyzed—observations to provide answers to theoretical controversies. For example, some economists supported price ceilings on domestically produced petroleum in the 1970s because they believed that higher oil prices do not stimulate greater supplies, but only serve to transfer wealth from the consumers of oil to those who supply it. (That is, they assumed a completely inelastic supply of oil.) Many who took this position had never performed a study of petroleum supply, but relied heavily on their "common sense" and on the relatively small production changes they observed following significant price increases in 1973–74. (These economists were surprised when, in 1981, the price ceiling was removed and oil production rose and reversed the downward trend in production established over the previous decade.)

The unstructured and undisciplined nature of casual empiricism virtually guarantees that on occasion the analyst will consider the evidence strong for a hypothesis that would actually be rejected by a more formal test. If variable Y is influenced by three other variables $X1$, $X2$, and $X3$, it is difficult through personal observation alone to measure the independent impact of each variable with any degree of accuracy. If the analyst is unaware of variables $X1$ and $X3$, he may be inclined to attribute all changes in Y to observed variations in $X2$. Another way of putting this is to say that economists typically make *ceteris paribus* predictions about events, but casual empiricism does not control for the many other factors that might intervene and therefore prevents the underlying relationship from being observed.

Like introspection, the advantage of personal observation is its low cost and quick availability. Only a few minutes' reflection may be enough to recall one or more real-world observations that correspond fairly well to a given theoretical argument, and those experiences may provide a "first approximation" guess about the validity of the argument.

Experimentation

Testable hypotheses are statements about relationships between variables (concepts), so if it were possible to manipulate the value of one variable and observe the response by a second, the analyst could learn about the existence of the hypothesized relationship. This is the nature of experimentation. Physical scientists frequently conduct experiments to test their hypotheses, but only a small fraction of social scientists use experiments.

For example, suppose you could snap your fingers and the price of gasoline would increase by 10¢ per gallon at every service station. With this power, you could implement a price increase and observe the response by consumers. Your experiment would allow us to observe changes in price and quantity consumed at a point in time; the observations would not include the effects of changes in consumer income, variations in the prices of related goods, or any number of other circumstances that ordinarily obscure the relationship between price and quantity consumed. The experiment holds other things constant, and permits the researcher to observe the relationship under investigation.

In fact, some economists do conduct experiments to test the validity of economic theories.* These researchers typically use evidence collected from experiments (sometimes structured as "games") conducted with students or volunteers. Sometimes experiments are conducted with animals (e.g., rats) to learn whether their behavior is consistent with principles of utility maximization. In a typical experiment, rats initially might be required to push a small lever three times to receive one unit of sugar water and it is observed that they "purchase" 12 units of sugar water per day. Later, the economist increases the price to five pushes of the lever for a unit of sugar water—and then the rats purchase only eight units a day. By controlling all variables in the experiment, the researcher can normally develop more accurate measures of key relationships.

Occasionally, sudden and significant changes in exogenous conditions provide a setting similar to those that an experimenter might arrange. Such cases provide a so-called "natural experiment" of the hypothesis that, one might argue, provides almost as useful results as an experiment conducted by a researcher. For example, in late 1979 monetary policy changed from expansionary to contractionary, then in mid-1980 monetary policy became expansionary again, and in 1981 it became contractionary. The real economy lagged only a few months behind monetary policy in each instance: recession in early 1980, expansion in late 1980, and recession again in 1981–82. This series of natural experiments convinced many that monetary policy could in fact influence short-run economic conditions.

Significance Tests

Elementary statistics courses examine methods used to test whether or not an observation (or the mean value of several observations) differs "significantly" from a specified value. For example, divide consumers into two groups: those with incomes less than $20,000 and those with incomes of $20,000 and up. Microeconomic theory predicts that the second group will purchase more clothing than those in the former group. To test this hypothesis, calculate the mean clothing expenditure of consumers in each group, subtract spending by the low income group from spending by the high income group to find the observed spending differential, then divide

---

*See Douglas Davis and Charles Holt, *Experimental Economics* (Princeton, N.J.: Princeton University Press, 1992); Vernon Smith, *Papers in Experimental Economics* (New York: Cambridge University Press, 1991); and R. Marc Isaac, *Research in Experimental Economics* (Greenwich, CT: JAI Press, 1991).

this differential by the standard error for the series to calculate a t-score (or a t-value).

If X_H is average clothing spending by the high-income group, X_L is average spending by the low-income group, and SE is the standard error of spending for all persons, then

$$t = \frac{X_H - X_L}{SE} \tag{1}$$

The t-score is a *ratio* between the observed spending difference and the normal variations in spending caused by all factors. If the ratio is "large," then the observed spending difference exceeds the amount that one might attribute to chance fluctuations alone, so the conclusion is that the spending difference is significantly greater than zero. If the ratio is "small," then the observed spending difference is "small" compared to normal spending fluctuations, so it would be unwise to conclude that the observed difference is meaningful. In this latter instance the observed spending difference may only be the result of random errors or due to changes in other variables besides income. As a rule of thumb, when the difference is about twice as large as its associated standard error most researchers say that the difference is significant. To be more precise, one must consult a table of critical t-scores.

In the example, a "large" t-score (a t-score of about 1.7 or greater) would suggest that clothing expenditures are positively related to income—that clothing is a normal good. Appendix 19 shows critical t-scores for various sample sizes.

Occasionally, tests of significance regarding the *variances* of two data series are conducted. For example, it might be reasoned that two firms that earn the same average rate of return over time will be valued differently by investors according to the variability of their earnings. Due to risk aversion, a firm that earns 8% every year is more desirable to investors than a firm that earns 0% half of the time and 16% the other half. To test whether a firm's earnings are more variable than average, calculate the *ratio* of earnings variance for the individual firm to the average variance of earnings for all firms. The ratio of variances weighted by relative sample sizes produces an F-statistic that can be compared to critical F-values to determine whether or not the variances differ significantly. Appendix 19 contains critical F-scores for various sample sizes.

A third statistic that researchers sometimes use is the *correlation coefficient*, a measure of the variance in one variable that occurs simultaneously with variance in another. If increases in X1 usually occur when X2 increases (and vice versa), the two variables are said to be highly correlated. The correlation coefficient, r, measures the share of their variation that X1 and X2 share in common ($0 \leq r \leq 1$). Appendix 19 contains critical r-values to test the significance of a calculated correlation coefficient.

Regression Analysis

Regression analysis is a more powerful technique than the simple tests of significance discussed above. With regression analysis a researcher can estimate the magnitude of change in a "dependent variable" (whose behavior the researcher seeks to understand) corresponding to one-unit changes in one or more "explanatory variables." Returning to the test of differential clothing purchases by low- and high-income consumers, a relatively large t-score indicates only that clothing is a normal good. Regression analysis could be used to estimate that for every $1 of incremental income, the typical family will spend 7¢ more on clothing. The positive relationship reveals that clothing is a normal good, while the size of the coefficient estimate indicates *how large* an impact clothing retailers are likely to experience this year if average consumer income rises by (say) $1,000. This is clearly more useful information than a significant t-score, because it answers more of our questions about the phenomenon being investigated.

A second advantage of regression analysis is its ability to estimate the independent impact of *multiple* explanatory variables on a key dependent variable. In practice, multiple regression is the most commonly used statistical technique in economic research. The major disadvantages of multiple regression include its significant data requirements and computational complexities that require the researcher to have access to computer hardware and software. Performance and diagnostic measures for regression analysis are discussed later in this chapter.

The Nature of Regression Analysis

Because regression analysis is the statistical technique used most frequently by economists to process empirical evidence and test the explanatory power of theoretical models, this chapter focuses on basic regression analysis and its refinements. The following discussion provides only a general introduction to the topic, not an exhaustive survey of technical issues. Additional information about regression analysis can be found in *econometrics* textbooks in your university library or bookstore. A few titles are mentioned in the bibliography to this chapter.

As noted above, regression analysis is a technique that uses real-world observations ("data") to estimate the statistical relationship between a dependent variable and one or more independent (explanatory) variables. This description of regression analysis corresponds closely to the empirical requirements of economic research. We saw in Chapter 10 that economic research involves both the theoretical development of testable propositions and the testing of those propositions against actual experience. For example, a testable hypothesis might state that: Condition X, which alters the cost or reward from engaging in activity Y, will result in more (or less) of activity Y. In this instance a test of the hypothesis calls for investigating the real-world relationship between condition X and activity Y. In this example, condition X is an explanatory variable and activity Y is the dependent variable that, in theory, is affected by X. *The coefficient estimate provided by regression analysis for each explanatory variable indicates the change in the Y variable corresponding to a one-unit change in that X variable, assuming that other relevant conditions remain unchanged.* This is precisely the information required to test the hypothesis.

The usefulness of regression analysis is even greater due to its ability to simultaneously estimate the independent impact of several explanatory

(X) variables on the dependent variable. For example, suppose economic theory predicts that private consumption spending by the nation's households *(C)* is a positive function of total disposable income *(Y_d)*, an inverse function of interest rates *(i)*, and a positive function of consumer sentiment (or confidence) about future economic conditions (*CS*, an index number developed by surveying households). The researcher might gather data on each of these variables for the past 40 years and use regression methods to estimate the relationship between *C*, the dependent variable, and the three explanatory variables Y_d, *i*, and *CS*. Suppose that is done and the following regression equation is estimated:

$$C = 75.5 + 0.825 \times Y_d - 32.5 \times i + 5.58 \times CS \qquad (2)$$

This particular equation indicates that if the values of all three explanatory variables were zero, then households would spend 75.5. Since expenditures are measured in billions of dollars in this particular exercise, the "constant" coefficient is interpreted as $75.5 billion. The coefficient estimate on Y_d indicates that a $1 increase in household income is associated with an 82.5 cent spending increase. In other words, 0.825 is the estimated value of the marginal propensity to consume. Assuming that *i* is measured in whole numbers (i.e., 10% is measured as "10"), then the coefficient on *i* indicates that a 1% increase in interest rates corresponds to a spending decrease of $32.5 billion. (The inverse relationship between consumption spending and interest rates is indicated by the negative coefficient on the latter variable.) Finally, the coefficient estimate on *CS* indicates that a one-unit rise in the index of consumer sentiment corresponds to a spending increase of nearly $5.6 billion.

Do these statistical estimates lend support to the *hypotheses* deduced from the theoretical analysis? One way of answering this question is to check the *signs* (positive or negative) of the coefficient estimates. It was assumed that economic analysis predicted a positive relationship between Y_d and *C*; an inverse (negative) relationship between *i* and *C*; and a positive relationship between *CS* and *C*. Because the signs on each of the estimated coefficients agree with those predicted by economic analysis, they provide evidence supporting the validity of the theoretical model.

Another test of a theory's validity rests on the "significance" of the regression's coefficient estimates. This is a t-test similar to the one discussed earlier (see equation (1) above). To perform this test, divide the coefficient estimate by its standard error. If the *ratio* (t-score) is relatively "large," then the estimate differs from zero by more than would be expected on the basis of sampling error alone. This is evidence that the explanatory variable has a "significant" empirical impact on the dependent variable. If the ratio of the coefficient estimate to its standard error is "small," this implies that the coefficient estimate differs from zero only by chance—that the observed difference between the coefficient estimate and zero is likely due to random sampling errors. Appendix 19 shows critical t-scores for various sample sizes.

The overall "goodness of fit" for the entire regression equation is indicated by *F* and R^2 statistics. The *F* statistic tests the hypothesis that none of the coefficients in the regression differ significantly from zero.

(Appendix 19 shows critical F-scores for this test.) *If it is impossible to reject this hypothesis* (with a sufficiently "large" *F* statistic), the conclusion is that *Y can be just as accurately described by its mean value as by a causal economic relationship* such as that in equation (2). The R^2 statistic (the "coefficient of determination") for the regression encompasses much of the same information as the *F* statistic. Formally, R^2 indicates the share of variation in the dependent (*Y*) variable away from its mean that is "explained" by the regression's independent (*X*) variables. As such, R^2 lies in the range between zero and one ($0 \leq R^2 \leq 1$), where larger values indicate that the regression has greater explanatory power.

Critics of regression analysis (correctly) point out that "correlation does not imply causation." The mere fact that a positive or negative coefficient is estimated for an *X* variable does not mean that the *X* variable is actually linked to *Y* in a *cause-and-effect relationship*. Regression analysis looks for the *statistical relationship* between variables, and is capable of identifying a statistical regularity between variables even where no cause-and-effect relationship exists. For example, one might estimate a statistically significant regression equation between the price of aluminum and the number of bananas consumed each year.

But statistical significance is not economic significance, and good economists all know that. Deductive economic research does not rest on the estimation of a regression equation. It begins with the development of a hypothesis using the methods discussed in Chapter 10. Finding a relationship between *X* and *Y* *after it was predicted by a theoretical model* supports the view that a causal relationship might exist; the mere estimation of regression coefficients with no theoretical context is not evidence of a causal link. And even a careful test of a properly developed hypothesis provides only limited evidence—not certain proof. As noted in Chapter 10, *repeated* successful tests covering various experiences (and with different statistical techniques) are usually required before a theory will be accepted as "conventional wisdom" by the economics profession.

Assumptions and Requirements of Regression Analysis

Basic ("classical") regression analysis estimates a statistical relationship between a variable of interest and one or more explanatory variables. In research investigations the choice of explanatory variables rests on theoretical considerations. Suppose a theoretical relationship can be expressed in the following form:

$$Y = b_0 + b_1 X1 + b_2 X2 + \epsilon \tag{3}$$

where *Y* is the dependent variable being investigated, *X1* and *X2* are variables whose behavior are believed to affect *Y*, ϵ is a *random disturbance term* that reflects changes in *Y* caused by random events, and b_i are coefficients whose values are estimated in the course of the regression exercise. Economic theory may predict the signs of these coefficients or even their specific values. If it does, the estimated values of the b_i terms can be tested to learn whether they are approximately equal to, or significantly different than, their predicted values. Using a computer and statistical software, the calculations necessary to estimate the coefficients can usually be completed within a few seconds. The researcher's job is to provide the correct information to the computer in the first instance and, once the calculations are completed, to interpret the findings.

For classical regression methods to yield unbiased and efficient estimates of b_i, certain conditions must be satisfied; otherwise, it is necessary to rely on more sophisticated statistical techniques. For example, to obtain reliable estimates of the coefficients the analyst must include all relevant explanatory variables in the regression equation. If $X1$ and $X2$ *both* cause variation in Y but variable $X1$ is not included in the regression model, then $X2$ may receive "credit" for causing variations in Y that actually might have been caused by changes in $X1$. In this instance the coefficient estimated for $X2$ will overstate that variable's influence. In more technical language, omitting a relevant explanatory variable from the regression will typically *bias* coefficient estimates on the regression's X variables. Including an $X3$ variable that in fact does not belong in the regression risks reducing the accuracy (increasing the variance) of the coefficient estimates on $X1$ and $X2$.

A second key assumption of regression analysis is that the impacts of X variables on Y are additive. That is, if $X1$ and $X2$ both vary, the impact of $X1$ on Y can be added to that of $X2$ in determining the total change in Y. A variety of tests can be performed to detect whether these assumptions are met, and in the event they aren't the researcher must make certain adjustments to the data to continue using linear regression methods. Such adjustments to the data are known generically as "data transformations."

A third assumption of regression analysis is that "errors" or unexplained variation in the dependent variable have a constant variance throughout the entire range of observations and that individual errors are randomly distributed (i.e., not correlated with each other or with the equation's independent variables). The errors presumably reflect the effects of "small" random events not included in the regression model. If a pattern is detected in the unexplained residuals of a regression equation, this may be a sign that a systematic outside force is affecting the Y variable, which suggests that a key explanatory variable may have been omitted from the equation, or that the relationship between Y and the explanatory variables is not linear.

A fourth assumption of regression analysis is that the explanatory variables are unrelated to each other. If $X1$ increases every time that $X2$ increases, then it becomes more difficult (or impossible) to accurately measure the independent impact of $X1$ on Y or the independent impact of $X2$ on Y.

Because these and other assumptions of the classical regression model are frequently not satisfied in real-world settings, an experienced econometrician spends most of his or her time diagnosing problems and making the correct modifications and adjustments so that regression estimates provide meaningful results, i.e., results that offer insights about the relationship of interest. The ability to diagnose and correct regression problems is what distinguishes skilled econometricians from the rest of the crowd.

Problems of Regression Analysis and Their Solutions

Suppose that one or more of the assumptions listed above *are violated* by the circumstances surrounding an actual regression exercise. In this setting it is the researcher's responsibility to diagnose (learn about the existence of) the problem, and decide which course of action will permit the exercise to be successfully completed. The objective is to obtain reliable coefficient estimates (b_i) for the explanatory variables and to test hypotheses deduced from economic analysis. The following nontechnical discussion describes a few of the most common violations of the basic regression model, explains how those problems can be *diagnosed* (identified), and suggests ways they can be *corrected*.

Nonlinear Relationships

Classical regression methods assume the existence of a *linear relationship* between the explanatory variables and the dependent variable. If linear regression methods are used to estimate a relationship that is actually nonlinear, the coefficient estimates do not accurately measure the change in Y resulting from one-unit changes in the X variables.

This case is illustrated in Exhibit 11–1. The same data points are graphed in both panels. In panel (a) a linear regression line is sketched through the data. The regression line implies that one-unit increases in $X1$ result in constant increases in Y, but a visual inspection reveals that increases in $X1$ cause Y to rise at a diminishing rate. For example, assume that $X1$ represents units of labor and Y represents units of production.

EXHIBIT 11–1 Nonlinear Relationships

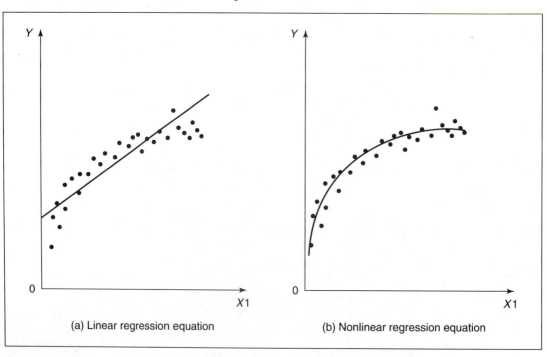

(a) Linear regression equation   (b) Nonlinear regression equation

Economic theory and the data itself suggest that labor is subject to diminishing marginal returns in production. In panel (b) a curve is sketched that more closely describes the actual nonlinear relationship between X1 and Y.

This example provides an important clue for identifying nonlinear relationships: *In many cases, economic theory will suggest when a nonlinear relationship is most likely.* The law of diminishing returns is well known, so one should expect the relationship between labor inputs and output to be a nonlinear one even before the data are graphed. Likewise, data pertaining to a firm's per unit production costs (ATC) might describe another nonlinear relationship, perhaps one that is U-shaped.

In some instances economic theory does not predict that a relationship will have a particular shape. To narrow the search, one might display the X1–Y combinations on a computer screen and then examine the data for a pattern that would indicate whether the relationship is linear or nonlinear. This approach may provide insights about the underlying relationship, but in some cases may seem to reveal a nonlinear relationship where none actually exists. In the left-hand panel of Exhibit 11–1, for example, the observed pattern of errors between actual data points and the regression line could have been caused by variation in X2 or other explanatory variables not accounted for by the graphical approach. Such possibilities suggest that whenever possible, economic analysis, rather than visual inspection, should be used to specify the functional form of a relationship.

Whether the possible existence of a nonlinear relationship is suggested by economic analysis or by the actual observation of nonlinearities in the data, the researcher may *correct* the problem by transforming the original data and then estimating a linear regression on the transformed data. For example, suppose that the relationship between Y and two explanatory variables is predicted to take a *multiplicative exponential* form:

$$Y = {}_AX1^BX2^C \tag{4}$$

where Y, X1, and X2 have the same definitions as before and $_A$, $_B$, and $_C$ are constants to be estimated in the regression. In this formulation Y equals the value of $_A$ multiplied by X1 raised to a power, then multiplied again by the value of X2 raised to a power. In the event $_B$ and $_C$ equal 1, the relationship is a simple multiplicative one between X1 and X2.

To estimate $_A$–$_C$ with linear regression methods, take natural logarithms of both sides of the equality in (4):

$$\log Y = (\log_A) + ({}_B \times \log X1) + ({}_C \times \log X2) \tag{5}$$

This equation is simplified by switching to new symbols. Let $\log Y$ be called Y^*, $\log A$ be called $_A{}^*$, $\log X1$ be called $X1^*$, and $\log X2$ be called $X2^*$. Now, equation (5) can be rewritten as:

$$Y^* = {}_A{}^* + {}_BX1^* + {}_CX2^* \tag{6}$$

Note the similarity between equations (6) and (3). You should see that *once the data have been transformed, the nonlinear relationship in (4) can be represented as a linear relationship between the transformed variables. Then the* *new regression can be estimated with ordinary linear regression techniques.* Once the coefficients for equation (6) have been estimated, values of B and C can be directly inserted into the multiplicative relationship in equation (4); and the antilog of A^* provides the value of A in (4). The lesson is that it is possible to estimate the nonlinear relationship in (4) with linear regression techniques. Although it takes a few minutes to describe the exercise, in practice it only takes a few seconds to carry it out:

1. Write down the multiplicative function to be estimated (such as equation (4)).

2. To transform the multiplicative function into an additive one, take the (natural) logarithm of all variables (as in equation (5)).

3. Estimate a linear regression on the transformed data set.

4. Substitute coefficients from the estimated regression back into the original multiplicative function. To estimate the constant (A) term in the original function, raise e, the base of the natural logarithm, to a power equal to the intercept term in the estimated regression. (For example, if $A^* = 4$, then $A = e^{A^*} = e^4 = 54.6$.)

The coefficients estimated on logged variables in regression equation (6)—which correspond to exponents in the multiplicative function (4)—have an interesting economic interpretation. They represent percentage changes in the Y variable that result from 1% changes in the Xi variables. In other words, the B and C terms in (4) and (6) are *elasticities:*

$$B = \%\Delta Y \div \%\Delta X1 \qquad C = \%\Delta Y \div \%\Delta X2$$

It follows that when a relationship can be characterized as a multiplicative exponential function, the researcher will estimate a relationship in which elasticities are assumed to remain constant throughout the range of observation. Because of this feature, economists frequently model a demand function as a multiplicative exponential relationship—say, with Y representing quantity consumed, $X1$ representing price, $X2$ representing consumer income, and $X3$ representing the price of a related good. The coefficient on $X1^*$ is own price elasticity, that on $X2^*$ is income elasticity, and that on $X3^*$ is cross-price elasticity.

Economic analysis may suggest that the relationship between Y and $X1$ is likely to be nonlinear but give no indication that a multiplicative relationship should exist between Y and the explanatory variables. Alternatively, economic analysis may suggest that the relationship between Y and $X1$ has different stages in which the relationship switches from positive to negative, or that the sign of the relationship remains unchanged but the slope of the relationship varies, such as occurs when a short-run production function switches from increasing to diminishing marginal returns after a certain quantity of labor has been employed.

In these cases, alternative transformation procedures (other than logs) can be used to modify the original data so that classical linear regression methods can be used to estimate the underlying nonlinear relationship. For example, a regression equation might include as explanatory variables $X1$, $X1^2$, and $X2$. Because this regression includes the squared value of $X1$, the coefficient estimates would describe a nonlinear relationship between $X1$ and Y but only a simple linear relationship between $X2$ and Y.

Regressions that include an independent variable raised to a power ($X1^2$, $X1^3$, etc.) are known as *polynomial models* (William Brown, *Introducing Econometrics*, p. 134). Researchers often use polynomial models when estimating producer cost functions, for example.* In these and other cases economic theory informs the choice of functional relationships, which in turn determines which data transformations are required so that classical regression procedures can still be used to obtain unbiased parameter estimates. Recall that reliable parameter estimates are necessary for testing predictions deduced from economic principles.

Heteroskedasticity

Another condition that must be satisfied for classical regression methods to yield satisfactory coefficient estimates is for a regression's residuals to have a constant variance. If this condition is satisfied, the errors are said to be *homo*skedastic; if the variance of the errors changes over the range of observations, the errors are said to be *hetero*skedastic. The two cases are illustrated in Exhibit 11–2.

EXHIBIT 11–2 Variance of the Regression's Residual (Error) Term

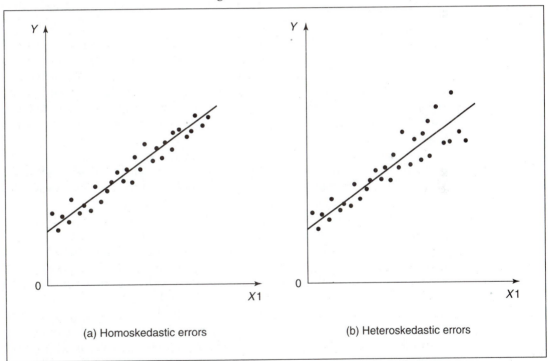

(a) Homoskedastic errors

(b) Heteroskedastic errors

The two regression lines in Exhibit 11–2 are identical and represent the relationship for data points plotted in each panel. In panel (a) the actual observations lie within a fairly compact band about the regression equation, so the errors do not appear to grow or shrink in any systematic way. Because the errors have a fairly constant variance throughout, they

---

*J. Johnston, *Statistical Cost Analysis* (New York: McGraw-Hill, 1960).

are homoskedastic. In panel (b) observations lie at increasing distances from the regression line as X1 increases. In this instance the errors grow, and their variance increases, in tandem with larger X1 values. Several things could account for this pattern, including measurement errors that are proportional to X1. Typically, but not always, heteroskedasticity occurs in cross-sectional data rather than in time-series data.

The increasing variance of errors as X1 increases does not bias coefficient estimates in one direction or the other, since outliers are as likely to lie above as to fall below the regression line. Yet, *heteroskedasticity does cause the standard errors* (SE) *of coefficient estimates to be biased downward*—although it is difficult to know in advance whether the bias is great or small.

This is particularly critical to researchers whose reason for estimating the regression equation is to test the impact of one particular variable on another. If theoretical analysis predicts that X1 and Y are positively related, this is equivalent to predicting that the regression coefficient on X1 is significantly greater than zero. To test whether or not a coefficient differs significantly from zero, form the t-ratio:

$$t = \frac{b_1 - 0}{SE} \qquad (7)$$

where b_1 is the estimated coefficient on X1 and *SE* is the standard error of the coefficient estimate. (Both statistics are provided by econometrics software packages.) To decide whether the coefficient estimate is "significant," compare the calculated t-score with the critical t-value (see Appendix 19). If the calculated t-value exceeds the critical t-value, then the estimate is significant. This can be interpreted as evidence for the original hypothesis.

The exercise breaks down if a problem (e.g., heteroskedasticity) imparts a downward *bias* on the standard error of the coefficient estimate. This artificially increases the calculated t-score and makes it impossible to conduct a reliable test of the hypothesis as in equation (7).

The nature of the problem can be illustrated by considering what might happen if the sample size were increased by one observation in panel 11–2(b). If the new observation corresponds to a small value for X1, it will probably lie fairly close to the original regression line and will not have a very large effect on the slope of the curve. If the new observation corresponds to a large value for X1, it will probably lie at a considerable distance from the regression line. Because the statistical method used to estimate coefficients is designed to minimize the total *squared* errors of the regression, large errors have a disproportionate impact on coefficient estimates. As a result of one additional observation, then, the coefficient on X1 could change by a large amount. The same logic suggests that removing one observation from the data set could also result in a large change in the estimated coefficient. When a coefficient estimate is so potentially sensitive to the number of observations, its calculated standard error may provide misleading signals about the stability of the relationship between X1 and Y. Consequently, tests of significance using this standard error are not reliable.

One way to *diagnose* heteroskedasticity is to plot the squared value of residuals from the original regression against corresponding values of each independent variable. Squaring the residuals makes their values positive and also tends to exaggerate differences between small and large residuals, therefore making it easier to detect a pattern of growing (or diminishing) residuals if one exists. A more sophisticated test involves regressing the absolute value of residuals from the original regression on various transformations of each X variable. Some regression programs have built-in routines that detect heteroskedasticity using such procedures, so you may not have to do anything more than examine the appropriate test statistic.

The *correction* for heteroskedasticity is to estimate a "weighted least squares" regression. This is a procedure in which the values of Y and X variables are divided by a variable corresponding to the pattern of residuals. This normalizes the residuals so that they do have a constant variance. As a rule of thumb, all data are divided by the square root of the independent variable most closely related to the size of the error term in the original (unweighted) regression.[*] Again, many regression programs are able to perform this step if the researcher issues the appropriate command. The standard errors of coefficient estimates in the weighted regression are not biased as those in the original regression were, so the standard error can be used in tests of hypotheses.

Autocorrelation

Another requirement of regression analysis is that the regression residuals for individual observations not be related to residuals for other observations. If this condition is not satisfied the data are said to be affected by autocorrelation (or serial correlation). A case of positive autocorrelation is illustrated by Exhibit 11–1(a) above, where residuals within three distinct ranges all have the same sign. Actual cases of autocorrelation arise frequently in time series studies, partly because the explanatory (X) variables may exert *prolonged effects* on the dependent (Y) variable or because of *inertia* in the Y variable. Occasionally autocorrelation is observed in cross-section data, such as when a significant event in one state affects economic conditions in neighboring states as well. This has been termed *spatial* autocorrelation.

Like heteroskedasticity, autocorrelation does not bias coefficient estimates but it does impart a (downward) bias to the standard errors of the coefficients. As a result, tests of hypotheses using the standard errors are not valid. Corrective action must be taken before regression results can be used to test hypotheses deduced in the theoretical analysis.

Recall that Exhibit 11–1 was originally used to illustrate the effects of applying the improper functional form to a regression, or a similar pattern of residuals could have been the result of omitting a relevant variable from the regression. Neither of these possibilities really qualifies as autocorrelation, however, and they are corrected by changing the functional form or adding additional variables to the regression.

Autocorrelation is *diagnosed* by examining the Durbin-Watson (DW) statistic provided with the regression estimate. A DW = 2 is ideal, but a rule of thumb is that when DW < 1 or DW > 3, autocorrelation is serious enough to require corrective action. It is possible that a DW statistic in the

---

[*]Peter Kennedy, *A Guide to Econometrics* (3rd ed.), p. 131.

problem range indicates that the model has been misspecified (i.e., is missing relevant explanatory variables or has the incorrect functional form), so these possibilities should be considered before treating the problem as autocorrelation.

Another method used to detect the presence of autocorrelation is to estimate an uncorrected regression equation, then collect residuals from this regression and use them to estimate a second regression. Autocorrelation refers to a situation in which residuals in the current period are related to residuals in previous periods, so if autocorrelation is present a statistically significant relationship should exist, possibly with the following form:

$$r_t = A \times r_{t-1} \tag{8}$$

where r_t is the residual in period t, r_{t-1} is the residual in period $t-1$, and A is a constant to be estimated. Autocorrelation typically arises in time-series regressions, so the residuals in (8) are written with time subscripts. If the estimated A coefficient is statistically significant, this suggests the presence of autocorrelation (or of a misspecified regression). More complex cases of autocorrelation are detected by adding r_{t-2} and other lagged residuals to the right-hand side of equation (8).

If autocorrelation is believed to exist, the problem can be *corrected* by transforming the original data set and then estimating a regression on the transformed variables. For the Y variable and each of the X variables, use the coefficient estimated in (8) to form a new variable Y^* or X^*:

$$Y_t^* = Y_t - A \times Y_{t-1} \qquad X_t^* = X_t - A \times X_{t-1} \tag{9}$$

This transformation is called quasi-differencing. If the A term happens to equal one, then Y^* and X^* are changes ("first differences") in Y and X from the previous period. On an intuitive level, the transformed variables equal Y_t and X_t minus the effects of inertia and events in previous periods whose effects carry over into the current period. In other words, Y^* and X^* are *the original variables purged of past effects*. The transformed variables should no longer include the effects that caused autocorrelation in the original regression.

Finally, after transforming the variables (data), estimate the regression using the transformed variables in the place of the untransformed variables. The coefficients and standard errors from this final regression are unbiased and will permit tests of hypotheses regarding the signs and magnitudes of coefficients.

These and even more sophisticated methods of diagnosing and correcting autocorrelation problems are incorporated in a number of econometrics software packages.

Multicollinearity

Another condition that must be satisfied before regression methods can provide the type of information needed for hypothesis testing is for the explanatory variables to be independent of each other—that they not be correlated. In the event two or more independent variables are highly correlated, classical regression techniques cannot distinguish between (or estimate) the independent influence of one explanatory variable on Y from that exerted by other explanatory variables. A certain amount of correlation between the Xi variables can be tolerated, but serious cases of multicollinearity pose a significant risk to hypothesis testing.

Exhibit 11–3 includes two specialized Venn diagrams, called "Ballentines," which can be used to illustrate the general nature of regression analysis as well as the impact of multicollinearity and a few other problems of regression analysis. In panel (a) the circle labeled Y represents observed variation in the dependent variable Y, the circle labeled X1 represents variation in the explanatory variable X1, and the circle labeled X2 represents variation in the explanatory variable X2. The blue area shows the variation that Y and X1 share in common—the independent influence of X1 on Y. Ideally, the information in the blue area is used to estimate the coefficient on X1. The coefficient estimate on a second explanatory variable uses information in the green area where the Y and X2 circles overlap.

The red area represents those observations in which X1 and X2 exerted a *joint influence* on Y. Regression methods do not use this information to develop coefficient estimates for X1 and X2 because of the difficulty of distinguishing the unique impact of X1 from that of X2. Because only the blue and green areas are used to estimate the impact of X1 and X2 on Y, while information represented by the red area is not used, the coefficient estimates for X1 and X2 are unbiased. The loss of the red area reduces the total amount of information available for estimating the coefficients,

EXHIBIT 11–3 Ballentine Diagrams in Regression Analysis

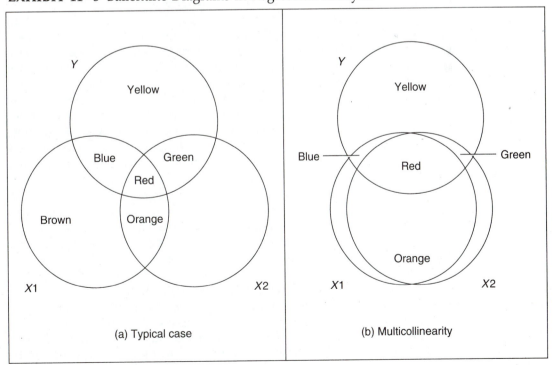

Source: Peter Kennedy, *A Guide to Econometrics* (1992), pp. 48–9.

however, and with less information available, the variances of coefficient estimates are increased. In the ideal case $X1$ and $X2$ are completely independent so no red overlapping area exists. Under normal circumstances some overlap between the $X1$ and $X2$ circles is present, but the red area is small enough that the *loss of efficiency* in coefficient estimates does not pose a threat to hypothesis testing.

Panel 11–3(b) illustrates a more severe case of multicollinearity, one in which variation in $X1$ can barely be distinguished from variation in $X2$. The relatively small amounts of information contained in the blue and green areas imply that the coefficient estimates on $X1$ and $X2$ have large variances (standard errors), which ordinarily rules out tests of hypotheses using the coefficient estimates. Although the blue and green areas appear relatively small, if the total sample is large enough the two areas may nevertheless contain a large amount of information regarding the relationships between Y and each of the X variables. Thus in large-sample cases relatively small variances may be obtained for the coefficient estimates even when multicollinearity is present. When working with small samples, however, multicollinearity must be corrected before using coefficient estimates to test hypotheses.

Multicollinearity can be *diagnosed* fairly easily. The easiest, but not the most powerful, test for multicollinearity is to calculate a correlation coefficient between $X1$ and $X2$. Correlations of 0.8 or more suggest that multicollinearity is a problem. Alternatively, one could regress each explanatory variable on all other explanatory variables. If one or more coefficient estimates are significant in these regressions, multicollinearity may be present.

As noted above, multicollinearity reduces the quantity of useful information available for estimating coefficients and causes them to have larger standard errors. Among other things, this means that changes in the sample size may cause significant fluctuations in coefficient estimates. Knowing this, one can test for multicollinearity by altering the sample size and checking to see if coefficient estimates change by a significant amount. For example, drop the first one-third of all observations and estimate the regression on the remaining observations; then drop the final one-third of all observations and estimate the regression on the former two-thirds. If the coefficient estimates are (fairly) stable over all samples, then as a practical matter whatever multicollinearity exists is not severe enough to require corrective steps. Another practical way of deciding whether multicollinearity is serious is to examine the t-scores that accompany coefficient estimates in the original regression (of Y on $X1$ and $X2$). A t-score equals the estimated coefficient divided by the standard error of the estimate; so if a "large" t-value is calculated, then one might conclude that the variance of the estimate is probably relatively small. This analysis also argues against taking corrective action.

Severe cases of multicollinearity can usually be *corrected* by adding more observations to the data set, then reestimating the regression. This is not always an easy thing to do, but more information would increase the absolute size of the blue and green areas in Exhibit 11–3(b) and help reduce the variance of coefficient estimates. Other methods of dealing with multicollinearity are more technical and will not be described here. (See G. S. Maddala, *Introduction to Econometrics* (2nd ed.), pp. 280–95.)

The Ballentine diagram can also be used to illustrate the effect of omitting a relevant explanatory variable from the regression. If $X2$ is omitted from the regression in panel 11–3(a), the coefficient estimate for $X1$ will include information contained in both the blue and red areas. Since the red area does not represent the *unique* variation that $X1$ and Y share in common (but only appears to do so because of the omission of $X2$), the coefficient estimate on $X1$ will be biased. But notice this: The relative size of the red area is larger in panel 11–3(b) than in 11–3(a), so the bias resulting from the omission of a relevant explanatory variable will be larger in the presence of multicollinearity than when multicollinearity is not present. This suggests that one sign of multicollinearity is the observation that coefficient estimates change by a significant amount as additional variables are added to or removed from the regression. As you estimate different versions of a relationship, remain aware of instances in which coefficients on a particular variable change by large amounts. This may be a sign of multicollinearity in the data set.

The Ballentine can also be used to interpret the R^2 statistic. R^2 equals the *ratio* of the blue-plus-red-plus-green area—the explained variation in Y—to the area of the entire Y circle—the total variation in Y. Because information represented by the red area is used to calculate R^2, multicollinearity (a larger red area and smaller blue and green areas) does not impair the calculation of accurate R^2 values. For this reason, *multicollinearity does not prevent the researcher from using a regression equation for forecasting purposes*. Regression-based forecasting methods depend more on the *overall fit* of the regression model—as indicated by higher R^2 values—than on precise coefficient estimates. If you are not interested in conducting significance tests on individual coefficients, multicollinearity presents little or no problem in forecasting.

In summary, regression analysis is almost ideally suited to testing hypotheses derived from economic theory. Unfortunately, classical regression analysis provides useful measures only when certain conditions (regarding the data set, the functional form of the relationship, etc.) are satisfied. In practice, econometricians often assume that those conditions *are* satisfied in the first instance, then use statistical results from preliminary regression estimates to diagnose the existence of problems which prevent standard regression techniques from yielding the kind of information (coefficient estimates, R^2, t-statistics) needed to test the relevant hypotheses. If a problem is diagnosed it can often be solved by transforming the data set before estimating a final (and more valid) regression equation.

Other Regression Issues

Qualitative Variables

Economists who conduct empirical research often need to rely on *qualitative* information to test a hypothesis. This refers to "data" whose value cannot be measured numerically. Such variables may include a few discrete choices: yes/no, high school/college, male/female, or Chrysler/ Ford/General Motors. Fortunately, regression analysis is capable of estimating coefficients on such variables. Although specialized methods not examined here are required when a qualitative variable serves as the *dependent (Y)* variable, qualitative variables can be easily introduced as *explanatory (X)* variables.* The present discussion focuses on this latter application of qualitative data in regression analysis.

Equation (3) stated the hypothesized relationship between a dependent variable and two independent variables:

$$Y = b_0 + b_1 X1 + b_2 X2 + \epsilon \tag{3}$$

When this regression was discussed earlier, it was implicitly assumed that each of the variables represented a *quantitative* data series—variables measured in units, feet, percentages, dollars. Consider an example that uses qualitative information. Let Y represent the dollar earnings of individual workers, let $X1$ represent the marginal productivity of those workers, and let $X2$ represent the gender of the workers. This regression might be estimated to test the hypothesis that worker pay is affected by the gender of the worker, or to measure the influence of productivity on worker pay.

To formulate a "gender" data series, assign to each worker a 0/1 code: female = 0 and male = 1 (or vice versa). Then estimate the regression with $X1$ and $X2$ as explanatory variables. Regression coefficients indicate the change in Y associated with a one-unit change in the corresponding X variable. In this instance, a one-unit change in the $X2$ variable corresponds to a change in the gender variable from female to male. So the coefficient on $X2$ provides an estimate of the pay differential associated with the difference in gender, holding worker productivity constant. If the coefficient is positive (and significant), this indicates that men are compensated more than women, *ceteris paribus*. If the coefficient is negative (and significant), this indicates that women are compensated more than men, *ceteris paribus*. If the coefficient does not differ significantly from zero, this indicates that gender is not a determinant of earnings in the workplace examined by the study. (In an actual study of earnings, additional variables would undoubtedly be included, e.g., years of experience, educational attainment.)

Qualitative variables are referred to in different ways: qualitative variables, dummy variables, binary variables, 0/1 variables. Despite the different terms, they all refer to the exercise described above. In general, regression *coefficients on qualitative variables provide less information about a phenomenon* than coefficients on quantitative variables. For this reason, researchers should use a quantitative measure rather than a qualitative one, if they have the choice to make. For example, use height in inches as a variable rather than a 0/1 designation for people who are shorter or taller than 68 inches.

Two additional features of qualitative variables are worth mentioning. First, qualitative variables should only take values of zero and one. If a

---

*Probit and logit regressions allow the use of a qualitative dependent variable. On this topic see Kennedy (1992), pp. 234–36.

qualitative phenomenon can take on three qualitative "values," then two binary variables are used. The rule is that *one fewer binary variables is used than the total number of categories* to be quantified. For example, to represent sales figures on a quarterly basis define three seasonal binary variables:

$S2$, a binary variable indicating whether the sales figure (Y variable) was drawn from the second quarter (=1) or another time of the year (=0)

$S3$, a binary variable indicating whether the sales figure (Y variable) was drawn from the third quarter (=1) or another time of the year (=0)

$S4$, a binary variable indicating whether the sales figure (Y variable) was drawn from the fourth quarter (=1) or another time of the year (=0)

In combination, these three variables provide the full range of coverage for all four quarters. The following shows how each variable would be coded throughout the year:

	Value of seasonal variables		
Sales quarter	$S2$	$S3$	$S4$
1st quarter	0	0	0
2nd quarter	1	0	0
3rd quarter	0	1	0
4th quarter	0	0	1

Note that the first quarter is coded 0,0,0. Because the first quarter was not assigned a binary variable of its own, first-quarter sales figures represent a benchmark against which sales figures from other quarters are compared. To estimate the impact of seasonal factors, add the three seasonal variables to a regression model such as that in equation (3). All data must be available on a quarterly basis, of course.

Once the regression is estimated, the coefficient on $S2$ will indicate the differential impact on sales associated with the second quarter compared to the first quarter, the coefficient on $S3$ will indicate the differential impact on sales associated with the third quarter (compared to the first quarter), and the coefficient on $S4$ will indicate the differential impact on sales associated with the fourth quarter (compared to the first quarter). The coefficients should be positive for quarters in which sales regularly exceed first-quarter sales, and negative for low-sales quarters (compared to the first-quarter). If the data represent retail sales figures, one might predict that the coefficient on $S4$ (which includes the Christmas shopping season) will be positive and larger than the coefficients on $S2$ and $S3$.

One can also use the coefficient estimates to develop a *seasonally adjusted data series*. To do this, *add* to actual (observed) quarterly retail sales figures the amount by which sales are normally depressed by seasonal factors or *subtract* from actual quarterly retail sales the amount by which sales are regularly inflated by seasonal factors. These adjustment amounts are merely the coefficient estimates on $S2$, $S3$, and $S4$. After the sales data have been increased or decreased to eliminate seasonal factors, the result is a series of seasonally adjusted sales figures. (This technique actually refers to an "additive seasonal" effect. A brief discussion of "multiplicative seasonal" effects was provided in Chapter 2.)

Another application of the 0/1 variable is to estimate *changes in the coefficients of explanatory variables* that occur because of some condition or event. For example, suppose the marginal propensity to consume for women is 0.8 and the marginal propensity to consume for men is 0.7. To measure this effect, estimate the regression:

$$C = b_0 + b_1 Y_d + b_2 D \times Y_d \tag{10}$$

where C is consumption spending, Y_d is disposable income, and D is a qualitative variable equal to 0 for male consumers and 1 for females. (Other explanatory variables would be included in a fully specified model.) Given the assumption above about male and female MPCs, the anticipated coefficient estimates are $b_1 = 0.7$ and $b_2 = 0.1$. To interpret these findings, consider male consumers. In this instance, $D = 0$ so the consumption function is:

$$\begin{aligned} C &= b_0 + 0.7 Y_d + 0.1(0) Y_d \\ &= b_0 + 0.7 Y_d \end{aligned}$$

For female consumers $D = 1$ so the consumption function is:

$$\begin{aligned} C &= b_0 + 0.7 Y_d + 0.1(1) Y_d \\ &= b_0 + 0.8 Y_d \end{aligned}$$

From this example and an earlier one, we have seen that the coefficient estimate on a stand-alone 0/1 variable measures a *shift* in the relationship between C and Y_d while the coefficient on a 0/1 variable multiplied by Y_d indicates a *change in the slope* of the relationship between C and Y_d. It is also legitimate to include both types of effects in a single regression if economic analysis suggests doing so.

Finally, qualitative variables can be used with data that have been transformed into log values. The 0/1 values themselves are not logged, however, since the log of 0 is undefined. It is legitimate to use a 0/1 variable if it is assumed that the underlying relationship between Y, $X1$ (a quantitative variable) and D (a binary variable) takes the form:

$$Y = {}_A X1^B e^{cD} \tag{11}$$

This is slightly different than the multiplicative expression in equation (4) above, which included only quantitative variables. In this particular case A–C are constants to be estimated in the regression and e is the base of natural logarithms ($= 2.7182 \cdots$). When natural logs are taken on both sides of the equality the relationship becomes:

$$\log Y = (\log_A) + ({}_B \times \log X1) + ({}_C \times D) \tag{12}$$

Using the (*) notation to indicate logs, the (linear) regression to be estimated is:

$$Y^* = {}_A{}^* + {}_B X1^* + {}_C D \tag{13}$$

The coefficient estimate on D indicates the *percentage* change in Y associated with a one-unit change in D. (A one-unit change in D is the difference between yes and no, male and female, etc.) Although this discussion demonstrates how qualitative variables can be used in regressions that employ log transformations, the exercise hinges on assuming the relationship between D and Y expressed in equation (11).

Limited Dependent Variables

Occasionally, issues are investigated in which a regression's *dependent* variable is constrained by some rule or condition so that it must take on values within a limited range. For example, consider a situation in which the dependent variable is a 0/1 variable whose values cannot exceed 1 or be less than zero. Alternatively, suppose the dependent variable is a percentage that cannot exceed 100%—say, the share of the population that own telephones. Exhibit 11–4 illustrates a hypothetical data set in which this problem is encountered. Along the vertical axis is measured the percent of households owning telephones in 42 nations and along the horizontal axis is measured per capita incomes in those nations. Note that when average money income reaches about $12,000 nearly all households in the nation have phones. Regressing telephone ownership on per capita income produces regression line 1. Standard regression techniques assume that observations are randomly distributed above and below the regression line, but in this case the observations for high-income nations fall significantly below regression line 1. For a high-income nation to fall above the line, well over 100% of all homes would have to own telephones, a physical impossibility. The fact that income does not affect telephone ownership beyond a certain level causes the relationship estimated with standard methods to be *biased* downward—causing the

EXHIBIT 11–4 Limited Dependent Variables

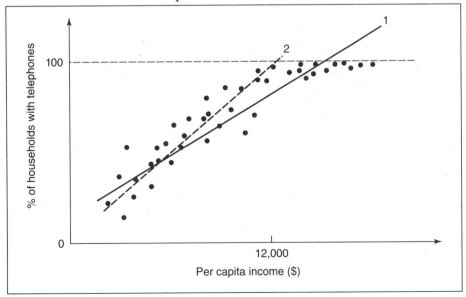

regression line to be relatively "flatter" than it would be if observations were used from low-income nations alone. A regression for only the low-income nations yields regression line 2, which indicates a larger impact of income on telephone ownership than line 1—at least for nations with low or moderate incomes.

This demonstration suggests that when the dependent variable is a *limited dependent variable*, it is not legitimate to employ classical linear regression techniques. The nonlinear relationship between telephone ownership and income requires that alternative statistical methods be employed. When the dependent variable is a quantitative variable whose range is limited, as in Exhibit 11–4, it is common to use *maximum likelihood estimation* (MLE) techniques. When the dependent variable is a qualitative (0/1) variable, *probit* or *logit* regression methods are used. These advanced methods are discussed in most econometrics texts, including several mentioned in the bibliography of this chapter. The present discussion has highlighted a few problems associated with regressions on limited dependent variables so that you will not make the mistake of using standard regression techniques in such instances, and so you will understand why researchers employ maximum likelihood, probit, or other econometric methods from time to time.

Simultaneous Equations

Occasionally a situation is encountered in which a dependent variable is determined by the simultaneous interaction of two or more relationships (represented by an equal number of regression equations). For example, suppose you possess information about the price *(P)* and quantity *(Q)* of bananas and hope to learn the shape of the demand function by estimating the regression equation:

$$Q = b_0 + b_1 \times P \tag{14}$$

Because the observed (equilibrium) price and quantity of bananas corresponds to points of intersection between the demand and supply curves, *the data reflect the joint interaction of both sides of the market*. Therefore it is not possible to estimate the demand relationship as planned.* Advanced techniques are required to estimate the coefficients of the demand function. In brief, those methods require the researcher to specify the other relationships that influence the data (i.e., supply), list other explanatory variables that may belong in the demand function (e.g., income, prices of related goods) and carry out a two-stage least squares (2SLS) exercise in which the results of one regression are used to estimate coefficients for a second. (This procedure was used in the Medoff article on abortion demand back in Chapter 9.) Most econometrics textbooks discuss the estimation of simultaneous equations, so consult one of those for assistance in such investigations. The primary reason for raising the issue here is to alert you to the possibility that some relationships must be

---

*Another way of describing this situation is to say that the explanatory variable in eq. (14) is endogenous, not exogenous, to the demand function.

jointly estimated with others in order to obtain reliable coefficient estimates.

Structural and Reduced-Form Regressions

Another way of dealing with simultaneous equation problems is to estimate a reduced-form regression instead. This method is fairly straightforward after all relevant terms have been defined. First, *structural equations* describe economic behavior, technological relationships, or other structures of the economic system. When two or more structural equations interact such that a dependent variable is influenced by the interaction, a *reduced-form regression* can be formed which includes *all of the explanatory* (X) *variables* from the relevant structural equations. For example, *structural equations* might be written for market demand and supply functions:

$$Q^d = b_0 + b_1 \times P + b_2 \times I \qquad Q^s = b_3 + b_4 \times P + b_5 \times R \qquad (15)$$

where Q^d and Q^s are quantities demanded and supplied of bananas, P is the market price of bananas, I is average income of consumers, and R is inches of rainfall in regions where bananas are grown. Here it is assumed that income and rainfall cause the demand and supply curves to shift. Assuming that equilibrium prevails in the market, $Q^d = Q^s$. This suggests that the demand and supply functions above can be set equal to each other and the entire expression can be solved for P, equilibrium price. The result of this exercise is a complex formula with price on the left-hand side and I and R on the right-hand side. The complex expression can be simplified and written as a regression equation:

$$P = c_0 + c_1 \times I + c_2 \times R \qquad (16)$$

This is a *reduced-form* regression in which price is a function of each of the explanatory variables (other than P) in the structural equations.

The coefficient estimates in the reduced-form regression (c_0, c_1, c_2) reflect the values of coefficients in the underlying structural equations (b_0, b_1, b_2, b_3, b_4, b_5), but in practice it is often impossible to break the reduced-form coefficients down into their constituent parts to obtain coefficients for the underlying structural equations. In many cases this problem does not prevent hypothesis testing, however, so researchers frequently estimate reduced-form regressions. (Reduced-form coefficients are most informative when variables enter only a single structural equation and when structural relationships are linear rather than non-linear.)

Methodological Issues in Empirical Work

Much of the research performed by academic and business economists incorporates a few of the statistical techniques discussed above. For the most part, the foregoing discussion highlighted methods brought into play when the researcher's data set fails to conform to certain standards assumed in classical linear regression theory. It is important for a researcher to have adequate statistical skills, but like other tools their usefulness is limited by the knowledge and intuition of the user. By critically examining your own work and by reading the reports of other researchers, you can develop a deeper understanding of research methods than is described in this or most other textbooks. To start you along this journey, a few methodological issues are discussed here.

Falsification

The procedure identified earlier as "testing the hypothesis" is also called *falsification*. By placing the predictions of a theory next to empirical observations, any differences between the two should become apparent. Darnell and Evans (ch. 2) summarize falsification in this way: "If the theory's predictions are refuted by material observations . . . then it is logically valid to conclude" that the underlying logic is false. This chain of reasoning is illustrated by the following logical syllogism:

1. If A_1 and A_2, A_3, , , and A_n are true then B is true;
2. B is false;
3. Therefore at least one of the propositions A_1 and A_2, A_3, , , and A_n is false (and therefore the theory encapsulated by these propositions is false).

In step 1, the propositions A_1 and A_2, A_3, , , and A_n refer to "tentative hypotheses," or all of the definitions, assumptions, and relationships used in theory development. In combination, they are used to predict condition or event B.* This prediction is then compared to actual experience. Empirical evidence that is contrary to the hypothesis ("B is false") suggests that the theory *encapsulated* by the propositions A_1 and A_2, A_3, , , and A_n is false, but does not indicate *which* of the propositions—a key relationship or one or more of the supporting assumptions—is false. Additional testing is required to answer this latter question, but in the first instance the evidence suggests that the theoretical argument (or model) is false.

On the other hand, a "successful" statistical test provides evidence for the power of a theory, but does not prove the theory's ultimate truth. Consider the following (flawed) syllogism, which suggests that truth is identified by successful empirical testing:

1. If A_1 and A_2, A_3, , , and A_n are true then B is true;
2. B is not falsified, nor has B ever been falsified;
3. Therefore A_1 and A_2, A_3, , , and A_n are true.

In step 2, empirical evidence is found (in the form of a regression estimate) which is consistent with the propositions A_1 and A_2, A_3, , , and A_n. However, these positive results do not permit us to rule out the possibility that they were produced by another set of propositions not accounted for by the theory (C_1 and C_2, C_3, , , and C_n). Therefore the conclusion

---

*Propositions and other theoretical building blocks were discussed in Chapter 10. See Exhibit 10–3 to review these issues.

contained in step 3 does not logically follow from steps 1 and 2. It would have been accurate to state step 3 as:

$3'$. Therefore B is consistent with A_1 and A_2, A_3, , , and A_n

and the theory *has not been rejected* by the empirical experience examined in this instance. This falls far short of "proof," yet it is the strongest statement that scientific inquiry is capable of producing.

Deductive and Inductive Empirical Analysis

This chapter has focused on regression analysis as a technique for *testing hypotheses* deduced by applying of economic theory to particular problems or situations. For example, if one's theoretical model predicts that consumers will respond to a higher price by purchasing a smaller quantity of some good, then the researcher would use data on price, quantity, and other variables to estimate one or more demand functions to test the validity of the hypothesis and the theory it was derived from. In this example the researcher's theoretical analysis is used to develop a prediction about a specific economic variable, so the research is *deductive* in nature, that is, proceeding from general principles to deduce a hypotheses about a particular situation. (Deductive logic was discussed at greater length in Chapter 10.)

Although the subject has not been discussed here, some researchers prefer to use regression analysis to *generate* hypotheses rather than to test them. This represents an *inductive* approach to empirical research. As described by Darnell and Evans, "the inductive method seeks to draw general conclusions based on a finite number of particular observations."[*] For example, you might first estimate various regressions in which consumption of several goods is regressed on consumer income, then conclude that as a general rule there is a positive relationship between consumption levels and consumer income.

In *deductive* research, the role played by statistical analysis is subsidiary to the theoretical work it follows. One observer calls this a "sterile" role for statistics, as opposed to the more exciting role of "empirical discovery" played by statistics when it is used *inductively*.[†] This chapter has not denied the possibility or desirability of engaging in exploratory statistical analysis for certain purposes, but has consciously avoided that approach and has highlighted the use of regression analysis in hypothesis testing. The remarks in Exhibit 11–5 provide different characterizations of the inductive approach to empirical research.

The inductive method highlighted in the exhibit, data reduction or data dredging, is described by proponents and opponents of the method. Data reduction requires the researcher to collect a data set that economic theory suggests might be related to the phenomenon being investigated; then to transform and creatively experiment with various configurations of the data until a regression equation can be estimated whose coefficients

---

[*]Adrian C. Darnell and J. Lynne Evans, *The Limits of Econometrics* (1990), p. 26.
[†]James J. Heckman, "Haavelmo and the Birth of Modern Econometrics . . . ," *Journal of Economic Literature* (1992: 884).

EXHIBIT 11–5 Econometric Methods as Tools of Discovery

Hendry and Ericsson: *Data Reduction*

[We see econometric] modeling . . . as an attempt to characterize data properties in simple parametric relationships that are interpretable in light of economic knowledge, remain reasonably constant over time, and account for the findings of preexisting models. . . .

The formal methodology [we use] is based on the statistical theory of data reduction. Empirical models arise from *transformations* and *reductions* of the data generation process (DGP, a shorthand for the actual mechanism that generated the observed data), which is characterized by the joint density of the observable variables.

The main steps producing models from the DGP are aggregation, algebraic transformation of data, marginalization, sequential conditioning, contemporaneous conditioning, truncation of lag length, and linearization. Each step entails a corresponding reduction and/or transformation of the parameters of the DGP to produce the reduced reparameterization in the econometric model. As a consequence, *all empirical models are derived entities.* . . .

[I]ndeed, Halbert White has shown that a sufficiently thorough testing procedure will arrive at a well-specified characterization of the DGP with confidence approaching certainty as the sample size grows without bound.

Feinstein: *Data Dredging*

A large number of statistical associations are explored in an automated manner for diverse individual groups, [variables] and outcomes. . . . Whenever a "statistically significant" result emerges during the myriads of computations, the event may be proposed as a cause-effect relationship.

Friedman and Schwartz: *A Critical View of Data Reduction*

Start with a collection of numerical data bearing on the question under study, subject them to sophisticated econometric techniques, place great reliance on tests of significance, and end with a single hypothesis (equation) . . . supposedly "encompassing" . . . all subhypotheses.

Adapted from: David F. Hendry and Neil R. Ericsson, "An Econometric Analysis of U.K. Money Demand . . . ," *American Economic Review* (1991): 18–20; Alvan R. Feinstein, "Scientific Standards in Epidemiologic Studies of the Menace of Daily Life," *Science* (December 1988): 1259; Milton Friedman and Anna Schwartz, "Alternative Approaches to Analyzing Economic Data," *American Economic Review* (1991): 39.

are unbiased and efficient, and which pass other tests discussed earlier in this chapter. Finally, the researcher uses regression estimates to infer properties and characteristics about the economic relationship under investigation. (The underlying relationship is what Hendry and Ericsson call the DGP—the economic process that generates the data we observe.)

Regressions Without Theory

Although both deductive and inductive approaches are valid for certain purposes, the greatest danger arises when the researcher does not explicitly distinguish between the two approaches and attempts to apply both in a single investigation. This confusion gives rise to empirical research that typically exhibits the following pattern: First, a theoretical model is developed, which suggests certain hypotheses the researcher attempts to test by estimating one or more regression equations. Finding that coefficient estimates have the "wrong" size or sign (or that the regression's R^2 is "too low," etc.), the researcher decides to collect data on additional variables or to transform data already on hand to create new variables, then inserts the additional variables into the original regression model to improve its performance. Possibly at the same time, or in a later estimate, the researcher drops a variable from the regression because of its poor performance in previous attempts. Other variables are added or dropped in succeeding trials, until eventually a "best" model is developed. Finally, the researcher includes the results of the best-performing regression in the final report *and modifies the preceeding theoretical argument* so that it focuses on the set of explanatory variables ultimately included in the report's empirical section. The actual process by which the final regression was developed may never be discussed, and the researcher may even describe the final set of explanatory variables *as if they were the only ones considered from the outset.*

This description actually highlights two problems. First, when the researcher alternates between hypothesis testing and data exploration, it is not an easy matter to interpret the statistical findings. Was the initial hypothesis rejected, and is that why additional variables were added or existing ones transformed? If the underlying economic theory is so open-ended that it permits an indeterminant number of changes, was that theory correctly developed in the first instance? If the hypothesis is consistent with evidence derived in the manner described above, is that convincing evidence of the theory's explanatory power, or merely weak evidence of its power? The answers to these questions depend on circumstances encountered in a particular setting, so no general answers are provided here. Nevertheless, it is important to explicitly consider such issues so that the final research report will provide a fair assessment of the evidence regarding the power of the theory from which the hypothesis was deduced.

Second, because of questions that have been raised about the validity of statistical estimates made under the mixed (deductive and inductive) approach, there is a tendency for researchers not to reveal much about their methods. This happened in the hypothetical example above, in which the research report discusses only the results of the "best" regression and mentions "the final set of explanatory variables as if they were the only ones considered from the outset." Regardless of the reasons one might have for blending deductive hypothesis testing with inductive data exploration, economic science progresses most rapidly when readers are made aware of the methods used to produce evidence for or against the hypothesis.

One way to avoid some of the pitfalls of blending inductive and deductive empirical analysis is to map out a course (or strategy) before estimating the first regression. In broad terms, the first step is to estimate the regression implied by the theoretical passage and then perform diagnostic tests to determine whether the data set is adequate for classical regression analysis. These issues were discussed earlier in this chapter under the heading of "Problems of Regression Analysis and Their Solutions" (p. 200). Assuming that the data set is adequate, if the results of the initial regression are consistent with the underlying economic theory, then the researcher is able to present that first set of results. If the original estimates reject the hypothesis, the proper interpretation is that the *original specification* of the theory is rejected. This permits the researcher to develop alternative specifications of the theoretical model by modifying simplifying assumptions incorporated in the theoretical and statistical analysis, e.g., considering the possibility that the relationship being estimated is nonlinear, adding a variable that controls for a variable whose importance for explaining the phenomenon was considered but judged doubtful, replacing one proxy operational variable with another when the former appears not to measure the theoretical concept it was assumed to correspond to. *The researcher should consider each of these possibilities in advance and specify a course of action for each contingency.* To the extent possible, new specifications of the model should reflect sound theoretical and econometric principles rather than spur-of-the-moment reactions to unexpected results.

Exhibit 11–6 outlines a strategy for a hypothetical regression session in which Y (consumption spending) is modeled as a function of $X1$ (disposable income) and $X2$ (the interest rate). First prepare the strategy, then when estimating the relationship limit yourself to the model adjustments specified in the strategy. In deductive research the general rule is that "statistical considerations are used to identify the *need* for re-specification, but economic theory dictates the *direction* of re-specification" (Darnell and Evans, *The Limits of Econometrics*, p. 69). The role of economic theory is emphasized by this process since the researcher considers various contingencies before estimating the first regression and identifies unresolved issues or key assumptions that could cause the hypothesis to be rejected. As we saw earlier, when the researcher has no overall strategy but reacts to each statistical problem as it develops, there is a strong tendency to transform a deductive study into an inductive one—either consciously or unconsciously.

Finally, the search strategy actually employed should be briefly described in an appropriate place of the final research report (Darnell and Evans, p. 69). Depending on circumstances this might be written in the text of the report, placed in a lengthy footnote, or included in a short appendix.

To the degree one does engage in "specification searches" or "data mining" to develop a best model, *testing its validity requires that it be estimated for a different data set than the one from which it was originally mined.* To do otherwise risks what Milton Friedman and others have called "pretest bias."* If test results from a fresh data set agree with those developed from the initial regression, the power of the regression model

---

*James J. Heckman, "Haavelmo and the Birth of Modern Econometrics: A Review of *The History of Econometric Ideas* by Mary Morgan," *Journal of Economic Literature* (1992): 882.

EXHIBIT 11–6 Strategy for a Hypothetical Regression Session*

Original regression to be estimated: $Y = b_0 + b_1 X1 + b_2 X2$

1. After estimating the original regression, perform diagnostic tests to determine whether multicollinearity, heteroskedasticity, or autocorrelation are present. If they are, either take corrective action or abandon the investigation.

2. If the hypothesis is supported by the coefficient estimates of the regression model as it was originally specified, or after corrective, measures have been taken, report those results.

3. If the hypothesis is rejected by the regression's coefficient estimates, modify the model's specification along the following lines:
    a. Take logarithms of Y, $X1$, and $X2$, then estimate a regression on the transformed variables. This would be appropriate if the underlying economic theory predicts the signs of b_1 and b_2 but not whether the relationship is linear or multiplicative.
    b. In the event b_1 is not statistically significant or diagnostic tests suggest that the relationship between $X1$ and Y is nonlinear, add a variable $X3$ to the regression, where $X3$ is the squared value of $X1$. This specification permits the estimation of a consumption function in which the MPC declines with rising income levels.
    c. Because consumer spending has various components—spending on nondurable goods, spending on durable goods, spending on services—there is some doubt regarding which interest rate is the theoretically appropriate one to use. Try the rate on consumer loans at banks, the home mortgage rate, and the interest rate on 5-year Treasury securities. Consider using a weighted average of all three rates.
    d. After estimating the coefficient on $X2$ (the nominal interest rate), divide that variable into its constituent parts, $X4$ (the real interest rate) and $X5$ (the expected rate of inflation), and substitute those for $X2$ in the original regression equation.
    e. An examination of the results for one or more regressions may indicate that the consumption function shifts downward during wartime. To test this auxiliary hypothesis include $X6$, a qualitative variable, in the regression. There is theoretical justification for including this variable: During wartime there are fewer young males in the domestic population, consumers may be pessimistic, and rationing may reduce the availability of consumer goods.
    f. The theoretical model predicts that consumption is a function of income, but disposable income is not the only possible income measure. For example, consumers may consider capital gains on assets a source of spendable funds. Replace $X1$ in the regression with a proxy variable $X7$, equal to $X1$ plus capital gains.

4. Report the findings of the investigation and the regression strategy that produced them. Regardless of the results, discuss how confident you are in the findings of the investigation. (In general, you should be *less confident* about accepting a hypothesis and more confident of rejecting one, the more *ad hoc* modifications made to the model in the hope of improving it.)

*The strategy should be developed prior to running the first regression.

is enhanced, and some support is found for the economic propositions and relationships which it is believed the regression model measures. Testing a hypothesis using two or more different data sets is called "cross validation." The view advanced here is that cross validation is an important part of the research process, whether conducted in conjunction with inductive methods (referred to as data reduction, data dredging, data mining, or specification searches) or deductive ones.

Social Sciences vs. Natural Sciences

The differences between studies of human behavior and interaction, on the one hand, and experimental investigations in the natural (physical) world, on the other, generate different types of data for researchers in the two areas to work with. Moreover, human behavior is the result of independent thought and action, whereas the natural world is largely controlled by regularities such as gravity, the changing of the seasons, and atomic weights, which, once "discovered," are more or less accepted by all without further argument or demonstration. If there are regularities in nature, then the job of the scientist is to understand and to measure them: Water boils at 212°, for example. This is fundamentally different from the law of demand, which seeks to explain human action. Even if higher prices have caused consumers to purchase fewer units of some good in every past instance, the free will of consumers could cause them to behave differently in the next case we encounter.

These observations suggest that research in the social sciences is typically less exact, and must incorporate the effects of a greater number of explanatory variables, than research in the natural sciences. In the natural sciences it is often possible to conduct repeated experiments, while experiments are often not practical in the social sciences. For each of these reasons, knowledge is generally more firmly established in the natural ("hard") sciences than in the social ("soft") sciences.*

In this environment, it is more likely that the normative values of a social scientist will influence his or her analysis than would be the case for a natural scientist. This provides yet another reason to view the results of individual research studies as merely *evidence* about the explanatory power of a theory, rather than *proof*. Many economists and other social scientists require that a preponderance of evidence from numerous investigations support a given theory before being convinced of its explanatory power—and even then continue to examine new evidence as it becomes available. (See the quote from Gordon Tullock that opens this chapter.)

Replication

In the natural sciences one of the requirements imposed on those who provide "evidence" for or against a theory is that they state all of the

---

*However, developments in experimental economics have strengthened our knowledge about economic behavior in recent years, and this trend seems likely to continue. For wide-ranging surveys of experimental economics see Douglas Davis and Charles Holt, *Experimental Economics* (Princeton, NJ: Princeton University Press, 1992); Vernon Smith, *Papers in Experimental Economics* (1991); and R. Marc Isaac, *Research in Experimental Economics* (Greenwich, CT: JAI Press, 1991).

procedures and experimental evidence on which their conclusions rest. This permits other researchers to conduct the same experiment, to *replicate* the same evidence for themselves. In recent years a growing number of economists have also demanded that researchers explain procedures and provide data so that others can replicate their findings.* For evidence to be accepted as credible, it should be accessible to those who wish to examine it. Among other things a research report should:

- Clearly define the variables contained in the theory to be tested.
- Disclose the data set used to test the theory, or provide the published source of the data.
- Indicate the exact specification of the regression equation (linear or nonlinear, structural or reduced form).
- Explain all methods used to carry out the exercise (transformation of variables, correction for autocorrelation or other problems, etc.).
- Identify the computer software used in the analysis.

Clear documentation permits other researchers to build on the findings of a particular study, or permits them to identify empirical or logical shortcomings they may want to avoid. Knowing that others may attempt to replicate their results may also make some researchers more careful and less willing to take shortcuts to complete a project more quickly. From many perspectives then, replication assists in the creation of economic knowledge.

Summary

This lengthy chapter has examined methods used to develop and present statistical "evidence" in empirically based research projects. The discussion has focused on regression analysis, including technical refinements that are commonly adopted when the available data set does not meet the requirements of classical regression theory. Although one needs strong mathematical skills to make theoretical contributions to econometrics, other researchers require fewer technical skills and rely more on a few widely used techniques such as those discussed here. Easy access to powerful econometric software means that in the future a growing share of economists will test theoretically derived hypotheses against actual experience.

---

*W. G. Dewald et al., "Replication in Empirical Economics . . . ," *American Economic Review* (September 1986): 587–603.

Exercises

Consider the following regression of Y on two variables, $X1$ and $X2$:

$$Y = 23.44 + 5.66X1 - 33.45X2 \qquad R^2 = 0.678$$
$$ (1.79) \quad (0.93) \quad (-4.56)$$

where the values of t-statistics for the coefficients are shown in parentheses. Use this information to answer questions 1–9.

Exercise 1: Interpret the coefficient estimates in the regression equation above with statements that begin, "If $X1$ (or $X2$) increases by one unit, then . . . "

Exercise 2: Which coefficient estimates in the regression equation are statistically significant? Explain your answer.

Exercise 3: Suppose the key explanatory variable in the analysis is $X2$. Assume that the value of $X1$ is zero and draw a graph of the estimated relationship between $X2$ and Y. Measure $X2$ along the graph's horizontal axis and Y along its vertical axis.

Exercise 4: Interpret the meaning of R^2 for this regression equation. Does R^2 indicate whether or not $X1$ and $X2$ are "significant"? Explain.

Exercise 5: Suppose you learn that the Durbin-Watson (DW) statistic for the regression equation equals 0.5. What does this indicate? Does this cause the coefficient estimates on $X1$ and $X2$ to be biased? Does it cause other problems that interfere with hypothesis testing? Explain.

Exercise 6: Suppose the correlation coefficient between $X1$ and $X2$ equals 0.45. Does this indicate the presence of multicollinearity? Explain your conclusion. If multicollinearity *is* present, how does this affect a test of the hypothesis regarding the value of the coefficient estimate on $X2$? Explain. How could one "solve" a multicollinearity problem?

Exercise 7: Suppose you now believe that the relationship between $X2$ and Y is nonlinear. Explain two ways to modify the regression to measure such a relationship.

Exercise 8: Modify the regression equation above by adding two binary variables, $D1$ and $D2$. The first ($D1$) should measure an exogenous change in Y resulting from event A, while the second ($D2$) should measure a change in the *slope* of the relationship between $X1$ and Y that results from event B.

Exercise 9: Suppose you learn that Y is a binary (0/1) variable. What impact does this have on the validity of the regression estimates? Explain.

Exercise 10: Select *one* of the regression equations estimated by E. W. Eckard in "The Effects of State Automobile Dealer Entry Regulation on New Car Prices" (p. 145) and interpret the coefficient signs, sizes, and significance as called for by Exercises 1 and 2 above.

Exercise 11: For Eckard's theoretical model to be empirically corroborated, what value or sign must be observed on the coefficient estimate for ROLD? Explain. For how many of his regressions is this condition satisfied?

Exercise 12: Does Eckard estimate a structural or reduced-form regression equation? How do you know? Does he use any binary (0/1) variables in his regression? If so, name them. Is his dependent variable a "limited dependent variable"? How do you know? Does Eckard report a Durbin-Watson statistic with his regression results? Why or why not?

Notes on Chapter 11

Use the space below to describe new concepts or methods that you learned in Chapter 11.

Bibliography

There are dozens of econometrics textbooks that examine issues raised in this chapter. The technical differences among econometrics texts are not as great as might be imagined; they tend to be written like cookbooks that contain all the best-known recipes. For nonspecialists the greatest difference among the texts is in the clarity of the writing—their ability to convey an intuitive understanding of the subject.

A text that emphasizes the intuitive approach to econometrics, and a personal favorite of mine, is Peter Kennedy's *A Guide to Econometrics* (Cambridge, MA: MIT Press, 1992). A good text that explains and applies technical econometric methods is G. S. Maddala's *Introduction to Econometrics* (New York: Macmillan, 1992). A book that examines the methodological status of econometrics is Adrian C. Darnell and J. Lynne Evans, *The Limits of Econometrics* (Brookfield, VT: Gower, 1990). The debate between deductive and inductive approaches is discussed by James J. Heckman, "Haavelmo and the Birth of Modern Econometrics . . . ," *Journal of Economic Literature* (June 1992): 876–886; David F. Hendry, *Econometrics: Alchemy or Science?* (Cambridge, MA: Blackwell, 1993); and Alvan R. Feinstein, "Scientific Standards in Epidemiologic Studies of the Menace of Daily Life," *Science* (December 1988): 1259–63.

For a glossary of statistical terms and methods see Patrick McC. Miller and Michael J. Wilson, *A Dictionary of Social Science Methods* (New York: John Wiley, 1983).

Several statistical software packages are available for personal computers. Two moderately priced programs are MicroTSP (student version) and MyStat. MicroTSP is $43.95 from Quantitative Micro Software (714-856-3368); MyStat is $19 from Course Technology (617-225-2595). Each program is a scaled-down version of a larger statistical package priced in the $500 range. In addition to simple statistical calculations (means, standard deviations, etc.) the programs include regression routines of the type discussed in this chapter. Of the two, TSP was especially designed for economic research and offers a longer list of desirable features.

Less technical research methods are appropriate for some investigations. For a discussion of these methods see the text by Corrine Glesne and Alan Peshkin, *Becoming Qualitative Researchers* (White Plains, NY: Longman, 1992).

CHAPTER 12

Reporting the Results of Economic Research

*Even if absolute truth remains elusive,
[we have] a responsibility to associate
[ourselves] with the search for truth, with a
positive valuation for objectivity and
detachment, and with a repugnance for gross,
demonstrable error.*
—Robert McC. Adams

Introduction

After conducting research on an issue or problem, the researcher traditionally describes the investigation and its findings in a research report. The report may be required in a course you are taking, prepared for publication as a professional journal article, or presented to a client (or employer) who financed the study. In projects involving empirical research, the final report is frequently structured as described in Chapter 9: (1) introductory remarks, (2) theoretical examination of the issue or problem, (3) empirical measures of relationships and tests of hypotheses deduced in the theoretical analysis, and (4) concluding remarks, including an interpretation or application of the study's findings. The *main body* of the report includes parts 2 and 3, the theoretical and empirical analysis. Those subjects were examined in Chapters 10 and 11. This chapter brings together all of the components of a research report, combining material from Chapters 9–11 with additional comments concerning the introductory and concluding sections of the report.

The Nature of the Research Report

The first characteristic of a good research report is that it have a *clearly defined purpose* that the reader is always aware of. Stated in reverse, the reader should never have to wonder what the report is about or where it is headed. A strong statement of purpose should appear early in the introductory section of the report; then the researcher should explain how key concepts, theoretical arguments, or statistical tests relate to the study's purpose as they are first mentioned. This will help the report stay "on track" and prevent it from wandering aimlessly through material irrelevant to the purpose at hand.

Second, a research report should incorporate *good science*. For beginning researchers, good science often means using the economic theories and statistical methods found in textbooks. More advanced researchers can develop new theories and methods, but even they must explain the logical steps leading up to a particular conclusion and justify the statistical methods they employ. For the reader to accept—to be convinced by—the findings of an investigation, he or she must have confidence in the logical reasoning and empirical evidence on which the findings rest.

A third characteristic of a good research report is that it *avoids subtleties*. Research reports are not murder mysteries that a person reads to the last page in anticipation of a surprise ending. The purpose of a research report is to communicate knowledge gained from a research study, and that is best accomplished by informing the reader about every major development leading up to the findings of the study. If relevant issues are not addressed explicitly the reader may feel that important points have been overlooked. This can raise doubts in the reader's mind about the validity of the entire study. If other researchers cannot understand what steps are taken in the study or the reasons for taking them, they may decide not to use the same approach in their own studies. This is especially detrimental in the case of academic research, where the main measure of success is the frequency with which other researchers adopt one's methods or cite one's findings.

Next, a good research report *should not promise more than it produces*. Among other things the introductory section of a report should describe the main findings of the investigation. A report that promises more than it delivers is a sign that the researcher does not have a clear understanding of what the investigation actually accomplished. Readers pay particular attention to statements about findings when deciding whether or not to read an entire report. The best way to disappoint them is to promise that some point will be demonstrated—and then never demonstrate it. When such a report is submitted to a professional journal to be considered for publication, the journal's editors and reviewers will almost certainly react negatively to unmet promises and reject the piece for that reason alone.

Finally, a research report should *efficiently communicate* the results of the investigation to the reader. In this instance efficiency refers to minimizing the effort required by the reader to understand the study's findings and the theoretical and empirical support that justify them. This means the researcher should employ a terse, get-to-the-point writing style and omit material that does not directly contribute to reporting the methods and findings of the investigation. Efficiency is also increased by structuring the report in a way that the reader expects and finds logically appealing. The material in a research report is challenging enough without disorienting the reader regarding the contribution each passage makes to the overall investigation.

Structure and Organization

In Chapter 9 an outline was provided for structuring a wide range of economic reports and research articles. The outline is shaped by the need to discuss each of the key elements of the research project itself and by the need to communicate effectively with readers. In this discussion the main parts of the report are given generic names: (1) introduction, (2) theoretical passage, (3) tests of hypotheses, and (4) concluding remarks. More specific section headings may be provided in actual research reports, and in longer reports it is common to subdivide some of the major parts into logical components. Exhibit 12–1 provides a graphical representation of a research report and its division into major functional parts. The following paragraphs elaborate on the specific contents of each part and provide a few suggestions for tying together the parts into a coherent whole.

EXHIBIT 12–1 Components of the Research Report

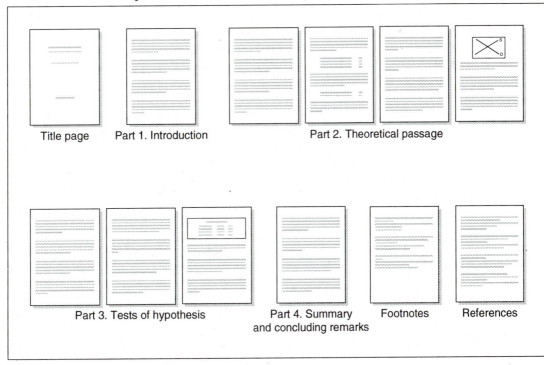

Introductory Remarks (Part 1 of the Report)

The introductory section of a research paper has several components. First, it announces the *topic* to be investigated and the *findings* of the author's research, usually within the first few sentences. This provides readers an overview of the study and invites them to continue reading if they are interested in knowing more about the theoretical and empirical justification for the findings. Less experienced researchers often are not certain about the specific contribution their efforts have produced, so having to provide a summary of findings at such an early stage may help focus the rest of their report. Only if the researcher focuses explicitly on the end-product of the research will he or she provide the most effective explanation of theoretical arguments and empirical evidence leading up to those findings. In practice it may be necessary to provide a few sentences of introductory remarks before stating the topic and findings of the investigation, but it is important to get to this matter very quickly.

A second component of the introductory section is a discussion of the problem or situation that is analyzed in the body of the report. For example, E.W. Eckard's article about auto dealer entry regulation (on p. 145) devotes several early paragraphs to describing the operation of auto dealerships and the operation of auto dealer entry restrictions. In addition to establishing a background which places the rest of the study in context, a discussion of the problem provides a useful place to introduce key terms that play a prominent role in the theoretical analysis of part 2. Recall from Chapter 10 that the building blocks of theoretical discussions are *concepts*, or terms corresponding to real-world phenomena. The introductory section of the report provides the occasion to introduce and define key concepts, and to mention their relationships to other concepts if those relationships will be used later in the theoretical discussion. Chapter 10 referred to definitions of concepts and relationships between concepts as *propositions*, another key element of the theory development in part 2 of the report. Except in lengthy reports it should normally be possible to summarize the essential nature of the problem or issue being studied a page or two. In longer studies (e.g., a dissertation or book) an entire chapter might be devoted to describing a problem and presenting its history or background.

Next, the introductory section should provide a "review of the literature" regarding work other researchers have done while investigating related issues. The literature review should highlight (a) research performed on the same *problem* or issue you are examining, (b) research related to the *theory* you plan to present in part 2, or (c) research employing the same *empirical methods* you will use in part 3.

Beginning researchers usually are not specialists in the area they are writing about, so they initially may be aware of very little existing research to cite. This provides an occasion for performing a literature search using some of the methods described in Chapter 3. Ideally, most of the literature review was performed at an earlier stage of the research project, rather than at the report-writing stage. When reading articles and books identified in the literature search, the researcher should prepare brief notes which can later be referred to while writing the report (see Chapter 4). Publications should be examined for theoretical ideas and statistical methods which might be used in the present investigation. A literature review informs readers about methods used by other specialists working in the same area, and this provides them with information they need to judge the value of the present contribution.

Sylvester Carter (1987, ch. 6) suggests including at least three pieces of information about each publication cited in the literature review: the author, the issue he or she investigated, and the findings of the study. It is also appropriate to mention the author's research methods if they are relevant to the present study. A citation can be brief and still convey quite a bit of information:

> Smith's (1991) study of factory workers presents regression estimates indicating that moderate levels of risk in the work environment cause money earnings to rise by 5–8% among experienced workers.

The fact that beginning researchers have to perform a literature search and then read the work of several other researchers before making much headway imposes a severe time constraint, which specialists do not confront. Many researchers specialize in a narrow range of issues to avoid incurring high start-up costs every time they commence a new study.

Finally, the introductory section can provide hints, but not an extended discussion, of the theoretical model and statistical methods found in the body of the report. Carter (p. 41) suggests providing only a few brief remarks on these matters, making use of "suggestive" terms and phrases. For example, the following sentence lets the reader know about the methods used to investigate the division of household work within families:

> The present study employs a wealth maximization model to explain the division of household responsibilities among family members, and a regression analysis is performed on survey data gathered from 500 urban families to test the model.

Statements of this type signal readers as to what they can expect later in the report without bogging them down in complex details they do not need to be exposed to at this stage of the discussion.

The writing style in the introductory section should make use of longer, more complex sentences than parts 2 and 3 of the report. This writing style is especially appropriate for describing a research topic or summarizing the work of other researchers (Carter, p. 42).

The Theoretical Passage (Part 2 of the Report)

The theoretical passage in part 2 provides the logical justification for the main findings of the study. First, begin the theoretical section by stating what will be demonstrated in the analysis. This reduces the effort expended by the reader in understanding where the discussion is heading. When the theoretical material is especially challenging, a clear statement of purpose can light the path through a theoretical maze which the reader might otherwise find impossible to navigate.

The Primary Focus of the Investigation

The theoretical section should be written so the reader can follow the researcher's logical analysis of the problem and arrive at the same conclusions. Although experienced researchers use various rhetorical devices to build a case for their findings, the standard technique is to develop a *deductive* argument that reasons from generally accepted principles and relationships to a specific conclusion.

Chapter 10 noted that the deductive approach identifies *concepts* about a real-world problem or situation and defines or links them to other concepts to form *propositions*. Presumably some of these propositions are part of the accepted body of economic knowledge. At this stage it is assumed that these propositions are true for the sake of constructing the theoretical argument. Then, propositions are used in combination with other propositions to deduce a conclusion whose empirical adequacy is tested against actual experience. Typically, the scientist combines propositions according to *transitive rules of logic,* which follow the general form: If X is related to Y and Y is related to Z, then X is related to Z. In this discussion X, Y, and Z are concepts, the statements about the relationships between X and Y and Y and Z are propositions, and deductive logic is used to reach the testable proposition (conclusion) that X is related to Z. Researchers often refer to a testable proposition as a *hypothesis.*

There is a good chance that many of the concepts and propositions used in part 2 of the report were introduced in part 1, where background information about the problem or issue was originally provided. Nevertheless, additional concepts and propositions typically will be introduced in the theoretical passage, combined with other propositions, and used to deduce a testable hypothesis.

In practice, researchers employ a variety of different rhetorical methods in their logical analysis, ranging from verbal (written) argument, to mathematical modeling, to graphical analysis.* The verbal/mathematical/graphical mix of the argument will vary according to the ability of the researcher, the nature of the issue being investigated, and the abilities of prospective readers. No simple rule dictates when the reader will consider a logical argument sufficiently well developed. The purpose of the theoretical passage is to logically justify the conclusions of the study, so a theory is adequate when the reader can understand all of the logical steps connecting the initial statement of the problem to the explanations, predictions, and conclusions provided later in the report. If the reader has to wonder about the validity of a conclusion or whether a certain prediction can be supported from the logical argument that preceded it, then gaps remain in the theoretical discussion, which are the researcher's responsibility to bridge. This is done by:

---

*See Donald M. McCloskey, "The Rhetoric of Economics," *Journal of Economic Literature,* v. 21 (June 1983): 481–517.

- including additional *concepts;*
- introducing additional *propositions* (or providing stronger empirical support for accepting them into the analysis);
- deducing additional *hypotheses;* or
- more carefully *explaining* or *rearranging* or *providing empirical support* for elements of the logical argument leading up to the hypothesis.

An essential part of the theoretical passage is difficult to classify— namely, *general information* a reader requires to understand the argument being presented. Define terms that might confuse the reader; explicitly mention assumptions about key variables (concepts); define symbols when mathematical notation is introduced; mention subtle facts about the problem or issue which the reader needs to know about to understand the theoretical argument. In a given situation perhaps a visual illustration—a graph of a key data series or a photograph of a difficult-to-describe object—would be the most effective way to communicate with the reader.

Finally, the main theoretical argument should end with a clear *statement of the hypothesis* to be tested against actual experience. The presumption is that if actual experience is consistent with the hypothesis, this provides support for the theoretical argument; if actual experience is at odds with the hypothesis, then the validity of the theoretical argument is in doubt.

Other Theoretically Relevant Variables and Relationships

Due to the nature of regression analysis, unbiased coefficient estimates —including those on key explanatory variables highlighted in the theoretical discussion—are obtained only if *all other* relevant explanatory variables are also included in the regression. For example, if one hopes to estimate the effect of the death penalty on the murder rate, it is not sufficient merely to include a death penalty variable in the regression; it is also necessary to include variables representing other factors that are believed to affect murders. These other variables might include things like the unemployment rate, the share of the male population age 16–30, and the degree of urbanization. These other variables have been identified by researchers of murder and violent crime—researchers whose work should already have been mentioned in the literature review of part 1.

In a study that investigates the impact of the death penalty on the murder rate, part 2 should contain a *general discussion* of murder and the many factors that contribute to or deter it, but *focus on* the explanatory variable emphasized in the present investigation. Because the other variables have been investigated by previous researchers, it is not necessary to provide a lengthy explanation for each of them. In most cases a two- or three-sentence explanation about the relationship between the explanatory variable and the present study's dependent variable, plus a comment about empirical support for this proposition, will suffice.

In the event coefficient estimates on some of the additional variables are no longer significant when your own variable is included in the regression equation, that is evidence (but not absolute proof) that the previous researchers' estimates were biased by the omission of a relevant variable—in this case, the variable your analysis suggests is important.*

In many instances it will be convenient to subdivide part 2—one section to examine the explanatory variable your investigation focuses on and another section to list and briefly discuss the explanatory variables identified by other researchers.

Preferred Writing Style

To avoid unnecessary confusion, sentences in the theory passage should be fairly short and uncomplicated. Use a high proportion of declarative sentences with few subordinate clauses and adjectives. Mention each step in the logical argument so that the reader will understand the source of your hypothesis. To communicate more effectively, omit all unnecessary words and sentences, and use no parenthetical remarks or footnotes that are not directly relevant to the central argument. Theoretical passages are difficult enough for readers to comprehend without also forcing them to struggle with unnecessarily complex sentences and extraneous material.

The theoretical passage of a research report is *not* the place to document the researcher's actual "discovery" of various ideas and conclusions. Readers are not interested in reading about the confusion and false starts you experienced during the course of an investigation; they prefer a passage that explains how they should think about a particular issue in order to reach the conclusion you want them to reach. This is not just a matter of reader preference, either. *Your analysis will have a far greater impact on (be more convincing to) readers when they are aware of each logical step leading to your findings and conclusions.* Sylvester Carter states that it is the researcher's responsibility to "have a completely integrated high-level view of the material" and then pass that view on to the reader (Carter, p. 49). In many cases the theoretical passage can be clarified by providing an illustrative example, then modifying it (possibly several times) as the theoretical argument unfolds. If it is not possible to use a "running example" throughout the discussion, a sprinkling of "for example" statements to illustrate the most abstract material will contribute to reader comprehension.

Tests of Hypotheses (Part 3 of the Report)

Chapter 11 examined a few of the methods commonly used to test hypotheses deduced by economic analysis. That discussion focused on the utility of regression analysis as well as some of the problems that one might expect to encounter when estimating regression equations.

The place to begin the empirical section of a report is to inform the reader about the *purpose* of the statistical exercises. For example, one might

---

*In the Ballentine graphic in Exhibit 11-3(a), suppose $X2$—the variable highlighted in *your* analysis—is not included in the previous researcher's regression equation. Now, the coefficient on $X1$ will measure the influence represented by the blue and red areas; since an unbiased coefficient estimate of $X1$ should only capture the effect of the blue area, his coefficient estimate is biased. This analysis also demonstrates why your regression should include both your own $X2$ variable as well as the $X1$ variable identified as important by other researchers.

reiterate the hypothesis developed in the theory passage and describe the general situation in which you propose to test it. This discussion "establishes the *context* into which all of the details about [statistical] arrangements and procedures will later be fitted" (Carter, p. 67).

Next, identify (name) the statistical method you intend to use and explain why you believe this approach is the appropriate one to test the hypothesis. If the reader is a professional economist it is not necessary to describe the basics of regression analysis, but you should explain why classical regression techniques are adequate under present circumstances or why certain considerations compel you to rely on some refinement of that analysis—two-stage least squares, reduced-form regression, logarithmic transformations, and so on. This goes well beyond simply naming the statistical test you plan to use; it requires that you *justify* your choice of technique to the reader. Statistical findings have greater validity when the proper methods are used to generate them, so the reader must understand and accept your choice of methods before being convinced by your findings. To guide your selection of statistical methods, consider the methods used by other researchers in the same area of inquiry. While you were putting together the literature review for part 1, you should have noticed the statistical procedures they used—and may even have identified weaknesses in their methods that you intend to rectify in your study. This is a good place to briefly review the statistical methods relied on in the other studies, even if you mentioned them earlier in the literature review.

In addition to justifying your statistical procedures, it is also necessary to discuss (and justify) the quality of the data you will employ. In the natural sciences hypotheses are most often tested with evidence (data) which the researcher generates experimentally. In that setting, emphasis is placed on the design of the experiment to ensure that the results are reliable and that the researcher is in fact measuring the phenomenon examined in the theoretical passage. Economists and other social scientists usually do not work with experimental data, but instead test their hypotheses on data that have been collected by others—often, governmental departments or agencies—for some other purpose. Being able to tap into "free" data is an advantage, but it does not relieve the researcher of the responsibility of ensuring that the data are appropriate for the test being conducted. Published data frequently do not exactly match the variables examined in the theoretical section of the report, so researchers use published data as proxies (substitutes) for the theoretically appropriate variables. It is important to inform the reader what proxies are being used and explain why those proxies are acceptable for present purposes. If the proxy variables have certain shortcomings, discuss the problems and explain their possible consequences. Later, during testing, if two operational proxy variables correspond to a single theoretical variable, test the hypothesis twice—once with each proxy—to determine how "fragile" or "robust" your empirical results are to changes in the variable's specification.* The reader has a right to know whether the researcher's choice of data has a significant impact on the findings of the study.

---

*One should not employ both proxy variables simultaneously, however. This method may result in multicollinearity problems. On this subject, see Chapter 11.

Fourth, write down the regression equation you plan to estimate and review the list of explanatory variables it includes. These variables were already discussed in part 2, so at this point it is sufficient merely to mention each variable and its predicted (hypothesized) relationship to the dependent variable.

Next, perform the statistical procedures required to test the hypothesis. If statistical problems (multicollinearity, autocorrelation, etc.) are encountered, take corrective steps and explain to the reader that, "Preliminary estimates revealed the presence of (say) heteroskedasticity. This problem was corrected by (say) weighting the data and estimating a new regression on the corrected data set," or something along those lines. Enough detail should be provided so that an informed reader will know what steps you have taken. Take care not to blur the distinction between the detection and correction of technical problems, and the actual test of the hypothesis. If a lengthy discussion is necessary to explain technical problems and steps taken to correct those problems, put the details of this discussion in a footnote. Even if no notable problems are encountered, readers will appreciate a statement that diagnostic tests were performed and no problems were detected. Without this type of statement, an alert reader may wonder whether or not you checked for potential problems. This raises questions about the reliability of your results.

In most instances regression results can be presented in one or two tables; a key relationship or trend may also be illustrated graphically. *Your discussion of results should include a careful interpretation of the coefficients estimated for the main regression equation.* In a (hypothetical) study of household spending behavior you might state that:

> In estimates using 1990 data, the coefficient on $X1$ indicates that a $1,000 increase in household real income is associated with an $871 increase in household real consumption spending; the coefficient on $X2$ suggests that a 1% increase in the real interest rate depresses spending by $84.43; and the coefficients on $X3$, $X4$, and $X5$ indicate that consumption spending rises, but at a decreasing rate, with increases in family size. The family size coefficients (on $X3$–$X5$) indicate that the second person added to a household increases real annual spending by $1,256, a third causes spending to rise by $812, and a fourth causes spending to rise by $567. The positive signs on all variables except the interest rate were as hypothesized. The t-statistics written below coefficient estimates are all significant at 95% or higher, and the coefficient on income is significant at 99%. The R^2 statistic indicates that slightly more than 82% of the variation in household consumption spending is explained by the regression.

A detailed discussion of the main regression equation should eliminate any uncertainty in the reader's mind about whether or not the hypothesis is rejected by the evidence. If you have estimated additional regressions in the study it is not necessary to provide such a detailed account of each coefficient as you provided for the first (main) regression. Even if subsidiary regressions are not discussed in as much detail, however, it is still necessary to provide an overview of their findings. Suppose that your study of spending behavior actually estimated spending equations for 1970, 1980, and 1990. After discussing your results for 1990 (above), you can briefly summarize those for 1970 and 1980:

Results for 1970 and 1980 were similar to those for 1990 (discussed above), but the coefficient on income appears to have declined over time (from 0.984 in 1970 to 0.964 in 1980 and 0.871 in 1990), while that on the interest rate seem to have risen somewhat. Only in one instance was a coefficient on a family size variable insignificant, so the evidence presented here provides strong support for the theoretical model developed in part 2.

Because the reader should be able to reproduce your results by using the same data and following the same procedures you followed, each step in the exercise should be clearly described. For the sake of efficiency, a brief statement rather than a lengthy explanation is called for when describing routine procedures. More lengthy explanations should only be provided for difficult-to-understand issues.

Like your theoretical remarks in part 2, the writing style in part 3 should be as direct and uncomplicated as possible. Parts 2 and 3 contain the most complex ideas and technical methods of the entire report, so great care should be taken to avoid confusing the reader with a difficult-to-comprehend writing style that crams as many ideas as possible into each sentence, or by failing to mention steps taken to test the hypothesis. Although it is not necessary to explain minor details to readers who are already familiar with the methods you are using, it is a good idea to *spell out every step in the first written draft* of the report and then later (during revision) remove those remarks that aim too low for the reader's experience and understanding.

In *revising the first draft* of the paper, try to remove *all* material that does not directly advance the purpose of your study. Omit parenthetical remarks or footnotes that are not directly relevant to the central argument. Terse, declarative sentences with few subordinate clauses and phrases are valued highly in this part of the report. Theoretical passages are difficult enough for readers to comprehend without also forcing them to struggle with unnecessarily complex sentences and extraneous material.

Concluding Remarks (Part 4 of the Report)

The fourth and final part of the research report should summarize and reflect on what has been accomplished by the investigation. The researcher may also be able to suggest ideas for additional research of the same issue, or for research of another problem using techniques employed in the present study.

The *summary* should provide a fast-paced commentary of the theoretical argument and empirical evidence developed more fully in the body of the report (parts 2 and 3) to provide a logical justification for the findings of the study. Those findings were announced in the introduction (part 1), but without the full explanation which you are now in a position to provide. Because the reader has already been exposed to the theoretical analysis and statistical evidence, the summary should highlight only the most important elements of that material—the body's skeleton, you might say. As a rule of thumb, the summary might weave two or three features of the theoretical argument together with two or three results of the empirical work, to show the reader the logic underlying the study's major findings.

Because summaries risk boring the reader, the discussion should omit all but the most essential elements of the logical argument. *A technique for writing fast-paced commentaries is to use longer, more complex sentences* that mention relationships between various ideas, or which summarize difficult points that originally took several paragraphs to demonstrate in the body of the report. Some sentences in the summary might recall conclusions or evidence discussed in earlier parts of the report without recounting every detail of those passages. Such sentences might begin: "It has been shown that . . ." or "The evidence presented above suggests that . . ." The summary might occupy only a few paragraphs, but if those paragraphs are well written they can leave the reader with a lasting memory of your investigation and its findings.

The second purpose of the concluding section is to suggest one or more *implications of the study's findings.* If the logical argument and empirical findings are correct, what does this imply about other issues of interest to economists? Recall Chapter 9, E. W. Eckard's study of auto dealer entry regulations. That investigation concluded that laws restricting entry cause significant increases in car prices, and transfer wealth from consumers to retailers. Eckard used this finding to suggest that a wider range of economic regulations might have similar effects. He specifically mentioned entry regulations in the airline and trucking industries, but the broader implication is that entry regulations generally have anticonsumer effects. Broader implications can be developed for the findings of most investigations.

Finally, the concluding remarks section should mention *opportunities for future research* in the area. In the course of conducting the study the researcher may have become aware of alternative techniques or data sets for testing the hypothesis, or may have considered modifications of the theoretical analysis that would have suggested different hypotheses. Or the researcher could point out limitations of the present study, and offer suggestions on overcoming them in future studies. The idea is to stimulate additional inquiry into the issue by showing other researchers where to begin.

In a sense, the purpose of a report's concluding remarks is the opposite of that of the report's introduction. Where the introduction brings together a broad range of research and observations to focus them on a single problem, the concluding remarks take a few specific ideas developed in the body of the report and project them outward to other problems and researchers who would benefit from them.

This perspective is illustrated in Exhibit 12–2, which resembles an hourglass lying on its side. At left, the introduction incorporates a broad range of material, much of it drawn from a review of work performed by others. *The literature review is most effective when it focuses the attention of the reader on the analysis contained in the body of the present report*—by suggesting effective theoretical models and empirical methods, or by identifying difficulties that other researchers have encountered in similar investigations (and their possible solutions). The concluding remarks indicate how the findings of the study may be useful in other settings and to other researchers.

EXHIBIT 12-2 Focus of the Research Report

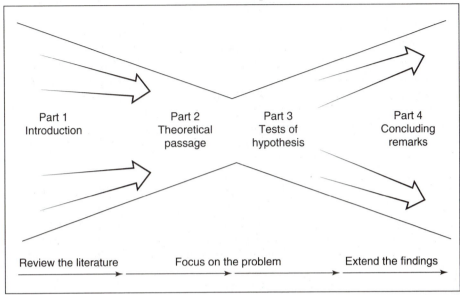

| Part 1 Introduction | Part 2 Theoretical passage | Part 3 Tests of hypothesis | Part 4 Concluding remarks |

Review the literature → Focus on the problem → Extend the findings →

The Title

The most important role performed by the title of a research report is to *announce the contribution of the study* to potential readers. When the study is performed to complete an assignment by a supervisor or course instructor, the nature of the report will be immediately known to the reader. For other reports, however, readers rely on clues provided by the author to evaluate the likely contents of a report. By using the title to announce the report's contribution, the author attracts the maximum number of readers interested in that topic and saves uninterested readers the trouble of reading part of the report to discover that they are not interested in the subject it examines. In both cases, a carefully written title promotes a more efficient allocation of time among readers.

The concern for efficiency should cause the author to avoid the use of "buzz words" and phrases that sound good but do a poor job of communicating the nature of the study's findings. Likewise, the title should not promise more than the report ultimately delivers; if a particular contribution or finding is announced in the title and again in the introduction (part 1), then by the end of the report the reader should agree that the finding has been logically demonstrated.

The title can also be used to indicate the *limits of the contribution;* for example, if a study develops a method of measuring worker productivity in the service sector, the title should not cause readers to believe that the method should also be used to measure productivity among manufacturing or construction workers.

Finally, the title can *hint at the theoretical or statistical methods* used in the body of the report. Thus the title might employ terms like "neoclassical," "regression," or "mathematical." Such clues help a prospective reader decide whether to invest the time necessary to read the report, and screen out readers who lack the interest or skills required to read it.

Footnotes and References

Footnote and reference styles are often established by publishers, by a supervisor or teacher for whom a report is written, or by custom. For that reason, no attempt is made here to suggest universal footnote and reference styles; consult appropriate guidelines in each particular case.

What can be discussed here is the suitability of including footnotes or reference citations in your report. Although at first you might think that more footnotes and references always make for a better report, that is definitely not the case. Each footnote entry or reference citation *distracts the reader* from the main discussion and makes it more difficult to comprehend a given passage. Thus the writer faces a trade-off between the value of information included in the footnote or citation and the incremental reading effort required by the distraction. These considerations suggest that footnotes and reference citations should *never* be added merely "for effect," and also that footnotes and reference citations that are only marginally relevant to the discussion should be omitted whenever possible.

Footnotes are used for various purposes: to provide technical material, to elaborate on ideas mentioned in the main text, or to offer less relevant observations that would be out of place in the text. The principle mentioned above—where footnote material must be of greater value than the reader distraction—suggests that the author should attempt to include relevant comments in the text whenever possible and should probably omit footnotes whose connection to the present study is tenuous. Unless externally imposed guidelines require it, footnotes should not be added merely to provide citations to published references.

Reference citations providing an author's name and year of publication can be included after a quote or after mentioning the author's work, such as (Smith, 1991, p. 6). Then the reader can refer to a list of references at the back of the report if he or she wishes additional publication information.

Longer reference citations might be used to compare the findings of the present study to those of earlier studies, to draw on information developed by other researchers, or to direct readers to related information that they might not be aware of. As with footnotes, a reference citation invites the reader to look away from the main text for additional information. To minimize reader distraction, as much relevant information as possible should be provided along with the citation. For example, one might state that, "Smith's (1991) study of labor force participation found that female participation rates rose by 23% between 1980 and 1990." The discussion of the literature review (in part 1) also advocated this type of citation.

Revising, Editing, Rewriting

Few people—almost no one—can write well enough to produce a finished product in a single draft. Most successful writers edit and rewrite their work several times to remove spelling and grammatical errors, clear up ambiguous statements, adjust the writing style to fit the reader's interest and ability, omit unnecessary material, add transitional remarks to make the prose flow more naturally from one paragraph to the next, and so forth.

Although the quality of the research is the single most important criterion for judging the value of a research report, it is also important for a research report to be packaged as attractively as possible to attract the maximum number of readers and to minimize the effort they have to expend to read and comprehend the conclusions of the study.* One technique used by many people is to write the first draft rapidly, not taking any special care to eliminate writing errors but sticking to the four-part outline (introduction, theoretical passage, tests of hypotheses, concluding comments) discussed earlier in this chapter. After the first draft is completed the researcher should then go through several iterations of revising and perfecting the report—working on the style of presentation, improving the readability, checking the accuracy of theoretical arguments and statistical methods used in the body, anticipating questions the reader is likely to have and providing answers to them.

Criteria for revising the first draft of your research report are suggested by Exhibit 12–3. This list was originally developed for a broad range of reports, letters, and other communications and has been adapted for use here. Most written reports violate to one or more of the infractions included on the list. By identifying these problems in advance, editing changes can be made and material can be added or eliminated before showing your final report to your reader.

Selecting a Research Topic

This chapter has paid considerable attention to organizing and writing a research report, but almost nothing has been said about how to select a research topic in the first instance. This is a difficult task for inexperienced researchers, but it gets easier with experience.

The easiest way to select a research topic is to have it assigned to you by a supervisor or a course instructor. "Hey, Jones," your boss might say, "why don't you collect a little information from around the city and tell us how much rent we ought to be charging tenants of that office building we own over at Second and Broadway." In this situation you don't have to select a research topic, but you should still contemplate alternative research strategies for completing the assignment. Can you handle this assignment or not?

Rather than tell your supervisor that you don't have a clue where to begin, jot down a few notes about various ways you might conduct the study. After focusing your attention on the assignment for an hour or two, you should either have a few ideas about where to begin or at least have several follow-up questions to ask your supervisor.

Here's one way to investigate office building rents: Look at newspaper advertisements and call several office building managers to perform a small-scale market study. This study may reveal that office space rents for about $12 per square foot per year. Or you may learn that an office

---

*"What is written without effort is in general read without pleasure"—Samuel Johnson.

EXHIBIT 12–3 Suggestions for Revising a Written Report*

READABILITY

Reader's Level
- Too specialized in approach
- Assumes too great a knowledge of subject
- So underestimates the reader that it belabors the obvious

Sentence Construction
- Unnecessarily long (in difficult material)
- Choppy, oversimple style (in simple material)
- Subject-verb-object word order too rarely used

Paragraph Construction
- Lack of topic sentences
- Too many ideas in a single paragraph
- Too long

Familiarity of Words
- Inappropriate jargon
- Pretentious language
- Unnecessarily abstract

Reader Direction
- Lack of "framing" (i.e., failure to tell the reader about purpose and direction of forthcoming discussion)
- Inadequate transitions between paragraphs
- Absence of subconclusions to summarize reader's progress at end of divisions in the discussion

Focus
- Unclear as to subject of letter/report

CORRECTNESS

Mechanics
- Shaky grammar
- Faulty punctuation
- Serious or abundant spelling errors

Format
- Careless appearance of documents
- Failure to structure report appropriately

Coherence
- Sentences seem awkward owing to illogical and ungrammatical yoking of unrelated ideas
- Failure to develop a logical progression of ideas through coherent, logically juxtaposed paragraphs

APPROPRIATENESS

Tact and Diplomacy
- Impolitic tone—too brusque, argumentative, or insulting
- Overbearing attitude toward reader
- Insulting and/or personal references

Supporting Detail
- Inadequate support for statements
- Too much indigested detail for busy reader

Opinion
- Adequate research but too great an intrusion of opinions
- Too few facts (and too little research) to entitle drawing of conclusions
- Pretense of unasked for but clearly implied recommendations

THOUGHT

Preparation
- Inadequate thought given to purpose of report prior to its final completion
- Inadequate preparation or use of data known to be available

Competence
- Subject beyond intellectual capabilities of writer

Fidelity to Assignment
- Failure to stick to topic
- Too little made of assignment
- Too much made of routine assignment

Analysis
- Failure to explain or qualify tenuous assertions
- Failure to identify and justify assumptions used
- Superficial examination of data leading to unconscious overlooking of important pieces of evidence
- Failure to draw obvious conclusions of important pieces of evidence
- Presentation of conclusions unjustified by evidence
- Bias, conscious or unconscious, which leads to distorted interpretation of data

Persuasiveness
- Seems less convincing than facts warrant
- Too ovious an attempt to sell ideas
- Too blunt an approach where subtlety and finesse are called for

building down the street is similar to yours, and is renting for $15. This may be exactly the kind of information your supervisor wants.

On the other hand, maybe the building down the street is managed by someone who is even more confused about market conditions than you are—so $15 is probably not the market clearing price. Your small-scale study (above) may tell you that the citywide average of $12 is for old and new buildings, one-story and high-rise buildings, buildings with large lobbies and elevators and buildings with small lobbies and stairs, buildings with their own parking lots and buildings with no parking, buildings in which utilities are included in the rent and buildings in which tenants pay their own utilities, buildings on the declining side of town and buildings in thriving neighborhoods. Are you really going to advise your boss to charge $12, Jones?

What's the big difference? you may be asking yourself. Charge $15, wait a few months, and adjust the price next year depending on whether a surplus or shortage of space emerges.

Unfortunately, that's not how the market for office space works. Tenants do not like to move to new offices and landlords do not like to deal with turnover among their tenants, so rental agreements are often long-term contracts—10 years would not be unusual. So if you are thinking about renting space in a 200,000-square-foot building on a 10-year contract, then each $1 error in your estimate is worth about $2 million over the life of the contract. Offer space at $15 when market conditions would support $16 and you've sacrificed the present value of $2 million; offer space at $15 when market conditions will support only $14 and you lose potential tenants who don't feel like paying an extra $2 million over the life of their contracts. If you discover your error later and begin offering space for $14, then tenants who originally agreed to pay $15 will be unhappy and may demand a $1 rebate.

Too bad, Jones. The boss is quickly losing confidence in your abilities.

After thinking about the assignment for a couple of hours, you might return to the supervisor with a few possibilities. First, you could check with the landlord of the building down the street to learn how much rent they charge there. Second, you could contact the landlords of six or eight buildings that are most similar to the one your company owns, then prepare an estimate from those figures. Finally, you could try to obtain information from about 75 to 100 local office buildings to conduct a study of the factors that determine office rents in your community, then use that information to place a value on your building. This third possibility may not be feasible if none of the data for such a study is readily available, but at that point you could revert to one of the earlier proposals. The question is whether the supervisor wants you to carry out a two-week study of the local market, *assuming that data can be found.*

If you earn $25,000 a year, then a two-week study would cost about $1,000 in labor time plus the cost of acquiring data. The firm may already have a computer and software for you to use on the project, but if it doesn't then additional costs will be incurred acquiring those. These costs are significant, but are small in comparison to the building's rental income. So there is a good chance that the supervisor will tell you, "Good idea, Jones. Let me know what you find out."

What you had better find out *first* is whether or not a study is even feasible. The structure for a four-part report discussed earlier identified several critical elements of a research study. *Unless certain information can be obtained, it is unlikely that the study can be brought to a successful conclusion:*

- **Economic content.** Is the problem you propose to investigate an economic issue? If it is, then the phenomenon of interest will be price, quantity, profit, unemployment, or some other issue mentioned in economics articles, courses, and texts. In this instance, rental price is the dependent variable being studied. Economists know quite a lot about the forces that influence market price. A list of topics that economists have expertise on was provided in Chapter 8.

- **Literature review.** Can you find articles and books that discuss the market for office rents? Articles from nonacademic publications might contain background information on the market for office buildings —long term leasing, factors that make office buildings more desirable, and so on. Books and journal articles about real estate management can be found in the local library. Not many books and journal articles by economists may focus on the market for office space, but many studies can be found regarding factors that influence market prices. Chapter 3 discussed methods used to locate published research, while a discussion of the literature review was provided earlier in this chapter.

- **Theoretical model.** Can you name one or more theories that economists commonly apply to problems like the one you intend to investigate? For example, price is determined by the intersection of supply and demand, so a supply and demand analysis could be used to examine factors that influence office rents (by shifting either of the two curves). A discussion of theory development was provided in Chapter 10 and earlier in this chapter.

- **Hypothesis.** Do you have a preliminary idea of the hypothesis you would be testing (or the phenomenon you would be measuring)? Write it down, and then revise it as your thoughts about the project continue to develop. This hypothesis should reflect your purpose for performing the study—a key consideration if you have been given a specific assignment to complete. The hypothesis must also flow from your theoretical model. The hypothesis was described as the final step in theory construction, discussed in Chapter 10 and earlier in this chapter.

- **Data.** Do you have, or can you acquire, data for the dependent variable and each of the explanatory variables discussed in your theoretical analysis? When investigating a "local" issue, local data sources should be consulted, such as information obtained from the county tax assessor's office, information from studies performed by the local Chamber of Commerce, or information from the city's "economic development" department. If the assignment warrants the cost, you may decide to collect original data by conducting a telephone or mail survey. Methods used to locate published data were discussed in Chapter 1.

- **Statistical technique.** Do you know what statistical method is appropriate for testing the hypothesis (or measuring the phenomenon)? Is this method consistent with the data you have access to? Will it yield estimates or statistics that can answer your questions? Several statistical techniques were discussed, but regression analysis was emphasized, in Chapter 11.

Although it may take a couple of weeks to prepare a complete report, two or three hours should be adequate to examine the assignment from the perspective suggested here to ensure that all of the necessary elements are in place to begin a formal research study. This preliminary work is critical to the success of the investigation; the worst thing that can happen is to get two-thirds of the way into the study before finding out that you won't be able to successfully complete it.

Later, *while actually conducting the study, return to these key elements to ensure that the inquiry is still viable.* Each "surprise" encountered during the research process can affect your ability to satisfy the standards listed above. For example, if you learn that you won't be able to find rents for more than a few office buildings, then you will not be able to analyze rents with regression analysis. Or it may mean that you should consider conducting a market survey to collect your own data. If you are uncertain whether rents are determined by current supply and demand conditions or by anticipated supply and demand conditions over the life of the contract, how do you modify the theoretical model? If your hypothesis and statistical estimates do not answer questions that you needed answers for, what will you do about it?

Once you have all of the key elements in place, then you are prepared to write a research report—which amounts to little more than writing a logically appealing "story" containing the background information, theoretical discussion, and empirical evidence you have collected. More specific guidelines for structuring the report were provided in Chapter 9 and earlier in this chapter.

The same requirements should be considered when selecting a topic for any empirical investigation, whether to satisfy the requirements of your job or to prepare a class project, master's thesis, dissertation, or journal article.

Summary

This chapter provides a "model" for reporting on economic research. The four-part reporting format advocated here begins by drawing together information about a problem or issue from various sources, examines relevant concepts and relationships from "the economic point of view" to derive one or more testable hypotheses, compares the hypotheses to actual experience to investigate the validity of the theory from which they were deduced, then announces the findings and places them in a context to maximize their usefulness to readers.

The research report is not a newspaper editorial or "opinion piece," but it does share one thing in common with that form of rhetoric: Its purpose is to provide a convincing argument to support certain findings or conclusions. If the investigation yields solid results, a report is written to explain those findings and provide logical and empirical justification for them. Exhibit 12–4 summarizes the main points that each report should touch on, and suggests how the report can be arranged so that each point exerts the greatest impact on the reader.

EXHIBIT 12–4 Content Checklist For a Four-part Research Report

Part 1—Introduction

Announce the topic and findings of the investigation you have conducted.

Discuss real-world aspects of the problem or issue examined by the study. Emphasize concepts that you have studied in economics courses—relative price, incentives, aggregate demand, marginal productivity, etc.

Review the literature on this subject. Point out what other researchers and writers have said about your topic or similar ones. Each citation should mention the author, the problem or issue investigated, and findings relevant to your inquiry.

Provide hints, but not an extended discussion, of the theoretical model and statistical techniques used later in your report.

Part 2—Theoretical Passage

Briefly *describe what you intend to demonstrate* in the theoretical discussion.

Develop a *deductive theoretical argument* that reasons from generally accepted principles and other relationships to a specific conclusion. A deductive argument uses concepts to describe the problem, defines and establishes relationships between concepts to form propositions, then combines propositions to deduce a testable prediction about the problem. "Economic theory" plays a key role in the statement and manipulation of propositions.

Provide all *supporting material* necessary to clarify the logical argument—definitions, examples, mathematical formulas, graphs, etc.

Explicitly state the *prediction or hypothesis* resulting from your analysis.

Briefly discuss the theoretical foundation for all *other explanatory variables* included in your regression model. In some cases it may be desirable to place this discussion in a subsection of part 2, apart from the main theoretical passage.

Part 3—Tests of Hypotheses

Describe the *purpose* of the statistical exercise to be carried out. Restating the hypothesis establishes a context for the statistical procedures that follow.

Describe the statistical method and explain why it is the appropriate one for testing the hypothesis.

Discuss the data used to test the hypothesis: Where did you obtain it? To what extent do the data correspond to theoretical concepts discussed in part 2?

Write down the *regression equation* to be estimated, review the list of explanatory variables it includes, and explain the expected relationship between each explanatory variable and the dependent variable.

Carry out the statistical exercise, including any corrective steps appropriate for the "problems" you encounter—multicollinearity, autocorrelation, etc.

Discuss and interpret the empirical estimates. Are they consistent with the hypothesis?

Part 4—Concluding Remarks

Briefly *summarize the theoretical argument and empirical evidence* presented in the body of the report.

Suggest the *implications* of the study's findings.

Mention *opportunities for future research* in the area.

Two additional issues discussed in this chapter are methods used to edit and revise a report and considerations to keep in mind when selecting a research topic. One should cut from the report all material that does not advance its objective. Extraneous information absorbs the reader's time for purposes that the reader may have no interest in; and even if the reader has unlimited time, he or she may become confused by unrelated material inserted in the middle of an already complex argument. A higher level of analysis, not a more difficult writing style, is what sets the research report apart from short essays of the type examined in Chapters 5–7 of this text.

Finally, the chapter examined issues relating to the choice of a research topic—that is, a topic that can fruitfully be explored using the methods examined in Chapters 9–12. In short, one should have a pretty good idea that the existing body of economic theory has something to say about the topic, have some idea what hypothesis might emerge from a theoretical analysis of the topic, and have access to a data set appropriate for testing the hypothesis. Considerable effort should be expended before officially beginning a project to ensure that all necessary ingredients for the study are present.

Exercise

Several research topics are described on the following pages. Each of these projects involves an "interesting" question or problem that can be investigated using the methods discussed in Chapters 9–12. Select one of the topics, read the comments and suggestions provided, research the topic, and *write a 20–25 page research report* describing your methods and findings. Your report should follow the outline/checklist provided in Exhibit 12–4; among other things, this implies that you should write a *four-part report* that follows the introduction-economic theory-statistical test-concluding remarks format. Use methods discussed in Chapters 1–3 to locate and transform data and to identify published materials that will be helpful in your study.

Good luck!

1. The Marginal Productivity Theory of Wages in Baseball

According to neoclassical economic theory, worker pay will tend toward the dollar contribution the worker makes to the employer's (net) revenues. This is the marginal productivity theory of wages. The question to be investigated in this instance is whether or not marginal productivity theory "explains" the earnings of major league baseball players.

The marginal productivity theory is discussed in most microeconomics and labor economics texts. The theoretical passage of your report should discuss the variables that most likely reflect the player's marginal productivity: performance (hitting ability, fielding ability, position played), personal characteristics (age, years of experience), the demand for baseball in the relevant market area (population, interest in baseball, advertising revenues of the team, ticket sales), or other factors (league played in, the player's race, all-star votes cast by fans for the player).

Player pay is the dependent variable. This information is reported each year when the baseball season begins; *USA Today* usually features this information in an article appearing about April 1. Information on the explanatory variables is published in a variety of sports almanacs and guides (e.g., see the *Sporting News* or some other sports guide in your library).

To keep the data requirements of the study from becoming too large, you may want to concentrate on hitter-fielders only (no pitchers) from 12 teams—six in each league. Do teams in one league seem to link pay and performance more closely than teams in the other league?

Players now have greater freedom to negotiate new deals than they did a decade ago, while many believe that in earlier years teams colluded to hold down wages. To the extent the change in free agency rules has had an effect, one might expect that wages now conform more closely to marginal productivity theory than they did in the past. By estimating the same regression for this year's teams and for teams in 1976 (say), it should be possible to determine whether wages today are more closely linked to marginal productivity than previously.

Researchers have discussed some of these issues elsewhere; e.g., see Gerald Scully's *American Economic Review* (December 1974) article and his recent book, *The Business of Major League Baseball* (Chicago: University of

Chicago Press, 1989). An academic article on wages is by Raymond (et al.), "Does Sex Still Matter? New Evidence from the 1980s," *Economic Inquiry* (January 1988).

2. The Prices of Academic Journals

What determines the price of a product, such as academic journals? Orthodox supply and demand theory suggests that prices are determined by factors that influence cost of production (supply) and the desire by consumers to purchase the good (demand).

Production costs for academic journals should reflect the cost of paper and ink, which is proportional to the number of pages, plus additional printing costs when special features (e.g., equations) are included. Economies of scale may affect the cost of publishing high-circulation journals. Third, journals affiliated to a professional organization (e.g., the American Economics Association sponsors the *American Economic Review*) may have lower overhead (fixed) costs if sponsoring organizations or universities provide subsidized office space or other facilities. Fourth, foreign publishers as a group may have higher or lower costs than American publishers because of differences in wages or postage costs. Finally, journals that levy a fee on article submissions recover some of their costs from authors, and may therefore charge subscribers less.

On the demand side of the market, the quality of research published in the journal may be important to subscribers. One demand-side variable may therefore be the journal's quality rating, and one would predict a positive impact of quality on price. Second, publishers may vary prices among groups of subscribers (according to their elasticity of demand). Do the journals charge all subscribers the same amount, do individuals pay less than institutions, or do low-income subscribers pay less than high-income subscribers? Price discrimination should permit the publisher to charge a lower *basic* subscription rate, while charging others a higher rate.

Supply and demand analysis assumes utility- and profit-maximizing behavior by market participants. To the extent these conditions are not satisfied, the analysis may perform poorly in empirical tests. Keep this in mind when writing the theory section of your report and when discussing your empirical findings.

Data for most of the variables in this study can be gathered from the journals themselves (subscription price, institutional affiliation, years published, price discrimination) and from reference books owned by most university libraries (ask the librarian in charge of ordering journals where he or she finds this information). For specific information about the market for academic journals refer to "Scientists Urged to Help Resolve Library 'Crisis' by Shunning High-Cost, Low-Quality Journals," *The Chronicle of Higher Education* (February 28, 1990): A6.

Estimate structural (supply, demand) equations separately, then estimate a reduced form regression that includes explanatory variables from both sides of the market. To narrow the investigation, concentrate exclusively on economics journals. (See a list of economics journals in Appendix 10 and a quality rating in Appendix 15.)

3. The Demand for Education (at Your University)

What do you suppose determines the number of students that attend your university this year? *At a given tuition price,* shifts in the demand curve will determine the quantity of services purchased—where "quantity" in this instance is the number of enrolled students.

Normally, one would state that quantity is determined by the *intersection* of a downward-sloping demand curve and an upward-sloping supply curve. In the case of most universities, however, the supply curve is usually perfectly elastic at the announced price. That price is not a profit-maximizing price, but probably reflects long-term average costs and the size of the subsidy received from taxpayers or donors. Since supply is perfectly elastic each year, tuition price can be modeled as an exogenous explanatory variable in the demand function of students.

Other variables that might explain enrollment include consumer (student) income, the value of time to students (which decreases during periods of high unemployment), the price of substitute goods, and the size of the relevant population. Maybe other factors—such as the football team's won-loss record or the availability of financial aid—are also important at your university. Tuition price, income, and prices of substitute goods should all be stated in *real* (inflation-adjusted) terms.

Since you will be investigating a consumer decision, your theory passage (part 3) should be consistent with theories of consumer behavior (in microeconomics texts).

Data specific to your university can probably be found in your university library or in an administrative office—say, the office of institutional research or the university records office. Personal income data for your state or county can be found in the *Survey of Current Business.* Population figures for various age groups are available from the U.S. Census Bureau. The U.S. Department of Education and the *Statistical Abstract of the U.S.* publish information about average tuition prices (which you may want to use as a substitute good price.)

After you have estimated a statistical demand function, interpret your results. (What elasticity of demand do you estimate? What is the income elasticity of demand?) Draw the demand curve implied by your regression results, and show the change in enrollment resulting from a hypothetical $100 fee increase. (Has your university's administration proposed raising fees lately? If so, then estimate the impact of the proposed increase on enrollments.)

As described, this is a time-series study. It will require at least 20–25 years of data, and more if possible. Include lagged enrollment as an explanatory variable in one specification of your regression model to investigate the effects of "inertia" on student decisions.

4. Does Alcohol and Drug Prohibition Increase Violent Crime?

Most people are aware that *using* alcohol and other drugs can harm the users, but are less aware of the harmful effects of *prohibiting* the production and sale of those substances. This project investigates the impact of alcohol and drug prohibition on murder, assault, and other violent crime rates.

As this subject is normally discussed, restrictions on the supply of alcohol and drugs cause prices to rise far above costs of production. This creates large profits for successful suppliers. The opportunity to earn these profits may cause suppliers to bribe, intimidate, or physically injure customers, competitors, police, judges, and others. The fact that suppliers cannot appeal to legal authorities to enforce their contracts and property rights means that they are more likely to enforce rights on their own. The fact that alcohol/drug prices are high during prohibition may also cause some consumers to engage in robbery and other illegal activities to pay for those products—which would not be expensive in an unregulated market.

You will learn of other ways that violence might result from prohibition as you read more about the subject. Several articles and books have been published on this subject recently; see Milton Friedman, "A War We're Losing," *Wall Street Journal* (March 3, 1991). Quite a bit has been written about the Eighteenth Amendment to the Constitution (ratified in 1919), so you should have no problem familiarizing yourself with the subject. Look at Henry Lee, *How Dry We Were* and David Kyvig, *Repealing National Prohibition*.

The theoretical passage of your report (part 2) should also include a brief analysis of *other* factors that might increase violence: high population density, the share of young males in the population, unemployment, low educational levels, and so on. Try to locate one or two references in the library that discuss factors that contribute to violent crime, and study them for additional explanatory variables to include in the theoretical discussion of violent crime.

Different dependent variables can be used to investigate the hypothesis: the murder rate, the violent crime rate, the assault rate, and so forth. Perhaps you will want to estimate regressions for each. Various *proxy variables* exist for *prohibition*—the key explanatory variable in this study. One is to use a 0/1 (qualitative) variable for alcohol prohibition years and another 0/1 variable for drug war years (which began in 1970, intensified in 1981, and reached a peak following President Bush's initiatives in 1989). An alternative proxy variable for prohibition activities is the number of alcohol/drug arrests. A third measure of prohibition is the government's budget outlays on anti-drug and -alcohol activities.

This is a time series study, so you should acquire data for as many years as possible. (See the *Statistical Abstract of the U.S., Uniform Crime Reports*, and *Historical Statistics of the U.S.*) If it is impossible to acquire information going back to the early part of the century, concentrate on measuring the impact of drug prohibition during the past 35–40 years.

Other Research Topics

1. Do **executive's salaries** reflect the financial performance of the corporations they manage? (This is a study that measures the degree to which earnings are explained by marginal productivity. See the comments above regarding the earnings of baseball players. *Business Week* and other publications provide data in survey articles on executive pay. Cross-sectional study.)

2. Is **consumer confidence** affected by current economic conditions? (See articles about consumer confidence indexes in Appendix 8. What other conditions influence consumer confidence? Time series study.)

3. To what extent do **housing prices** in your community reflect home size, the number of bedrooms, lot size, location, and other variables? (Check your library for books on real estate valuation. Data regarding home prices—or "assessed valuation"—and characteristics can usually be found in records maintained by the county tax assessor's office. Cross-sectional study.)

4. Do **used car prices** reflect the ratings of *Consumer Reports* magazine? (See the annual car buyer's guide in *Consumer Reports* for data on the study's main explanatory variable. Include original purchase price and car age as other explanatory variables. Used car prices are published in guides available in most commercial bookstores; find a guide that also shows the car's *original purchase price*. Cross-sectional study.)

5. What variables influence the **national saving rate**? Has something happened in recent years to change the *preference* of Americans for saving, or have *economic and demographic conditions* caused the saving rate to decline? (Since saving is the residual of income not spent, the factors that influence saving are similar to those that influence spending. Will the aging of the "baby boom" generation cause the national savings rate to rise over the next 20 years? Do people reduce saving when they realize investment gains in the stock markets? Consult the many journal articles, conference reports, and magazine articles that have discussed the saving rate in recent years. Time series study.)

6. Does a **minimum wage** increase teenage unemployment as economic theory predicts? (Test the prediction of supply and demand analysis against actual experience. Because low-skilled labor is a *substitute* for high-skilled labor, the impact of a higher minimum wage may depend on the *ratio* of the minimum wage to the wage of high-skilled workers. Unemployment is also affected by macroeconomic conditions, so one or more explanatory variables in the unemployment model should be proxies for aggregate demand or supply conditions. Check the hypothesis for different groups—males, females, whites, minorities, teens. Time series study.)

Notes on Chapter 12

Use the space below to describe new concepts or methods that you learned in Chapter 12.

Bibliography

This chapter draws on several discussions of research report writing. I have made greatest use of Sylvester Carter's excellent book about the writing of professional journal articles, *Writing for Your Peers* (New York: Praeger, 1987). According to Carter, the research article must meet standards of scientific rigor, professional ethics and efficiency in reporting (p. 8). Readers who desire a more in-depth discussion of research report writing should consult Carter.

This chapter also borrows from other authors. Francis C. Dane's *Research Methods* (Belmont, CA: Wadsworth, 1990) discusses the literature review (chapter 4) and report organization (chapter 12). Willam G. Zikmund's *Business Research Methods* (Chicago: Dryden Press, 1988) discusses the organization of research reports. A good discussion of the use of concepts, propositions, and deduction in theory development can be found in Chava Frankfort-Nachmias and David Nachmias, *Research Methods in the Social Sciences* (New York: St. Martin's Press, 1992): 41–43. Jacqueline Fawcett and Florence Down's *The Relationship Between Theory and Research* (Norwalk, CT: Appleton-Century-Crofts, 1986) provides a careful discussion and many examples of the close integration between theory and evidence required in research.

Appendices

Appendix 17: The Keynesians Return to Washington

Appendix 18: Guidelines for Giving an Oral Report

Appendix 19: Statistical Tables (t, F, p, and DW)

Appendix 20: Glossary of Economic Terms

APPENDIX 1

What Should Economists Know?

The material in the present text is structured around key skills (or proficiencies) which W. Lee Hansen has argued are critical for economics graduates to possess. Hansen developed his list of skills by surveying students, faculty, and employers. This article is from the *American Economic Review* (May 1986): 149–52. A later article by Hansen reaches similar conclusions regarding graduate students. See his "The Education and Training of Economics Doctorates," *Journal of Economic Literature* (September 1991): 1054–87.

The following article is reprinted by permission of The American Economic Review, *What Knowledge is Most Worth Knowing—For Economics Majors?* by, W. Lee Hansen.

What Knowledge Is Most Worth Knowing—
For Economics Majors?

By W. Lee Hansen*

This essay resurrects an old question but asks it in a new context. The old question is a paraphrase of the title of Herbert Spencer's famous essay "What Knowledge Is of Most Worth?" The new context is to pose the question for undergraduate students majoring in economics. My intent is to engage you in reflecting about what kinds of knowledge and skills our economics majors should master—what proficiencies they should be able to demonstrate—by the time they graduate from college. My focus is on not the select few who plan to enter graduate economics programs, but rather the vast majority who go out into the world and will become the next generation of leaders. I propose a list of knowledge and skills, perhaps a better word is proficiencies, that we might reasonably expect our majors to demonstrate upon graduation. This is by no means a final or definitive list; rather it is offered to stimulate discussion about the meaning of the economics major and how to give it more meaning.

This question, to the best of my knowledge, has not recently been raised in a serious way by the economics profession. It was touched on briefly more than 30 years ago in a special supplement to the *American Economic Review* on undergraduate education (see Horace Taylor, 1950). The silence since then is peculiar in light of significant professional interest in examining the outcomes of a wide variety of public programs through cost-benefit analysis, program analysis, and the like. It now seems timely to raise the question because of the growing concern about what a college degree represents, not in some grand philosophical sense but in readying young people for

a fuller and more productive life (see the Association of American Colleges, 1985).

What do we expect of our graduating economics majors? We take as given their need to meet the requirements for graduation established by their colleges. Usually, this entails four years of course work beginning with general education courses in the first two years followed by completion of the major and other breadth requirements during the final two years. It is the major, however, that gives focus to the college experience. Typically, majors are required to take somewhere between 24 and 40 credit hours, or from 8 to 13 economics courses—elementary, intermediate, and advanced. These courses must usually include intermediate theory and statistics and perhaps also other distributional requirements (see John Siegfried and James Wilkinson, 1982). It goes without saying that students must earn passing grades in these courses.

What do our majors know after all this? About all we as members of economics department faculties can claim for our majors is their ability to answer our examination questions with some facility. Implicit in our approach is the assumption that exposure to a range of courses produces learning, learning that enables students not only to apply their knowledge to a variety of questions and issues they will confront as citizens but also to prepare them for employment as economists (albeit junior economists), or in related jobs that may utilize the skills acquired by economics majors. Whether graduating economics majors can in fact apply their knowledge as citizens or employees is not clear, to us and perhaps to them either.

Some economists might well dispute whether improved citizenship and job

*University of Wisconsin, Madison, WI 53706.

preparation are uppermost in the minds of economics majors or their instructors. They would assert that as members of economics departments we should not be concerned with such questions. The undergraduate degree is essentially a liberal arts degree that prepares students to think critically about the great and small issues of mankind; its purpose is not vocational; and most students end up doing work that is at most only loosely related to their undergraduate majors. Continuing, they would argue that the purpose of economics instruction is to offer an opportunity for students to be exposed to different facets of the discipline and to learn how economists go about their work. Responsibility for figuring out how to put together what is learned rests with students. How pervasive this view is remains to be ascertained. Whatever the case, economics is seen by many students as a discipline that can offer enlightenment about how the economics system operates as well as improved employment prospects after graduation. Indeed, numerous departments tout their programs as providing these opportunities.

While it may still be unclear who is responsible for what, this leaves unanswered the question of what we might hope or expect our majors to be able to do as a result of their heavy investment in schooling. Remember that they had extensive contact with the economics literature, the fundamentals of economic analysis, and applications to a variety of economic issues and problems. They have participated in somewhere between 300 and 600 hours of classroom instruction by professional economists. At the same time they have experienced a heavy diet of multiple choice examinations. Few have been subjected to any serious grilling in the classroom because of the dominance of lecturing. And not many have had to write papers in their courses. While we like to say that we have tried to teach them how economists think, we have almost no evi-

dence as to our success. In fact, except for the exams they took, there may be little that distinguishes graduating economics majors from those in, say, biology or political science.

How do we specify what it is that economics majors should know? We can begin by examining statements of the competencies expected of college entrants. Perhaps the most comprehensive statement is that prepared by The College Board (1983) to describe for prospective college students what is most worth knowing. Less has been done at the college level though there is a strong move by some institutions to specify what students should have mastered in the general education phase—the first two years—of college. Statements about the general competencies expected of college graduates are usually quite vague. Even less has been done by academic disciplines to spell out how their instructional programs for majors enhance, or are intended to enhance, the capacities of students to demonstrate their knowledge and skills. Thus, the existing literature provides little or no guidance.

This gap offers a bold opportunity to set out a list of proficiencies for graduating economics majors. This list is based on thinking about the question for some years and on occasional efforts in my undergraduate teaching to build the competencies of my students. It also reflects the responses to surveys of our recently graduated majors, conversations with employers who hire our majors, and discussions with a range of other people— colleagues in economics, faculty members from other disciplines, and high-level executives in both business and government.

This list of proficiencies moves from what might be called lower to higher levels of cognitive activity, as suggested by the groupings of the items on the list.

1) *Gaining Access to Existing Knowledge:* Locate published research in economics and related fields; locate information on particular topics and issues in economics;

search out economic data as well as information about the meaning of the data and how they are derived.

2) *Displaying Command of Existing Knowledge:* Summarize (in a 2-minute monologue or a 300-word written statement) what is known about the current condition of the economy; summarize the principal ideas of an eminent living economist; summarize a current controversy in the economics literature; state succinctly the dimensions of a current economic policy issue; explain key economic concepts and describe how they can be used.

3) *Displaying Ability to Draw Out Existing Knowledge:* Write a precis of a published journal article; read and interpret a theoretical analysis, including simple mathematical derivations, reported in an economics journal article; read and interpret a quantative analysis, including regression results, reported in an economics journal article; show what economic concepts and principles are used in economic analyses published in articles from daily newspapers and weekly newsmagazines.

4) *Utilizing Existing Knowledge to Explore Issues:* Prepare a written analysis (of say, 5 pages) of a current economic problem; prepare a decision memorandum (of say, 2 pages) for a superior that recommends some action on an economic decision faced by the organization.

5) *Creating New Knowledge:* Identify and formulate a question or series of questions about some economic issue that will facilitate investigation of the issue; prepare a 5-page proposal for a research project; complete a research study whose results are contained in a polished 20-page paper.

Several comments need to be made. First, these proficiencies probably strike most of us as being quite reasonable. Indeed, most if not all economics faculty members would hope that students, by the time they begin work in the major, already possess the generic proficiencies indicated here. This would allow faculty members to be concerned with sharpening these proficiencies within the context of economics. Second, these proficiencies are quite neutral with respect to the content of the economics major, except perhaps for students planning to enter graduate school. Thus, an emphasis on these proficiencies need not intrude on the intellectual focus of the major.

At the same time, problems arise. First, how can we determine whether students have acquired these proficiencies by the time they graduate; put another way, how would we test for these proficiencies? The obvious answer would be to devote the final several weeks of the senior year of college to a hands-on testing program that would permit students to demonstrate their proficiencies. Second, how might we structure the major and its related teaching program so as to provide reasonable assurance that students develop these proficiencies? In fact, relatively little might have to be done except to incorporate the acquisition of these proficiencies into individual courses or groups of courses. A senior research seminar would be helpful, however, in giving students experience with the development of new knowledge. Third, how do we enlist faculty support for a focus on the development of proficiencies among our economics majors? This is no doubt the toughest question to answer because many faculty members are likely to view a focus on proficiencies as simply another attempt to increase the costs of their undergraduate teaching, with no off-setting increase in benefits to them as faculty members.

Rather than attempting to resolve all of these questions here, it is probably best to think about whether the list of proficiencies presented above is reflective of the proficiencies we would like to see in our graduating majors, and how we might take some small steps to facilitate the acquisition of these proficiencies by our undergraduate majors.

Do these proficiencies reflect what we think is important? Even if we believe they do, what do recent and long-time graduates have to say about the appropriateness of these proficiencies? What do employers think about this approach and these proficiencies? Will these proficiencies enhance the employability of graduating seniors? Will they contribute to the career development of our seniors? If we agree on these questions, how do we go about answering them?

On the assumption that these proficiencies are viewed as important, how do we encourage their acquisition? It seems clear that economics faculty members are not going to rise up overnight and embrace the concept of proficiencies. This means we have to find ways of making it easier for individual faculty members to promote the notion of competencies in their own teaching. What can be done? One approach is to develop materials that can be helpful to instructors. Of particular value would be sample assignments and evaluations of actual student responses, both to show how to implement a proficiency approach and how to evaluate student achievement of these proficiencies. Another approach is to specify how the cumulative acquisition of these proficiencies can be assured. This requires development of a sequence of materials that would be integrated across courses in the major. None of these tasks is easy; indeed, implementation is the most difficult of all.

In developing these materials and integrating them into the major, it is important to assess whether the stress on proficiencies will subtract from the economic content of the major. It seems probable that adoption of the proficiency approach will lead to some restructuring of our teaching. The likely result is that students will be taught less, but will learn more, and learn what they do learn better than they do now. The impact on faculty members is more difficult to speculate about, but they could find this approach a stimulating one.

To sum up, if we are concerned about the public's understanding of economics, and everyone judges it to be low, perhaps we should concentrate on increasing the capacity of those students with whom we have the greatest contact, our majors. The proficiency approach outlined here should do at least as well as we now do and probably much better.

References

Siegfried, John J. and Wilkinson, James T., "The Economics Curriculum in the United States: 1980," *American Economic Review Proceedings*, May 1982, *72*, 125–38.

Taylor, Horace, "The Teaching of Undergraduate Economics: Report of the Committee on the Undergraduate Teaching of Economics and Training of Economists," *American Economic Review*, December 1950, *40*, Suppl., Part 2.

Association of American Colleges, *Integrity in the College Curriculum: A Report to the Academic Community*, Washington, D.C., February 1985.

The College Board, *Academic Preparation for College: What Students Need to Know and Be Able to Do*, New York, 1983.

APPENDIX 2

Calendar of Release Dates for Economic Indicators

Most of the following data series are reported in the *Wall Street Journal* (on the day following release of data); others can be found in the *Survey of Current Business*. Release dates are approximate.

Frequently Released Data

Commodity prices	Daily (newspapers report previous day prices)
Foreign exchange rates	Daily (newspapers report previous day rates)
Interest rates	Daily (newspapers report previous day rates)
Initial unemployment claims	Weekly (for two weeks prior)
Jobless claims	Weekly (for two weeks prior)
Money supply	Thursdays (for week ended Monday of previous week)
Treasury bill auction results	Tuesday (for Monday auction)
Treasury bill rates	Daily (most major newspapers)

Monthly Data

Auto sales	1st week of month (for previous month)
Balance of trade	45 days following close of reporting month
Building permits	16th–20th of month (for previous month)
Capacity utilization rate	14th–17th of month (for previous month)
Construction spending	1st business day of month (for two months prior)
Consumer confidence	1st week of month (for previous month)
Consumer price index (CPI)	9th–18th of month (for previous month)
Consumer installment credit	5th business day (for two months prior)
Consumption spending	22nd–31st of month (for previous month)
Durable goods orders	22nd–28th of month (for previous month)
Employment (payroll employment)	2nd–8th of month (for previous month)
Factory orders	1st–6th of month (for two months prior)
Federal expenditures, receipts, and deficit	Final week in month (for previous month)
Help-wanted index	1st week of month (for two months prior)
Housing starts and building permits	16th–20th of month (for previous month)
Industrial production	Mid-month (for previous month)
Inventories	2nd week of month (for previous month)
Leading, coincident, and lagging indicators	1st business day of month (for two months prior)
Machine tool orders and shipments	Last day of month (for previous month)
Manufacturers' orders (nondefense capital goods)	1st–6th of each month (for two months prior)
New home sales	28th–4th of month (for two months prior)
Personal income	23rd–31st of month (for previous month)
Producer price index (PPI)	8th–14th of month (for previous month)
Productivity	45 days following each quarter (for previous quarter)
Purchasing managers' report	1st business day of month (for previous month)
Retail sales	11th–14th of month (for previous month)
Unemployment rate	1st week of month (for previous month)

Quarterly Data (Q1 = Jan.–Mar.; Q2 = Apr. –Jun.; Q3 = Jul.–Sep.; Q4 = Oct.–Dec.)

Corporate profits, revised estimate   22nd–30th of final month in quarter (for previous quarter)

Corp. profits by firm   Early February, May, August, November (*Wall Street Journal* feature article, for the previous quarter)

GDP, advance estimate   25th–30th of first month in quarter (for previous quarter)

GDP, preliminary estimate   25th–30th of second month in quarter (for previous quarter)

GDP, final (revised) estimate   22nd–30th of final month in quarter (for previous quarter)

Merchandise trade   8th week of quarter (for previous quarter)

State personal income   4th week of quarter (for two quarters prior)

Annual Data

GDP (complete accounts for several years, revised data)   July (*Survey of Current Business*)

Metropolitan area personal income   Late May (for two years prior)

State per capita personal income (revised)   Late August (for previous year)

Appendix 3

Economic Data and Publications Directory

Federal Reserve System

Board of Governors of the Federal Reserve System / Publications Services / MS-138 / Washington, DC 20551 / (202) 452-3244

District 1: Federal Reserve Bank of **Boston** / Public Services Department / P.O. Box 2076 / Boston, MA 02106-2076 / (617) 973-3459

District 2: Federal Reserve Bank of **New York** / Public Information Department / 33 Liberty Street / New York, NY 10045 / (212) 720-6134

District 3: Federal Reserve Bank of **Philadelphia** / Public Information Department / P.O. Box 66 / Philadelphia, PA 19105 / (215) 574-6115

District 4: Federal Reserve Bank of **Cleveland** / Public Affairs Department / P.O. Box 6387 / Cleveland, OH 44101-1387 / (216) 579-2047

District 5: Federal Reserve Bank of **Richmond** / Public Services Department / P.O. Box 27622 / Richmond, VA 23261 / (804) 697-8109

District 6: Federal Reserve Bank of **Atlanta** / Public Affairs Department / 104 Marietta Street, NW / Atlanta, GA 30303-2713 / (404) 521-8020

District 7: Federal Reserve Bank of **Chicago** / Public Information Center / 230 South LaSalle Street / P.O. Box 834 / Chicago, IL 60690-0834 / (312) 322-5111

District 8: Federal Reserve Bank of **St. Louis** / Public Information Office / P.O. Box 442 / St. Louis, MO 63166 / (314) 444-8444 ext. 545

Federal Reserve System (continued)

District 9: Federal Reserve Bank of **Minneapolis** / Public Affairs Department / 250 Marquette Avenue / Minneapolis, MN 55401-0291 / (612) 340-2446

District 10: Federal Reserve Bank of **Kansas City** / Public Affairs Department / 925 Grand Avenue / Kansas City, MO 64198-0001 / (816) 881-2683

District 11: Federal Reserve Bank of **Dallas** / Public Affairs Department / 2200 North Pearl Street / Dallas, TX 75222 / (214) 651-6289 or -6266

District 12: Federal Reserve Bank of **San Francisco** / Public Information Department / P.O. Box 7702 / San Francisco, CA 94120 / (415) 974-2163

U.S. Commerce Department

Recorded Telephone Messages—Brief recorded telephone messages summarizing key estimates immediately after their release. The messages are available 24 hours a day for several days following release. The usual time of release (Eastern time) and telephone numbers to call are:

Leading Indicators (8:30 a.m.)   (202) 898-2450

The message is updated weekly, usually on Monday, to include recently available component data that will be incorporated into the next release.

Gross Domestic Product (8:30 a.m.)   -2451
Personal Income and Outlays (10 a.m.)   -2452
Merchandise Trade, Balance of Payments (10 a.m.)   -2453

Economic Bulletin Board—On-line computer access to news releases, data, and other information is available from the Commerce Department's Economic Bulletin Board (EBB). Selected estimates and articles from *Survey of Current Business* are available on EBB, as are financial data from the Federal Reserve. A $35 annual fee includes 2 hours of connect time on the system; additional time is charged by the minute. Instant hook-up via modem is available. For more information call (202) 377-1986.

Contact Persons—Bureau of Economic Analysis staff can answer specific questions about the availability or preparation of data. (For actual data, refer to sources above.) A few contacts are listed here; for additional names consult "A User's Guide to BEA Information," *Survey of Current Business* (January).

U.S. Commerce Department (continued)

GDP/GNP	(202) 523-0824
Business cycle indicators (*SCB* "yellow pages")	-0800
Current business statistics (*SCB* "blue pages")	-0500
Personal income	-0832
Wealth estimates	-0837
Personal consumption expenditures	-0819
GDP by industry	-0517
Capital (investment) expenditures	-0791
Input-output tables (annual)	-0867
Federal government receipts and expenditures	-3472
State and local government receipts and expenditures	-0728
Pollution abatement and control spending	-0687
Wages and salaries	-0809
Gross state product	-9180
International current-account (analysis)	-0621
International travel	-0609
Capital-account transactions	-0603
State personal income (quarterly)	254-6640

U.S. Government Printing Office (Publications and Subscriptions)

Superintendent of Documents / Government Printing Office / Washington, DC 20402-9325 / (202) 783-3238 / fax: (202) 275-0019

Key publications: *Survey of Current Business, Statistical Abstract of the U.S., Monthly Labor Review,* and other publications of government departments and agencies.

President's Council of Economic Advisers

Council of Economic Advisers / Office of Public Affairs / Executive Office Building / Washington, DC 20506 / (202) 395-5084

Key publication: *Economic Report of the President.*

U.S. Treasury Department

U.S. Department of the Treasury / Office of Public Affairs / 15th Street & Pennsylvania Avenue / Washington, DC 20220 / (202) 566-2041

Key publication: *Treasury Bulletin.*

International Monetary Fund (IMF)

International Monetary Fund / Publication Services / Washington, DC
20431 / (202) 623-7430

Key publications: *International Financial Statistics, International Financial
Statistics Yearbook, Balance of Payments Statistics, Government Finance Statistics Yearbook, Direction of Trade Statistics.*

Council of State Governments

The Council of State Governments / Order Department / Iron Works
Pike / P.O. Box 11910 / Lexington, KY 40578-1910 / (606) 231-1850

Key publication: *Book of the States.*

Advisory Commission on Intergovernmental Relations (ACIR)

Advisory Commission on Intergovernmental Relations / 800 K St., NW /
South Building, Suite 450 / Washington, DC 20575 / (202) 659-4073

Key publication: *Significant Features of Fiscal Federalism* (information on
state and local government).

APPENDIX 4

On-Line Databases for Economists

1. U.S. Department of Commerce—**Economic Bulletin Board** (EBB). A computer–based electronic bulletin board. You can reach EBB from a personal computer equipped with a modem and standard communications software. The EBB's menus help you locate and read press releases and data files. EBB includes the latest *statistical releases* from the Bureau of Economic Analysis (Commerce Department), the Bureau of the Census, the Bureau of Labor Statistics, the Federal Reserve Board, the Department of the Treasury, and other Federal agencies. EBB *data files* include but are not limited to the following topics: national income and product accounts (GDP), price indexes, productivity, money supply, federal budget, international trade, employment, industry performance.

The EBB can be reached 24 hours a day, 7 days a week at (202) 377-3870 using your personal computer. Set your PC's communications software to no parity, word length = 8 bits and 1 stop bit, and a baud rate of 300/1200/2400 bps. A demonstration is available by typing GUEST when prompted for a user ID.

EBB charges run 20¢ (weekday mornings), 15¢ (weekday afternoons), and 5¢ (evening and weekends) per minute, not including long distance telephone charges. An annual subscription rate of $35 is also charged (which includes $12 worth of connect time). Instant subscriptions can be arranged by calling (202) 377-1986 and providing a credit card number.

2. Federal Reserve Bank of St. Louis—**Federal Reserve Electronic Data** (FRED). An electronic database that provides up-to-the-minute information on the money supply and its major components, interest rates, bank loans, and a range of other financial and economic data. FRED also includes regional business and banking data for the St. Louis Federal Reserve district (Missouri, Arkansas, Kentucky, and Tennessee).

FRED is available 24 hours a day, 7 days a week by dialing (314) 621-1824. The service is free; you pay only for the phone call. Set your PC's communications software to no parity, word length = 8 bits and 1 stop bit, and a baud rate of 300/1200/2400/9600 bps. First-time callers will be asked to enter some information about themselves. (Your first call should be placed on some day of the week *other than* Thursday.)

3. Federal Reserve Bank of Minneapolis—**KIMBERELY.** An electronic database that provides financial and economic data, press releases, and information from the Federal Reserve Bank of Minneapolis.

KIMBERELY is accessed by dialing (612) 340-2489. The service is free; you pay only for the phone call. Set your PC's communications software to no parity, word length = 8 bits and 1 stop bit, and a baud rate of 300/1200/2400/9600 bps. For more information call (612) 340-2443.

4. Federal Reserve Bank of Dallas—**FED FLASH.** An electronic database that provides economic data and information from the Federal Reserve Bank of Dallas.

FED FLASH is accessed by dialing (214) 922-5199. The service is free; you pay only for the phone call. Set your PC's communications software to no parity, word length = 8 bits and 1 stop bit, and a baud rate of 300/1200/2400/9600 bps. For more information call (214) 922-5171.

5. CompuServe Information Service—**CompuServe.**® This commercial database contains a wide range of services including financial data, news, weather, hobby and special-interest information, dissertation abstracts, games, movie reviews, retail shopping, and software. After logging on, access to information and other services is gained by selecting menu choices or by typing the name of the service desired. For example, GO BASICQUOTES is a request for current prices on corporate stocks, options, and stock indexes.

CompuServe "Basic Services" provides unlimited access to a basic list of services for $8.95 per month; additional services can be accessed by basic service subscribers for a fee. Other service levels are also available. For more information call (800) 848-8990. Charges are billed against your credit card account.

A sample of CompuServe services and GO commands include:

To find a topic: GO INDEX
Federal Reserve policy analysis and briefings on economic data: GO MMS
Stock quotes: GO BASICQUOTES
Stock market highlights (previous trading day): GO MARKET
Fundwatch (*Money Magazine* mutual fund database): GO FUNDWATCH
Value Line Corporate Reports: GO VLINE
Spot and futures prices for commodities: GO COMMODITIES
Associated Press News: GO APQ
Academic American Encyclopedia: GO ENCYCLOPEDIA
Dissertation abstracts: GO DISSERTATION
Census Bureau data: GO CENDATA
Demographic and economic information by zip code: GO NEIGHBORHOOD
Newspaper library: GO NEWSLIB
Journal Graphics (television broadcast transcripts): GO TRANSCRIPTS
Government publications (GPO catalog and orders): GO GPO
Peterson's College Database (college information): GO PETERSONS
Instructions and fees: GO FINHELP

6. DIALOG Information Services, Inc.—**DIALOG.** This commercial database provides a powerful and comprehensive offering of online

information. DIALOG is actually an intermediary between users and over 400 individual database services. Subscribers provide key words or other information to search individual databases or groups of databases. The databases on the DIALOG system contain about 350 million records. Records include directory-type listings, tables of data, bibliographic citations, and full-text articles.

DIALOG has two levels of service: full service, which is the more expensive service, and evening and weekend service, which is less expensive. The fee for a 10-minute daytime session will cost about $6–$16. Most university libraries already subscribe to DIALOG and have experienced operators.

To select a hypothetical database named XYZ, type BEGIN XYZ. After gaining access to the database, search for topics by typing SELECT followed by one or more key words. Another way of searching DIALOG is to type the command BEGIN MENUS and select relevant options from the menus that appear.

A sample of DIALOG databases and BEGIN commands include:

ECONOMIC LITERATURE INDEX index of articles and books: BEGIN 139
ECONBASE economic data and forecasts: BEGIN 565
MEDIA GENERAL PLUS financial data on 5,300 corporations: BEGIN 546
MONEYCENTER current news and economic data: BEGIN MONEYCEN
ECONBASE time series data and forecasts: BEGIN 565
PETERSON'S GRADLINE information about graduate programs: BEGIN 273
PTS U.S. TIME SERIES economic data for many topics: BEGIN 82
PAPERS index of major newspapers and full-text articles: BEGIN PAPERS
SOCIAL SCISEARCH index to literature in the social sciences: BEGIN 7

APPENDIX 5

Recent U.S. Business Cycles

The dates of business cycle peaks and troughs are determined by the Business Cycle Dating Committee of the National Bureau of Economic Research, a private research organization. The committee currently includes seven economists and is headed by Robert Hall of Stanford University. Although a rule of thumb states that a recession occurs when real GDP declines for two consecutive quarters, in practice the Dating Committee considers many factors in arriving at its decisions.

On December 22, 1992, the Business Cycle Dating Committee declared that the most recent recession had ended more than a year and a half earlier. The long delay between the onset of recovery in April 1991 and the declaration that the recession had ended is explained by the mildness of the recovery. "Only by December did the overall pattern of economic activity appear to be strong enough to warrant the determination of the trough date," the committee said.*

---

*See "Panel Says Recession Ended in March 1991," *Wall Street Journal* (Dec. 23, 1992): A2.

Business Cycle Summary

Trough	Peak	Duration (in months)	
		Contraction (to trough from previous peak)	Expansion (trough to peak)
Nov. 1927	Aug. 1929	13	21
Mar. 1933	May 1937	43	50
June 1938	Feb. 1945	13	80
Oct. 1945	Nov. 1948	8	37
Oct. 1949	July 1953	11	45
May 1954	Aug. 1957	10	39
Apr. 1958	Apr. 1960	8	24
Feb. 1961	Dec. 1969	10	106
Nov. 1970	Nov. 1973	11	36
Mar. 1975	Jan. 1980	16	58
July 1980	July 1981	6	12
Nov. 1982	July 1990	16	92
Mar. 1991	?	8	?
Average (Nov. 1927–Mar. 1991)		13.3	50

Source: National Bureau of Economic Research

APPENDIX 6

Selected Economic Data

1. Gross domestic product and income, *Federal Reserve Bulletin* (December 1993).
2. Gross domestic product by industry, in constant dollars, *Survey of Current Business* (May 1993).
3. Gross state product, by industry, *Statistical Abstract of the U.S.* (1993).
4. Personal consumption expenditures, by type of product, *Survey of Current Business* (August 1993).
5. Consumer price indexes for major expenditure classes, *Economic Report of the President* (1993).
6. Population and labor force, *Economic Report of the President* (1993).
7. Employment by selected industry, *Statistical Abstract of the U.S.* (1993).
8. Unemployment rates, by industry, *Statistical Abstract of the U.S.* (1993).
9. Unemployment rates, approximating U.S. concepts, in nine countries, *Monthly Labor Review* (November 1993).
10. Mean money earnings of persons, by educational attainment, sex and age, *Statistical Abstract of the U.S.* (1993).
11. Federal minimum hourly wage rates, of US (1993).
12. Gross stock of fixed private capital, by industry, *Statistical Abstract of the U.S.* (1992).
13. Interest rates in money and capital markets, *Federal Reserve Bulletin* (December 1993).
14. Flow of funds accounts—assets and liabilities of households, *Statistical Abstract of the U.S.* (1993).
15. Money stock, liquid assets, and debt measures, *Federal Reserve Bulletin* (December 1993).
16. U.S. domestic exports and general imports of selected commodities, by area, *Statistical Abstract of the U.S.* (1993).
17. Foreign exchange rates, *Federal Reserve Bulletin* (December 1993).
18. Insured commercial banks—assets and liabilities, *Statistical Abstract of the U.S.* (1993).

19. Insured commercial banks—assets, deposits, and problem banks, by state, *Statistical Abstract of the U.S.* (1993).
20. National health expenditures, by object, *Statistical Abstract of the U.S.* (1993).
21. Federal and state and local government receipts and expenditures, *Economic Report of the President* (1993).
22. Federal receipts, outlays and debt (fiscal years), *Economic Report of the President* (1993).
23. The government of the United States (organization chart), *Statistical Abstract of the U.S.* (1993).

TABLE 1

2.16 GROSS DOMESTIC PRODUCT AND INCOME

Billions of current dollars except as noted; quarterly data at seasonally adjusted annual rates

Account	1990[r]	1991[r]	1992[r]	1992[r] Q2	1992[r] Q3	1992[r] Q4	1993[r] Q1	1993[r] Q2
GROSS DOMESTIC PRODUCT								
1 Total	**5,546.1**	**5,722.9**	**6,038.5**	**5,991.4**	**6,059.5**	**6,194.4**	**6,261.6**	**6,327.6**
By source								
2 Personal consumption expenditures	3,761.2	3,906.4	4,139.9	4,099.9	4,157.1	4,256.2	4,296.2	4,359.9
3 Durable goods	468.2	457.8	497.3	487.8	500.9	516.6	515.3	531.6
4 Nondurable goods	1,229.2	1,257.9	1,300.9	1,288.2	1,305.7	1,331.7	1,335.3	1,344.8
5 Services	2,063.8	2,190.7	2,341.6	2,323.8	2,350.5	2,407.9	2,445.5	2,483.4
6 Gross private domestic investment	808.9	736.9	796.5	799.7	802.2	833.3	874.1	874.1
7 Fixed investment	802.0	745.5	789.1	786.8	792.5	821.3	839.5	861.0
8 Nonresidential	586.7	555.9	565.5	566.3	569.2	579.5	594.7	619.1
9 Structures	201.6	182.6	172.6	174.5	170.8	171.1	172.4	177.6
10 Producers' durable equipment	385.1	373.3	392.9	391.7	398.4	408.3	422.2	441.6
11 Residential structures	215.3	189.6	223.6	220.6	223.3	241.8	244.9	241.9
12 Change in business inventories	6.9	−8.6	7.3	12.9	9.7	12.0	34.6	13.1
13 Nonfarm	3.8	−8.6	2.3	6.2	4.4	9.5	33.0	16.8
14 Net exports of goods and services	−71.4	−19.6	−29.6	−33.9	−38.8	−38.8	−48.3	−65.1
15 Exports	557.1	601.5	640.5	632.4	641.1	654.7	651.3	660.0
16 Imports	628.5	621.1	670.1	666.3	679.9	693.5	699.6	725.0
17 Government purchases of goods and services	1,047.4	1,099.3	1,131.8	1,125.8	1,139.1	1,143.8	1,139.7	1,158.6
18 Federal	426.5	445.9	448.8	444.6	452.8	452.4	442.7	447.5
19 State and local	620.9	653.4	683.0	681.2	686.2	691.4	697.0	711.1
By major type of product								
20 Final sales, total	5,539.3	5,731.6	6,031.2	5,978.6	6,049.9	6,182.5	6,227.1	6,314.5
21 Goods	2,178.4	2,227.0	2,305.5	2,278.4	2,308.6	2,365.6	2,362.9	2,395.0
22 Durable	933.6	934.3	975.8	963.2	978.4	1,008.3	1,003.5	1,037.8
23 Nondurable	1,244.8	1,292.8	1,329.6	1,315.1	1,330.2	1,357.3	1,359.3	1,357.1
24 Services	2,849.5	3,032.7	3,221.1	3,196.2	3,239.3	3,296.1	3,341.8	3,388.1
25 Structures	511.5	471.9	504.7	504.0	501.9	520.8	522.4	531.5
26 Change in business inventories	6.9	−8.6	7.3	12.9	9.7	12.0	34.6	13.1
27 Durable goods	−2.1	−12.9	2.1	16.7	5.7	−1.2	15.0	2.7
28 Nondurable goods	9.0	4.3	5.3	−3.8	4.0	13.2	19.5	10.4
MEMO								
29 Total GDP in 1987 dollars	**4,897.3**	**4,861.4**	**4,986.3**	**4,956.5**	**4,998.2**	**5,068.3**	**5,078.2**	**5,102.1**
NATIONAL INCOME								
30 Total	**4,491.0**	**4,598.3**	**4,836.6**	**4,814.6**	**4,800.8**	**4,975.8**	**5,038.9**	**5,104.0**
31 Compensation of employees	3,297.6	3,402.4	3,582.0	3,558.1	3,603.6	3,658.6	3,705.1	3,750.6
32 Wages and salaries	2,745.0	2,814.9	2,953.1	2,933.6	2,970.7	3,015.8	3,054.3	3,082.7
33 Government and government enterprises	516.0	545.3	567.5	566.9	569.7	574.2	584.1	586.3
34 Other	2,229.0	2,269.6	2,385.6	2,366.8	2,401.0	2,441.6	2,470.2	2,496.3
35 Supplement to wages and salaries	552.5	587.5	629.0	624.5	632.9	642.8	650.7	668.0
36 Employer contributions for social insurance	278.3	290.6	306.3	304.6	306.9	311.3	312.2	321.4
37 Other labor income	274.3	296.9	322.7	319.9	326.0	331.5	338.5	346.6
38 Proprietors' income[1]	363.3	376.4	414.3	411.1	408.1	431.2	444.1	439.4
39 Business and professional[1]	321.4	339.5	370.6	366.2	371.3	383.6	388.4	392.4
40 Farm[1]	41.9	36.8	43.7	44.9	36.8	47.6	55.7	47.0
41 Rental income of persons[2]	−14.2	−12.8	−8.9	−7.2	−18.5	−1.2	7.5	12.7
42 Corporate profits[1]	380.6	369.5	407.2	411.7	367.5	439.5	432.1	458.1
43 Profits before tax[3]	365.7	362.3	395.4	409.5	357.9	409.9	419.8	445.6
44 Inventory valuation adjustment	−11.0	4.9	−5.3	−13.7	−7.8	4.9	−12.7	−12.2
45 Capital consumption adjustment	25.9	2.2	17.1	16.0	17.4	24.7	25.1	24.7
46 Net interest	463.7	462.8	442.0	440.8	440.1	447.7	450.1	443.2

1. With inventory valuation and capital consumption adjustments.
2. With capital consumption adjustment.

3. For after-tax profits, dividends, and the like, see table 1.48.
SOURCE. U.S. Department of Commerce, *Survey of Current Business*.

TABLE 2

Table 12.—Gross Domestic Product by Industry in Constant Dollars, Fixed 1987 Weights [1]

[Billions of 1987 dollars]

	Line	1977	1978	1979	1980	1981	1982	1983	1984	1985	1986	1987*	1987*	1988	1989	1990
Gross domestic product	1	3,533.3	3,703.5	3,796.8	3,776.3	3,843.1	3,760.3	3,906.6	4,148.5	4,279.8	4,404.5	4,539.9	4,539.9	4,718.6	4,838.0	4,877.5
Private industries	2	3,017.3	3,169.7	3,238.1	3,202.7	3,272.6	3,246.3	3,361.8	3,620.4	3,759.2	3,871.2	4,019.4	4,019.4	4,188.0	4,288.8	4,311.4
Agriculture, forestry, and fisheries	3	63.7	59.2	62.4	63.2	72.7	73.3	68.4	71.5	81.9	84.5	88.5	88.5	85.1	88.0	94.2
Farms	4	53.8	48.2	50.4	51.0	60.8	60.2	53.7	55.1	64.2	64.3	66.0	66.0	63.2	66.2	70.5
Agricultural services, forestry, and fisheries	5	9.8	11.1	12.0	12.2	11.9	13.1	14.8	16.4	17.7	20.2	22.5	22.5	21.9	21.8	23.7
Mining	6	83.5	85.0	71.9	79.9	74.2	73.1	71.3	82.0	83.3	83.0	83.0	83.0	94.4	83.7	87.7
Metal mining	7	1.7	1.5	1.6	1.6	2.5	2.6	2.7	2.8	2.5	2.9	2.6	2.6	4.4	5.4	6.0
Coal mining	8	9.5	8.9	8.5	10.1	10.3	11.1	10.2	11.5	11.3	13.0	12.5	12.5	13.8	14.8	15.6
Oil and gas extraction	9	65.7	67.1	54.7	61.8	56.1	54.5	52.9	60.9	63.2	60.2	60.8	60.8	69.1	56.2	58.6
Nonmetallic minerals, except fuels	10	6.7	7.5	7.0	6.4	5.3	4.8	5.4	6.8	6.3	6.9	7.2	7.2	7.1	7.3	7.6
Construction	11	190.8	198.8	200.3	185.4	174.7	164.9	170.0	190.9	209.0	209.1	213.0	213.0	211.2	212.8	208.5
Manufacturing	12	741.6	773.1	777.1	725.4	746.7	711.1	733.8	791.4	810.5	819.1	878.4	877.8	924.6	932.4	922.8
Durable goods	13	440.9	460.9	458.0	424.3	429.7	392.4	402.5	458.4	468.1	471.5	503.2	501.9	537.0	543.0	535.0
Lumber and wood products	14	23.1	23.3	23.4	21.6	19.5	19.3	22.5	25.3	24.9	27.5	31.0	31.3	30.3	29.4	28.7
Furniture and fixtures	15	11.1	12.0	11.1	11.6	11.8	11.0	12.3	13.5	14.3	14.3	15.2	15.2	15.2	15.4	14.2
Stone, clay, and glass products	16	25.8	26.8	26.7	23.8	22.3	18.2	22.0	23.9	24.5	25.9	24.8	24.0	25.1	26.0	26.0
Primary metal industries	17	54.7	58.0	54.1	49.2	51.0	38.0	32.3	37.7	35.3	38.5	36.3	36.3	34.5	33.3	35.1
Fabricated metal products	18	52.7	54.9	57.3	54.6	55.2	49.1	50.6	56.4	57.6	56.4	59.2	59.3	61.9	61.1	59.0
Machinery, except electrical	19	81.8	85.0	85.9	81.2	81.6	69.4	66.8	73.7	77.9	74.6	87.1	...	...	...	...
Industrial machinery and equipment	20	...	...	...	...	...	...	...	...	...	...	...	88.2	97.3	102.6	102.0
Electric and electronic equipment	21	54.1	60.1	64.3	69.8	72.7	66.9	70.6	80.4	83.4	83.8	91.3	...	...	...	...
Electronic and other electric equipment	22	...	...	...	...	...	...	...	...	...	...	...	76.8	84.6	90.8	87.9
Motor vehicles and equipment	23	66.7	68.1	60.5	39.8	45.0	39.4	47.2	59.3	62.8	58.0	58.5	58.7	63.0	56.5	48.1
Other transportation equipment	24	35.3	36.5	38.2	38.3	32.3	44.2	41.8	45.5	46.7	51.2	57.5	56.6	58.3	61.0	64.3
Instruments and related products	25	22.1	23.1	24.3	24.2	26.1	25.3	26.1	27.9	26.7	27.3	27.3	40.4	49.8	49.6	52.7
Miscellaneous manufacturing industries	26	13.6	13.2	12.1	10.4	12.2	11.6	10.2	14.7	14.1	14.0	15.0	15.0	17.0	17.3	17.1
Nondurable goods	27	300.7	312.2	319.2	301.1	317.1	318.7	331.3	333.0	342.4	347.7	375.2	375.9	387.6	389.4	387.8
Food and kindred products	28	56.6	60.9	62.4	64.3	65.9	73.3	72.2	71.2	74.7	73.1	78.9	78.9	82.4	79.5	81.4
Tobacco manufactures	29	18.9	19.9	19.8	19.7	20.9	17.3	15.7	14.7	14.4	14.5	13.0	13.0	12.2	10.4	10.0
Textile mill products	30	17.0	17.3	17.8	17.3	17.2	16.3	18.1	18.3	18.0	19.3	20.3	20.3	20.0	20.9	21.2
Apparel and other textile products	31	18.7	20.5	21.5	20.4	19.9	18.6	20.4	21.0	20.9	21.9	22.6	22.6	23.5	24.7	23.7
Paper and allied products	32	32.8	33.9	33.5	30.9	31.0	31.9	34.4	35.4	35.7	36.9	38.7	38.5	39.7	39.5	42.2
Printing and publishing	33	49.1	51.5	54.5	52.7	53.6	53.8	54.9	57.4	58.9	58.6	61.0	61.0	63.1	64.1	62.2
Chemicals and allied products	34	65.1	67.7	65.1	57.5	62.0	63.8	68.1	66.4	67.0	74.8	82.3	82.3	83.2	84.1	88.0
Petroleum and coal products	35	21.0	17.6	21.1	15.0	21.4	19.6	21.7	20.6	23.3	19.4	25.9	25.9	29.7	30.4	22.8
Rubber and miscellaneous plastics products	36	16.5	17.8	18.9	18.5	20.4	19.4	21.3	24.2	26.1	26.0	29.0	29.9	30.0	32.2	32.5
Leather and leather products	37	4.9	5.1	4.5	4.8	4.7	4.6	4.2	4.0	3.6	3.2	3.5	3.5	3.7	3.7	3.9
Transportation and public utilities	38	314.3	325.1	335.5	336.3	337.1	331.3	351.7	377.6	381.8	386.9	419.9	419.8	431.5	443.0	456.0
Transportation	39	117.2	121.2	126.2	120.2	116.5	115.5	127.3	136.6	137.4	142.6	152.8	152.7	150.1	154.7	160.9
Railroad transportation	40	16.1	17.6	18.2	18.5	17.9	15.6	17.3	19.6	19.6	19.5	21.7	21.7	23.1	22.1	23.5
Local and interurban passenger transit	41	9.9	9.6	9.5	8.5	7.7	7.3	7.4	8.3	8.3	8.6	8.7	8.7	8.1	8.7	8.7
Trucking and warehousing	42	52.7	52.5	53.5	50.8	47.1	46.1	52.2	57.2	58.2	59.5	61.0	61.0	57.8	60.7	60.7
Water transportation	43	8.6	9.2	9.3	9.3	9.7	9.0	8.5	8.6	8.4	8.2	8.0	8.0	7.7	7.8	8.1
Transportation by air	44	17.0	20.0	21.7	19.2	19.1	21.5	25.5	26.5	25.5	30.2	35.1	35.1	34.8	35.6	39.9
Pipelines, except natural gas	45	6.1	4.5	5.7	5.3	5.9	6.7	6.3	5.4	5.4	4.3	5.2	5.2	4.8	5.0	4.9
Transportation services	46	6.8	7.8	8.3	8.7	9.0	9.3	10.0	11.0	12.0	12.5	13.1	13.1	13.8	14.7	15.0
Communications	47	73.5	80.7	86.2	94.4	98.7	101.0	107.6	116.3	115.8	117.8	127.6	127.6	135.1	135.7	140.4
Telephone and telegraph	48	60.6	67.2	72.6	80.9	85.0	87.0	93.6	101.7	102.5	105.6	113.7	111.2	117.0	116.2	121.2
Radio and television	49	12.9	13.5	13.5	13.5	13.7	13.9	14.0	14.6	13.3	12.2	13.9	16.4	18.1	19.5	19.2
Electric, gas, and sanitary services	50	123.7	123.2	123.1	121.6	121.9	114.9	116.8	124.7	128.6	126.5	139.5	139.5	146.3	152.6	154.8
Wholesale trade	51	170.1	185.8	195.8	190.5	207.5	218.2	224.2	259.5	273.0	307.1	302.6	303.1	313.4	329.4	323.1
Retail trade	52	318.0	338.1	334.8	320.1	330.6	336.8	365.1	397.7	421.4	453.2	440.1	441.8	467.0	483.7	478.0
Finance, insurance, and real estate	53	596.5	631.0	667.4	692.8	704.7	708.4	727.9	762.1	776.4	776.6	809.9	809.7	847.4	869.0	868.3
Banking	54	92.6	96.9	102.3	107.1	111.2	113.0	113.4	114.4	116.2	118.1	118.7	...	...	...	...
Depository institutions	55	...	...	...	...	...	...	...	...	...	...	...	134.7	134.6	135.5	135.2
Credit agencies other than banks	56	18.0	19.7	20.9	21.4	22.1	22.1	24.4	26.9	28.8	31.7	34.0	...	...	...	...
Nondepository institutions	57	...	...	...	...	...	...	...	...	...	...	...	17.4	17.4	17.3	18.1
Security and commodity brokers	58	12.8	15.2	15.6	17.5	20.0	17.9	24.4	22.6	26.7	26.5	37.8	37.9	36.4	41.7	39.9
Insurance carriers	59	53.8	57.0	58.6	61.1	56.9	53.4	52.9	58.8	58.7	55.4	51.2	51.2	60.9	66.2	57.6
Insurance agents, brokers, and service	60	21.3	21.5	21.6	22.5	23.6	25.6	25.6	27.1	27.1	27.5	30.1	30.2	31.2	30.8	32.9
Real estate	61	389.0	411.4	438.3	453.0	460.2	464.8	475.2	499.2	504.7	502.0	521.3	521.5	549.4	560.2	566.3
Nonfarm housing services	62	275.4	288.3	301.9	321.7	333.4	339.6	340.3	350.2	358.4	360.5	368.9	368.9	378.4	385.0	390.4
Other real estate	63	113.6	123.0	136.4	131.3	126.8	125.2	135.0	149.0	146.3	141.5	152.4	152.6	170.9	175.2	176.0
Holding and other investment offices	64	9.0	9.4	10.1	10.2	10.7	11.7	11.9	13.2	14.2	15.5	16.9	16.9	17.4	17.4	18.4
Services	65	538.9	573.5	592.8	609.0	624.4	629.2	649.5	687.8	722.0	751.7	784.0	782.5	813.5	846.8	872.9
Hotels and other lodging places	66	33.3	34.8	33.7	31.0	30.9	31.6	34.6	37.0	39.2	40.7	42.6	42.6	43.1	45.3	44.2
Personal services	67	28.4	28.8	28.1	27.6	27.1	26.5	27.4	28.4	31.1	32.0	32.2	31.0	32.8	32.2	30.7
Business services	68	79.5	88.4	97.2	103.9	109.9	113.2	121.6	138.6	151.2	162.6	174.6	141.6	152.3	163.2	172.3
Auto repair, services, and parking	69	28.9	31.2	32.6	31.7	31.4	30.3	31.9	34.8	39.3	39.0	38.2	38.2	39.3	38.2	39.2
Miscellaneous repair services	70	11.0	12.2	12.6	13.5	13.0	12.4	12.8	14.3	12.6	14.0	13.7	13.7	14.9	16.0	16.1
Motion pictures	71	7.6	10.2	9.4	9.0	9.3	10.0	9.9	10.5	11.1	12.0	12.9	13.7	13.0	15.1	14.1
Amusement and recreation services	72	16.5	17.3	18.4	19.5	20.5	21.2	22.6	22.8	24.9	25.8	27.4	28.1	29.1	31.4	34.4
Health services	73	176.0	182.4	187.6	196.1	202.1	206.4	208.2	209.6	213.6	216.1	228.9	228.9	229.9	232.8	237.6
Legal services	74	46.1	49.6	50.6	51.5	51.6	52.3	51.6	54.8	56.5	61.0	61.1	61.1	66.0	66.0	65.9
Educational services	75	24.7	25.5	25.6	26.3	25.9	26.2	26.8	27.8	28.4	28.7	30.4	30.3	31.6	32.3	33.0
Social services and membership organizations	76	33.9	35.8	36.9	37.8	38.1	38.0	39.0	40.3	41.4	43.5	45.7	45.7	50.1	54.4	57.1
Miscellaneous professional services	77	44.0	48.0	52.1	53.9	57.9	54.3	56.5	61.5	65.1	68.3	68.8	...	...	...	...
Other services	78	...	...	...	...	...	...	...	...	...	...	...	100.0	103.0	111.4	119.6
Private households	79	9.1	9.3	8.1	7.2	6.7	6.6	6.6	7.5	7.5	7.8	7.7	7.7	8.2	8.7	8.8
Government	80	475.7	488.3	498.6	508.9	511.6	507.1	512.5	516.9	527.5	536.4	545.3	545.3	555.9	567.0	581.7
Federal	81	171.7	176.5	175.7	178.7	179.6	176.2	179.8	180.6	182.6	182.9	185.4	185.4	188.3	189.9	193.3
General government	82	137.0	138.4	137.5	139.2	140.9	142.4	144.8	146.4	148.6	149.0	151.4	151.4	153.5	154.2	156.3
Government enterprises	83	34.7	38.0	38.2	39.4	38.7	33.8	35.0	34.2	34.0	33.9	34.0	34.0	34.8	35.7	37.1
State and local	84	304.0	311.8	322.9	330.3	332.0	330.9	332.7	336.3	344.9	353.5	360.0	360.0	367.6	377.0	388.4
General government	85	278.6	285.8	295.0	301.1	303.0	301.8	302.6	305.4	313.2	320.8	327.3	327.3	333.9	342.7	353.5
Government enterprises	86	25.4	26.0	27.9	29.2	29.1	29.1	30.1	30.9	31.7	32.7	32.7	32.7	33.7	34.3	34.9
Statistical discrepancy [2]	87	19.4	12.2	20.6	19.0	13.6	–8.7	11.5	–9.8	–14.7	1.3	–24.8	–24.8	–27.4	.9	4.9
Residual [3]	88	20.8	33.4	39.6	45.7	45.3	15.6	20.8	21.0	7.7	–4.4	0	0	2.1	–18.6	–20.5

* Estimates for the year 1987 are shown on the basis of both the 1972 and 1987 Standard Industrial Classification (SIC). The estimate based on the 1972 SIC is shown first and is comparable with estimates back to 1977; the estimate based on the 1987 SIC is shown second and is comparable with estimates after 1987.

1. Constant 1987 dollar values are equal to fixed-weighted quantity indexes with 1987 weights divided by 100 and multiplied by the 1987 value of current-dollar GDP.

2. Equals the current-dollar statistical discrepancy deflated by the implicit price deflator for gross domestic business product.

3. Equals GDP in constant dollars measured as the sum of expenditures less the statistical discrepancy in constant dollars and GDP in constant dollars measured as the sum of gross product originating by industry.

TABLE 3

No. 685. Gross State Product, by Industry: 1989

[In billions of dollars. For definition of gross state product, see text, section 14. Industries based on *1972 Standard Industrial Classification Manual*; see text, section 13]

DIVISION AND STATE	Total [1]	Farms, forestry, and fisheries [2]	Construction	Manufacturing	Transportation and public utilities	Wholesale trade	Retail trade	Finance, insurance, and real estate	Services	Government [3]
U.S. . . .	5,165	113	248	966	461	339	486	897	971	604
N.E.	312	3	16	63	22	21	31	58	68	29
ME	23	1	2	5	2	1	3	4	4	3
NH	25	(Z)	1	6	2	1	3	5	5	2
VT	12	(Z)	1	2	1	1	1	2	2	1
MA	145	1	8	27	10	11	14	24	36	13
RI	19	(Z)	1	4	1	1	2	3	4	2
CT	89	1	4	19	7	6	9	19	17	8
M.A.	872	7	42	149	78	64	73	181	186	90
NY	441	3	20	62	37	33	35	102	99	49
NJ	203	1	11	37	19	17	17	42	40	19
PA	228	3	10	49	23	14	21	37	47	22
E.N.C.	849	16	35	216	75	57	79	141	146	81
OH	212	3	8	58	19	13	20	34	36	20
IN	105	3	5	30	10	6	10	16	15	9
IL	256	5	12	51	26	21	23	45	50	23
MI	182	2	7	50	13	11	17	31	31	18
WI	94	4	3	26	7	6	8	16	14	9
W.N.C.	349	19	13	69	35	24	33	59	57	37
MN	94	4	3	20	8	7	9	17	16	9
IA	53	5	2	11	4	3	5	10	8	5
MO	100	2	4	23	11	7	10	15	18	10
ND	11	1	1	1	1	1	1	2	2	1
SD	11	1	(Z)	1	1	1	1	2	2	1
NE	31	4	1	4	3	2	3	5	5	4
KS	49	3	2	9	6	3	5	8	7	6
S.A.	865	17	49	145	78	54	88	135	161	132
DE	15	(Z)	1	4	1	1	1	3	2	2
MD	99	1	6	11	8	6	11	17	22	17
DC	39	(Z)	3	1	2	1	2	3	12	16
VA	136	2	9	22	12	7	12	22	24	25
WV	28	(Z)	1	4	4	1	2	5	4	3
NC	130	3	5	39	11	8	13	18	17	16
SC	60	1	2	15	5	3	6	13	8	9
GA	130	2	6	25	14	12	13	20	21	16
FL	227	6	16	23	20	16	28	38	51	28
E.S.C.	264	7	11	64	24	15	25	39	39	34
KY	66	2	3	15	6	3	6	10	9	8
TN	92	2	4	22	7	6	10	14	15	11
AL.	68	2	2	16	7	4	6	10	10	10
MS	38	1	2	11	4	2	4	5	5	5
W.S.C.	509	12	21	86	57	32	46	76	83	58
AR	37	2	2	9	4	2	4	5	5	4
LA.	79	1	4	12	9	4	7	12	12	8
OK	52	2	2	7	6	3	5	7	8	8
TX	340	7	14	57	38	23	30	51	57	39
Mt.	254	8	15	29	26	13	26	40	51	35
MT	13	1	1	1	1	1	1	2	2	2
ID	16	2	(Z)	3	2	1	2	2	3	2
WY	11	(Z)	1	(Z)	2	(Z)	1	2	1	1
CO	66	2	3	9	7	4	7	10	14	9
NM	25	1	1	2	3	1	2	4	5	5
AZ	65	2	5	8	6	3	7	11	13	9
UT	28	1	1	5	3	2	3	4	5	4
NV	28	(Z)	3	1	2	1	3	4	10	3
Pac.	891	23	45	146	66	59	86	168	179	107
WA	96	4	6	16	8	7	11	14	16	14
OR	52	2	2	10	5	4	5	9	9	6
CA	697	16	34	118	49	46	66	139	146	78
AK	20	1	1	1	1	(Z)	1	1	2	4
HI	26	1	2	1	2	3	3	3	6	5

Z Less than $500 million.   [1] Includes mining, not shown separately.   [2] Includes agricultural services.   [3] Includes Federal civilian and military, State and local government.

Source: U.S Bureau of Economic Analysis, *Survey of Current Business*, December 1991.

TABLE 4

No. 699. Personal Consumption Expenditures, by Type of Expenditure, in Current and Constant (1987) Dollars: 1970 to 1991

[In billions of dollars]

TYPE OF EXPENDITURE	CURRENT DOLLARS				CONSTANT (1987) DOLLARS			
	1970	1980	1990	1991	1970	1980	1990	1991
Personal consumption expenditures [1]	646.5	1,748.1	3,748.4	3,887.7	1,813.5	2,447.1	3,260.4	3,240.8
Food and tobacco [1]	152.9	362.6	644.7	665.4	431.0	487.5	552.7	547.2
Food purchased for off-premise consumption	104.4	241.7	398.4	407.4	283.6	307.5	343.4	339.0
Purchased meals and beverages [2]	34.9	93.4	191.4	198.5	105.8	132.3	167.3	166.7
Tobacco products	10.8	20.9	43.4	47.8	33.5	38.7	31.9	31.5
Clothing, accessories, and jewelry [1]	57.6	131.8	258.6	260.6	107.8	157.1	229.0	222.5
Shoes	7.8	17.4	31.3	31.1	14.4	19.9	28.0	27.5
Clothing	39.8	89.8	175.5	177.7	66.3	106.0	159.1	
Jewelry and watches	4.1	15.0	31.1	30.1	8.4	16.8	25.2	23.6
Personal care	11.8	26.9	59.5	62.2	34.0	38.0	52.5	53.0
Housing [1]	94.0	255.2	547.5	574.0	269.3	399.4	474.7	478.2
Owner-occupied nonfarm dwellings-space rent	61.3	178.4	379.8	399.1	174.4	278.7	326.9	330.7
Tenant-occupied nonfarm dwellings-space rent	26.0	61.8	140.8	147.3	75.1	98.2	125.2	126.5
Household operation [1]	84.8	233.6	434.7	441.7	239.2	315.3	406.1	401.9
Furniture [3]	8.6	20.7	35.3	33.4	17.8	25.8	33.5	31.4
Semidurable house furnishings [4]	4.9	10.6	21.3	21.4	12.2	14.9	20.0	19.7
Cleaning and polishing preparations	8.2	22.9	51.5	52.8	26.4	31.2	45.3	45.0
Household utilities	22.7	81.1	136.4	143.2	92.3	111.7	124.1	126.2
Electricity	9.6	37.2	70.7	75.2	33.3	54.0	66.1	67.8
Gas	5.6	19.1	26.9	28.4	27.0	27.6	26.3	27.4
Water and other sanitary services	3.2	9.4	26.1	28.0	11.7	16.2	21.6	21.4
Fuel oil and coal	4.4	15.4	12.6	11.7	20.2	14.0	10.1	9.7
Telephone and telegraph	10.1	27.6	53.2	54.3	19.9	41.1	54.4	55.1
Medical care [1]	60.0	207.2	595.9	656.0	208.7	346.5	482.4	497.3
Drug preparations and sundries [5]	8.1	21.8	60.3	64.6	23.5	38.8	49.0	48.9
Physicians	14.0	42.8	134.2	148.1	52.7	72.9	108.8	113.4
Dentists	4.9	13.7	32.2	34.5	16.0	22.4	26.6	26.5
Hospitals and nursing homes [6]	23.4	98.7	269.0	296.5	87.1	164.0	217.5	223.9
Health insurance	4.4	12.8	35.6	38.3	13.9	23.0	25.0	24.3
Medical care [7]	2.1	7.6	30.0	31.9	10.0	17.7	19.4	19.4
Personal business [1]	32.0	101.6	297.4	317.7	119.5	175.5	250.1	252.8
Expense of handling life insurance [8]	7.1	23.4	57.1	59.7	22.6	37.8	49.7	50.1
Legal services	4.9	13.6	49.7	51.4	21.7	26.6	42.0	41.0
Funeral and burial expenses	2.3	4.6	8.3	8.9	8.2	8.8	7.2	7.2
Transportation	81.1	235.7	453.7	438.2	219.5	274.8	403.2	377.4
User-operated transportation [1]	74.2	214.9	413.5	398.4	198.8	247.4	368.9	343.4
New autos	21.9	46.4	96.7	79.5	47.4	60.2	91.6	72.6
Net purchases of used autos	4.8	10.8	33.7	35.8	20.9	20.8	33.4	35.0
Tires, tubes, accessories, etc.	6.1	14.9	22.5	23.0	10.8	15.3	21.4	21.6
Repair, greasing, washing, parking, storage, rental, and leasing	12.3	33.7	82.5	83.7	39.3	48.3	72.6	70.8
Gasoline and oil	21.9	86.7	108.5	105.5	62.9	72.0	864.0	85.2
Purchased local transportation	3.0	4.8	8.9	9.1	8.8	7.8	7.8	7.6
Mass transit systems	1.8	2.9	5.7	5.7	5.3	5.3	5.0	4.9
Taxicab	1.2	1.9	3.2	3.4	3.5	2.5	2.8	2.7
Purchased intercity transportation [1]	4.0	16.1	31.2	30.7	11.9	19.7	26.5	26.4
Railway (commutation)	0.2	0.3	0.7	0.7	0.8	0.5	0.6	0.6
Bus	0.5	1.4	1.4	1.5	2.3	2.4	1.3	1.3
Airline	3.1	13.5	26.5	25.8	8.1	15.2	22.4	22.3
Recreation [1] [9]	43.1	117.6	280.7	289.7	91.3	149.1	257.3	258.7
Magazines, newspapers, and sheet music	4.1	12.0	24.1	24.6	13.2	18.4	21.2	20.3
Nondurable toys and sport supplies	5.5	14.6	31.4	32.2	9.5	17.4	28.1	28.4
Radio and television receivers, records, and musical instruments	8.5	19.9	49.6	50.2	8.8	17.6	53.2	56.2
Education and research	12.5	33.6	86.4	92.8	41.6	51.7	73.8	74.9
Religious and welfare activities	12.1	38.6	102.1	107.7	35.4	51.3	90.4	92.1

[1] Includes other expenditures not shown separately. [2] Consists of purchases (including tips) of meals and beverages from retail, service, and amusement establishments, hotels, dining and buffet cars, schools, school fraternities, institutions, clubs, and industrial lunch rooms. Includes meals and beverages consumed both on and off-premise. [3] Includes mattresses and bedsprings. [4] Consists largely of textile house furnishings including piece goods allocated to house furnishing use. Also includes lamp shades, brooms, and brushes. [5] Excludes drug preparations and related products dispensed by physicians, hospitals, and other medical services. [6] Consists of (1) current expenditures (including consumption of fixed capital) of nonprofit hospitals and nursing homes, and (2) payments by patients to proprietary and government hospitals and nursing homes. [7] Consists of (1) premiums, less benefits and dividends, for health, hospitalization and accidental death and dismemberment insurance provided by commercial insurance carriers, and (2) administrative expenses (including consumption of fixed capital) of Blue Cross and Blue Shield plans and of other independent prepaid and self-insured health plans. [8] Consist of (1) operating expenses of life insurance carriers and private noninsured pension plans, and (2) premiums, less benefits and dividends of fraternal benefit societies. Excludes expenses allocated by commercial carriers to accident and health insurance. [9] For additional details, see table 398.

Source: U.S. Bureau of Economic Analysis, *National Income and Product Accounts, volume 2, 1959-88*, and *Survey of Current Business*, July 1992.

TABLE 5

TABLE B-56.—*Consumer price indexes for major expenditure classes, 1950–92*

[For all urban consumers; 1982–84 = 100]

| Year or month | All items (CPI–U) | Food and beverages | | Housing | | | | Apparel and upkeep | Transportation [2] | Medical care [2] | Entertainment | Other goods and services | Energy [3] |
		Total [1]	Food [2]	Total	Shelter [2]	Fuel and other utilities [2]	Household furnishings and operation						
1950	24.1		25.4					40.3	22.7	15.1			
1951	26.0		28.2					43.9	24.1	15.9			
1952	26.5		28.7					43.5	25.7	16.7			
1953	26.7		28.3		22.0	22.5		43.1	26.5	17.3			
1954	26.9		28.2		22.5	22.6		43.1	26.1	17.8			
1955	26.8		27.8		22.7	23.0		42.9	25.8	18.2			
1956	27.2		28.0		23.1	23.6		43.7	26.2	18.9			
1957	28.1		28.9		24.0	24.3		44.5	27.7	19.7			21.5
1958	28.9		30.2		24.5	24.8		44.6	28.6	20.6			21.5
1959	29.1		29.7		24.7	25.4		45.0	29.8	21.5			21.9
1960	29.6		30.0		25.2	26.0		45.7	29.8	22.3			22.4
1961	29.9		30.4		25.4	26.3		46.1	30.1	22.9			22.5
1962	30.2		30.6		25.8	26.3		46.3	30.8	23.5			22.6
1963	30.6		31.1		26.1	26.6		46.9	30.9	24.1			22.6
1964	31.0		31.5		26.5	26.6		47.3	31.4	24.6			22.5
1965	31.5		32.2		27.0	26.6		47.8	31.9	25.2			22.9
1966	32.4		33.8		27.8	26.7		49.0	32.3	26.3			23.3
1967	33.4	35.0	34.1	30.8	28.8	27.1	42.0	51.0	33.3	28.2	40.7	35.1	23.8
1968	34.8	36.2	35.3	32.0	30.1	27.4	43.6	53.7	34.3	29.9	43.0	36.9	24.2
1969	36.7	38.1	37.1	34.0	32.6	28.0	45.2	56.8	35.7	31.9	45.2	38.7	24.8
1970	38.8	40.1	39.2	36.4	35.5	29.1	46.8	59.2	37.5	34.0	47.5	40.9	25.5
1971	40.5	41.4	40.4	38.0	37.0	31.1	48.6	61.1	39.5	36.1	50.0	42.9	26.5
1972	41.8	43.1	42.1	39.4	38.7	32.5	49.7	62.3	39.9	37.3	51.5	44.7	27.2
1973	44.4	48.8	48.2	41.2	40.5	34.3	51.1	64.6	41.2	38.8	52.9	46.4	29.4
1974	49.3	55.5	55.1	45.8	44.4	40.7	56.8	69.4	45.8	42.4	56.9	49.8	38.1
1975	53.8	60.2	59.8	50.7	48.8	45.4	63.4	72.5	50.1	47.5	62.0	53.9	42.1
1976	56.9	62.1	61.6	53.8	51.5	49.4	67.3	75.2	55.1	52.0	65.1	57.0	45.1
1977	60.6	65.8	65.5	57.4	54.9	54.7	70.4	78.6	59.0	57.0	68.3	60.4	49.4
1978	65.2	72.2	72.0	62.4	60.5	58.5	74.7	81.4	61.7	61.8	71.9	64.3	52.5
1979	72.6	79.9	79.9	70.1	68.9	64.8	79.9	84.9	70.5	67.5	76.7	68.9	65.7
1980	82.4	86.7	86.8	81.1	81.0	75.4	86.3	90.9	83.1	74.9	83.6	75.2	86.0
1981	90.9	93.5	93.6	90.4	90.5	86.4	93.0	95.3	93.2	82.9	90.1	82.6	97.7
1982	96.5	97.3	97.4	96.9	96.9	94.9	98.0	97.8	97.0	92.5	96.0	91.1	99.2
1983	99.6	99.5	99.4	99.5	99.1	100.2	100.2	100.2	99.3	100.6	100.1	101.1	99.9
1984	103.9	103.2	103.2	103.6	104.0	104.8	101.9	102.1	103.7	106.8	103.8	107.9	100.9
1985	107.6	105.6	105.6	107.7	109.8	106.5	103.8	105.0	106.4	113.5	107.9	114.5	101.6
1986	109.6	109.1	109.0	110.9	115.8	104.1	105.2	105.9	102.3	122.0	111.6	121.4	88.2
1987	113.6	113.5	113.5	114.2	121.3	103.0	107.1	110.6	105.4	130.1	115.3	128.5	88.6
1988	118.3	118.2	118.2	118.5	127.1	104.4	109.4	115.4	108.7	138.6	120.3	137.0	89.3
1989	124.0	124.9	125.1	123.0	132.8	107.8	111.2	118.6	114.1	149.3	126.5	147.7	94.3
1990	130.7	132.1	132.4	128.5	140.0	111.6	113.3	124.1	120.5	162.8	132.4	159.0	102.1
1991	136.2	136.8	136.3	133.6	146.3	115.3	116.0	128.7	123.8	177.0	138.4	171.6	102.5
1991: Jan	134.6	135.9	135.8	131.8	144.0	114.8	114.1	123.8	125.5	171.0	135.5	166.5	107.1
Feb	134.8	136.0	135.5	132.4	144.6	114.7	115.6	126.2	123.7	172.5	136.2	167.4	102.8
Mar	135.0	136.3	135.8	132.6	145.2	114.1	115.7	128.8	122.3	173.7	136.7	167.9	99.7
Apr	135.2	137.2	136.7	132.5	145.2	113.1	115.9	130.1	122.2	174.4	137.7	168.8	99.5
May	135.6	137.3	136.8	132.8	145.2	114.2	116.3	129.4	123.3	175.2	137.8	169.1	102.1
June	136.0	137.7	137.2	133.4	145.8	115.8	115.9	126.9	123.7	176.2	138.1	170.0	103.5
July	136.2	137.1	136.5	134.2	146.8	116.4	116.3	125.2	123.4	177.5	138.6	170.8	102.7
Aug	136.6	136.6	136.0	134.5	147.3	116.2	116.2	127.6	123.8	178.9	139.2	172.2	102.9
Sept	137.2	136.7	136.0	134.7	147.4	116.8	116.4	131.3	123.8	179.7	140.2	175.8	103.6
Oct	137.4	136.5	135.8	134.7	147.7	115.7	116.4	132.7	124.0	180.7	140.5	176.2	101.8
Nov	137.8	136.9	136.2	134.7	147.9	115.3	116.5	132.9	125.0	181.8	140.4	176.9	101.8
Dec	137.9	137.3	136.7	135.0	148.2	116.0	116.3	129.6	125.3	182.6	139.9	177.6	101.9
1992: Jan	138.1	137.9	137.2	135.7	149.2	116.2	116.7	127.9	124.5	184.3	140.1	178.6	100.1
Feb	138.6	138.1	137.5	136.1	149.8	115.9	117.3	130.2	124.1	186.2	140.7	179.4	99.0
Mar	139.3	138.8	138.1	136.6	150.4	115.8	117.7	133.4	124.4	187.3	141.2	179.8	98.9
Apr	139.5	138.8	138.1	136.5	150.2	115.8	118.0	133.3	125.2	188.1	142.0	180.3	99.5
May	139.7	138.3	137.4	136.7	150.2	116.8	117.9	133.1	126.3	188.7	142.0	181.3	102.4
June	140.2	138.3	137.4	137.7	151.1	119.0	118.2	131.0	126.9	189.4	142.0	181.5	105.9
July	140.5	138.1	137.2	138.3	151.8	119.4	118.4	129.2	127.2	190.7	142.4	182.3	106.0
Aug	140.9	138.8	138.0	138.6	152.3	119.4	118.3	130.2	126.9	191.5	142.6	183.9	105.4
Sept	141.3	139.3	138.5	138.6	151.9	119.8	118.3	133.3	126.8	192.3	143.2	187.0	105.9
Oct	141.8	139.2	138.3	138.5	152.5	118.5	118.4	135.0	128.0	193.3	143.5	187.9	104.5
Nov	142.0	139.1	138.3	138.5	152.4	118.3	118.5	134.5	129.2	194.3	143.7	188.0	104.5

[1] Includes alcoholic beverages, not shown separately.
[2] See table B-57 for components.
[3] Household fuels—gas (piped), electricity, fuel oil, etc.—and motor fuel. Motor oil, coolant, etc. also included through 1982. See table B-57 for the components.

Note.—Data beginning 1983 incorporate a rental equivalence measure for homeowners' costs.

Source: Department of Labor, Bureau of Labor Statistics.

TABLE 6

TABLE B-30.—*Population and the labor force, 1929-92*

[Monthly data seasonally adjusted, except as noted]

Year or month	Civilian noninsti- tutional popula- tion [1]	Resi- dent Armed Forces [1]	Labor force includ- ing resident Armed Forces	Employ- ment includ- ing resident Armed Forces	Civilian labor force					Unemploy- ment rate		Civil- ian labor force par- tici- pation rate [4]	Civil- ian em- ploy- ment/ pop- ula- tion ratio [5]
					Total	Employment			Un- em- ploy- ment	All work- ers [2]	Civil- ian work- ers [3]		
						Total	Agri- cul- tural	Non- agri- cultural					
			Thousands of persons 14 years of age and over									**Percent**	
1929					49,180	47,630	10,450	37,180	1,550		3.2		
1933					51,590	38,760	10,090	28,670	12,830		24.9		
1939					55,230	45,750	9,610	36,140	9,480		17.2		
1940	99,840				55,640	47,520	9,540	37,980	8,120		14.6	55.7	47.6
1941	99,900				55,910	50,350	9,100	41,250	5,560		9.9	56.0	50.4
1942	98,640				56,410	53,750	9,250	44,500	2,660		4.7	57.2	54.5
1943	94,640				55,540	54,470	9,080	45,390	1,070		1.9	58.7	57.6
1944	93,220				54,630	53,960	8,950	45,010	670		1.2	58.6	57.9
1945	94,090				53,860	52,820	8,580	44,240	1,040		1.9	57.2	56.1
1946	103,070				57,520	55,250	8,320	46,930	2,270		3.9	55.8	53.6
1947	106,018				60,168	57,812	8,256	49,557	2,356		3.9	56.8	54.5
			Thousands of persons 16 years of age and over										
1947	101,827				59,350	57,038	7,890	49,148	2,311		3.9	58.3	56.0
1948	103,068				60,621	58,343	7,629	50,714	2,276		3.8	58.8	56.6
1949	103,994				61,286	57,651	7,658	49,993	3,637		5.9	58.9	55.4
1950	104,995	1,169	63,377	60,087	62,208	58,918	7,160	51,758	3,288	5.2	5.3	59.2	56.1
1951	104,621	2,143	64,160	62,104	62,017	59,961	6,726	53,235	2,055	3.2	3.3	59.2	57.3
1952	105,231	2,386	64,524	62,636	62,138	60,250	6,500	53,749	1,883	2.9	3.0	59.0	57.3
1953 [6]	107,056	2,231	65,246	63,410	63,015	61,179	6,260	54,919	1,834	2.8	2.9	58.9	57.1
1954	108,321	2,142	65,785	62,251	63,643	60,109	6,205	53,904	3,532	5.4	5.5	58.8	55.5
1955	109,683	2,064	67,087	64,234	65,023	62,170	6,450	55,722	2,852	4.3	4.4	59.3	56.7
1956	110,954	1,965	68,517	65,764	66,552	63,799	6,283	57,514	2,750	4.0	4.1	60.0	57.5
1957	112,265	1,948	68,877	66,019	66,929	64,071	5,947	58,123	2,859	4.2	4.3	59.6	57.1
1958	113,727	1,847	69,486	64,883	67,639	63,036	5,586	57,450	4,602	6.6	6.8	59.5	55.4
1959	115,329	1,788	70,157	66,418	68,369	64,630	5,565	59,065	3,740	5.3	5.5	59.3	56.0
1960 [6]	117,245	1,861	71,489	67,639	69,628	65,778	5,458	60,318	3,852	5.4	5.5	59.4	56.1
1961	118,771	1,900	72,359	67,646	70,459	65,746	5,200	60,546	4,714	6.5	6.7	59.3	55.4
1962 [6]	120,153	2,061	72,675	68,763	70,614	66,702	4,944	61,759	3,911	5.4	5.5	58.8	55.5
1963	122,416	2,006	73,839	69,768	71,833	67,762	4,687	63,076	4,070	5.5	5.7	58.7	55.4
1964	124,485	2,018	75,109	71,323	73,091	69,305	4,523	64,782	3,786	5.0	5.2	58.7	55.7
1965	126,513	1,946	76,401	73,034	74,455	71,088	4,361	66,726	3,366	4.4	4.5	58.9	56.2
1966	128,058	2,122	77,892	75,017	75,770	72,895	3,979	68,915	2,875	3.7	3.8	59.2	56.9
1967	129,874	2,218	79,565	76,590	77,347	74,372	3,844	70,527	2,975	3.7	3.8	59.6	57.3
1968	132,028	2,253	80,990	78,173	78,737	75,920	3,817	72,103	2,817	3.5	3.6	59.6	57.5
1969	134,335	2,238	82,972	80,140	80,734	77,902	3,606	74,296	2,832	3.4	3.5	60.1	58.0
1970	137,085	2,118	84,889	80,796	82,771	78,678	3,463	75,215	4,093	4.8	4.9	60.4	57.4
1971	140,216	1,973	86,355	81,340	84,382	79,367	3,394	75,972	5,016	5.8	5.9	60.2	56.6
1972 [6]	144,126	1,813	88,847	83,966	87,034	82,153	3,484	78,669	4,882	5.5	5.6	60.4	57.0
1973 [6]	147,096	1,774	91,203	86,838	89,429	85,064	3,470	81,594	4,365	4.8	4.9	60.8	57.8
1974	150,120	1,721	93,670	88,515	91,949	86,794	3,515	83,279	5,156	5.5	5.6	61.3	57.8
1975	153,153	1,678	95,453	87,524	93,775	85,846	3,408	82,438	7,929	8.3	8.5	61.2	56.1
1976	156,150	1,668	97,826	90,420	96,158	88,752	3,331	85,421	7,406	7.6	7.7	61.6	56.8
1977	159,033	1,656	100,665	93,673	99,009	92,017	3,283	88,734	6,991	6.9	7.1	62.3	57.9
1978 [6]	161,910	1,631	103,882	97,679	102,251	96,048	3,387	92,661	6,202	6.0	6.1	63.2	59.3
1979	164,863	1,597	106,559	100,421	104,962	98,824	3,347	95,477	6,137	5.8	5.8	63.7	59.9
1980	167,745	1,604	108,544	100,907	106,940	99,303	3,364	95,938	7,637	7.0	7.1	63.8	59.2
1981	170,130	1,645	110,315	102,042	108,670	100,397	3,368	97,030	8,273	7.5	7.6	63.9	59.0
1982	172,271	1,668	111,872	101,194	110,204	99,526	3,401	96,125	10,678	9.5	9.7	64.0	57.8
1983	174,215	1,676	113,226	102,510	111,550	100,834	3,383	97,450	10,717	9.5	9.6	64.0	57.9
1984	176,383	1,697	115,241	106,702	113,544	105,005	3,321	101,685	8,539	7.4	7.5	64.4	59.5
1985	178,206	1,706	117,167	108,856	115,461	107,150	3,179	103,971	8,312	7.1	7.2	64.8	60.1
1986 [6]	180,587	1,706	119,540	111,303	117,834	109,597	3,163	106,434	8,237	6.9	7.0	65.3	60.7
1987	182,753	1,737	121,602	114,177	119,865	112,440	3,208	109,232	7,425	6.1	6.2	65.6	61.5
1988	184,613	1,709	123,378	116,677	121,669	114,968	3,169	111,800	6,701	5.4	5.5	66.2	62.3
1989	186,393	1,688	125,557	119,030	123,869	117,342	3,199	114,142	6,528	5.2	5.3	66.5	63.0
1990	188,049	1,637	126,424	119,550	124,787	117,914	3,186	114,728	6,874	5.4	5.5	66.4	62.7
1991	189,765	1,564	126,867	118,440	125,303	116,877	3,233	113,644	8,426	6.6	6.7	66.0	61.6
1992	191,576	1,566	128,548	119,164	126,982	117,598	3,207	114,391	9,384	7.3	7.4	66.3	61.4

[1] Not seasonally adjusted.
[2] Unemployed as percent of labor force including resident Armed Forces.
[3] Unemployed as percent of civilian labor force.
[4] Civilian labor force as percent of civilian noninstitutional population.
[5] Civilian employment as percent of civilian noninstitutional population.
See next page for continuation of table.

TABLE 7

No. 648. Employment by Selected Industry, 1975 to 1990, and Projections, 2005

[In thousands, except percent. Figures may differ from those in other tables since these data exclude establishments not elsewhere classified (SIC 99); in addition, agriculture services (SIC 074, 5, 8) are included in agriculture, not services. See source for details. N.e.c. means not elsewhere classified. Minus sign (-) indicates decrease]

1987 SIC [1] code	INDUSTRY	EMPLOYMENT 1975	EMPLOYMENT 1990	EMPLOYMENT 2005 [2]	ANNUAL AVERAGE RATE OF CHANGE 1975-1990	ANNUAL AVERAGE RATE OF CHANGE 1990-2005 [2]
(X)	**Total**.	**87,666**	**122,570**	**147,190**	**2.3**	**1.2**
(X)	Nonfarm wage and salary.	76,680	109,319	132,647	2.4	1.3
(X)	Goods-producing (excluding agriculture).	22,600	24,958	25,241	0.7	0.1
10-14	Mining	752	711	668	-0.4	-0.4
15,16,17	Construction	3,525	5,136	6,059	2.5	1.1
20-39	Manufacturing	18,323	19,111	18,514	0.3	-0.2
24,25,32-39	Durable manufacturing	10,662	11,115	10,517	0.3	-0.4
24	Lumber and wood products	627	741	722	1.1	-0.2
25	Furniture and fixtures.	417	510	618	1.4	1.3
32	Stone, clay and glass products	598	557	516	-0.5	-0.5
33	Primary metal industries.	1,139	756	643	-2.7	-1.1
331	Blast furnaces/basic steel products	548	275	222	-4.5	-1.4
34	Fabricated metal products	1,453	1,423	1,238	-0.1	-0.9
35	Industrial machinery and equipment	2,076	2,095	1,941	0.1	-0.5
3571,2,5,7	Computer equipment	210	396	345	4.3	-0.9
36	Electronic and other electric equipment [3]	1,442	1,673	1,567	1.0	-0.4
3661	Telephone and telegraph apparatus	148	128	110	-1.0	-1.0
3674	Semiconductors and related devices.	122	238	235	4.6	-0.1
37	Transportation equipment.	1,700	1,980	1,889	1.0	-0.3
371	Motor vehicles and equipment . .	792	809	744	0.1	-0.6
38	Instruments and related products [3]	804	1,004	1,018	1.5	0.1
382	Measuring/controlling devices, watches. . . .	326	334	271	0.2	-1.4
3841-3	Medical instruments and supplies	109	206	282	4.3	2.1
39	Miscellaneous manufacturing industries	407	377	364	-0.5	-0.2
20-23,26-31	Nondurable manufacturing.	7,661	7,995	7,998	0.3	-
20	Food and kindred products.	1,658	1,668	1,560	-	-0.4
21	Tobacco manufactures	76	49	34	-2.9	-2.5
22	Textile mill products	868	691	596	-1.5	-1.0
23	Apparel and other textile products	1,243	1,043	848	-1.2	-1.4
26	Paper and allied products.	633	699	727	0.7	0.3
27	Printing and publishing.	1,083	1,574	1,900	2.5	1.3
28	Chemicals and allied products.	1,015	1,093	1,098	0.5	-
29	Petroleum and coal products	194	158	122	-1.4	-1.7
30	Rubber/misc. plastics products	643	889	1,043	2.2	1.1
31	Leather and leather products	248	132	72	-4.1	-4.0
(X)	Service producing	54,080	84,363	107,405	3.0	1.6
40-42,44-49	Transportation, communications, utilities	4,542	5,826	6,689	1.7	0.9
40-42,44-47	Transportation.	2,634	3,554	4,427	2.0	1.5
48	Communications	1,176	1,311	1,143	0.7	-0.9
49	Electric, gas, and sanitary services	733	961	1,119	1.8	1.0
50,51	Wholesale trade	4,430	6,205	7,210	2.3	1.0
52-59	Retail trade	12,630	19,683	24,804	3.0	1.6
58	Eating and drinking places	3,380	6,565	8,712	4.5	1.9
60-67	Finance, insurance, and real estate	4,165	6,739	8,129	3.3	1.3
70-87,89	Services	13,627	27,588	39,058	4.8	2.3
70	Hotels and other lodging places	898	1,649	2,174	4.1	1.9
72	Personal services [3]	782	1,113	1,338	2.4	1.2
73	Business services [3]	1,697	5,241	7,623	7.8	2.5
731	Advertising	122	238	345	4.6	2.5
734	Services to buildings	391	809	995	5.0	1.4
736	Personnel supply services	242	1,559	2,068	13.2	1.9
737	Computer and data processing services	143	784	1,494	12.0	4.4
75	Auto repair, services, and garages	439	928	1,245	5.1	2.0
76	Miscellaneous repair shops	218	390	480	4.0	1.4
78	Motion pictures	206	408	476	4.7	1.0
784	Video tape rental	(NA)	132	150	(NA)	0.8
79	Amusement and recreation services	613	1,089	1,428	3.9	1.8
80	Health services	4,134	7,844	11,519	4.4	2.6
801,2,3,4	Offices of health practitioners	936	2,180	3,470	5.8	3.1
805	Nursing and personal care facilities	759	1,420	2,182	4.3	2.9
806	Hospitals, private	2,274	3,547	4,605	3.0	1.8
807,8,9	Health services, n.e.c..	165	697	1,262	10.1	4.0
81	Legal services.	341	919	1,427	6.8	3.0
82	Educational services	1,001	1,652	2,326	3.4	2.3
83	Social services	690	1,811	2,874	6.6	3.1
84,86,8733	Museums, zoos, and membership organizations	1,573	2,149	2,488	2.1	1.0
87,89	Engineering, management, and services n.e.c. [4] .	(NA)	2,396	3,660	(NA)	2.9
(X)	Government.	14,686	18,322	21,515	1.5	1.1
(X)	Federal government.	2,748	3,085	3,184	0.8	0.2
(X)	State and local government.	11,937	15,237	18,331	1.6	1.2
01,02,07,08,09	Agriculture.	3,459	3,276	3,080	-0.4	-0.4
88	Private households	1,362	1,014	700	-1.9	-2.4
(X)	Nonagriculture self-employed and unpaid family	6,165	8,961	10,763	2.5	1.2

- Represents or rounds to zero.   NA Not available.   X Not applicable.   [1] 1987 Standard Industrial Classification; see text, section 13.   [2] Based on assumptions of moderate growth; see source.   [3] Includes other industries, not shown separately.   [4] Excludes SIC 8733.

Source: U.S. Bureau of Labor Statistics, *Monthly Labor Review*, November 1991.

TABLE 8

No. 655. Unemployment Rates, by Industry, 1975 to 1992, and by Sex, 1980 and 1992

[**In percent.** For civilian noninstitutional population 16 years old and over. Annual averages of monthly figures. Rate represents unemployment as a percent of labor force in each specified group. Data for 1985-91, and also beginning 1992, not strictly comparable with other years due to changes in industrial classification]

INDUSTRY	1975	1980	1985	1989	1990	1991	1992	MALE		FEMALE	
								1980	1992	1980	1992
All unemployed [1]	**8.5**	**7.1**	**7.2**	**5.3**	**5.5**	**6.7**	**7.4**	**6.9**	**7.8**	**7.4**	**6.9**
Industry: [2]											
Agriculture	10.4	11.0	13.2	9.6	9.7	11.6	12.3	9.7	12.1	15.1	13.1
Mining	4.1	6.4	9.5	5.8	4.8	7.7	7.9	6.7	8.3	4.5	5.7
Construction	18.0	14.1	13.1	10.0	11.1	15.4	16.7	14.6	17.2	8.9	11.0
Manufacturing	10.9	8.5	7.7	5.1	5.8	7.2	7.8	7.4	7.2	10.8	8.8
Transportation and public utilities . . .	5.6	4.9	5.1	3.9	3.8	5.3	5.5	5.1	5.8	4.4	4.7
Wholesale and retail trade	8.7	7.4	7.6	6.0	6.4	7.6	8.4	6.6	7.7	8.3	9.1
Finance, insurance, and real estate .	4.9	3.4	3.5	3.1	3.0	4.0	4.5	3.2	4.4	3.5	4.6
Services	7.1	5.9	6.2	4.8	5.0	5.7	6.5	6.3	7.4	5.8	5.9
Government	4.1	4.1	3.9	2.7	2.6	3.2	3.5	3.9	4.0	4.3	3.1

[1] Includes the self-employed, unpaid family workers, and persons with no previous work experience, not shown separately.
[2] Covers unemployed wage and salary workers.
Source: U.S. Bureau of Labor Statistics, *Employment and Earnings,* monthly, January issues.

TABLE 9

47. Unemployment rates, approximating U.S. concepts, in nine countries, quarterly data seasonally adjusted

Country	Annual average		1991	1992					1993	
	1991	1992	IV	I	II	III	IV		I	II
United States	6.7	7.4	7.0	7.3	7.5	7.5	7.3		7.0	7.0
Canada	10.3	11.3	10.3	10.7	11.3	11.5	11.5		11.0	11.4
Australia	9.6	10.8	10.3	10.5	10.7	10.9	11.2		11.0	10.8
Japan	2.1	2.2	2.1	2.1	2.1	2.2	2.3		2.3	2.4
France	9.6	10.2	9.9	10.0	10.2	10.2	10.4		10.6	11.0
Germany	4.4	4.7	4.4	4.4	4.6	4.8	5.0		5.4	5.8
Italy[1]	6.9	7.3	6.9	6.9	7.0	7.0	8.3		9.4	10.8
Sweden[2]	2.6	4.7	3.2	3.7	5.1	5.0	5.2		7.2	8.0
United Kingdom	8.8	10.0	9.4	9.6	9.8	10.2	10.5		10.6	10.5

[1] Quarterly rates are for the first month of the quarter. Break in series beginning in 1993.
[2] Break in series beginning in 1993. Data for 1993 are not seasonally adjusted.
NOTE: Quarterly figures for France, Germany, and the United Kingdom are calculated by applying annual adjustment factors to current published data and therefore should be viewed as less precise indicators of unemployment under U.S. concepts than the annual figures. See "Notes on the data" for information on breaks in series.

TABLE 10

No. 731. Average Earnings of Persons, by Educational Attainment, Sex, and Age: 1991
[In dollars. For year-round, full-time workers 25 years old and over. As of March 1992]

AGE AND SEX	Total	Less than 9th grade	HIGH SCHOOL		COLLEGE		
			9th to 12th grade (no diploma)	High school graduate (includes equivalency)	Some college, no degree	Associate degree	Bachelor's degree or more
Male, total	**35,850**	**19,632**	**23,765**	**28,230**	**33,758**	**35,500**	**50,747**
25 to 34 years old	28,742	15,853	19,596	24,045	28,135	29,923	39,765
35 to 44 years old	37,882	19,972	23,770	28,984	34,377	37,887	52,130
45 to 54 years old	41,676	20,713	25,277	32,468	41,121	41,796	56,918
55 to 64 years old	38,868	22,274	29,491	32,484	35,291	32,695	59,089
65 years old and over. . . .	35,303	16,479	18,926	27,165	30,365	(B)	56,164
Female, total	**23,778**	**12,570**	**15,352**	**19,336**	**22,633**	**25,554**	**33,144**
25 to 34 years old	22,429	12,521	13,849	18,269	20,993	23,120	29,614
35 to 44 years old	25,277	12,255	15,037	19,824	24,100	27,329	35,214
45 to 54 years old	24,521	12,319	16,854	20,342	23,369	26,035	36,264
55 to 64 years old	22,451	13,201	15,116	18,914	24,049	28,168	34,363
65 years old and over. . . .	18,590	(B)	15,833	17,757	(B)	(B)	23,332

B Base figure too small to meet statistical standards for reliability of derived figure.

Source: U.S. Bureau of the Census, *1990 Census of Population and Housing,* Summary Tape File 3C on CD-ROM.

TABLE 11

Effective Federal Minimum Hourly Wage Rates

| In Effect | Wages Rates In Current Dollars | | | Wages Rates In August 1993 $ | | | CPI–U |
| | Nonfarm Workers | | | Nonfarm Workers | | | |
	Covered^	Newly Covered#	Farm Workers+	Covered^	Newly Covered#	Farm Workers+	(1982–84=100.0)
October 24, 1938	$0.25	$ —	$ —	$2.59	$ —	$ —	14.0
October 24, 1939	0.30	—	—	3.10	—	—	14.0
October 24, 1945	0.40	—	—	3.20	—	—	18.1
January 25, 1950	0.75	—	—	4.62	—	—	23.5
March 1, 1956	1.00	—	—	5.40	—	—	26.8
September 3, 1961	1.15	1.00	—	5.55	4.83	—	30.0
September 3, 1963	1.25	—	—	5.90	—	—	30.7
September 3, 1964	—	1.15	—	—	5.35	—	31.1
September 3, 1965	—	1.25*	—	—	5.73	—	31.6
February 1, 1967	1.40*	1.00	1.00	6.16	4.40	4.40	32.9
February 1, 1968	1.60	1.15	1.15	6.77	4.87	4.87	34.2
February 1, 1969	—	1.30	1.30	—	5.26	5.26	35.8
February 1, 1970	—	1.45	—	—	5.53	—	38.0
February 1, 1971	—	1.60	—	—	5.81	—	39.9
May 1, 1974	2.00	1.90	1.60	5.96	5.66	4.77	48.6
January 1, 1975	2.10	2.00	1.80	5.84	5.56	5.00	52.1
January 1, 1976	2.30	2.20	2.00	5.99	5.73	5.21	55.6
January 1, 1977	—	2.30	2.20	—	5.69	5.45	58.5
January 1, 1978	2.65	2.65	2.65	6.14	6.14	6.14	62.5
January 1, 1979	2.90	2.90	2.90	6.15	6.15	6.15	68.3
January 1, 1980	3.10	3.10	3.10	5.77	5.77	5.77	77.8
January 1, 1981	3.35	3.35	3.35	5.58	5.58	5.58	87.0
April 1, 1990	3.80	3.80	3.80	4.27	4.27	4.27	128.9
April 1, 1991	4.25	4.25	4.25	4.55	4.55	4.55	135.2
August, 1993							144.8

^ Applies to workers covered prior to 1961 Amendments and, after Sept. 1965, to workers covered by 1961 Amendments. Rates set by 1961 Amendments were: Sept. 1961, $1.00; Sept. 1964, $1.15; and Sept. 1965, $1.25

Applies to workers newly covered by Amendments of 1966, 1974, and 1977, and Title IX of Education Amendments of 1972.

+ Included in coverage as of 1966, 1974 and 1977 Amendments.

* All job categories covered prior to the 1966 amendments were raised to $1.40 per hour in February 1967.

Sources: (1) Federal Reserve Bank of Kansas City, "Economic Review," January 1978, p. 4.
(2) U.S. Department of Commerce, Bureau of the Census, "Statistical Abstract of the United States, 1992, Table No. 658, p. 415.

TABLE 12

No. 860. Gross Stock of Fixed Private Capital, Nonresidential and Residential, by Industry: 1970 to 1990

[In billions of dollars. Estimates as of Dec. 31. Based on the *1987 Standard Industrial Classification Manual;* see text, section 13]

INDUSTRY	CURRENT DOLLARS				CONSTANT (1987) DOLLARS			
	1970	1980	1985	1990	1970	1980	1985	1990
Fixed private capital.	2,689.0	9,364.1	12,746.6	16,821.0	8,131.2	11,584.7	13,322.3	15,214.5
Nonresidential	1,469.6	5,072.1	7,156.4	9,433.0	4,250.1	6,263.6	7,388.5	8,459.1
Agriculture, forestry and fisheries	96.7	333.2	398.2	418.1	300.6	436.1	418.5	369.5
Farms	90.7	308.6	363.1	370.6	282.6	405.0	382.0	326.9
Agr. serv., forestry and fisheries	6.0	24.6	35.1	47.6	18.0	31.1	36.6	42.5
Mining	83.5	403.3	541.4	516.1	282.4	383.7	495.8	445.7
Metal mining	6.9	30.6	40.0	42.0	21.3	39.6	41.7	37.0
Coal mining	4.7	31.0	46.0	49.9	15.1	39.3	47.8	43.9
Oil and gas extraction.	67.2	323.2	431.4	395.5	231.2	280.8	381.4	339.7
Nonmetallic minerals, exc. fuels	4.7	18.4	23.9	28.8	14.8	24.0	25.0	25.1
Construction.	28.1	91.8	96.4	113.3	87.3	120.0	102.4	100.9
Manufacturing.	338.4	1,144.5	1,598.6	2,088.7	1,001.1	1,480.7	1,694.1	1,873.3
Durable goods.	184.0	622.6	873.1	1,122.2	533.7	797.9	922.5	1,013.7
Lumber and wood products	7.8	31.0	37.1	41.8	24.2	40.5	39.5	37.3
Furniture and fixtures.	2.6	9.6	13.7	19.1	7.7	12.6	14.5	17.3
Stone, clay, glass products	14.6	47.8	57.9	63.1	44.9	61.4	61.4	57.5
Primary metal industries	49.0	143.2	178.0	203.3	144.3	185.6	188.7	179.9
Fabricated metal products	19.8	70.0	95.5	124.4	57.6	90.2	101.6	111.6
Machinery, exc. electrical	28.2	99.8	148.1	194.0	75.7	123.2	155.1	178.9
Elec. and elec. equipment	16.5	65.4	115.6	167.4	46.8	84.8	121.2	152.0
Motor vehicles and equipment	22.4	73.3	95.1	116.5	65.8	93.6	101.3	104.6
Other transp. equipment	12.7	41.2	65.4	95.9	36.6	53.1	68.9	86.4
Instruments, related products	7.1	29.5	51.4	77.8	20.4	37.6	54.1	71.3
Misc. mfg. industries	3.4	11.8	15.2	18.9	9.8	15.3	16.2	16.9
Nondurable goods	154.4	521.9	725.5	966.5	467.4	682.8	771.7	859.6
Food and kindred products.	33.9	103.8	141.8	189.2	103.5	137.2	151.8	168.6
Tobacco manufacturers	1.4	5.3	10.7	14.5	4.0	7.0	11.3	13.0
Textile mill products	11.5	34.7	43.4	51.1	36.9	47.1	47.0	45.6
Apparel; other textile products.	3.2	11.8	15.3	18.0	9.4	15.4	16.4	16.1
Paper and allied products.	20.8	69.8	98.7	143.4	63.9	91.9	105.0	126.5
Printing and publishing.	10.7	36.1	52.7	81.0	33.3	47.8	56.2	74.2
Chemicals, allied products	41.0	149.6	202.6	271.5	119.5	192.1	213.9	239.3
Petroleum and coal products	21.7	71.4	107.5	127.0	65.6	92.6	113.4	112.8
Rubber; misc. plastic products	9.3	36.7	49.4	66.9	28.3	48.0	52.9	59.9
Leather and leather products	1.0	2.8	3.5	4.0	3.2	3.7	3.8	3.6
Transportation and public utilities	483.2	1,498.3	1,940.5	2,423.9	1,348.7	1,810.2	1,978.5	2,143.3
Transportation.	192.6	492.4	572.1	617.1	555.1	603.1	580.5	553.0
Railroad transportation.	114.1	232.0	253.1	251.4	332.6	281.1	252.0	226.0
Local, interurban pass. transit	5.1	8.9	10.3	12.6	14.4	11.2	10.7	11.5
Trucking and warehousing	20.7	77.5	100.9	106.4	60.5	101.6	105.2	96.1
Water transportation	14.5	46.6	51.0	54.8	39.3	56.5	53.3	48.5
Transportation by air	19.0	64.0	83.1	106.2	51.5	78.9	85.5	95.7
Pipelines, exc. natural gas	9.8	33.3	37.4	41.3	28.5	40.1	37.9	35.8
Transportation services	9.3	30.0	36.4	44.4	28.2	33.8	35.9	39.4
Communication	101.8	360.2	492.9	622.2	249.7	426.7	505.8	561.4
Telephone and telegraph	95.8	336.4	444.6	539.5	233.3	395.3	455.5	485.9
Radio and TV broadcasting	6.0	23.8	48.4	82.7	16.5	31.4	50.3	75.5
Elec., gas, and sanitary services.	188.7	645.7	875.5	1,184.6	544.0	780.4	892.2	1,028.9
Electric services	136.5	492.6	677.1	916.4	391.7	596.3	690.2	791.8
Gas services	46.6	135.3	170.7	210.1	136.2	163.6	174.0	183.2
Sanitary services	5.6	17.8	27.7	58.2	16.0	20.4	28.0	53.8
Wholesale trade	40.7	160.5	276.3	394.8	107.6	199.6	286.6	366.7
Retail trade	75.8	259.6	412.8	606.2	216.5	334.8	432.3	547.8
Finance, insurance, real estate	216.8	794.3	1,302.7	2,031.9	619.8	1,006.3	1,362.9	1,842.3
Banking	22.4	126.1	235.4	407.9	60.9	151.2	244.5	377.7
Credit agencies other than banks	6.2	39.1	58.2	105.5	16.7	44.8	59.9	95.9
Security and commodity brokers and services	1.1	3.8	8.6	12.9	2.6	4.4	8.8	12.4
Insurance carriers	5.6	21.8	56.2	122.4	13.4	25.3	57.2	120.2
Insurance agents, brokers, and services . . .	1.9	4.8	5.4	5.9	3.9	5.0	5.5	5.7
Real estate.	177.5	589.6	919.5	1,349.6	517.8	765.5	967.4	1,203.4
Holding, other investment companies	2.1	9.0	19.3	27.7	4.6	10.2	19.6	27.0
Services.	106.3	386.7	589.6	840.1	286.1	492.1	617.3	769.7
Hotels, other lodging places	20.1	63.2	96.0	129.5	60.0	82.4	101.0	115.4
Personal services	7.9	20.7	24.2	32.1	19.9	26.0	25.2	29.7
Business services	18.7	88.4	149.7	216.9	48.0	111.2	157.2	198.3
Auto repair; serv., garages.	16.3	68.2	103.4	145.6	43.8	86.5	107.8	136.8
Misc. repair services.	2.4	9.4	12.3	14.9	7.0	12.0	12.9	13.5
Motion pictures	2.8	9.0	11.4	19.8	6.8	10.8	12.1	18.4
Amusement, recreation services.	10.0	28.5	34.8	41.7	27.3	36.4	36.3	37.5
Other services.	28.1	99.5	157.8	239.6	73.3	126.8	164.8	220.0
Health services	14.0	50.6	83.0	130.0	38.8	64.9	86.9	117.7
Legal services	2.8	7.9	14.5	25.5	7.0	9.9	15.1	24.2
Educational services	1.4	2.6	3.6	5.5	2.9	3.1	3.8	5.0
Other [1]	9.8	38.4	56.7	78.6	24.6	48.9	59.0	73.0
Residential	1,219.4	4,292.0	5,590.2	7,387.9	3,881.1	5,321.2	5,933.8	6,755.4
Farms.	50.9	129.1	144.7	159.8	161.6	160.8	153.1	146.4
Real estate	1,168.5	4,162.9	5,445.5	7,228.1	3,719.5	5,160.4	5,780.7	6,609.0

[1] Consists of social services, membership organizations, and miscellaneous professional services.

Source: U.S. Bureau of Economic Analysis, *Survey of Current Business,* January 1992.

TABLE 13

1.35 INTEREST RATES Money and Capital Markets

Averages, percent per year; figures are averages of business day data unless otherwise noted

Item	1990	1991	1992	1993				1993, week ending				
				June	July	Aug.	Sept.	Aug. 27	Sept. 3	Sept. 10	Sept. 17	Sept. 24
MONEY MARKET INSTRUMENTS												
1 Federal funds[1,2,3]	8.10	5.69	3.52	3.04	3.06	3.03	3.09	2.98	3.08	2.99	3.03	3.12
2 Discount window borrowing[2,4]	6.98	5.45	3.25	3.00	3.00	3.00	3.00	3.00	3.00	3.00	3.00	3.00
Commercial paper[3,5,6]												
3 1-month	8.15	5.89	3.71	3.19	3.15	3.14	3.14	3.11	3.14	3.12	3.14	3.15
4 3-month	8.06	5.87	3.75	3.25	3.20	3.18	3.16	3.14	3.16	3.13	3.15	3.16
5 6-month	7.95	5.85	3.80	3.38	3.35	3.33	3.25	3.27	3.27	3.22	3.24	3.26
Finance paper, directly placed[3,5,7]												
6 1-month	8.00	5.73	3.62	3.12	3.08	3.08	3.07	3.03	3.07	3.05	3.07	3.08
7 3-month	7.87	5.71	3.65	3.16	3.12	3.13	3.09	3.11	3.11	3.09	3.09	3.09
8 6-month	7.53	5.60	3.63	3.16	3.15	3.16	3.11	3.15	3.13	3.10	3.11	3.11
Bankers acceptances[3,5,8]												
9 3-month	7.93	5.70	3.62	3.16	3.12	3.10	3.07	3.08	3.08	3.06	3.08	3.08
10 6-month	7.80	5.67	3.67	3.28	3.26	3.23	3.17	3.20	3.18	3.16	3.18	3.17
Certificates of deposit, secondary market[3,9]												
11 1-month	8.15	5.82	3.64	3.13	3.10	3.09	3.09	3.09	3.09	3.08	3.09	3.10
12 3-month	8.15	5.83	3.68	3.21	3.16	3.14	3.12	3.14	3.13	3.11	3.12	3.11
13 6-month	8.17	5.91	3.76	3.36	3.34	3.32	3.24	3.27	3.26	3.22	3.26	3.24
14 Eurodollar deposits, 3-month[3,10]	8.16	5.86	3.70	3.21	3.17	3.14	3.08	3.13	3.11	3.06	3.08	3.06
U.S. Treasury bills *Secondary market[3,5]*												
15 3-month	7.50	5.38	3.43	3.07	3.04	3.02	2.95	3.00	2.99	2.96	2.96	2.93
16 6-month	7.46	5.44	3.54	3.20	3.16	3.14	3.06	3.10	3.09	3.06	3.07	3.06
17 1-year	7.35	5.52	3.71	3.39	3.33	3.30	3.22	3.24	3.21	3.18	3.24	3.26
Auction average[3,5,11]												
18 3-month	7.51	5.42	3.45	3.10	3.05	3.05	2.96	3.02	3.02	2.95	2.98	2.93
19 6-month	7.47	5.49	3.57	3.23	3.15	3.17	3.06	3.12	3.11	3.03	3.06	3.06
20 1-year	7.36	5.54	3.75	3.40	3.42	3.30	3.27	3.30	n.a.	n.a.	n.a.	3.27
U.S. TREASURY NOTES AND BONDS												
Constant maturities[12]												
21 1-year	7.89	5.86	3.89	3.54	3.47	3.44	3.36	3.37	3.34	3.32	3.38	3.39
22 2-year	8.16	6.49	4.77	4.16	4.07	4.00	3.85	3.88	3.83	3.79	3.88	3.90
23 3-year	8.26	6.82	5.30	4.53	4.43	4.36	4.17	4.22	4.16	4.09	4.19	4.22
24 5-year	8.37	7.37	6.19	5.22	5.09	5.03	4.73	4.87	4.76	4.66	4.73	4.80
25 7-year	8.52	7.68	6.63	5.61	5.48	5.35	5.08	5.18	5.09	5.00	5.10	5.16
26 10-year	8.55	7.86	7.01	5.96	5.81	5.68	5.36	5.51	5.41	5.28	5.35	5.44
27 30-year	8.61	8.14	7.67	6.81	6.63	6.32	6.00	6.16	6.06	5.90	5.98	6.09
Composite												
28 More than 10 years (long-term)	8.74	8.16	7.52	6.55	6.34	6.18	5.94	6.08	5.97	5.84	5.93	6.03
STATE AND LOCAL NOTES AND BONDS												
Moody's series[13]												
29 Aaa	6.96	6.56	6.09	5.35	5.27	5.37	n.a.	5.33	5.33	5.33	5.27	5.23
30 Baa	7.29	6.99	6.48	5.80	5.74	5.84	n.a.	5.82	5.82	5.82	5.78	5.74
31 *Bond Buyer series[14]*	7.27	6.92	6.44	5.63	5.57	5.45	5.29	5.35	5.35	5.24	5.27	5.30
CORPORATE BONDS												
32 Seasoned issues, all industries[15]	9.77	9.23	8.55	7.66	7.50	7.19	6.98	7.04	6.95	6.87	6.96	7.08
Rating group												
33 Aaa	9.32	8.77	8.14	7.33	7.17	6.85	6.66	6.71	6.61	6.51	6.66	6.79
34 Aa	9.56	9.05	8.46	7.51	7.35	7.06	6.85	6.91	6.82	6.74	6.85	6.96
35 A	9.82	9.30	8.62	7.74	7.53	7.25	7.05	7.11	7.02	6.95	7.02	7.15
36 Baa	10.36	9.80	8.98	8.07	7.93	7.60	7.34	7.43	7.34	7.26	7.33	7.43
37 A-rated, recently offered utility bonds[16]	10.01	9.32	8.52	7.59	7.43	7.16	6.94	6.97	6.83	6.85	6.99	7.07
MEMO *Dividend–price ratio[17]*												
38 Preferred stocks	8.96	8.17	7.46	6.97	6.89	6.83	6.70	6.85	6.85	6.79	6.76	6.76
39 Common stocks	3.61	3.24	2.99	2.81	2.81	2.76	2.73	2.73	2.71	2.75	2.72	2.76

1. The daily effective federal funds rate is a weighted average of rates on trades through New York brokers.
2. Weekly figures are averages of seven calendar days ending on Wednesday of the current week; monthly figures include each calendar day in the month.
3. Annualized using a 360-day year or bank interest.
4. Rate for the Federal Reserve Bank of New York.
5. Quoted on a discount basis.
6. An average of offering rates on commercial paper placed by several leading dealers for firms whose bond rating is AA or the equivalent.
7. An average of offering rates on paper directly placed by finance companies.
8. Representative closing yields for acceptances of the highest-rated money center banks.
9. An average of dealer offering rates on nationally traded certificates of deposit.
10. Bid rates for Eurodollar deposits at 11:00 a.m. London time. Data are for indication purposes only.
11. Auction date for daily data; weekly and monthly averages computed on an issue-date basis.

12. Yields on actively traded issues adjusted to constant maturities. Source: U.S. Treasury.
13. General obligations based on Thursday figures; Moody's Investors Service.
14. General obligations only, with twenty years to maturity, issued by twenty state and local governmental units of mixed quality. Based on figures for Thursday.
15. Daily figures from Moody's Investors Service. Based on yields to maturity on selected long-term bonds.
16. Compilation of the Federal Reserve. This series is an estimate of the yield on recently offered, A-rated utility bonds with a thirty-year maturity and five years of call protection. Weekly data are based on Friday quotations.
17. Standard & Poor's corporate series. Preferred stock ratio is based on a sample of ten issues: four public utilities, four industrials, one financial, and one transportation. Common stock ratio is based on the 500 stocks in the price index.
NOTE. Data in this table also appear in the Board's H.15 (519) weekly and G.13 (415) monthly statistical releases. For ordering address, see inside front cover.

TABLE 14

No. 787. Flow of Funds Accounts—Assets and Liabilities of Households: 1980 to 1992

[As of **December 31**. Includes personal trusts and nonprofit organizations. See also *Historical Statistics, Colonial Times to 1970*, series X 114-147]

TYPE OF INSTRUMENT	TOTAL (bil. dol.)							PERCENT DISTRIBUTION		
	1980	1985	1988	1989	1990	1991	1992	1980	1990	1992
Total financial assets	**6,391**	**9,819**	**12,356**	**13,804**	**13,984**	**15,434**	**16,181**	**100.0**	**100.0**	**100.0**
Deposit and market instrument [1]	2,140	3,526	4,534	4,959	5,219	5,099	5,143	33.5	37.3	31.8
Checkable deposits and currency. . .	260	380	479	494	516	560	672	4.1	3.7	4.2
Small time and savings deposits . . .	1,141	1,830	2,137	2,225	2,279	2,283	2,215	17.8	16.3	13.7
Money market fund shares	65	211	302	388	433	461	462	1.0	3.1	2.9
Large time deposits.	112	72	129	142	109	61	2	1.8	0.8	(Z)
Credit market instruments.	562	1,033	1,485	1,710	1,882	1,735	1,792	8.8	13.5	11.1
U.S. Government securities	241	427	584	680	771	658	650	3.8	5.5	4.0
Treasury issues.	194	340	381	393	441	355	344	3.0	3.2	2.1
Savings bonds.	73	80	110	118	126	138	157	1.1	0.9	1.0
Other Treasury	122	260	271	275	315	217	186	1.9	2.2	1.2
Agency issues	47	87	203	288	330	303	306	0.7	2.4	1.9
Tax-exempt obligations	102	303	465	527	558	579	600	1.6	4.0	3.7
Corporate and foreign bonds	69	53	81	116	151	150	131	1.1	1.1	0.8
Mortgages	107	127	182	213	215	245	302	1.7	1.5	1.9
Open-market paper	43	122	174	173	188	103	109	0.7	1.3	0.7
Mutual fund shares.	52	207	418	492	515	680	898	0.8	3.7	5.5
Other corporate equities	1,111	1,611	1,719	2,004	1,842	2,349	2,535	17.4	13.2	15.7
Life insurance reserves	216	257	326	354	380	402	434	3.4	2.7	2.7
Pension fund reserves [2]	916	1,992	2,755	3,211	3,303	4,223	4,586	14.3	23.6	28.3
Equity in noncorporate business	1,865	2,059	2,373	2,525	2,449	2,368	2,264	29.2	17.5	14.0
Security credit	16	35	41	53	62	87	80	0.3	0.4	0.5
Miscellaneous assets	74	133	191	206	215	225	242	1.2	1.5	1.5
Total liabilities	**1,466**	**2,373**	**3,284**	**3,619**	**3,892**	**4,060**	**4,281**	**100.0**	**100.0**	**100.0**
Credit market instruments	1,406	2,271	3,177	3,508	3,781	3,926	4,141	95.9	97.1	96.7
Mortgages	950	1,460	2,219	2,483	2,732	2,867	3,067	64.8	70.2	71.6
Installment consumer credit	302	526	673	729	749	742	741	20.6	19.2	17.3
Other consumer credit	53	75	69	63	61	55	58	3.6	1.6	1.4
Tax-exempt debt	17	81	80	82	86	95	101	1.1	2.2	2.4
Bank loans, not elsewhere classified	30	44	41	53	43	47	47	2.0	1.1	1.1
Other loans	55	84	97	99	110	120	127	3.7	2.8	3.0
Security credit	25	51	44	43	39	55	57	1.7	1.0	1.3
Trade credit . . . . [3] . . .	22	36	47	51	56	61	64	1.5	1.4	1.5
Unpaid life insurance premiums [3]	13	15	16	16	17	18	20	0.9	0.4	0.5

Z Less than .05 percent. [1] Excludes corporate equities. [2] See also table 839. [3] Includes deferred premiums.

Source: Board of Governors of the Federal Reserve System, *Annual Statistical Digest*.

TABLE 15

1.21   MONEY STOCK, LIQUID ASSETS, AND DEBT MEASURES[1]
Billions of dollars, averages of daily figures

Item	1989 Dec.	1990 Dec.	1991 Dec.	1992 Dec.r	1993 June r	1993 July r	1993 Aug.	1993 Sept.
				Seasonally adjusted				
Measures[2]								
1 M1	794.6	827.2	899.3	1,026.6	1,073.1	1,085.3	1,094.8	1,107.6
2 M2	3,233.3	3,345.5	3,445.8	3,494.9	3,510.9	3,516.8	3,521.9	3,534.5
3 M3	4,056.1	4,116.8r	4,168.1	4,162.5	4,167.5	4,165.1	4,167.9	4,180.7
4 L	4,886.1	4,966.6	4,982.3r	5,039.5	5,070.2	5,068.4	5,075.2	n.a.
5 Debt	10,030.7r	10,670.1r	11,141.9r	11,718.6	11,972.0	12,025.9	12,079.5	n.a.
M1 components								
6 Currency[3]	222.7	246.7	267.2	292.3	306.8	309.6	312.6	316.4
7 Travelers checks[4]	6.9	7.8	7.8	8.1	8.0	7.9	7.8	7.8
8 Demand deposits[5]	279.8	278.2	290.5	340.8	360.5	365.7	370.7	376.5
9 Other checkable deposits[6]	285.3	294.5	333.8	385.2	397.8	402.2	403.8	406.9
Nontrgnsaction components								
10 In M2[7]	2,438.7	2,518.3	2,546.6	2,468.3	2,437.8	2,431.4	2,427.1	2,426.9
11 In M3[8]	822.8	771.3r	722.3	667.7	656.6	648.3	645.9	646.2
Commercial banks								
12 Savings deposits, including MMDAs	541.4	582.2	666.2	756.1	769.0	769.5	773.9	777.4
13 Small time deposits[9]	534.9	610.3	601.5	506.9	488.7	483.8	479.5	476.4
14 Large time deposits[10, 11]	387.7	368.8r	341.3	288.1	276.0	271.6	272.3	270.7
Thrift institutions								
15 Savings deposits, including MMDAs	349.6	338.6	376.3	429.9	429.8	430.6	431.2	431.7
16 Small time deposits[9]	617.8	562.0	463.2	360.4	338.0	333.8	330.7	327.1
17 Large time deposits[10]	161.1	120.9	83.4	67.5	63.8	63.6	63.1	63.1
Money market mutual funds								
18 General purpose and broker–dealer	317.4	350.5	363.9	342.3	336.2	335.9	334.3	332.4
19 Institution-only	108.8	135.9	182.1	202.3	198.1	195.0	193.3	194.1
Debt components								
20 Federal debt	2,247.6r	2,490.7r	2,763.8r	3,068.4	3,207.9	3,227.8	3,252.2	n.a.
21 Nonfederal debt	7,783.1r	8,179.4r	8,378.1r	8,650.2	8,764.1	8,798.1	8,827.4	n.a.
				Not seasonally adjusted				
Measures[2]								
22 Ms18	811.5	843.7	916.4	1,045.7	1,072.6	1,084.1	1,088.4	1,099.3
23 M2	3,245.1	3,357.0	3,457.9	3,509.1	3,506.5	3,513.3	3,514.7	3,520.8
24 M3	4,066.4	4,126.3	4,178.1	4,174.6	4,162.6	4,158.6	4,165.7	4,168.0
25 L	4,906.0	4,988.0	5,004.2	5,064.0	5,057.1	5,050.4	5,062.4	n.a.
26 Debt	10,026.5r	10,667.7r	11,141.0r	11,717.2	11,937.8	11,984.5	12,040.4	n.a.
M1 components								
27 Currency[3]	225.3	249.5	269.9	295.0	307.4	311.0	312.8	314.8
28 Travelers checks[4]	6.5	7.4	7.4	7.8	8.2	8.4	8.4	8.2
29 Demand deposits[5]	291.5	289.9	302.9	355.2	359.4	365.4	367.4	373.0
30 Other checkable deposits[6]	288.1	296.9	336.3	387.7	397.5	399.1	399.8	403.3
Nontrgnsaction components								
31 In M2[7]	2,433.6	2,513.2	2,541.5	2,463.4	2,434.0	2,429.2	2,426.3	2,421.5
32 In M3[8]	821.3r	769.3	720.1	665.5	656.1	645.3	651.0	647.1
Commercial banks								
33 Savings deposits, including MMDAs	543.0	580.1	663.3	752.3	772.3	772.2	774.5	775.3
34 Small time deposits[9]	533.8	610.5	602.0	507.7	486.9	483.7	479.6	477.1
35 Large time deposits[10, 11]	386.9	367.7	340.1	287.1	277.5	271.2	273.4	271.1
Thrift institutions								
36 Savings deposits, including MMDAs	347.4	337.3	374.7	427.8	431.6	432.1	431.6	430.5
37 Small time deposits[9]	616.2	562.1	463.6	360.9	336.8	333.8	330.8	327.6
38 Large time deposits[10]	162.0	120.6	83.1	67.3	64.1	63.6	63.4	63.2
Money market mutual funds								
39 General purpose and broker–dealer	315.7	348.4	361.5	340.0	333.0	331.7	331.5	329.8
40 Institution-only	109.1	136.2	182.4	202.4	194.3	191.8	193.3	190.7
Repurchase agreements and Eurodollars								
41 Overnight	77.5	74.7	76.3	74.8	73.5	75.7	78.3	81.3
42 Term	178.4	158.3	130.1	126.2	140.6	140.7	141.8	142.4
Debt components								
43 Federal debt	2,247.5	2,491.3	2,765.0	3,069.8	3,188.9	3,201.8	3,229.4	n.a.
44 Nonfederal debt	7,779.0r	8,176.3r	8,376.0r	8,647.4	8,748.9	8,782.7	8,810.9	n.a.

Footnotes appear on following page.

TABLE 16

No. 1350. U.S. Exports and General Imports of Selected Commodities—Value, by Area: 1991

[**In millions of dollars.** Includes nonmonetary gold. Exports are f.a.s. (free alongside ship) transaction value basis; imports are customs value basis. N.e.s. = Not elsewhere specified]

SELECTED MAJOR COMMODITIES	Total [1]	WESTERN HEMISPHERE		WESTERN EUROPE				ASIA		
		Canada	Mexico	United Kingdom	Germany [1]	France	Italy	Japan	China: Taiwan	South Korea
Exports, total	**421,730**	**85,150**	**33,277**	**22,046**	**21,302**	**15,345**	**8,570**	**48,125**	**13,182**	**15,505**
Meat and meat preparations	3,653	587	508	6	8	49	14	1,593	21	209
Fish (except marine mammal) crustaceans, etc., preparations	3,181	410	36	139	61	99	37	1,879	44	158
Cereals and cereal preparations	10,927	367	686	71	47	64	125	2,165	746	399
Vegetables and fruit	5,908	2,278	155	266	300	139	82	1,050	166	81
Feeding stuff for animals not including unmilled cereal	3,281	404	164	74	58	104	83	430	52	20
Miscellaneous edible products and preparations	1,364	318	74	12	13	17	2	99	99	39
Tobacco and tobacco manufactures	6,028	18	4	48	264	21	68	1,579	152	119
Hides, skins, and furskins, raw	1,389	60	140	3	13	10	38	282	130	603
Oil seeds and oleaginous fruits	4,320	100	390	111	202	30	59	891	467	244
Cork and wood	5,131	690	227	95	134	45	203	2,490	140	280
Pulp and waste paper	3,627	239	290	144	224	188	331	702	206	345
Textile fibers & their wastes (excluding wool tops, etc)	3,704	169	113	46	122	11	164	533	132	386
Crude fertilizers & crude minerals [2]	1,433	251	95	39	71	26	51	326	46	76
Metalliferous ores and metal scrap	4,163	1,002	178	103	68	34	55	709	228	600
Crude animal and vegetable materials, n.e.s.	1,128	210	133	40	70	27	33	155	16	31
Coal, coke and briquettes	4,781	489	22	286	69	389	516	536	190	171
Petroleum, petroleum products, and related materials	6,770	673	744	58	50	241	261	537	233	497
Organic chemicals	11,044	1,140	708	368	489	208	226	1,179	1,028	594
Inorganic chemicals	4,141	510	260	134	239	67	44	1,139	94	201
Dyeing, tanning and coloring materials	1,662	489	114	90	53	28	17	113	58	68
Medicinal and pharmaceutical products	4,679	564	121	235	325	288	361	812	61	65
Essential oils, etc; toilet, polishing, preparations	2,430	534	120	145	90	64	39	284	72	71
Fertilizers [3]	2,994	202	52	7	27	56	13	166	3	75
Plastics in primary forms	7,560	1,279	608	235	222	74	63	519	360	312
Plastics in nonprimary forms	2,821	772	357	125	125	80	46	197	58	71
Chemical materials and products, n.e.s.	6,098	1,230	314	260	354	257	140	666	104	202
Rubber manufactures, n.e.s.	2,326	1,037	286	72	68	29	16	225	20	37
Cork and wood manufactures other than furniture	1,292	306	158	130	129	12	22	111	55	57
Paper, paperboard and articles	6,034	1,564	778	240	233	102	101	520	121	147
Textile yarn, fabrics, made-up articles, n.e.s.	5,610	1,410	547	307	196	99	134	266	67	124
Nonmetallic mineral manufactures, n.e.s.	4,720	1,215	246	167	120	84	55	447	94	103
Iron and steel	4,457	1,471	879	108	64	67	48	285	135	334
Nonferrous metals	5,822	1,285	426	294	136	120	58	1,778	425	210
Manufactures of metals, n.e.s.	6,700	2,360	1,109	326	295	129	116	395	90	182
Power generating machinery and equipment	17,368	4,175	1,082	1,200	851	2,354	226	881	351	869
Machinery specialized for particular industries	17,192	3,027	1,239	862	786	553	296	973	284	600
Metalworking machinery	2,805	448	244	169	217	98	64	243	91	181
General industrial machinery, equipment, parts	17,567	4,852	1,599	853	764	560	278	1,089	536	795
Office machines and automatic data processing machines	29,461	4,589	1,131	3,058	2,995	1,484	646	3,746	499	632
Telecommunications, sound recording, reproduction apparatus and equipment	10,896	1,763	1,643	581	433	230	288	1,086	432	420
Electrical machinery, apparatus, and appliances, n.e.s.	34,479	7,936	4,340	1,866	1,666	1,049	635	2,815	1,704	1,420
Road vehicles (incl. air-cushion vehicles)	33,133	17,648	3,650	394	1,596	345	106	1,344	838	361
Transport equipment, n.e.s.	37,188	1,870	754	3,167	2,966	2,196	1,025	3,278	1,150	1,457
Furniture, bedding, mattresses, etc.	2,172	941	536	72	58	36	7	95	11	14
Articles of apparel and clothing accessories	3,316	273	547	95	70	79	71	431	8	7
Professional scientific and control instruments and apparatus	14,062	1,990	1,028	982	1,154	834	489	1,821	335	519
Photo apparatus, equipment and optical goods n.e.s.; watch and clocks	4,247	647	220	527	232	390	101	656	67	37
Miscellaneous manufactured articles	21,212	4,459	1,335	1,710	1,644	854	323	2,499	439	542
Special transactions and commodities not classified by kind	3,737	1,264	187	138	105	43	13	213	94	145
Gold, nonmonetary (excluding ores and concentrates	3,337	411	80	608	61	328	5	81	55	8
Shipments under $10,000 and under $1,500 documented exports	9,854	1,493	1,423	690	556	415	204	621	181	140

See footnotes at end of table.

TABLE 16 (continued)

No. 1350. U.S. Exports and General Imports of Selected Commodities—Value, by Area: 1990—Continued

[**In millions of dollars.** See headnote, page 811]

SELECTED MAJOR COMMODITIES	Total [1]	WESTERN HEMISPHERE		WESTERN EUROPE				ASIA		
		Canada	Mexico	United Kingdom	Ger-many[1]	France	Italy	Japan	China: Taiwan	South Korea
Imports, total	**487,129**	**91,064**	**31,130**	**18,413**	**26,137**	**13,333**	**11,764**	**91,511**	**23,023**	**17,018**
Meat and meat preparations	2,908	603	2	(Z)	2	3	6	4	1	(Z)
Fish (except marine mammal) crustaceans, etc., preps	5,638	1,230	291	19	2	22	2	127	168	131
Vegetables and fruit	5,391	273	1,382	12	92	20	36	41	60	14
Coffee, tea, cocoa, spices manufactures thereof	3,347	167	363	24	88	10	16	3	7	1
Beverages	3,609	569	234	602	158	812	340	31	4	5
Cork and wood	3,057	2,715	143	1	1	3	2	(Z)	4	(Z)
Pulp and waste paper	2,163	1,870	1	(Z)	6	(Z)	-	(Z)	1	-
Metalliferous ores and metal scrap	3,561	942	202	61	37	32	1	18	6	1
Petroleum, petroleum products, and related materials	49,762	6,636	4,564	1,391	54	303	447	19	(Z)	35
Gas, natural and manufactured	3,497	3,074	108	7	4	4	5	(Z)	(Z)	-
Organic chemicals	8,133	757	248	917	1,139	449	385	979	52	74
Inorganic chemicals	3,296	1,024	182	197	429	260	53	185	9	4
Medicinal and pharmaceutical products	3,047	118	18	587	403	128	216	268	4	2
Chemical materials and products, n.e.s.	2,122	302	55	201	331	139	42	280	11	3
Rubber manufactures, n.e.s.	3,334	913	55	88	197	151	91	942	193	216
Cork and wood manufactures other than furniture	1,988	666	102	10	24	45	45	11	251	8
Paper, paperboard and articles	8,021	6,111	119	173	228	131	60	218	63	65
Textile yarn, fabrics, made-up articles, n.e.s.	6,981	500	324	269	327	184	499	615	500	554
Nonmetallic mineral manufactures, n.e.s.	9,678	672	435	537	411	313	578	701	362	102
Iron and steel	9,333	1,531	304	333	764	567	235	2,049	135	588
Nonferrous metals	8,430	3,636	330	343	417	136	30	352	26	5
Manufactures of metals, n.e.s.	8,834	1,270	569	260	548	257	223	1,724	1,585	503
Power generating machinery and equipment	14,195	2,324	1,131	1,698	1,507	2,200	227	3,123	89	100
Machinery specialized for particular industries	10,864	1,109	140	819	2,608	441	646	2,909	342	67
Metalworking machinery	3,605	232	7	173	718	61	134	1,562	144	26
General industrial machinery, equipment, parts	14,396	1,792	831	896	2,088	362	720	3,904	848	319
Office machines and automatic data processing machines	30,019	2,283	724	989	644	282	150	11,831	3,752	1,289
Telecommunications, sound recording, reproduction apparatus and equipment	23,446	1,000	2,944	246	180	146	67	9,394	1,202	1,745
Electrical machinery, apparatus and appliances, n.e.s.	35,067	3,626	4,838	973	2,055	569	262	9,352	2,228	2,432
Road vehicles (incl air-cushion vehicles)	70,576	25,577	4,273	867	5,425	712	528	28,344	804	1,223
Transport equipment, n.e.s.	8,197	2,428	33	1,075	169	1,441	502	633	43	84
Furniture, bedding, mattresses, etc.	4,936	1,066	651	100	175	56	444	208	1,106	50
Travel goods, handbags and similar containers	2,346	16	52	5	12	78	190	9	370	379
Articles of apparel and clothing accessories	26,202	315	910	177	127	179	857	138	2,658	2,762
Footwear	9,554	45	163	40	43	46	787	7	1,168	1,987
Professional scientific and control instruments and apparatus	6,733	577	643	624	1,012	274	75	1,796	194	83
Photo apparatus, equipment and optical goods, n.e.s.; watch and clocks	7,469	221	150	270	353	214	303	2,996	355	152
Miscellaneous manufactured articles, n.e.s.	24,846	1,340	911	1,346	898	703	1,500	4,018	3,025	1,535
Special transactions and commodities not classified by kind	11,718	3,761	1,083	1,092	757	522	171	820	118	133
Estimate of low valued import transactions	3,424	879	302	201	323	115	108	543	160	38

- Represents zero.   Z Less than $500,000.   [1] Effective October 3, 1990 East Germany ceased to exist as a sovereign state and became a part of West Germany. However, trade statistics for Germany comprise of statistics for West Germany and East Germany combined for the period shown. [2] Other than fertilizers covered in SITC division 56 (Fertilizers). [3] Other than crude fertilizers covered in SITC division 272.

Source: U.S. Bureau of the Census, *U.S. Merchandise Trade: Exports, General Imports, and Imports for Consumption*, series FT 927.

TABLE 17

3.28 FOREIGN EXCHANGE RATES[1]

Currency units per dollar except as noted

Country/currency unit	1990	1991	1992	1993 May	June	July	Aug.r	Sept.	Oct.
1 Australia/dollar[2]	78.069	77.872	73.521	69.859	67.492	67.788	67.736	65.167	66.100
2 Austria/schilling	11.331	11.686	10.992	11.305	11.637	12.071	11.920	11.402	11.540
3 Belgium/franc	33.424	34.195	32.148	33.044	34.009	35.483	35.985	34.847	35.674
4 Canada/dollar	1.1668	1.1460	1.2085	1.2698	1.2789	1.2820	1.3080	1.3215	1.3263
5 China, P.R./yuan	4.7921	5.3337	5.5206	5.7392	5.7504	5.7756	5.7906	5.8015	5.8013
6 Denmark/krone	6.1899	6.4038	6.0372	6.1751	6.3380	6.6531	6.8976	6.6336	6.6379
7 Finland/markka	3.8300	4.0521	4.4865	5.4847	5.5674	5.8464	5.8315	5.7868	5.7554
8 France/franc	5.4467	5.6468	5.2935	5.4180	5.5700	5.7852	5.9298	5.6724	5.7541
9 Germany/deutsche mark	1.6166	1.6610	1.5618	1.6071	1.6547	1.7157	1.6944	1.6219	1.6405
10 Greece/drachma	158.59	182.63	190.81	218.12	225.45	234.77	237.64	232.56	237.93
11 Hong Kong/dollar	7.7899	7.7712	7.7402	7.7290	7.7362	7.7556	7.7515	7.7384	7.7307
12 India/rupee	17.492	22.712	28.156	31.613	31.668	31.600	31.612	31.578	31.505
13 Ireland/pound[2]	165.76	161.39	170.42	151.65	147.47	140.83	139.05	143.40	143.19
14 Italy/lira	1,198.27	1,241.28	1,232.17	1,475.66	1,505.05	1,586.02	1,603.75	1,569.10	1,600.93
15 Japan/yen	145.00	134.59	126.78	110.34	107.41	107.69	103.77	105.57	107.02
16 Malaysia/ringgit	2.7057	2.7503	2.5463	2.5661	2.5696	2.5672	2.5514	2.5475	2.5478
17 Netherlands/guilder	1.8215	1.8720	1.7587	1.8026	1.8559	1.9299	1.9062	1.8214	1.8438
18 New Zealand/dollar[2]	59.619	57.832	53.792	54.290	53.949	54.900	55.261	55.157	55.260
19 Norway/krone	6.2541	6.4912	6.2142	6.8027	6.9986	7.3179	7.3579	7.0829	7.1755
20 Portugal/escudo	142.70	144.77	135.07	151.89	157.63	167.87	173.27	166.28	169.60
21 Singapore/dollar	1.8134	1.7283	1.6294	1.6136	1.6175	1.6206	1.6100	1.5972	1.5735
22 South Africa/rand	2.5885	2.7633	2.8524	3.1787	3.2408	3.3518	3.3660	3.4135	3.3924
23 South Korea/won	710.64	736.73	784.58	803.19	805.91	809.58	811.94	811.84	813.45
24 Spain/peseta	101.96	104.01	102.38	121.30	127.11	134.93	138.51	130.54	132.18
25 Sri Lanka/rupee	40.078	41.200	44.013	47.965	48.073	48.643	48.750	48.854	48.954
26 Sweden/krona	5.9231	6.0521	5.8258	7.3271	7.4541	7.9802	8.0466	8.0170	8.0195
27 Switzerland/franc	1.3901	1.4356	1.4064	1.4504	1.4769	1.5147	1.4966	1.4182	1.4432
28 Taiwan/dollar	26.918	26.759	25.160	25.978	26.267	26.682	26.950	26.931	26.865
29 Thailand/baht	25.609	25.528	25.411	25.234	25.214	25.331	25.191	25.196	25.269
30 United Kingdom/pound[2]	178.41	176.74	176.63	154.77	150.82	149.55	149.14	152.48	150.23
MEMO									
31 United States/dollar[3]	89.09	89.84	86.61	90.24	91.81	94.59	94.32	92.07	93.29

1. Averages of certified noon buying rates in New York for cable transfers. Data in this table also appear in the Board's G.5 (405) monthly statistical release. For ordering address, see inside front cover.
2. Value in U.S. cents.
3. Index of weighted-average exchange value of U.S. dollar against the currencies of ten industrial countries. The weight for each of the ten countries is the 1972–76 average world trade of that country divided by the average world trade of all ten countries combined. Series revised as of August 1978 (see *Federal Reserve Bulletin*, vol. 64 (August 1978), p. 700).

TABLE 18

No. 797. Insured Commercial Banks—Assets and Liabilities: 1980 to 1992

[**In billions of dollars, except as indicated**. As of **Dec. 31**. Includes outlying areas. Except as noted, includes foreign branches of U.S. banks. See *Historical Statistics, Colonial Times to 1970*, series X 588-609, for related data]

ITEM	1980	1985	1986	1987	1988	1989	1990	1991	1992 [1]
Number of banks	14,435	14,417	14,209	13,722	13,137	12,713	12,345	11,926	11,461
Assets, total	**1,856**	**2,731**	**2,941**	**3,000**	**3,131**	**3,299**	**3,389**	**3,431**	**3,506**
Net loans and leases.	1,006	1,608	1,728	1,779	1,886	2,004	2,054	1,998	1,978
Real estate loans.	269	438	516	600	675	762	830	851	868
Commercial and industrial loans . . .	391	578	600	589	600	619	615	559	536
Loans to individuals	187	309	336	351	378	401	403	392	385
Farm loans.	32	36	32	29	30	31	33	35	35
Other loans and leases.	137	270	273	259	249	246	229	216	207
Less: Reserve for losses.	10	23	29	50	47	54	56	55	54
Temporary investments	(2)	452	464	451	466	482	451	499	541
Securities over 1 year in length	(2)	298	358	397	383	402	450	514	569
Other	[2]849	374	392	373	397	411	434	420	418
Domestic office assets.	1,533	2,326	2,532	2,575	2,726	2,897	2,999	3,033	3,110
Foreign office assets.	323	406	409	425	405	402	390	398	396
Liabilities and capital, total	1,856	2,731	2,941	3,000	3,131	3,299	3,389	3,431	3,506
Noninterest-bearing deposits [3] . . .	432	471	532	478	479	483	489	480	541
Interest-bearing deposits [4]	1,049	1,646	1,751	1,858	1,952	2,065	2,162	2,207	2,158
Subordinated debt.	7	15	17	18	17	19	24	25	34
Other liabilities	260	429	458	466	486	526	496	486	510
Equity capital	108	169	182	181	197	205	219	232	264
Domestic office deposits.	1,187	1,796	1,970	1,994	2,117	2,237	2,357	2,383	2,412
Foreign office deposits.	294	322	314	342	315	312	293	305	287

[1] Preliminary.   [2] Temporary investments and securities over one year in length included in other.   [3] Prior to 1985, demand deposits.   [4] Prior to 1985, time and savings deposits.
Source: U.S. Federal Deposit Insurance Corporation, *The FDIC Quarterly Banking Profile, Annual Report*, and *Statistics on Banking*, annual.

TABLE 19

No. 799. Insured Commercial Banks, 1991, and Banks Closed or Assisted, 1992, by State and Other Area

[**In billions of dollars, except as indicated**. Includes foreign branches of U.S. banks]

STATE	COMMERCIAL BANKS, [1] 1991			BANKS CLOSED OR ASSISTED, [2] 1992		STATE	COMMERCIAL BANKS, [1] 1991			BANKS CLOSED OR ASSISTED, [2] 1992	
	Number	Assets	Deposits	Number	Deposits		Number	Assets	Deposits	Number	Deposits
Total	11,926	3,430.1	2,687.6	122	41.2	WV	169	18.6	15.7	-	-
U.S. . . .	11,908	3,412.9	2,672.9	121	41.1	NC	81	79.6	59.7	-	-
Northeast . . .	814	1,125.0	826.5	45	29.0	SC	83	25.6	19.0	-	-
N.E.	219	162.9	126.5	31	7.5	GA	405	71.0	54.9	2	0.1
ME	21	8.8	7.4	-	-	FL	421	138.9	119.9	2	(Z)
NH	32	8.5	6.9	3	0.2	**E.S.C.**	912	155.0	128.1	1	(Z)
VT	24	6.0	5.3	-	-	KY	320	42.5	34.1	-	-
MA	73	92.0	67.8	15	3.9	TN	250	49.1	41.3	-	-
RI	13	14.4	10.9	3	1.1	AL	219	41.2	33.6	-	-
CT	56	33.2	28.2	10	2.4	MS	123	22.1	19.1	1	(Z)
M.A.	595	962.1	700.0	14	21.5	**W.S.C**	2,021	258.2	226.2	36	8.3
NY	189	694.8	480.7	7	14.4	AR	262	23.5	20.9	1	(Z)
NJ	117	95.5	81.2	5	3.8	LA	226	37.5	33.0	2	0.1
PA	289	171.9	138.1	2	3.2	OK	411	28.3	24.8	2	(Z)
Midwest	5,194	758.2	610.4	13	2.3	TX	1,122	168.9	147.5	31	8.2
E.N.C.	2,313	525.2	417.6	3	0.1	**West**	1,466	570.5	464.0	17	1.3
OH	280	119.0	92.2	-	-	**Mt.**	814	127.0	103.5	4	0.1
IN	284	59.2	48.5	1	(Z)	MT	145	7.5	6.5	1	(Z)
IL	1,061	199.1	157.0	2	(Z)	ID	22	9.8	7.6	-	-
MI	230	98.8	78.7	-	-	WY	62	4.8	4.3	-	-
WI	458	49.0	41.3	-	-	CO	387	28.1	24.4	-	-
W.N.C	2,881	233.0	192.7	10	2.2	NM	83	12.1	10.7	-	-
MN	608	54.9	45.0	1	(Z)	AZ	41	35.6	30.4	3	(Z)
IA	553	36.3	30.8	-	-	UT	55	13.8	10.5	-	-
MO	532	65.4	54.4	7	2.2	NV	19	15.2	9.1	-	-
ND	146	7.7	6.8	-	-	**Pac**	652	443.5	360.5	13	1.2
SD	125	17.6	11.3	-	-	WA	93	39.6	33.4	-	-
NE	389	21.4	18.6	-	-	OR	51	25.7	20.3	-	-
KS	528	29.8	25.9	2	(Z)	CA	480	352.8	287.1	12	1.2
South	4,434	959.2	771.9	46	8.6	AK	8	4.6	3.5	-	-
S.A.	1,501	546.1	417.7	9	0.2	HI	20	20.8	16.2	1	(Z)
DE	42	74.5	36.0	-	-						
MD	102	54.7	44.0	1	(Z)	AM . . .	1	(Z)	(Z)	-	-
DC	24	14.8	12.7	2	(Z)	PR . . .	14	16.5	14.0	1	(Z)
VA	174	68.5	55.8	2	0.1	GU . . .	2	0.6	0.6	-	-
						Pac. Is .	1	(Z)	(Z)	-	-

- Represents zero.   Z Less than $50 million.   [1] As of December 31.   [2] Includes Bank Insurance Fund-insured savings banks.
Source of tables 798 and 799: U.S. Federal Deposit Insurance Corporation, *Annual Report; Statistics on Banking*, annual; and *FDIC Quarterly Banking Profile*.

TABLE 20

No. 150. National Health Expenditures, by Object: 1970 to 1991

[See headnote, table 149. See also *Historical Statistics, Colonial Times to 1970*, series B 221-235]

OBJECT OF EXPENDITURE	EXPENDITURE (bil. dol.)								PERCENT	
	1970	1980	1985	1987	1988	1989	1990	1991	1970	1991
Total	74.4	250.1	422.6	494.2	546.1	604.3	675.0	751.8	100.0	100.0
Spent by—										
Consumers	42.3	132.9	228.6	264.0	293.8	323.3	358.7	388.6	56.9	51.7
Government	27.7	105.2	174.6	208.0	227.1	253.3	285.1	330.0	37.2	43.9
Other [1]	4.4	12.1	19.4	22.2	25.2	27.7	31.3	33.2	5.9	4.4
Spent for—										
Health services and supplies	69.1	238.9	407.2	476.9	526.2	583.6	652.4	728.6	92.8	96.9
Personal health care expenses	64.9	219.4	369.7	439.3	482.8	530.9	591.5	660.2	87.3	87.8
Hospital care	27.9	102.4	168.3	194.2	212.0	232.4	258.1	288.6	37.6	38.4
Physicians' services.	13.6	41.9	74.0	93.0	105.1	116.1	128.8	142.0	18.3	18.9
Dentists' services	4.7	14.4	23.3	27.1	29.4	31.6	34.1	37.1	6.3	4.9
Other professional services [2].	1.5	8.7	16.6	21.1	23.8	27.1	30.7	35.8	2.0	4.8
Home health care	0.1	1.3	3.8	4.1	4.5	5.6	7.6	9.8	0.2	1.3
Drugs/other medical nondurables	8.8	21.6	36.2	43.2	46.3	50.5	55.6	60.7	11.8	8.1
Vision products/other med. durables [3] .	2.0	4.6	7.1	9.1	10.1	10.4	11.7	12.4	2.7	1.6
Nursing home care	4.9	20.0	34.1	39.7	42.8	47.5	53.3	59.9	6.5	8.0
Other health services.	1.4	4.6	6.4	7.8	8.7	9.8	11.5	14.0	1.8	1.9
Net cost of insurance and admin. [4]	2.8	12.2	25.2	23.0	26.9	33.8	38.9	43.9	3.7	5.8
Government public health activities	1.4	7.2	12.3	14.6	16.6	18.9	22.0	24.5	1.9	3.3
Medical research.	2.0	5.4	7.8	9.0	10.3	11.0	11.9	12.6	2.6	1.7
Medical facilities construction	3.4	5.8	7.6	8.2	9.5	9.7	10.8	10.6	4.5	1.4

[1] Includes nonpatient revenues, privately funded construction, and industrial inplant.   [2] Includes services of registered and practical nurses in private duty, visiting nurses, podiatrists, optometrists, physical therapists, clinical psychologists, chiropractors, naturopaths, and Christian Science practitioners.   [3] Includes expenditures for eyeglasses, hearing aids, orthopedic appliances, artificial limbs, crutches, wheelchairs, etc.   [4] Includes administrative expenses of federally financed health programs.

Source: U.S. Health Care Financing Administration, *Health Care Financing Review,* winter 1992.

TABLE 21

TABLE B-77.—*Federal and State and local government receipts and expenditures, national income and product accounts, 1959–92*

[Billions of dollars; quarterly data at seasonally adjusted annual rates]

Year or quarter	Total government			Federal Government			State and local government		
	Receipts	Expendi-tures	Surplus or deficit (−), national income and product accounts	Receipts	Expendi-tures	Surplus or deficit (−), national income and product accounts	Receipts	Expendi-tures	Surplus or deficit (−), national income and product accounts
1959	128.8	131.9	−3.1	90.6	93.2	−2.6	45.0	45.5	−0.5
1960	138.8	135.2	3.6	97.0	93.4	3.5	48.3	48.3	.0
1961	144.1	147.1	−3.0	99.0	101.7	−2.6	52.4	52.7	−.4
1962	155.8	158.7	−2.9	107.2	110.6	−3.4	56.6	56.1	.5
1963	167.5	165.9	1.6	115.5	114.4	1.1	61.1	60.6	.4
1964	172.9	174.5	−1.6	116.2	118.8	−2.6	67.1	66.1	1.0
1965	187.0	185.8	1.2	125.8	124.6	1.3	72.3	72.3	.0
1966	210.7	211.6	−1.0	143.5	144.9	−1.4	81.5	81.1	.5
1967	226.4	240.2	−13.7	152.6	165.2	−12.7	89.8	90.9	−1.1
1968	260.9	265.5	−4.6	176.8	181.5	−4.7	102.7	102.6	.1
1969	294.0	284.0	10.0	199.6	191.0	8.5	114.8	113.3	1.5
1970	299.8	311.2	−11.5	195.2	208.5	−13.3	129.0	127.2	1.8
1971	318.9	338.1	−19.2	202.6	224.3	−21.7	145.3	142.8	2.5
1972	364.2	368.1	−3.9	232.0	249.3	−17.3	169.7	156.3	13.4
1973	408.5	401.6	6.9	263.7	270.3	−6.6	185.3	171.9	13.4
1974	450.7	455.2	−4.5	294.0	305.6	−11.6	200.6	193.5	7.1
1975	465.8	530.6	−64.8	294.8	364.2	−69.4	225.6	221.0	4.6
1976	532.6	570.9	−38.3	339.9	392.7	−52.9	253.9	239.3	14.6
1977	598.4	615.2	−16.8	384.0	426.4	−42.4	281.9	256.3	25.6
1978	673.2	670.3	2.9	441.2	469.3	−28.1	309.3	278.2	31.1
1979	754.7	745.3	9.4	504.7	520.3	−15.7	330.6	305.4	25.1
1980	825.7	861.0	−35.3	553.0	613.1	−60.1	361.4	336.6	24.8
1981	941.9	972.3	−30.3	639.0	697.8	−58.8	390.8	362.3	28.5
1982	960.5	1,069.1	−108.6	635.4	770.9	−135.5	409.0	382.1	26.9
1983	1,016.4	1,156.2	−139.8	660.0	840.0	−180.1	443.4	403.2	40.3
1984	1,123.6	1,232.4	−108.8	725.8	892.7	−166.9	492.2	434.1	58.1
1985	1,217.0	1,342.2	−125.3	788.6	969.9	−181.4	528.7	472.6	56.1
1986	1,290.8	1,437.5	−146.8	827.2	1,028.2	−201.0	571.2	517.0	54.3
1987	1,405.2	1,516.9	−111.7	913.8	1,065.6	−151.8	594.3	554.2	40.1
1988	1,492.4	1,590.7	−98.3	972.3	1,109.0	−136.6	631.3	593.0	38.4
1989	1,622.6	1,700.1	−77.5	1,059.3	1,181.6	−122.3	681.5	636.7	44.8
1990	1,704.4	1,840.5	−136.1	1,107.4	1,273.6	−166.2	729.3	699.2	30.1
1991	1,746.8	1,940.1	−193.3	1,122.2	1,332.7	−210.4	777.9	760.7	17.1
1982: IV	965.9	1,122.8	−156.9	632.3	815.7	−183.4	417.9	391.4	26.5
1983: IV	1,043.7	1,180.0	−136.3	671.1	855.7	−184.6	459.5	411.1	48.3
1984: IV	1,147.1	1,274.9	−127.8	739.8	926.6	−186.8	505.1	446.1	59.0
1985: IV	1,243.8	1,374.7	−130.9	803.6	990.8	−187.2	544.8	488.4	56.3
1986: IV	1,335.4	1,461.6	−126.2	856.8	1,034.3	−177.5	582.4	531.1	51.2
1987: IV	1,445.7	1,561.5	−115.8	943.5	1,096.3	−152.7	605.1	568.1	37.0
1988: IV	1,535.8	1,630.5	−94.7	1,000.6	1,135.5	−134.9	648.2	607.9	40.2
1989: I	1,597.9	1,664.0	−66.1	1,050.9	1,160.8	−110.0	662.8	618.9	43.9
II	1,625.4	1,686.9	−61.5	1,064.5	1,174.2	−109.7	678.0	629.8	48.2
III	1,622.8	1,705.1	−82.3	1,053.6	1,181.5	−128.0	687.4	641.7	45.7
IV	1,644.1	1,744.3	−100.2	1,068.3	1,209.8	−141.5	697.7	656.4	41.3
1990: I	1,671.7	1,803.4	−131.7	1,086.7	1,254.5	−167.8	713.1	677.0	36.1
II	1,699.5	1,822.6	−123.1	1,109.6	1,266.5	−156.9	722.1	688.3	33.8
III	1,724.1	1,839.4	−115.3	1,119.9	1,265.5	−145.6	735.4	705.0	30.3
IV	1,722.3	1,896.8	−174.4	1,113.3	1,307.9	−194.6	746.6	726.4	20.2
1991: I	1,724.3	1,859.6	−135.3	1,114.6	1,264.4	−149.9	754.0	739.4	14.6
II	1,734.7	1,930.4	−195.6	1,117.3	1,329.4	−212.2	769.3	752.8	16.5
III	1,757.8	1,963.3	−205.6	1,127.7	1,348.7	−221.0	783.5	768.1	15.4
IV	1,770.4	2,007.0	−236.6	1,129.4	1,388.1	−258.7	804.6	782.5	22.0
1992: I	1,796.0	2,068.6	−272.6	1,143.3	1,432.5	−289.2	817.8	801.2	16.6
II	1,809.6	2,094.9	−285.2	1,149.8	1,452.7	−302.9	834.0	816.3	17.7
III	1,821.5	2,116.6	−295.2	1,155.4	1,459.8	−304.4	840.0	830.8	9.2

Note.—Federal grants-in-aid to State and local governments are reflected in Federal expenditures and State and local receipts. Total government receipts and expenditures have been adjusted to eliminate this duplication.

Source: Department of Commerce, Bureau of Economic Analysis.

TABLE 22

TABLE B-75.—*Federal receipts, outlays, and debt, fiscal years 1981-93*

[Millions of dollars; fiscal years]

Description	Actual					Estimates
	1988	1989	1990	1991	1992	1993
RECEIPTS AND OUTLAYS:						
Total receipts	908,954	990,691	1,031,308	1,054,264	1,091,631	1,147,588
Total outlays	1,064,140	1,143,172	1,252,691	1,323,785	1,381,791	1,474,935
Total surplus or deficit (−)	−155,187	−152,481	−221,384	−269,521	−290,160	−327,347
On-budget receipts	667,463	727,026	749,652	760,380	789,205	828,183
On-budget outlays	861,449	932,261	1,027,626	1,082,098	1,129,475	1,208,120
On-budget surplus or deficit (−)	−193,986	−205,235	−277,974	−321,719	−340,270	−379,937
Off-budget receipts	241,491	263,666	281,656	293,885	302,426	319,405
Off-budget outlays	202,691	210,911	225,065	241,687	252,316	266,815
Off-budget surplus or deficit (−)	38,800	52,754	56,590	52,198	50,110	52,590
OUTSTANDING DEBT, END OF PERIOD:						
Gross Federal debt	2,600,760	2,867,537	3,206,347	3,598,993	4,002,669	4,410,475
Held by Government accounts	550,507	678,210	795,990	911,060	1,004,039	1,100,758
Held by the public	2,050,252	2,189,327	2,410,357	2,687,933	2,998,630	3,309,717
Federal Reserve System	229,218	220,088	234,410	258,591	296,397	....
Other	1,821,034	1,969,239	2,175,947	2,429,342	2,702,234	....
RECEIPTS: ON-BUDGET AND OFF-BUDGET	908,954	990,691	1,031,308	1,054,264	1,091,631	1,147,588
Individual income taxes	401,181	445,690	466,884	467,827	476,465	510,388
Corporation income taxes	94,508	103,291	93,507	98,086	100,270	105,501
Social insurance taxes and contributions	334,335	359,416	380,047	396,016	413,689	435,831
On-budget	92,845	95,751	98,392	102,131	111,263	116,426
Off-budget	241,491	263,666	281,656	293,885	302,426	319,405
Excise taxes	35,227	34,386	35,345	42,402	45,569	47,539
Estate and gift taxes	7,594	8,745	11,500	11,138	11,143	12,594
Customs duties and fees	16,198	16,334	16,707	15,949	17,359	18,176
Miscellaneous receipts:						
Deposits of earnings by Federal Reserve System	17,163	19,604	24,319	19,158	22,920	13,090
All other	2,747	3,225	2,997	3,688	4,215	4,469
OUTLAYS: ON-BUDGET AND OFF-BUDGET	1,064,140	1,143,172	1,252,691	1,323,785	1,381,791	1,474,935
National defense	290,361	303,559	299,331	273,292	298,361	289,299
International affairs	10,471	9,573	13,764	15,851	16,106	18,704
General science, space, and technology	10,841	12,838	14,444	16,111	16,409	17,142
Energy	2,297	2,706	3,341	2,436	4,509	4,807
Natural resources and environment	14,606	16,182	17,067	18,552	20,017	21,462
Agriculture	17,210	16,919	11,958	15,183	14,997	21,533
Commerce and housing credit	18,815	29,211	67,142	75,639	9,514	22,141
On-budget	18,815	29,520	65,516	74,321	8,877	20,514
Off-budget	....	−310	1,626	1,317	636	1,627
Transportation	27,272	27,608	29,485	31,099	33,337	36,380
Community and regional development	5,294	5,362	8,498	6,811	7,411	10,086
Education, training, employment, and social services	31,938	36,674	38,755	43,354	45,248	52,292
Health	44,487	48,390	57,716	71,183	89,570	104,979
Medicare	78,878	84,964	98,102	104,489	119,024	132,839
Income security	129,332	136,031	147,019	170,301	198,073	207,433
Social security	219,341	232,542	248,623	269,015	287,545	304,747
On-budget	4,852	5,069	3,625	2,619	6,127	6,023
Off-budget	214,489	227,473	244,998	266,395	281,418	298,724
Veterans benefits and services	29,428	30,066	29,112	31,349	34,133	35,575
Administration of justice	9,236	9,474	9,995	12,276	14,450	15,229
General government	9,464	9,017	10,734	11,661	12,939	14,728
Net interest	151,838	169,266	184,221	194,541	199,429	202,771
On-budget	159,253	180,661	200,212	214,763	223,066	229,793
Off-budget	−7,416	−11,395	−15,991	−20,222	−23,637	−27,022
Undistributed offsetting receipts	−36,967	−37,212	−36,615	−39,356	−39,280	−37,213
On-budget	−32,585	−32,354	−31,048	−33,553	−33,179	−30,698
Off-budget	−4,382	−4,858	−5,567	−5,804	−6,101	−6,515

See *Budget Baselines, Historical Data, and Alternatives for the Future,* January 1993, for additional information.
Sources: Department of the Treasury and Office of Management and Budget.

TABLE 23

Figure 10.1
The Government of the United States
(As of July 1, 1992)

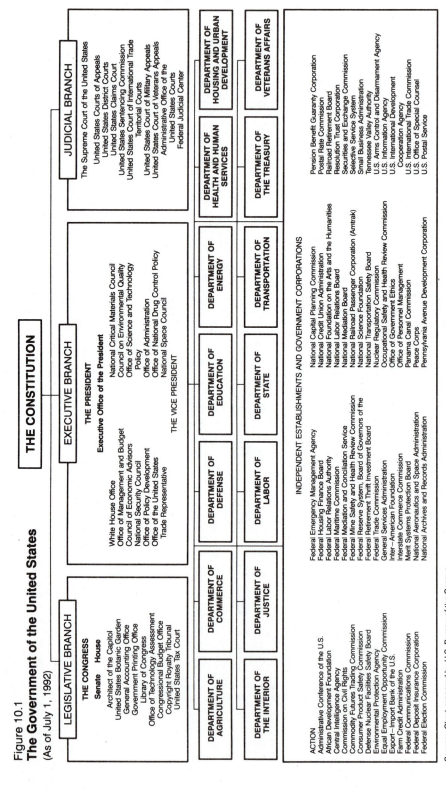

Source: Chart prepared by U.S. Bureau of the Census.

APPENDIX 7

Economic Forecasts

1. "Economic Assumptions Underlying the Fiscal Year 1994 Budget," from Karl Galbraith, "Federal Budget Estimates, Fiscal Year 1994," *Survey of Current Business* (April 1993), p. 46. These forecasts are used by administration economists to project federal outlays and receipts in upcoming years. Consult future *SCB* articles on the federal budget for updated forecasts.

2. "Economic Projections for 1993 and 1994," from Alan Greenspan, "Monetary Policy Report to the Congress," *Federal Reserve Bulletin* (September 1993), p. 830. Forecasts of economic activity by Federal Reserve officials. These forecasts are included in the Federal Reserve's semiannual report to Congress, published every six months in the *Federal Reserve Bulletin*.

3. "The Livingston Survey," Federal Reserve Bank of Philadelphia (December 1993). The oldest continuous survey of forecasts by economists. The survey reflects forecasts by 50 academic and business economists. A subscription is available from the Philadelphia Fed (see Appendix 3 for the address).

4. "A Sampling of Interest-Rate, Economic and Currency Forecasts," *Wall Street Journal* (January 3, 1994). Forecasts of real GDP growth, inflation, interest rates, and exchange rates by 40–50 business economists. This table is published semiannually, during the first week of January and July.

TABLE 1

Table 1.—Economic Assumptions Underlying the Fiscal Year 1994 Budget

	Calendar year		
	Actual	Estimates	
	1992	1993	1994
	Billions of dollars		
GDP:			
Current dollars	5,951	6,254	6,594
1987 dollars	4,923	5,054	5,204
Incomes:			
Personal income	5,058	5,308	5,617
Wages and salaries	2,918	3,055	3,226
Corporate profits before taxes	372	432	457
	Percent change from preceding year		
GDP in current dollars:			
Annual average	4.8	5.2	5.4
Fourth quarter	5.6	5.4	5.4
GDP in 1987 dollars:			
Annual average	2.1	2.8	3.0
Fourth quarter	2.5	2.8	3.0
GDP implicit price deflator:			
Annual average	2.6	2.4	2.4
Fourth quarter	3.3	2.5	2.4
Consumer Price Index: [1]			
Annual average	3.0	3.0	2.7
Fourth quarter	3.1	2.8	2.7
	Percent		
Unemployment rate: [2]			
Annual average	7.4	7.1	6.6
Fourth quarter	7.3	6.9	6.4
Interest rate (annual average): [3]			
91-day Treasury bills	3.5	3.2	3.7
10-year Treasury notes	7.0	6.7	6.6

1. Consumer Price Index for urban wage earners and clerical workers.
2. Percent of labor force, including armed forces residing in the United States.
3. Average rate on new issues within a year.
Source: The Budget of the United States Government. Fiscal Year 1994.

TABLE 2

Economic Projections for 1993 and 1994

		FOMC Members and Other FRB Presidents	
1993		Range	Central Tendency
Percentage change, fourth quarter to fourth quarter:	Nominal GDP	4¾ to 6¼	5 to 5¾
	Real GDP	2 to 3½	2¼ to 2¾
	Consumer price index	3 to 3½	3 to 3¼
Average level in the fourth quarter, percent:	Civilian unemployment rate	6½ to 7	6¾
1994		Range	Central Tendency
Percentage change, fourth quarter to fourth quarter:	Nominal GDP	4½ to 6¾	5 to 6½
	Real GDP	2 to 3¼	2½ to 3¼
	Consumer price index	2 to 4¼	3 to 3½
Average level in the fourth quarter, percent:	Civilian unemployment rate	6¼ to 7	6½ to 6¾

TABLE 3

THE LIVINGSTON SURVEY, DECEMBER 1993
(mean forecast)

Quarterly Indicators	Q4 1993	Q2 1994	Q4 1994	Annual Average 1993	Annual Average 1994	1995
Real Gross Domestic Product (billions, SAAR)	$5186.1	5257.3	5333.2	5125.2	5278.6	5421.3
Gross Domestic Product (bil. '87, SAAR)	$6496.2	6661.9	6849.4	6370.9	6721.8	7112.2
Real Nonresidential Fixed Investment (bil. '87, SAAR)	$607.1	627.1	646.4	587.0	632.7	668.7
Corporate Profits after taxes (billions, SAAR)	$281.7	291.4	301.2	268.7	292.5	308.5

Monthly Indicators	Dec 1993	June 1994	Dec 1994	Annual Average 1993	Annual Average 1994	1995
Industrial Production (1987=100)	113.3	115.2	117.1	111.0	115.3	118.9
Total Private Housing Starts (millions, SAAR)	1.390	1.402	1.408	1.281	1.395	1.420
Producer Prices - Finished Goods	124.5	126.2	128.0	124.8	126.8	130.5
Consumer Prices	146.0	148.2	150.6	144.7	148.9	154.0
Unemployment Rate (%)	6.5	6.4	6.2	6.8	6.4	6.1
Average Weekly Earnings in Manufacturing	$498.10	505.57	516.33	483.61	503.51	523.20
Retail Trade (billions,SAAR)	$179.4	184.3	189.8	173.7	184.4	193.9
Automobile Sales, including foreign (millions, SAAR)	9.1	9.2	9.2	8.7	9.2	9.4

Interest Rates & Stock Prices (End of Period)	Dec 1993	June 1994	Dec 1994	Dec 1995
Prime Interest Rate (%)	6.0	6.1	6.4	6.8
30-Yr U.S. Treasury Bond (%)	6.2	6.3	6.4	6.7
90-Day U.S. Treasury Bill (%)	3.1	3.4	3.7	4.2
Stock Prices (S&P 500)	466.6	476.3	484.4	502.8

SAAR - Seasonally Adjusted Annual Rate

TABLE 4

A Sampling of Interest-Rate, Economic and Currency Forecasts

(In percent except for the dollar vs. yen)

	JUNE 1993 SURVEY					NEW FORECASTS FOR 1994									
	3-MO. TREASURY BILLS-a 12/31	30-YR. BONDS 12/31	GDP-b 2nd HALF 1993	CPI-c 2nd HALF 1993	DLR. vs. YEN 12/31	3-MONTH TREASURY BILLS-a 6/30	3-MONTH TREASURY BILLS-a 12/31	30-YEAR TREASURY BONDS 6/30	30-YEAR TREASURY BONDS 12/31	GDP-d 1st HALF	GDP-d 2nd HALF	INFLATION RATE-e MAY 1994	INFLATION RATE-e NOV 1994	DOLLAR vs. YEN JUNE	DOLLAR vs. YEN DEC
Maureen Allyn, Scudder Stevens Clark	3.30	6.75	3.4	3.0	114	3.55	4.60	5.90	6.90	0.7	2.9	2.8	3.2	119	126
Robert Barbera, Lehman Brothers	3.50	6.80	3.5	3.5	118	3.70	4.20	6.40	6.60	3.6	3.4	3.0	3.3	115	125
Richard Berner, Mellon Bank	3.75	6.80	3.6	2.9	110	3.55	3.75	5.75	5.90	2.5	3.2	2.0	3.0	112	115
David Berson, Fannie Mae	3.20	7.10	3.6	3.0	115	3.50	3.90	6.40	6.55	3.1	2.5	2.9	3.2	113	120
Paul Boltz, T. Rowe Price	3.30	6.90	3.0	3.1	105	3.63	4.13	6.63	6.88	3.1	3.2	2.7	2.8	108	103
David Bostian, Herzog, Heine, Geduld	N.A.	N.A.	N.A.	N.A.	N.A.	3.45	3.60	6.40	6.75	2.4	3.2	3.2	3.4	109	114
Philip Braverman, DKB Securities	2.9	6.25	2.3	3.0	105	2.95	2.60	5.75	5.50	1.5	1.8	2.2	2.0	100	95
William Brown, J.P. Morgan	3.50	6.50	3.5	2.8	115	3.90	4.40	6.40	6.50	3.1	3.5	2.5	2.8	117	120
Ed Campbell, Brown Bros.	N.A	N.A.	N.A.	N.A.	N.A.	3.10	3.25	6.00	6.25	3.2	3.4	2.5	2.7	110	115
Gary Ciminero, Fleet Financial Group	3.19	6.98	2.4	3.4	115	3.36	3.59	6.51	6.77	2.2	2.7	2.8	3.2	112	114
James Coons, Huntington Natl Bank	N.A.	N.A.	N.A.	N.A.	N.A.	3.15	3.15	6.10	5.85	3.0	3.0	2.4	2.6	115	118
Michael Cosgrove, The Econoclast	3.40	7.36	3.3	3.3	120	3.40	3.70	6.50	6.90	2.2	2.5	3.5	4.0	112	110
Dewey Daane, Vanderbilt Univ.	3.50	7.25	3.2	3.4	110	3.70	3.95	6.85	7.25	3.4	3.1	3.3	3.7	115	108
Robert Dederick, Northern Trust	3.60	6.85	3.4	3.0	110	3.70	4.20	6.25	6.40	3.3	3.1	2.4	2.8	115	120
Michael Englund, MMS Intl	N.A.	N.A.	N.A.	N.A.	N.A.	3.35	3.60	5.50	6.00	3.3	3.5	2.9	2.9	115	116
Michael Evans, Evans Group	N.A.	N.A.	N.A.	N.A.	N.A.	3.00	3.15	6.10	6.30	1.7	1.8	2.9	3.4	105	110
Gail Fosler, Conference Board	3.10	6.80	2.6	3.5	105	3.50	3.80	6.50	6.50	3.4	3.0	3.5	3.9	110	113
Lyle Gramley, Mortg. Bankers Assn.	3.60	7.00	3.7	3.1	115	3.70	4.30	6.40	6.60	3.1	2.9	2.9	3.1	110	112
Maury Harris, PaineWebber Inc.	3.30	6.50	3.0	2.5	110	3.10	3.20	5.70	6.20	2.1	3.1	2.5	2.5	110	115
H.E. Heinemann, Ladenburg, Thal.	3.50	7.50	2.5	3.9	104	3.60	4.50	6.70	7.70	2.4	1.8	3.1	4.6	109	104
Richard Hoey, Dreyfus Corp.	3.30	6.80	3.2	2.7	110	3.35	3.60	6.30	6.50	2.9	2.2	2.6	3.4	115	118
William Hummer, Wayne Hummer	3.30	7.00	2.8	3.2	111	3.80	4.10	6.80	7.10	3.3	3.4	3.2	3.6	113	120
Edward Hyman, ISI Group Inc.	3.10	6.30	3.0	2.0	110	3.80	3.80	5.50	5.50	2.5	3.0	2.0	2.0	118	120
Saul Hymans, Univ. of Michigan	3.12	6.80	1.9	3.1	105	3.07	3.19	6.51	6.54	2.6	1.9	2.6	3.2	107	108
Mieczyslaw Karczmar, Deutsche Bank	3.30	7.15	3.1	3.5	110	3.50	4.00	7.00	7.25	3.2	2.7	3.2	3.5	115	125
Kurt Karl, WEFA Group	N.A.	N.A.	N.A.	N.A.	N.A.	3.30	3.50	6.40	6.50	2.9	3.0	2.6	3.3	120	124
Irwin Kellner, Chemical Bank	3.30	7.00	2.3	2.8	100	3.15	3.25	6.10	6.00	2.1	1.7	1.5	1.5	105	100
Michael Keran, Prudential Insurance	N.A.	N.A.	N.A.	N.A.	N.A.	3.06	2.80	5.80	5.80	2.5	2.5	2.4	2.5	110	110
Lawrence Kudlow, Bear Stearns	4.00	7.40	4.5	3.8	120	3.40	3.60	6.90	7.30	3.5	2.3	2.7	3.7	112	115
Carol Leisenring, CoreStates Fin'l	3.70	6.90	3.3	2.4	115	3.40	4.00	6.10	6.50	2.7	2.8	2.4	2.5	115	108
Mickey Levy, NationsBank Cap.Mkts	3.20	6.50	2.9	3.2	107	3.30	3.60	5.90	6.10	3.1	3.0	2.2	3.0	115	112
John Lonski, Moody's Investors Svc	N.A.	N.A.	N.A.	N.A.	N.A.	3.37	3.68	6.50	6.80	3.2	3.6	3.0	3.4	112	115
Arnold Moskowitz, Moskowitz Capital	3.50	6.75	3.2	3.3	114	3.20	3.30	5.75	5.70	2.2	1.7	2.6	2.4	106	105
David Munro, High Frequency Econ.	N.A.	N.A.	N.A.	N.A.	N.A.	3.50	3.80	6.10	5.90	2.8	2.9	2.1	2.2	N.A	N.A.
Elliott Platt, Donaldson Lufkin	3.06	7.00	3.5	3.3	115	3.30	3.30	6.38	5.75	3.5	3.0	3.0	3.0	117	115
Donald Ratajczak, Georgia State Univ.	3.20	7.07	3.3	2.9	105	3.42	4.05	6.45	6.65	2.7	3.5	2.7	2.9	109	107
Lynn Reaser, First Interstate Bancorp	3.62	6.70	3.5	3.5	112	3.55	3.75	6.30	6.40	3.1	2.7	2.7	3.2	114	117
David Resler, Nomura Securities Int'l	3.10	6.50	3.2	2.8	115	3.30	3.60	6.00	5.75	3.0	2.7	2.5	2.7	111	115
Alan Reynolds, Hudson Institute	4.00	7.50	3.7	4.0	115	3.60	4.00	6.90	7.30	3.3	2.3	2.9	3.8	112	116
Richard Rippe, Prudential Securities	3.60	7.00	3.2	2.8	115	3.55	4.10	6.50	6.75	3.0	2.7	2.6	3.2	115	110
Norman Robertson, Carnegie Mellon	3.30	6.70	2.8	3.0	115	3.60	4.00	6.30	6.40	2.9	3.1	2.9	3.2	110	115
A. Gary Shilling, Shilling & Co.	2.50	6.00	2.0	2.2	130	2.50	2.50	5.50	5.00	1.5	2.0	1.9	2.0	140	160
Allen Sinai, Lehman Bros.	3.18	6.50	2.3	3.0	107	3.20	3.47	6.35	6.64	2.4	3.5	2.2	2.7	117	121
Neal Soss, First Boston Corp.	3.25	5.99	3.0	3.2	100	3.50	3.75	6.25	6.50	2.8	3.4	2.8	3.2	115	125
Susan Sterne, Economic Analysis	N.A.	N.A.	N.A.	N.A.	N.A.	4.00	3.50	7.00	6.50	3.4	1.1	3.2	3.7.	N.A.	N.A.
Donald Straszheim, Merrill Lynch	3.10	6.65	3.6	2.5	110	3.65	3.90	6.15	5.90	2.9	3.2	2.3	2.7	106	100
Anthony Vignola, Kidder Peabody	3.50	7.00	3.3	3.2	113	3.50	4.00	6.50	6.75	3.2	2.8	2.8	3.3	114	117
John Williams, Bankers Trust	3.00	6.30	2.8	2.5	100	3.10	3.15	6.15	6.00	2.7	2.8	2.6	2.8	125	135
Raymond Worseck, A.G. Edwards	3.80	7.00	3.5	3.7	120	3.30	3.60	6.10	6.40	2.8	2.8	3.0	3.0	117	122
David Wyss, DRI/McGraw-Hill	3.50	6.90	3.1	3.2	103	3.25	3.70	6.20	6.30	2.9	2.7	2.7	3.2	111	105
Edward Yardeni, C.J. Lawrence	3.50	7.08	3.0	2.0	120	3.00	3.00	5.75	5.25	3.0	3.2	2.0	2.0	115	119
AVERAGE-f	3.36	6.83	3.1	3.1	111	3.40	3.67	6.26	6.39	2.8	2.8	2.7	3.0	113	115
Closing Rates as of 12/31/93-g	3.05	6.34	N.A.	N.A.	112										

N.A.-Not available, did not participate in prior survey. a-Treasury bill rates are on a bond-equivalent basis. b-Gross domestic product, annualized rate. c-Consumer price index, annual rate. d-Annualized rate based on rounded average of quarter to prior quarter estimates. e-CPI vs. 12 months earlier. f-Averages for the June survey are for the analysts polled at that time. g-Government estimates of second half gross domestic product and inflation are not yet available.

APPENDIX 8

Macroeconomic Methods and Issues Reading List

Aggregate Income, Growth, and the NIPA Accounts

"Index to the NIPA Tables," *Survey of Current Business* (August 1993). [Published annually, July or August; use this index to locate detailed entries in the national income and product accounts, featured each month in the *Survey of Current Business (SCB)*.]

"A Look at How BEA Presents the NIPA's," *Survey of Current Business* (February 1993): 30–32.

"Principal Source Data and Estimating Methods Used in Preparing Current-Dollar Estimates of GDP," *Survey of Current Business* (July 1992): 25–36.

Roy H. Webb, "The National Income and Product Accounts," *Economic Review*, Federal Reserve Bank of Richmond (May/June 1986). [Reprinted in *Macroeconomic Data: A User's Guide* (Federal Res. Bank of Richmond, 1991).]

Richard M. Beemiller and Ann Dunbar, "Gross State Product, 1977–90," *Survey of Current Business* (December 1993): 28–49.

Linnea Hazen, "State Personal Income, Revised Estimates for 1990–92," *Survey of Current Business* (September 1993): 70–85. [State personal income, by industry of employment.]

Richard D. Raddock, "Recent Developments in Industrial Capacity and Utilization," *Federal Reserve Bulletin* (June 1990): 411–435. [In addition, each issue of the *Bulletin* contains a brief article and data on industrial production.]

David M. Gould and Roy J. Ruffin, "What Determines Economic Growth?" *Economic Review*, Federal Reserve Bank of Dallas (1993, 2nd quarter): 25–40. [A survey of theories about the causes of long-term economic growth.]

Stanley L. Engerman and Robert E. Gallman (ed.), *Long-Term Factors in American Economic Growth* (Chicago: University of Chicago Press, 1986).

Mark A. Wynne, "The Comparative Growth Performance of the U.S. Economy in the Postwar Period," *Economic Review*, Federal Reserve Bank of Dallas (January 1992): 1–16. [The "convergence theory" of economic growth.]

The Business Cycle and Forecasting

Craig Carlock, "Business Cycle Theories," *Cross Sections*, Federal Reserve Bank of Richmond (Winter 1990/91): 6–9. Reprinted in this text, Chapter 6.

Marie Hertzberg and Barry A. Beckman, "Business Cycle Indicators: Revised Composite Indexes," *Survey of Current Business* (January 1989): 23–28.

George R. Green and Barry A. Beckman, "The Composite Index of Coincident Indicators and Alternative Coincident Indicators," *Survey of Current Business* (June 1992): 42–45.

"Diffusion Indexes of Industrial Production" *Federal Reserve Bulletin* (July 1991): 534–536.

George Hildebrand, *Business Cycle Indicators and Measures: A Complete Guide to Interpreting the Key Economic Indicators* (Chicago: Probus Publishing Co., 1992). [Snapshots of about 200 economic indicators.]

Handbook of Cyclical Indicators (Washington: U.S. Department of Commerce, 1984).

"A Better Entrail," *The Economist* (February 10, 1990): 65. [An article highlighting "the probability of recession" index for the U.S. economy.]

Herb Taylor, "The Livingston Surveys: A History of Hopes and Fears," *Business Review*, Federal Reserve Bank of Philadelphia (January/February 1992).

Tom Herman, "A Sampling of Interest-Rate, Economic and Currency Forecasts," *Wall Street Journal* (January 3, 1994): A2. [Semiannual survey of economists, reprinted in Appendix 7 of this text.]

Stephen K. McNees, "How Large are Economic Forecast Errors?" *New England Economic Review* (July/August 1992): 25–42.

Stephen K. McNees, "Man vs. Model? The Role of Judgment in Forecasting," *New England Economic Review*, Federal Reserve Bank of Boston (July/August 1990): 41–52.

Francis X. Diebold, "Are Long Expansions Followed by Short Contractions?" *Business Review*, Federal Reserve Bank of Philadelphia (July/August 1993): 3–11. [Experience suggests that the length of a recession can be fairly accurately predicted by knowing the length of the previous expansion.]

Lawrence R. Klein (ed.), *Comparative Performance of U.S. Econometric Models* (Oxford Univ. Press, 1991).

Prices and Inflation

John K. Hill and Kenneth J. Robinson, "Money, Wages and Factor Scarcity as Predictors of Inflation," *Economic Review*, Federal Reserve Bank of Dallas (May 1989): 21–29.

Roy H. Webb and Rob Willemese, "Macroeconomic Price Indexes," *Economic Review*, Federal Reserve Bank of Richmond (July/August 1989).

[Reprinted in *Macroeconomic Data: A User's Guide* (Federal Reserve Bank of Richmond, 1991).]

"Consumer Price Index," *BLS Handbook of Methods* (Washington, DC: U.S. Department of Labor, 1988): ch. 19.

"Producer Prices," *BLS Handbook of Methods* (Washington, DC: U.S. Department of Labor, 1988): ch. 16.

American Chamber of Commerce Researchers Association, "Cost of Living Index—Selected Metropolitan Areas," *Statistical Abstract of the United States: 1993* (Washington: U.S. Government Printing Office, 1993). [An index of relative living costs in most metropolitan areas.]

Jeffrey J. Hallman, Richard D. Porter, and David H. Small, "M2 per Unit of Potential GNP as an Anchor for the Price Level," Federal Reserve Staff Study (1989): number 157. [A summary of this study appeared in the *Federal Reserve Bulletin* (April 1989): 263–264.]

Frank de Leeuw, "A Price Index for New Multifamily Housing," *Survey of Current Business* (February 1993): 33–42.

Labor Markets

Janice Shack-Marquez, "Issues in Labor Supply," *Federal Reserve Bulletin* (June 1991): 375–387.

Roy H. Webb and William Whelpley, "Labor Market Data," *Economic Review*, Federal Reserve Bank of Richmond (November/December 1989). [Reprinted in *Macroeconomic Data: A User's Guide* (Federal Reserve Bank of Richmond (1991).]

"Labor Force, Employment, and Unemployment from the Current Population Survey," *BLS Handbook of Methods* (Washington, DC: U.S. Department of Labor, 1988): ch. 1.

Phillip B. Levine, "CPS Contemporaneous and Retrospective Unemployment Compared," *Monthly Labor Review* (August 1993): 33–39. [Compares unemployment rates as measured by two different surveys.]

Alfred L. Malabre and Lindley H. Clark, "Productivity Statistics for the Service Sector May Understate Gains," *Wall Street Journal* (August 12, 1992): A.1.

John E. Breffer and Cathryn S. Dippo, "Overhauling the Current Population Survey: Why is it Necessary to Change?" *Monthly Labor Review* (September 1993): 3–9. [A discussion of the Census Bureau's monthly survey of household employment and unemployment patterns.]

"Major Agreements Expiring Next Month," *Monthly Labor Review* (September 1993): 43. [A list of collective bargaining agreements that expire during the month; used by labor economists to monitor wage trends, non-wage benefits and strike situations. This item appears each month in the *MLR*.]

"Productivity Measures: Business Sector and Major Subsectors," *BLS Handbook of Methods* (Washington, DC: U.S. Department of Labor, 1988): ch. 10.

Consumer Spending, Saving, and Confidence

David W. Wilcox, "Household Spending and Saving: Measurement, Trends and Analysis," *Federal Reserve Bulletin* (January 1991): 1–17.

"Consumer Expenditures and Income," *BLS Handbook of Methods* (Washington, DC: U.S. Department of Labor, 1988): ch. 18.

Arthur Kennickell and Janice Shack-Marquez, "Changes in Family Finances from 1983–1989: Evidence from the Survey of Consumer Finances," *Federal Reserve Bulletin* (January 1992): 1–18.

Dawn M. Spinozza, "Two Indexes Track Consumer Confidence," *Cross Sections*, Federal Reserve Bank of Richmond (Summer 1991): 8–9.

C. Alan Garner, "Forecasting Consumer Spending: Should Economists Pay Attention to Consumer Confidence Surveys?" *Economic Review*, Federal Reserve Bank of Kansas City (May/June 1991): 57–71.

Jeffrey C. Fuhrer, "What Role Does Consumer Sentiment Play in the U.S. Macroeconomy?" *New England Economic Review*, Federal Reserve Bank of Boston (January/February 1993): 32–44.

Business and Industry

Robert P. Parker, "Gross Product by Industry, 1977–90," *Survey of Current Business* (May 1993): 33–54. [Contribution to GDP by major industries.]

Stephen Oliner, "The Formation of Private Business Capital: Trends, Recent Developments and Measurement Issues," *Federal Reserve Bulletin* (December 1989): 771–783.

"Corporate Performance Review," *Wall Street Journal* (February, May, August, November). [Quarterly profit report for most major companies in the U.S.]

Richard Kopcke, "The Determinants of Business Investment: Has Capital Spending Been Surprisingly Low?" *New England Economic Review*, Federal Reserve Bank of Boston (January 1993). [Review of investment theories and evidence.]

Kevin L. Kliesen, "Restructuring and Economic Growth: Taking the Long-Term View," *The Regional Economist*, Federal Reserve Bank of St. Louis (July 1993): 5–9. [Corporate downsizing makes firms more efficient, but confuses policy makers about the economy's true direction.]

Allan D. Brunner and William English, "Profits and Balance Sheet Developments at U.S. Commercial Banks in 1992," *Federal Reserve Bulletin* (July 1993): 649–73. [Annual article reporting on the condition of the banking industry.]

Credit Markets and Interest Rates

Steven Russell, "Understanding the Term Structure of Interest Rates," *Review*, Federal Reserve Bank of St. Louis (July/August 1992): 36–50.

William D. Jackson, "Federal Deficits, Inflation, and Monetary Growth: Can they Predict Interest Rates?" *Economic Review*, Federal Reserve Bank of Richmond (September/October 1976). [Explanation and empirical test of the loanable funds model of interest rates.]

Milton P. Reid and Stacey L. Schreft, "Credit Aggregates from the Flow of Funds Accounts," *Economic Quarterly*, Federal Reserve Bank of Richmond (Summer 1993): 49–63.

Federal Reserve Board, *Introduction to Flow of Funds* (Washington, DC: Board of Governors of the Federal Reserve System, 1980).

Government Finance

Karl Galbraith, "Federal Budget Estimates, Fiscal Year 1994," *Survey of Current Business* (April 1993): 46–52. [Annual article; summary of the president's budget proposals for the coming fiscal year.]

The Budget System and Concepts (Washington, D.C.: U.S. Government Printing Office, 1993). [Explanation of concepts and methods used to prepare the U.S. Government's annual budget. This is a companion volume to the *Budget of the United States Government,* prepared by the Office of Management and Budget.]

Roy H. Webb, "The Stealth Budget: Unfunded Liabilities of the Federal Government," *Economic Review,* Federal Reserve Bank of Richmond (May/June 1991): 23–33.

Robert F. Graboyes, "State Revenues Fall Short: Problems May Be Long-Term," *Cross Sections,* Federal Reserve Bank of Richmond (Summer 1991):1–3.

Laura S. Rubin, "The State and Local Government Sector: Long-Term Trends and Recent Fiscal Pressures," *Federal Reserve Bulletin* (Dec. 1992): 892–901.

David F. Sullivan, "State and Local Government Fiscal Position in 1992," *Survey of Current Business* (March 1993): 42–46.

Tax Foundation, *Facts and Figures on Government Finance* (Washington, DC). [Reference book containing historical data on government expenditures and tax collections.]

Laurence J. Kotlikoff, *Generational Accounting: Knowing Who Pays, and When, for What We Spend* (New York: Free Press, 1992).

International Economics

Robert F. Graboyes, "International Trade and Payments Data: An Introduction," *Economic Review,* Federal Reserve Bank of Richmond (September/October 1991). [Reprinted in *Macroeconomic Data: A User's Guide* (Federal Reserve Bank of Richmond, 1991).]

Victor B. Bailey and Sara R. Bowen, *Understanding United States Foreign Trade Data* (Washington, DC: U.S. Department of Commerce, 1985).

Roger M. Kubarych, *Foreign Exchange Markets in the United States* (New York: Federal Reserve Bank of New York, 1983). [Description of foreign exchange market, role of various participants, instruments traded.]

United Nations, *World Economic Survey 1992: Current Trends and Policies in the World Economy* (New York: United Nations, 1992). [Annual U.N. survey of national policy initiatives to encourage economic development.]

Stephen L. Parente and Edward C. Prescott, "Changes in the Wealth of Nations," *Quarterly Review,* Federal Reserve Bank of Minneapolis (Spring 1993):3–16.

Craig S. Hakkio, "Is Purchasing Power Parity a Useful Guide to the Dollar?" *Economic Review,* Federal Reserve Bank of Kansas City (1992, 3d qtr.): 37–51.

Geoffrey M. B. Tootell, "Purchasing Power Parity within the United States," *New England Economic Review* (July/August 1992): 15–24.

Geoffrey H. Moore and Melita H. Moore, *International Economic Indicators* (Westport, CT: Greenwood Press, 1985).

B. Dianne Pauls, "U.S. Exchange Rate Policy: Bretton Woods to Present," *Federal Reserve Bulletin* (November 1990): 891–908.

The Balance of Payments of the U.S.: Concepts, Data Sources, and Estimating Procedures (Washington, DC: U.S. Department of Commerce, 1990).

William L. Helkie, "U.S. International Transactions in 1992," *Federal Reserve Bulletin* (May 1993): 379–388. [Annual articles appear on this subject.]

Christopher L. Bach, "U.S. International Transactions, Fourth Quarter and Year 1992," *Survey of Current Business* (March 1993): 66–107. [Annual articles appear on this subject.]

Anthony J. DiLullo and Obie G. Whichard, "U.S. International Sales and Purchases of Services," *Survey of Current Business* (September 1990): 37–72.

Alicia M. Quijano, "A Guide to BEA Statistics on Foreign Direct Investment in the United States," *Survey of Current Business* (February 1990): 29–37.

Russell B. Scholl, Jeffrey H. Lowe, and Sylvia E. Bargas, "The International Investment Position of the United States in 1992," *Survey of Current Business* (June 1993): 42–55. [Annual articles appear on this subject.]

Stephen A. Meyer, "The U.S. as a Debtor Country: Causes, Prospects, and Policy Implications," *Business Review*, Federal Reserve Bank of Philadelphia (November/December 1989): 19–31.

Marla L. Kessler, "International Organizations Promote Global Monetary Stability and Free Trade," *Cross Sections*, Federal Reserve Bank of Richmond (Fall 1993): 6–8. [Description of International Monetary Fund, World Bank, OECD and other organizations associated with international trade and finance.]

Macroeconomic Policy Making

Alan Greenspan, "Monetary Policy Report to the Congress," *Federal Reserve Bulletin* (March 1993): 167–87. [Semiannual report to Congress. See later issues of the *Federal Reserve Bulletin* for updated reports.]

Joseph A. Ritter, "The FOMC in 1992: A Monetary Conundrum," *Review*, Federal Reserve Bank of St. Louis (May/June 1993): 31–49. [Annual review of Federal Open Market Committee meetings and policy decisions.]

Walter W. Heller, *New Dimensions of Political Economy* (New York: Norton, 1966).

Sherman J. Maisel, *Managing the Dollar* (New York: Norton, 1973).

George P. Schultz and Kenneth W. Dam, *Economic Policy Beyond the Headlines* (New York: Norton, 1977).

Arthur F. Burns, *Reflections of an Economic Policy Maker* (Washington: American Enterprise Institute, 1978).

Herbert Stein, *Washington Bedtime Stories* (New York: Free Press, 1986).

Shaghil Ahmed, "Does Money Affect Output?" *Business Review*, Federal Reserve Bank of Philadelphia (July/August 1993): 13–28. [Review article of research on the impact of money growth on short-run real GDP.]

Other Topics

Edmund S. Phelps, *Seven Schools of Macroeconomic Thought* (New York: Oxford University Press, 1990).

Ernst R. Berndt and Jack E. Triplett (eds.), *Fifty Years of Economic Measurement* (Chicago: University of Chicago Press, 1990). [Leading researchers offer comments on the measurement of labor productivity, the price level, aggregate output, saving, and other economic variables.]

Daniel J. Slottje, et al., *Measuring the Quality of Life Across Countries* (Boulder, CO: Westview Press, 1991).

John C. Musgrave, "Fixed Reproducible Tangible Wealth in the United States, 1982–89," *Survey of Current Business* (September 1990):99–106. [Less detailed but more recent data can be found in an article of the same title, *Survey of Current Business* (August 1992): 37–43.]

Paula C. Young, "Benchmark Input-Output Accounts for the U.S. Economy, 1982," *Survey of Current Business* (July 1991): 30–71.

Cletus C. Coughlin and Thomas B. Mandelbaum, "A Consumer's Guide to Regional Economic Multipliers," *Review,* Federal Reserve Bank of St. Louis (January/February 1991): 19–32.

Regional Multipliers: A User Handbook for the Regional Input-Output Modeling System (Washington, DC: U.S. Department of Commerce, May 1986).

"The Underground Economy: Introduction," *Survey of Current Business* (July 1984): 106–17.

Gary L. Rutledge and Mary L. Leonard, "Pollution Abatement and Control Expenditures, 1987–91," *Survey of Current Business* (May 1993): 55–62. For a longer-term perspective see an article by the same authors, "Pollution Abatement and Control Expenditures, 1972–90," *Survey of Current Business* (June 1992): 25–41.

James H. Morsink, "Seasonal Adjustment," *Macroeconomic Data: A User's Guide* (Federal Reserve Bank of Richmond, 1991).

APPENDIX 9

Present and Future Value

If placed in a bank account or other interest-bearing instrument, an original investment of P dollars will grow in value as shown by the following relationship:

$$F_n = P \times (1 + i)^n \tag{1}$$

where F_n is the **future value** of the investment n years hence, i is the annual interest rate earned by the investment (in decimals; e.g., 10% = 0.10), and n is the length of the investment in years. This formula assumes that the investor does not receive interest as it is earned, but allows it to accrue in the investment until its full maturity. (If the investor receives interest as it is earned, the investment will not increase in value over time; P dollars continue earning interest, but nothing is added to the account.)

Consider a three-year, $1,000 investment that earns 8% per year. The value of the investment at the end of the three-year period is:

$$
\begin{aligned}
F_3 &= \$1,000 \times (1 + 0.08)^3 \\
&= \$1,000 \times (1.08)^3 \\
&= \$1,000 \times (1.259712) \\
&= \$1,259.71
\end{aligned}
$$

Interest on the original $1,000 is $80 per year, or $240 over the life of the investment. This *simple interest* increases the value of the investment from $1,000 to $1,240. The additional $19.71 received by the investor represents interest earnings on interest accrued in earlier years; for example, the $80 of interest earned in year 1 earns $0.08 \times \$80 = \$6.40$ in year 2. Interest received on interest previously earned (but not received) is known as *compound interest*.

When interest compounds more often than once a year, two of the terms (i and n) in equation (1) must be modified. Rather than 8% annual interest, suppose that the investment pays 2% per quarter. Now, i

represents the quarterly interest rate and n is the number of quarter-year periods the investment will exist: 4×3 years $= 12$ interest periods. Now:

$$
\begin{aligned}
F_{3\text{ years}} &= \$1,000 \times (1 + 0.02)^{12} \\
&= \$1,000 \times (1.02)^{12} \\
&= \$1,000 \times (1.268242) \\
&= \$1,268.24
\end{aligned}
$$

Because of more frequent compounding, the investment earns $8.53 more over the three years than the investment above where interest compounds annually.

Another application of the relationship in equation (1) is seen by solving for P, the **present value** of F dollars, n years hence:

$$
P = \frac{F_n}{(1 + i)^n} \tag{2}
$$

Equation (2) states that the *present value* of an amount to be received n years in the future (F_n) is found by dividing that future value by $(1 + i)^n$. The denominator exceeds one, so the present value of the investment is less than the investment's future value. For this reason, the procedure in equation (2) is frequently described as *discounting future dollars to their present value*.

The easiest way to illustrate eq. (2) is with figures from the earlier example. Consider an investment that promises to return $1,259.71 to the investor three years hence. Suppose also that the investor is willing to accept an 8% annual yield on his or her funds. Then the investment has a present value of $1,259.71 $\div$ $(1.08)^3$ = $1,000. The equal sign in the equation indicates that *the investor is indifferent between having $1,000 immediately or the promise of receiving $1,259.71 three years hence.* Consequently, the investor would be willing to pay a maximum of $1,000 for the investment.

Figures in the accompanying table show the present value of $1,000 to be received at various points in the future, discounted at interest rates ranging between 5% and 10%. The figures in the table can be multiplied by five to calculate the present value of a future $5,000 payment, and the same method is used to scale the figures for other future amounts.

Both equation (2) and the figures in the table indicate that the present value of an investment declines with increases in n or i; that is, the longer the lender must wait to receive the promised amount, or the greater the interest rate the lender requires on his or her funds. The interest rate also reflects a risk premium to compensate the lender for the possibility that interest or principal may not actually be received as promised; more default risk causes the investor to require a higher interest rate.

Many investments promise to pay a *series* of future payments. In this case, each payment is treated as a separate F_n amount in equation (2) and its present value is calculated. The total value of the investment equals the summed present values of all future payments. For example, the purchaser of a bond receives the promise of regular interest payments plus the face (par) value of the bond on the date of maturity. Each interest

Present Value of a Future $1,000 Receipt or Payment

Years Hence	Interest Rate (annual)					
	5%	6%	7%	8%	9%	10%
1	$952.38	$943.40	$934.58	$925.93	$917.43	$909.09
2	907.03	890.00	873.44	857.34	841.68	826.45
3	863.84	839.62	816.30	793.83	772.18	751.31
4	822.70	792.09	762.90	735.03	708.43	683.01
5	783.53	747.26	712.99	680.58	649.93	620.92
10	613.91	558.39	508.35	463.19	422.41	385.54
15	481.02	417.27	362.45	315.24	274.54	239.39
20	376.89	311.80	258.42	214.55	178.43	148.64
30	231.38	174.11	131.37	99.38	75.37	57.31
50	87.20	54.29	33.95	21.32	13.45	8.52
100	7.60	2.95	1.15	0.45	0.18	0.07

payment plus the bond's face value is treated as a separate future payment (F_n) and their present values are computed; the bond's current market price equals the summed present values of all of the payments.

The present value of an investment in an apartment building would be calculated in a similar way, but in this case anticipated operating and maintenance expenses are subtracted from expected rental receipts to calculate future net receipts, F_n. The discounted present value of all future net receipts, plus the net resale value of the property, is the maximum amount one would pay to purchase the building today. As these examples illustrate, a wide range of applications require future dollars to be discounted to present value.

Economists played an important role in developing the discounting technique.* Although the mathematics is not complicated and most people are aware that a dollar in hand is more valuable than a dollar to be received in the future, it can be a challenging assignment to apply the present value method to real-world problems. The practicing economist should be familiar with these methods and be prepared to apply them in cases where dollars are to be paid or received at different points in time.

---

*Gerald R. Faulhaber and William J. Baumol, "Economists as Innovators: Practical Products of Theoretical Research," *Journal of Economic Literature* (June 1988): 577–600.

Economics Journals Grouped by Subject Area

General Economics

American Economic Review
Applied Economics
Atlantic Economic Journal
Cambridge Journal of Economics
Canadian Journal of Economics
Eastern Economic Journal
Economic and Social Review
Economic Inquiry
Economic Journal
Economic Notes
Economic Record
Economic Studies Quarterly
Economica
Economics Letters
European Economic Review
International Review of Applied Economics
Journal of Economic Issues
Journal of Economic Literature
Journal of Economic Perspectives
Journal of Economic Studies
Journal of Economic Surveys
Journal of Economic Theory
Journal of Political Economy
Kyklos
*Manchester School of Economic and Social
    Studies*
Margin, The
*Nebraska Journal of Economics and
    Business*
Oxford Bulletin of Economics and Statistics

Oxford Economic Papers
Quarterly Journal of Economics
Review of Economic Studies
Review of Economics and Statistics
Scandinavian Journal of Economics
Scottish Journal of Political Economy
Southern Economic Journal

History of Economic Thought

History of Political Economy
Journal of the History of Economic Thought

Econometrics and Statistics

Econometric Reviews
Econometric Theory
Econometrica
Empirica
Empirical Economics
International Journal of Forecasting
Journal of the American Statistical Association
Journal of Applied Econometrics
Journal of Business and Economic Statistics
Journal of Econometrics
*Journal for Studies in Economics and
    Econometrics*

Mathematical Economics

Economic Modelling
Games and Economic Behavior
International Journal of Game Theory
Journal of Mathematical Economics

Journal of Quantitative Economics
Mathematical Social Sciences

Microeconomics
Information Economics and Policy
Journal of Consumer Research
Journal of Economic Behavior and Organization
Managerial and Decision Economics
Marketing Science
Metroeconomica

Macroeconomics and Monetary Economics
Brookings Papers on Economic Activity
Economic Trends (F.R. Bank of Cleveland)
Federal Reserve Bank of Atlanta Economic Review
Federal Reserve Bank of Dallas Economic Review
Federal Reserve Bank of Kansas City Economic Review
Federal Reserve Bank of Minneapolis Quarterly Review
Federal Reserve Bank of New York Quarterly Review
Federal Reserve Bank of Richmond Economic Quarterly
Federal Reserve Bank of St. Louis Review
Federal Reserve Bank of San Francisco Economic Review
Federal Reserve Bulletin
Fiscal Studies
Journal of Macroeconomics
Journal of International Money and Finance
Journal of Monetary Economics
Journal of Money, Credit, and Banking
Journal of Post Keynesian Economics
Lloyds Bank Review
New England Economic Review (FR Bank of Boston)
OECD Economic Studies
Survey of Current Business

International Economics
International Economic Journal
International Economic Review
International Monetary Fund Staff Papers
Japan and the World Economy
Journal of Common Market Studies
Journal of International Economics
Journal of World Trade

Public Finance and Public Choice
Constitutional Political Economy
Economics and Politics
Journal of Public Economics
National Tax Journal
Public Budgeting and Finance
Public Choice
Public Finance
Public Finance Quarterly

Public Policy Issues
Carnegie-Rochester Conference Series on Public Policy
CATO Journal
Challenge
Congressional Quarterly Weekly Report
Contemporary Policy Issues
Journal of Consumer Affairs
Journal of Economic and Social Measurement
Journal of Policy Analysis and Management
Policy Analysus
Policy Sciences
Policy Studies
Public Interest
Public Policy
Rand Journal of Economics
Social Choice and Welfare

Health, Education, and Welfare
Economics of Education Review
Inquiry
Journal of Health Economics
Review of Income and Wealth
Social Security Bulletin

Labor Economics
Industrial and Labor Relations Review
Industrial Relations
International Labor Review
Journal of Human Resources
Journal of Labor Economics
Journal of Labor Research
Labour
Labour Economics
Labor History
Monthly Labor Review

Law and Economics
International Review of Law and Economics
Journal of Law and Economics
Journal of Law, Economics, and Organization

Journal of Forensic Economics
Journal of Legal Economics
Journal of Legal Studies
Journal of World Trade Law
Michigan Law Review
Yale Law Journal

Industrial Organization and Regulation

Antitrust Bulletin
Bell Journal of Economics
International Journal of Industrial Organization
Journal of Industrial Economics
Journal of Regulatory Economics
Review of Industrial Organization
Yale Journal on Regulation

Economic Development and Growth

Canadian Journal of Development Studies
Developing Economies
Development and Change
Economic Development and Cultural Change
Finance and Development
Growth and Change
Journal of Comparative Economics
Journal of Developing Areas
Journal of Development Economics
Journal of Development Studies
Journal of Economic Development
Population and Development Review
Problems of Economic Transition
World Bank Economic Review
World Bank Research Observer
World Development
World Economy

Urban and Regional Economics

American Real Estate and Urban Economics Association Journal
Anals of Regional Science
Economic Geography
Economics of Planning
International Regional Science Review
Journal of Real Estate Finance and Economics
Journal of Regional Science
Journal of Urban Economics
Land Economics
Regional Science Perspectives
Regional Science and Urban Economics
Regional Studies
Review of Regional Studies
Urban Studies

Energy, Natural Resources and the Environment

Ecological Economics
Energy Economics
Energy Journal
Environment and Planning
Journal of Energy and Development
Journal of Environmental Economics and Management
Marine Resource Economics
Natural Resource Journal
Natural Resource Modeling
Resource and Energy Economics
Resources and Energy
Water Resources Research

Transportation Economics

International Journal of Transport Economics
Journal of Transport Economics and Policy
Logistics and Transportation Review

Financial Economics

Finance
Financial Review
Insurance: Mathematics and Economics
Journal of Banking and Finance
Journal of Empirical Finance
Journal of Finance
Journal of Financial Economics
Journal of Financial Intermediation
Journal of Financial and Quantitative Analysis
Journal of Financial Research
Journal of Financial Services Research
Quarterly Review of Economics and Finance
Review of Financial Studies

Business Economics

Business Economics
Journal of Accounting and Economics
Journal of Business
Journal of Economics and Business
Journal of Business Economics
Quarterly Journal of Business and Economics
Quarterly Review of Economics and Business
Sloan Management Review

Economic History

Business History Review
Economic History Review
Explorations in Economic History
Journal of Economic History

Journal of European Economic History
Scandinavian Economic History Review

Population Economics
Demography
Journal of Population Economics
Population Research and Policy Review
Population Studies

Agricultural Economics
Agricultural Economics
American Journal of Agricultural Economics
Canadian Journal of Agricultural Economics
European Review of Agricultural Economics
Journal of Agricultural Economics
Journal of Agricultural Economics Research
Journal of Agricultural and Resource Economics
Review of Marketing and Agricultural
    Economics
Southern Journal of Agricultural Economics

Economics and the Social Sciences
American Journal of Economics and Sociology
Economics and Philosophy
International Journal of Social Economics
Journal of Conflict Resolution
Journal of Cultural Economics
Journal of Economic Psychology
Journal of Socio-economics
Review of Social Economy
Social and Economic Studies
Social Science Quarterly
Social Philosophy and Policy

Other (unclassified)
Economic Design
Journal of Economic Education
Journal of Institutional and Theoretical
    Economics
Journal of Media Economics
Review of Black Political Economy
Review of Radical Political Economics
Soviet Economy

Non-U.S. Journals (English language)
Asian Economic Journal
Asian-Pacific Economic Literature
Australian Bulletin of Labor

Australian Economic History Review
Australian Economic Papers
Australian Economic Review
Australian Journal of Agricultural Economics
Australian Tax Forum
Banca Nazionale del Lavoro Quarterly Review
Bangladesh Development Studies
Bank of Japan Monetary and Economic Studies
British Journal of Industrial Relations
British Review of Economic Issues
Bulletin of Indonesian Economic Studies
Canadian Public Policy
Chinese Economic Studies
Eastern Africa Economic Review
Eastern European Economics
Economia (Catholic University of Peru)
Economia (Portuguese Catholic University)
Economic Review (Keizai Kenkyu)
Finnish Economic Papers
Greek Economic Review
Indian Economic Journal
Indian Economic Review
Indian Economic and Social History Review
Indian Journal of Quantitative Economics
Middle East Business and Economic Review
Middle East Technical University Studies
    in Development
Oxford Review of Economic Policy
Pakistan Development Review
Pakistan Economic and Social Review
Pakistan Journal of Applied Economics
Philippine Review of Economics and Business
Review of Economic Conditions in Italy
Russian and East European Finance and Trade
Singapore Economic Review
South African Journal of Economics
Weltwirtschaftliches Archiv

Nonacademic Periodicals
Agricultural Outlook
Asian Wall Street Journal
Barrons
Business Week
Economist, The
Forbes
Fortune
Reason
Wall Street Journal

APPENDIX 11

Survey Articles in the *Journal of Economic Literature*, 1984–1993

The *Journal of Economic Literature* features articles that review the professional literature in specific subdisciplines of economics. The following list includes regular review articles and selected notes and comments published in the *JEL* since 1984. Many of the survey articles are accompanied by extensive bibliographies, so the researcher may want to consult those sources for useful background material information. Terms highlighted in **boldface type** below are key words that suggest the general topic of the article. To conduct on-line searches of *JEL* information, see Appendix 4 (DIALOG: Economic Literature Index).

- December 1993 (v. 31, no. 4)
  Stoker, Thomas M., Empirical Approaches to the **Problem of Aggregation Over Individuals**. 1827–74.
  Chirinko, Robert S., Business Fixed **Investment Spending**: Modeling Strategies, Empirical Results, and Policy Implications. 1875–1911.
  Viscusi, W. Kip, The **Value of Risks to Life** and Health. 1912–46.
  Sugden, Robert, Welfare, Resources, and Capabilities: A Review of *Inequality Reexamined* **by Amartya Sen**. 1947–62.
- September 1993 (v. 31, no. 3)
  Winston, Clifford, **Economic Deregulation**: Days of Reckoning for Microeconomists: 1263–89.
  Bonin, John P., Jones, Derek. C., and Putterman, Louis, Theoretical and Empirical Studies of **Producer Cooperatives**: Will Ever the Twain Meet? 1290–1320.
  Eichengreen, Barry, European **Monetary Unification**: 1321–57.
  Edwards, Sebastian, Openness, **Trade Liberalization, and Growth** in Developing Countries: 1358–93.
  Rebitzer, James B., Radical Political Economy and the **Economics of Labor Markets**: 1394–1434.

- June 1993 (v. 31, no. 2)

  Hausman, Daniel M. and McPherson, Michael S., Taking Ethics Seriously: Economics and **Contemporary Moral Philosophy**: 671–731.

  Benassy, Jean-Pascal, **Nonclearing Markets**: Microeconomic Concepts and Macroeconomic Applications: 732–761.

  Burgess, Robin and Stern, Nicholas, **Taxation and Development**: 762–830.

  Sattinger, Michael, Assignment Models of **the Distribution of Earnings**: 831–880.

  Dornbusch, Rudiger, The End of **the German Miracle**: 881–85.

- March 1993 (v. 31, no. 1)

  McKinnon, Ronald I., The Rules of the Game: **International Money** in Historical Perspective: 1–44.

  Kennan, John and Wilson, Robert B., **Bargaining** with Private Information: 45–104.

  Silvestre, Joaquim, The **Market-Power Foundations** of **Macroeconomic** Policy: 105–41.

  Seater, John J., **Ricardian Equivalence**: 142–90.

  Anderson, Robert M., EP Seeks EP: A Review of *Sex and Reason* by Richard A. Posner: 191–98.

  Teece, David J., The **Dynamics of Industrial Capitalism**: Perspectives on Alfred Chandler's *Scale and Scope:* 199–225.

- December 1992 (v. 30, no. 4)

  Nelson, Richard R. and Wright, Gavin, The Rise and Fall of **American Technological Leadership**: The Postwar Era in Historical Perspective: 1931–64.

  Otsuka, Keijiro, Chuma, Hiroyuki, and Hayami, Yujiro, **Land and Labor Contracts** in Agrarian Economies: Theory and Facts: 1965–2018.

  Walstad, William B., **Economics Instruction** in High Schools: 2019–2051.

  Bloomfield, Arthur I., On the Centenary of **Jacob Viner**'s Birth: A Retrospective View of the Man and His Work: 2052–85.

  Barnett, William A., Fisher, Douglas, and Serletis, Apostolos, Consumer Theory and the **Demand for Money**: 2086–2119.

  Cooper, Richard N., Fettered to **Gold**? Economic **Policy in the Interwar Period**: 2120–28.

  Friedman, Milton, Do Old **[Statistical] Fallacies** Ever Die? 2129–32.

- September 1992 (v. 30, no. 3)

  Levy, Frank and Murnane, Richard J., U.S. **Earnings Levels and Earnings Inequality**: A Review of Recent Trends and Proposed Explanations: 1333–81.

  Radner, Roy, Hierarchy: The **Economics of Managing**: 1382–1415.

  Scherer, F. M., **Schumpeter** and Plausible Capitalism: 1416–33.

  Browning, Martin, **Children and Household Economic Behavior**: 1434–75.

  Phelps, Edmund S., A Review of *Unemployment*: 1476–90.

  Bateman, Bradley W., The **Education of Economists**: A Different Perspective: 1491–95.

- June 1992 (v. 30, no. 2)

  Cropper, Maureen L. and Oates, Wallace, **Environmental Economics**: A Survey: 675–740.

  Barr, Nicholas, Economic Theory and the **Welfare State**: A Survey and Interpretation: 741–803.

  Baldwin, Robert E., Are Economists' Traditional **Trade Policy Views** Still Valid? 804–29.

  Ehrenberg, Ronald G., The Flow of **New Doctorates**: 830–75.

  Heckman, James J., Haavelmo and the **Birth of Modern Econometrics**: A Review of *The History of Econometric Ideas* by Mary Morgan: 876–86.

- March 1992 (v. 30, no. 1)

  Moffitt, Robert, Incentive Effects of the U.S. **Welfare** System: A Review: 1–61.

  Gardner, Bruce L., Changing Economic Perspectives on the **Farm Problem**: 62–101.

  MacKinnon, James, **Model Specification Tests** and Artificial Regressions: 102–46.

  Frank, Robert, Melding **Sociology and Economics**: James Coleman's *Foundations of Social Theory*: 147–70.

  Fischel, William A., **Property Taxation and the Tiebout Model**: Evidence for the Benefit View from Zoning and Voting: 171–77.

- December 1991 (v. 29, no. 4)

  Donohue, John J. III and Heckman, James, Continuous Versus Episodic Change: The **Impact of Civil Rights Policy** on the Economic Status of Blacks: 1603–43.

  Blejer, Mario I. and Cheasty, Adrienne, The Measurement of **Fiscal Deficits**: Analytical and Methodological Issues: 1644–78.

  Atkinson, Anthony and Micklewright, John, **Unemployment Compensation** and Labor Market Transitions: A Critical Review: 1679–1727.

  Fishlow, Albert, Review of **Handbook of Development Economics**: 1728–37.

- September 1991 (v. 29, no. 3)

  Krueger, Anne O., et al., Report of the Commission on **Graduate Education in Economics**: 1035–53.

  Hansen, W. Lee., The Education and **Training of Economics Doctorates**: Major Findings of the American Economic Association's Commission on Graduate Education in Economics: 1054–87.

  Kasper, Hirschel, et al., The **Education of Economists**: From Undergraduate to Graduate Study: 1088–1109.

  Pindyck, Robert S., Irreversibility, Uncertainty, and **Investment**: 1110–1148.

  Stigler, George J., **Charles Babbage**: 1149–52.

  Wright, Gavin, **Understanding the Gender Gap**: A Review Article: 1153–63.

- June 1991 (v. 29, no. 2)

  Juster, F. Thomas and Stafford, Frank P., The **Allocation of Time**: Empirical Findings, Behavioral Models, and Problems of Measurement: 471–522.

  Weisbrod, Burton A., The **Health Care** Quadrilemma: An Essay on Technological Change, Insurance, Quality of Care, and Cost Containment: 523–52.

Porter, Robert H., A Review Essay on *Handbook of* **Industrial Organization**: 553–72.

Dorfman, Robert, Review Article: **Economic Development** from the Beginning to Rostow: 573–91.

● March 1991 (v. 29, no. 1)

Caldwell, Bruce J., Clarifying **Popper**: 1–33.

Manski, Charles F., **Regression**: 34–50.

Williamson, Jeffrey G., **Productivity** and American Leadership: A Review Article: 51–68.

Judd, Kenneth L., A Review of **Recursive Methods** in **Economic Dynamics**: 69–77.

● December 1990 (v. 28, no. 4)

Mankiw, N. Gregory, A Quick Refresher Course in **Macroeconomics**: 1645–60.

Griliches, Zvi, **Patent Statistics** as Economic Indicators: A Survey: 1661–1707.

Baumol, William J., Sir John Versus the **Hicksians**, or Theorist Malgre Lui? 1708–15.

● September 1990 (v. 28, no. 3)

Heilbroner, Robert, Analysis and Vision in the History of **Modern Economic Thought**: 1097–1114.

Gordon, Robert J., What is **New-Keynesian Economics**? 1115–71.

● June 1990 (v. 28, no. 2)

Hurd, Michael D., Research on **the Elderly**: Economic Status, Retirement, and Consumption and Saving: 565–637.

Gardner, Roy, L. V. Kantorovich: The Price Implications of Optimal **Planning**: 638–48.

Wildasin, David, Haig: Pioneer Advocate of **Expenditure Taxation**? 649–54.

Laband, David, Measuring the Relative **Impact of Economics Book Publishers** and Economics Journals: 655–60.

● March 1990 (v. 28, no. 1)

Aoki, Masahiko, Toward an Economic Model of the **Japanese Firm**: 1–27.

Bodie, Zvi, **Pensions** as Retirement Income Insurance: 28–49.

Sandmo, Agnar, **Buchanan on Political Economy**: A Review Article: 50–65.

● December 1989 (v. 27, no. 4)

LeRoy, Stephen F., Efficient **Capital Markets** and Martingales: 1583–1621.

Machina, Mark J., Dynamic Consistency and Non-Expected Utility Models of **Choice Under Uncertainty**: 1622–68.

● September 1989 (v. 27, no. 3)

Cooter, Robert D. and Rubinfeld, Daniel L., Economic Analysis of **Legal Disputes** and Their Resolution: 1067.

Mieszkowski, Peter and Zodrow, George R., **Taxation and the Tiebout Model**: The Differential Effects of Head Taxes, Taxes on Land, Rents and Property Taxes: 1098–1146.

Laidler, David, Dow and Saville's *Critique of* **Monetary Policy**—A Review Essay: 1147–59.

Baumol, William J. and Tobin, James, The **Optimal Cash Balance** Proposition: Maurice Allais' Priority: 1160–62.

- June 1989 (v. 27, no. 2)

Smith, James P., and Welch, Finis R., **Black Economic Progress** After Myrdal: 519–64.

Duffie, Darrell and Sonnenschein, Hugo, Arrow and **General Equilibrium Theory**: 565–98.

- March 1989 (v. 27, no. 1)

Blackburn, Keith and Christensen, Michael, **Monetary Policy** and Policy Credibility: Theories and Evidence: 1–45.

Gunderson, Morley, **Male-Female Wage Differentials** and Policy Responses: 46–72.

- December 1988 (v. 26, no. 4)

Eisner, Robert, **Extended Accounts for National Income** and Product: 1611–84.

Kelley, Allen C., Economic Consequences of **Population** Change in the Third World: 1685–1728.

Stigler, George J., **Palgrave's Dictionary** of Economics: 1729–36.

- September 1988 (v. 26, no. 3)

Sawhill, Isabel V., **Poverty** in the U.S.: Why Is It So Persistent? 1073–1119.

Dosi, Giovanni, Sources, Procedures, and Microeconomic Effects of **Innovation**: 1120–71.

- June 1988 (v. 26, no. 2)

Faulhaber, Gerald R. and Baumol, William J., **Economists as Innovators**: Practical Products of Theoretical Research: 577–600.

Perkins, Dwight Heald, Reforming **China's Economic System**: 601–45.

Kiefer, Nicholas M., Economic **Duration** Data and Hazard Functions: 646–79.

- March 1988 (v. 26, no. 1)

Helliwell, John F., Comparative Macroeconomics of **Stagflation**: 1–28.

Smith, Lawrence B., Rosen, Kenneth T., and Fallis, George, Recent Developments in Economic Models of **Housing Markets**: 29–64.

Alchian, Armen A. and Woodward, Susan, **The Firm** Is Dead; Long Live the Firm: A Review of Oliver E. Williamson's *The Economic Institutions of Capitalism*: 65–79.

- December 1987 (v. 25, no. 4)

Ofer, Gur, **Soviet Economic Growth**: 1928–1985: 1767–1833.

Piore, Michael J., Historical Perspectives and the Interpretation of **Unemployment**: 1834–50.

- September 1987 (v. 25, no. 3)

Kniesner, Thomas J. and Goldsmith, Arthur H., A Survey of Alternative Models of the **Aggregate** U.S. **Labor Market**: 1241–80.

Novshek, William and Sonnenschein, Hugo, **General Equilibrium with Free Entry**: A Synthetic Approach to the Theory of Perfect Competition: 1281–1306.

- June 1987 (v. 25, no. 2)

Maddison, Angus, **Growth and Slowdown in Advanced Capitalist Economies**: Techniques of Quantitative Assessment: 649–98.

McAfee, R. Preston and McMillan, John, **Auctions** and Bidding: 699–738.

- March 1987 (v. 25, no. 1)

Stiglitz, Joseph E., The Causes and Consequences of the Dependence of **Quality** on Price: 1–48.

Nelson, Robert H., The Economics Profession and the **Making of Public Policy**: 49–91.

Starrett, David A., *Production and Capital:* **Kenneth Arrow**'s Contributions in Perspective—A Review Article: 92–102.

Malinvaud, Edmond, The **Overlapping Generations Model** in 1947: 103–05.

- December 1986 (v. 24, no. 4)

Kornai, Janos, The **Hungarian Reform** Process: Visions, Hopes, and Reality: 1687–1737.

Greenwood, Michael J. and McDowell, John M., The Factor Market Consequences of U.S. **Immigration**: 1738–72.

Dorfman, Robert, Comment: P. A. Samuelson, "**Thunen** at Two Hundred": 1773–76.

Samuelson, Paul A., Yes to Robert Dorfman's Vindication of **Thunen 's Natural-Wage Derivation**: 1777–85.

- September 1986 (v. 24, no. 3)

Hanushek, Eric A., The **Economics of Schooling**: Production and Efficiency in the Public Schools: 1141–77.

Comanor, William S., The Political Economy of the **Pharmaceutical Industry**: 1178–1217.

- June 1986 (v. 24, no. 2)

Rees, Albert, An Essay on **Youth Joblessness**: 613–28.

Pauly, Mark V., Taxation, Health Insurance, and Market Failure in **the Medical Economy**: 629–75.

- March 1986 (v. 24, no. 1)

Norton, R. D., **Industrial Policy** and American Renewal: 1–40.

Freeman, Richard B., **Unionism** Comes to the Public Sector: 41–86.

- December 1985 (v. 23, no. 4)

Coats, A. W., The **American Economic Association and the Economics Profession**: 1697–1727.

Ekwurzel, Drucilla and Saffran, Bernard, **Online Information Retrieval** for Economists—The **Economic Literature Index**: 1728–63.

Sen, Amartya, *Social Choice* and *Justice:* A Review Article: 1764–76.

- September 1985 (v. 23, no. 3)

Griffin, Keith and Gurley, John, **Radical Analyses of** Imperialism, the Third World, and the Transition to Socialism: A Survey Article: 1089–1143.

Rosen, Sherwin, **Implicit Contracts**: A Survey: 1144–75.

Salant, Walter S., *Keynes and the Modern World:* A Review Article: 1176–85.

- June 1985 (v. 23, no. 2)

Zarnowitz, Victor, Recent Work on **Business Cycles** in Historical Perspective: A Review of Theories and Evidence: 523–80.

Pollak, Robert A., A Transaction Cost Approach to **Families and Households**: 581–608.

- March 1985 (v. 23, no. 1)

  Lundberg, Erik, The Rise and Fall of the **Swedish Model**: 1–36.

  Lindbeck, Assar, The **Prize in Economic Science** in Memory of Alfred **Nobel**: 37–56.

  Winston, Clifford, Conceptual Development in the Economics of **Transportation**: An Interpretive Survey: 57–94.

- December 1984 (v. 22, no. 4)

  Scitovsky, Tibor, **Lerner**'s Contribution to Economics: 1547–71.

  Colander, David, **Was Keynes a Keynesian** or a Lernerian? 1572–75.

  Kotlikoff, Laurence J., **Taxation and Savings**: A Neoclassical Perspective: 1576–1629.

- September 1984 (v. 22, no. 3)

  Shoven, John B. and Whalley, John, Applied General Equilibrium Models of **Taxation and International Trade**: An Introduction and Survey: 1007–51.

  Bergson, Abram, **Income Inequality** Under **Soviet Socialism**: 1052–99.

  Gately, Dermot, A Ten-Year Retrospective: **OPEC** and the **World Oil Market**: 1100–14.

- June 1984 (v. 22, no. 2)

  Cooter, Robert and Rappoport, Peter, Were the **Ordinalists** Wrong About **Welfare Economics**? 507–30.

  Mellor, John W. and Johnston, Bruce F., The World Food Equation: Interrelations Among **Development, Employment and Food Consumption**: 531–74.

  Caldwell, Bruce J. and Coats, A.W., The **Rhetoric of Economists**: A Comment on McCloskey: 575–78.

  McCloskey, Donald N., **Reply** to Caldwell and Coats: 579–80.

- March 1984 (v. 22, no. 1)

  Kravis, Irving B., **Comparative** Studies of **National Income** and Prices: 1–39.

  Marris, Robin, **Comparing the Incomes of Nations**: A Critique of the International Comparison Project: 40–57.

  Hoover, Kevin D., Two Types of **Monetarism**: 58–76.

  Liebowitz, S. J. and Palmer, J. P., Assessing the Relative **Impacts of Economics Journals**: 77–88.

APPENDIX 12

Selected Readings for Economists

Graduate Study

Abedi, J. and Benkin, E., "The Effects of Students, Academic, Financial and Demographic Variables on Time to Doctorate," *Research in Higher Education* (1987): 3–14.

Barbezat, Debra, "The Market for New Ph.D. Economists," *Journal of Economic Education* (Summer 1992): 262–76.

Bowen, William G. and Rudenstine, Neil L., *In Pursuit of the PhD* (Princeton, NJ: Princeton University Press, 1992).

Coats, A.W., "Changing Perceptions of American Graduate Education in Economics, 1953–1991," *Journal of Economic Education* (Fall 1992): 341–52.

Colander, David and Klamer, Arjo, *The Making of an Economist* (Boulder, CO: Westview Press, 1990). See an article with the same title in *Journal of Economic Perspectives* (Fall 1987).

Colander, David and Reuven, Brenner (eds.), *Educating Economists* (Ann Arbor: University of Michigan Press, 1992).

Diamond, Arthur M. and Haurin, Donald R., "The Dissemination of Research Agendas Among Young Economists," *Journal of Economic Education* (Winter 1993): 53–61.

Hansen, W. Lee, "The Education and Training of Economics Doctorates," *Journal of Economic Literature* (September 1991): 1054–87.

Owen, Wyn F. and Cross, Larry R., *Guide to Graduate Study in Economics and Agricultural Economics* (Boulder, CO: Economics Institute, 1982).

Quddus, Munir, "Changing Perceptions of American Graduate Education in Economics," *Journal of Economic Education* (Fall 1992):357–61.

Reagan, Barbara B., "Stocks and Flows of Academic Economists," *American Economic Review* (May 1979): 143–47.

Rudestam, K. E. and Newton, R. R., *Surviving Your Dissertation* (Newbury Park, CA: Sage, 1992).

Scott, Charles E., "The Market for Ph.D. Economists: The Academic Sector," *American Economic Review* (May 1979): 137–42.

Solow, Robert M., "Educating and Training New Economics Ph.D.'s: How Good a Job Are We Doing?" *American Economic Review* (May 1990): 437–50.

Tower, Edward, *Macro, Monetary & Financial Economics Reading Lists* (Durham, NC: Eno River Press, 1990). Reading lists, course outlines, exams, and problems used by economists at leading universities. *Additional titles are available* for microeconomics, public finance, international trade, etc.

Famous Economists

Blaug, Mark and Sturges, Paul, *Who's Who in Economics* (Cambridge: MIT Press, 1982).

Breit, William and Spencer, Roger, *Lives of the Laureates: Seven Nobel Economists* (Cambridge: MIT Press, 1986). Reviewed in *JEL*, December 1987.

Buchanan, James M., *Better than Plowing and Other Personal Essays* (Chicago, IL: University of Chicago Press, 1992).

Coughlin, Ellen K., "Defying the Odds: Chicago's Run on the Nobel Economics Prize," *Chronicle of Higher Education*, October 28, 1992: A6–9.

Klamer, Arjo, *Conversations with Economists: New Classical Economists and Their Opponents Speak Out on the Current Controversy in Macroeconomics* (Totowa, NJ: Rowman & Allanheld, 1983). Reviewed in *JEL*, June 1985.

Lindbeck, Assar, "The Prize in Economic Science in Memory of Alfred Nobel," *Journal of Economic Literature* (March 1985): 37–56.

Nasar, Sylvia, "Nobels Pile Up for Chicago, but Is the Glory Gone?" *New York Times* (November 4, 1993): C1.

Simon, Herbert A., *Models of My Life* (New York: HarperCollins, 1991).

Stigler, George, *Memoirs of an Unregulated Economist* (Chicago: University of Chicago Press, 1985).

Szenberg, Michael (ed.), *Eminent Economists: Their Life Philosophies* (New York: Cambridge University Press, 1992).

Wasson, Tyler (ed.), *Nobel Prize Winners* (New York: H.W. Wilson Co., 1987).

Economics as a Discipline

Bernholz, Peter, *Economic Imperialism* (New York: Paragon House, 1987).

Coats, A.W., "The American Economic Association and the Economics Profession," *Journal of Economic Literature* (December 1985): 1697–1727.

Colander, David, *Why Aren't Economists as Important as Garbagemen? Essays on the State of Economics* (Armonk, NY: ME Sharpe, 1991).

Frey, Bruno, Pommerehne, Werner W. and Gygi, Beat, "Economics Indoctrination or Selection? Some Empirical Results," *Journal of Economic Education* (Summer 1993): 271–81. Argues that those who decide to study economics tend to prefer the price system to allocate resources more than the general public.

Hausman, Daniel M., *The Inexact and Separate Science of Economics* (New York: Cambridge University Press, 1992). Evaluates the standing of economics as a science.

Hey, John D., *The Future of Economics* (Cambridge, MA: Blackwell, 1992). Opinions of leading economists about the future of the discipline.

Kamarck, Andrew M., *Economics and the Real World* (Philadelphia: University of Pennsylvania Press, 1983). Reviewed in *JEL* (Dec. 1985): 1786–88.

McCloskey, Donald, *If You're So Smart: The Narrative of Economic Expertise* (Chicago: University of Chicago Press, 1990).

Rhoads, Steven E., *The Economist's View of the World* (New York: Cambridge University Press, 1985). Reviewed in *JEL* (September 1986): 1223–25.

Viner, Jacob, *Essays on the Intellectual History of Economics* (Princeton, NJ: Princeton University Press, 1991).

Economic Methodology and Rhetoric

Caldwell, Bruce J. "Clarifying Popper," *Journal of Economic Literature* (March 1991): 1–33.

Debreu, Gerard, "The Mathematization of Economic Theory," *American Economic Review* (March 1991): 1–7.

de Marchi, Neil (ed.), *Post-Popperian Methodology of Economics* (Boston: Kluwer, 1992).

Dewald, W. G., et al., "Replication in Empirical Economics . . . ," *American Economic Review* (September 1986): 587–603.

Drakopoulos, S.A., *Values and Economic Theory* (Brookfield, VT: Glower Publishing Co., 1991).

Hausman, Daniel M., "Economic Methodology in a Nutshell," *Journal of Economic Perspectives* (Spring 1989): 115–27.

Hausman, Daniel M., *Essays on Philosophy and Economic Methodology* (New York: Cambridge University Press, 1992).

Klamer, Arjo; McCloskey, Donald N.; and Solow, Robert M. (eds.), *The Consequences of Economic Rhetoric* (New York: Cambridge University Press, 1988). Reviewed in *JEL* (March 1991): 85–7.

Leontief, Wassily, "Theoretical Assumptions and Non-Observed Facts," *American Economic Review* (1971):1–7.

Mayer, Thomas, *Truth versus Precision in Economics* (Brookfield, VT: Edward Elgar, 1993).

McCloskey, Donald M., *The Rhetoric of Economics* (Madison: University of Wisconsin Press, 1985). Reviewed in *JEL* (March 1987): 110. See an article with the same title in *Journal of Economic Literature* (June 1983): 481–517.

Morgan, Theodore, "Theory versus Empiricism in Academic Economics: Update and Comparisons," *Journal of Economic Perspectives* (Fall 1988): 159–64.

Sayer, Andrew, *Method in Social Science*, 2nd ed. (London: Routledge, 1992).

Economists at Work: Teaching, Researching, Advising

Bowen, William G. and Sosa, Julie Ann, *Prospects for Faculty in the Arts and Sciences* (Princeton, NJ: Princeton University Press, 1989).

Cabell, David E.W. (ed.), *Cabell's Directory of Publishing Opportunities in Business and Economics* (Beaumont, TX: Cabell Publishing Co., 1990).

Colander, David and Coats, A.W. (eds.), *The Spread of Economic Ideas* (New York: Cambridge University Press, 1989). Reviewed in *JEL* (June 1991): 592.

Faulhaber, Gerald R. and Baumol, William J., "Economists as Innovators: Practical Products of Theoretical Research," *Journal of Economic Literature* (June 1988): 577–600. Historical development of techniques and methods used by applied economists (e.g., marginal analysis, present value, econometric forecasting).

Furner, Mary O. and Supple, Barry, *The State and Economic Knowledge: The American and British Experiences* (New York: Cambridge University Press, 1990). Government's role in the supply and demand for economic knowledge.

Hamermesh, Daniel S., "Professional Etiquette for the Mature Economist," *American Economic Review* (May 1993): 34–38.

Harberger, Arnold C., "The Search for Relevance in Economics," *American Economic Review* (May 1993): 1–16.

Humphrey, Thomas M., "Economists Help Fed Presidents Prepare for Monetary Policymaking," *Cross Sections* (Federal Reserve Bank of Richmond, Winter 1988/89): 3–4.

McCallin, Nancy J., "The Business Economist at Work: The Economics Function at the Colorado Legislative Council," *Business Economics* (January 1992), 55–57. This is only one of many articles published in *Business Economics* about the careers of economists working in non-academic jobs.

Miller, A. Carolyn and Punsalan, Victoria J., *Refereed and Nonrefereed Economic Journals* (New York: Greenwood Press, 1988).

NABE, *Careers in Business Economics* (Cleveland, OH: National Association of Business Economists, 1989).

Nelson, John; Megill, Allan; and McCloskey, Donald (eds.), *The Rhetoric of the Human Sciences: Language and Argument in Scholarship and Public Affairs* (Madison: University of Wisconsin Press, 1987). Reviewed in *JEL* (March 1989): 73.

Nelson, Robert H., "The Economics Profession and the Making of Public Policy," *Journal of Economic Literature* (March 1987): 49–91.

Orr, Daniel, "Reflections on the Hiring of Faculty," *American Economic Review* (May 1993): 39–43.

Saunders, Philip and Walstad, William B., *The Principles of Economics Course: A Handbook for Instructors* (New York: McGraw Hill, 1990).

Stein, Herbert, *Presidential Economics: The Making of Economic Policy from Roosevelt to Reagan and Beyond* (Washington, DC: American Enterprise Institute, 1988).

Walsh, Richard G., *Recreation Economic Decisions* (State College, PA: Venture Publishing, Inc., 1986). This text discusses and applies economic methods to a variety of situations.

Economics Dictionaries, Encyclopedias, Reference Books

Bureau of Labor Statistics, *BLS Handbook of Methods* (U.S. Department of Labor, 1988).

Eatwell, J.; Milgate, M.; and Newman, P., *The New Palgrave: The World of Economics* (New York: Norton, 1991).

Henderson, David R. (ed.), *The Fortune Encyclopedia of Economics* (New York: Warner Books, 1993).

James, Simon, *A Dictionary of Economic Quotations* (Totowa, NJ: Barnes & Noble Books, 1981).

Jong, Frits J. de, *Quadrilingual Economics Dictionary: English/American, French, German, Dutch* (Boston: Kluwer, 1980).

Knopf, Kenyon A., *A Lexicon of Economics* (New York: Academic Press, 1991).

Kruschchke, Earl R. and Jackson, Byron M., *The Public Policy Dictionary* (Santa Barbara, CA: ABC-CLIO, 1987).

Mai, Ludwig H., *Men and Ideas in Economics: A Dictionary of World Economists, Past and Present* (Totowa, NJ: Littlefield, Adams, 1975).

Miller, Patrick McC. and Wilson, Michael J., *A Dictionary of Social Science Methods* (New York: John Wiley and Sons, 1983).

Moffat, Donald W., *Economics Dictionary* (New York: Elsevier, 1983).

Nemmers, Erwin E., *Dictionary of Economics and Business* (Totowa, NJ: Littlefield, Adams, 1978).

Pearce, David W., *The MIT Dictionary of Modern Economics* (Cambridge: MIT Press, 1986).

Rutherford, Donald, *Dictionary of Economics* (London: Routledge, 1992).

Skrapek, Wayne A., *Mathematical Dictionary for Economics and Business Administration* (Boston: Allyn and Bacon, 1976).

APPENDIX 13

Careers in Economics

Information is provided on the following pages regarding market conditions for recipients of undergraduate and graduate economics degrees. In general, economics graduates earn above-average salaries whether they work in business or academia. Estimates by the Bureau of Labor Statistics indicate that employment of economists will grow at about the same rate as for other occupations between now and 2005, but those figures do not account for the fact that many economics graduates do not pursue economics, narrowly defined, as an occupation. Results from one alumni survey indicate that bachelor's degree economics graduates work in a wide variety of occupations.

The 1990–2005 Job Outlook for Economists

Every two years the Bureau of Labor Statistics publishes a summary of the expected change in employment for about 250 occupations. Here are the most recent projections for **"Economists and marketing research analysts."**

Estimated employment, 1990:	37,000
Projected change in employment, 1990–2005:	21%
Numerical change in employment, 1990–2005:	8,000
Employment prospects:	Employment is expected to increase as fast as average [for all occupations], reflecting increased reliance on quantitative methods to analyze business trends, forecast sales, and plan purchasing and production. For economists, master's and doctoral degree holders will have the best opportunities. Bachelor's degree holders will face competition; those skilled in quantitative techniques have the best prospects.

Source: Jay M. Berman and Theresa A. Cosca, "The 1990–2005 Job Outlook in Brief," *Occupational Outlook Quarterly* (Spring 1992): 18.

The Supply of Doctorate Economists

Number of economics doctorates employed in 1987*		17,837
Academic employment	11,778	
Nonacademic employment	6,059	
Number of economics doctorates awarded in 1986#		861
Number of economics graduate students in 1986#		12,830
Percent U.S. citizens	55.3%	
Percent female	25.9%	
Percent full-time	71.2%	
Mean years of registered time to Ph.D. in 1986#§		6.3 years
GRE scores among students intending to study economics, 1986#		
Quantitative	612	
Economics	601	

*W. Lee Hansen, "The Education and Training of Economics Doctorates," *Journal of Economic Literature* (September 1991): 1060.
#Hansen: 1057.
§Following receipt of the B.A. or B.S.

Average Monthly Earnings by Field of Degree, Spring 1990*

Field of Degree	Bachelor's degree	Advanced degree
Agriculture/Forestry	$2,537	—
Biology	2,409	—
Business/Management	2,447	$3,802
Economics	*2,528*	—
Education	1,532	2,597
Engineering	2,953	3,780
English/Journalism	1,607	2,055
Home Economics	906	—
Law	—	5,608
Liberal Arts/Humanities	1,592	2,383
Mathematics/Statistics	2,569	2,953
Medicine/Dentistry	—	5,651
Nursing/Pharmacy/Technical Health	1,898	2,683
Physical/Earth Sciences	2,399	3,982
Psychology	2,021	2,416
Religion/Theology	—	2,073
Social Sciences	1,841	2,617
Other	2,369	2,550
All fields	2,116	3,334

*Average monthly salary of all workers with degree indicated, not including fringe benefits. Blank entries denote fewer than 200,000 persons in category.
Source: Robert Kominski and Rebecca Sutterlin, *What's It Worth?* (Washington, DC: U.S. Department of Commerce, Current Population Reports, 1993).

Average Annual Salary Offers Received by New Graduates, 1993*

Field of Degree	Bachelor's degree	Master's degree
Accounting	$27,775	$30,488
Agribusiness	22,471	—
Architectural and environmental design	23,668	—
Biology	22,101	27,500
Business admin./management	24,456	36,657#
Chemistry	29,637	34,471
Civil engineering	29,234	34,098
Communications	21,821	25,900
Computer science	31,195	37,920
Economics and finance	26,979	34,868
Elementary education	20,112	27,660
Geology	27,970	36,800
Health sciences	22,856	30,576
History	22,970	—
Human resources and labor relations	22,895	30,493
Industrial engineering	32,868	39,298
Management information systems	29,465	36,871
Marketing/marketing management	24,638	38,275
Mathematics and statistics	26,100	33,811
Nursing	31,876	39,634
Physics	22,728	33,000
Political science/government	24,663	—
Psychology	20,503	33,530
Sociology	21,436	—

*Average salary offers (not including bonuses, fringe benefits, or overtime pay) received by *new graduates* in the first half of 1993. Data are combined for men and women.

#MBA (for a graduate with a nontechnical undergraduate degree and one year or less of experience).

Source: *CPC Salary Survey* (Bethlehem, PA: College Placement Council, July 1993).

Fields of Specialization Cited in *Job Openings for Economists*, 1992

The following table shows the number of jobs advertised in *JOE* during 1992. Most of the positions advertised in *JOE* are in colleges and universities. According to the table, most positions are offered in international economics, macro and monetary economics, microeconomics, mathematical and quantitative economics, and industrial organization. Such information may be useful to those contemplating a career as a professional economist.

Fields of Specialization Cited: 1992

Code	Fields	February	April	June	August	October	November	December	Totals
A	General Economics and Teaching	9	6	4	4	20	11	13	67
B	Methodology and History of Economic Thought	2	2	—	—	5	3	3	15
C	Mathematical and Quantitative Methods	27	18	14	17	66	42	65	249
D	Microeconomics	17	20	19	26	72	32	72	258
E	Macroeconomics and Monetary Economics	23	15	14	20	84	47	72	275
F	International Economics	25	17	9	18	85	56	76	286
G	Financial Economics	14	11	8	6	40	22	32	133
H	Public Economics	13	5	6	5	38	18	29	114
I	Health, Education, and Welfare	10	4	2	7	29	22	37	111
J	Labor and Demographic Economics	14	13	5	9	38	28	47	154
K	Law and Economics	4	1	1	—	8	4	7	25
L	Industrial Organization	19	16	13	20	65	41	64	238
M	Business Administration; Business Economics; Marketing, Accounting	6	4	1	2	15	5	11	44
N	Economic History	4	2	2	2	4	5	5	24
O	Economic Development, Technological Change	17	11	8	17	43	26	46	168
P	Economic Systems	6	2	3	2	7	6	7	33
Q	Agricultural and Natural Resource Economics	17	12	18	16	47	21	42	173
R	Urban, Rural, and Regional Economics	8	7	5	4	16	14	8	62
Z	Other Special Topics	2	—	—	—	1	2	2	7
AF	Any Field	6	4	3	7	46	3	35	104
ZZ	Administrative Positions	5	2	3	4	7	8	7	36
	Totals	248	172	138	186	736	416	680	2,576

Note: Fields of specialization codes are from the *Journal of Economic Literature.*
Source: C. Elton Hinshaw, Report of the Director, *Job Openings for Economists, American Economic Review* (May 1993), p. 503.

Average Salaries* of Academic Economists, 1988–1993

	Professor	Associate Prof.	Assistant Prof.
1992–93			
Ph.D. granting departments	$74,350	$53,071	$44,441
Master's degree departments	59,214	46,530	40,490
Bachelor's degree departments	55,900	43,557	37,449
1991–92			
Ph.D. granting departments	$71,190	$50,843	$42,871
Master's degree departments	66,718	48,817	41,688
Bachelor's degree departments	53,108	42,020	36,754
1990–91			
Ph.D. granting departments	68,890	49,161	41,834
Master's degree departments	55,367	43,942	38,180
Bachelor's degree departments	52,003	40,861	35,086
1989–90			
Ph.D. granting departments	66,006	47,056	39,199
Master's degree departments	52,728	42,401	35,640
Bachelor's degree departments	48,753	38,620	33,094
1988–89			
Ph.D. granting departments	63,902	45,945	37,064
Master's degree departments	51,534	39,866	33,750
Bachelor's degree departments	46,045	36,157	30,247

*Academic year (9 month) salaries, not including fringe benefits.
Source: American Economic Association (annual surveys). For 1992–93 the table includes reports from 80 Ph.D. departments, 28 master's departments, and 142 bachelor's departments.

Contribution of Undergraduate Economics to Working Careers*

Survey question: "If your [undergraduate] economics major has helped your career, describe that contribution."

Year of Graduation	Comment	Current Career
1971	Economics provided me with a greater overall understanding of life.	Real estate general mgr.
1972	Economics provided me with a well-rounded career preparation.	Director of hospital admin.
1973	Economics increased my analytical skills, which has helped me in my business	Restaurant owner
1974	Economics helped me understand how to solve problems and communicate the attendant information to others.	Government program analyst
1977	The ability to think clearly and to deal with abstract models/concepts . . . has been integral to my career.	Senior pricing specialist
1980	It taught me to recognize that more than one solution exists for every problem.	Securities analyst
1983	Economics helps me understand what motivates individuals and organizations.	Insurance district mgr.
1985	Economics gave me the ability to analyze and understand the supply/demand determinants of price.	Market director
1985	Economics provided me with a look at the bigger picture in the business world, and helped me understand why things happen.	Pharmaceutical area sales mgr.
1986	Economics has offered insights into my decision making and the social and political environment in which I operate.	Sales, heating & cooling
1986	My [economics] background has helped me analyze diverse material.	Land use planner
1987	Economics has proved invaluable to me in working with my clients.	Corp. tax consultant

*A selection of comments provided by former undergraduate economics students at Southwest Missouri State University (Springfield, MO). Comments above reflect the views and careers of bachelor's graduates at SMSU. Alumni quoted are 27–43 years old (early- to mid-career).

Source: Fall 1992 alumni survey conducted by Larry G. Cox, Economics Department, Southwest Missouri State University.

Careers in Economics: Selected Readings

Hansen, W. Lee, "The Education and Training of Economics Doctorates," *Journal of Economic Literature* (September 1991): 1054–87. Table 12 provides results of employer surveys regarding skills needed by Ph.D. economists in their careers.

McCallin, Nancy J., "The Business Economist at Work: The Economics Function at the Colorado Legislative Council," *Business Economics* (January 1992): 55–57. *Business Economics* regularly publishes articles about the careers of economists working in the business sector. The McCallin article cited here is provided only for illustration; check other issues of *Business Economics* regarding careers that appeal to your interests.

NABE, *Careers in Business Economics* (Cleveland: National Association of Business Economists, 1989). A collection of personal histories written by practicing business economists. Single copies of this booklet are free of charge. Contact NABE at 28790 Chagrin Blvd., Suite 300, Cleveland, OH 44122, (216) 464-7986.

National Employment Business Weekly (Dow Jones). A weekly newspaper that lists jobs in major corporations and other organizations and provides strategies and advice for job searchers. Jobs listed in *NEBW* are usually appropriate for experienced workers, rather than for new college graduates. Jobs of interest to economists include "industry analyst," "forecast manager," "business analyst," or "real estate analyst." Sold at newsstands or by subscription ($52/year). For subscription information call (800) 842-7900.

APPENDIX 14

The Top Economics Departments and MBA Programs

Many studies have been performed over the years to rate the quality of departments and graduate programs. Most rankings are based on the volume of publications by faculty, the number of times other researchers cite articles by the department's faculty, publication success of former students, and so on. *These measures may or may not be relevant measures of quality to students contemplating graduate study.* For additional rankings consult Lynn C. Hattendorf, *Educational Rankings Annual, 1993* (Detroit: Gale Research, Inc., 1993).

Ratings of Economics Departments

These departmental ratings are based on the number of pages published by the department's faculty in the three most highly ranked economics journals (listed in Appendix 15) between 1983 and 1988. These rankings correlate highly with rankings based on other criteria. See table footnote for source information.

1978–88 Rank	University	1983–88 Rank	1978–83 Rank
1	Chicago	4	1
2	MIT	1	2
3	Harvard	3	3
4	Princeton	2	9
5	Stanford	6	5
6	Yale	9	4
7	Pennsylvania	5	6
8	Northwestern	7	8
9	California—Los Angeles	8	13
10	Columbia	13	12
11	Rochester	14	11
12	California—Berkeley	10	16
13	Carnegie-Mellon	11	14
14	Minnesota	21	7
15	Michigan	12	15
16	California—San Diego	29	10
17	Wisconsin—Madison	17	17
18	Virginia	15	18
19	Washington—Seattle	18	19
20	New York (N.Y.U.)	16	21
21	California—Santa Barbara	30	20
22	Ohio State	20	26
23	Cornell	23	25
24	Duke	18	41
25	Michigan State	24	29

(continued)

1978–88 Rank	University	1983–88 Rank	1978–83 Rank
26	California Tech. Inst.	32	24
27	Iowa	22	40
28	Brown	42	22
29	Boston	27	38
30	California—Davis	33	27
31	Maryland	31	35
32	Houston	25	49
33	Florida	35	30
34	Illinois—Urbana/Champaign	59	23
35	S.U.N.Y.—Stony Brook	37	34
36	Texas A&M	27	48
37	S.U.N.Y.—Buffalo	34	39
38	Arizona	41	32
39	Virginia Tech. (V.P.I.)	40	35
40	Indiana—Bloomington	26	68
41	Southern Calif. (U.S.C.)	47	37
42	Rutgers	72	28
43	Illinois—Chicago	67	31
44	Purdue	67	33
45	North Carolina State	45	44
46	Pittsburgh	35	64
47	Texas—Austin	37	64
48	Boston College	56	43
49	Kansas	61	42
50	Dartmouth	43	58

Source: Mark C. Berger and Frank A. Scott, "Changes in U.S. and Southern Economics Department Rankings Over Time," *Growth and Change* (Summer 1990): table 1. Rankings for departments outside the U.S. can be found in Barry T. Hirsch et al., "Economics Departmental Rankings: Comment," *American Economic Review* (September 1984): 825.

Ratings of Economics Departments by Field

The table rates departmental quality in specific areas of economics. The ratings are based on the volume of publications by current (1985) faculty in the leading 27 economics journals. Faculty publications are counted for the decade 1975–1984.

Rank	Micro	Macro/Money	Econometrics	Public Fin.	International
1	Harvard	Harvard	Stanford	Harvard	MIT
2	Princeton	MIT	Minnesota	Princeton	Columbia
3	Stanford	Car.-Mellon	UC—S. Diego	Stanford	Ohio State
4	Yale	Yale	Michigan State	MIT	Princeton
5	MIT	Minnesota	Yale	Pennsylvania	Chicago
6	Pennsylvania	Princeton	Princeton	Michigan	Illinois
7	Minnesota	Rochester	Duke	Columbia	Pennsylvania
8	UCLA	Chicago	Illinois	Illinois	Duke
9	Chicago	Columbia	Wisconsin	Yale	Harvard
10	Illinois	Stanford	Pennsylvania	Virginia	Wisconsin
11	Tex. A&M	Illinois	UCLA	Minnesota	Rochester
12	UC—Berkeley	N. Carolina	N. Carolina	Duke	Yale*
13	Michigan	Brown	Florida	UC—Berkeley	Minnesota
14	UC—S. Diego	Pennsylvania*	MIT*	Delaware	Michigan
15	Car.-Mellon	Virginia	Ohio State	UC—S. Barb.*	Iowa State
16	USC	Washington	Chicago	Cornell	Maryland*
17	Iowa	UC—Berkeley	Cornell	Tex. A&M	NYU*
18	NYU	Ohio State	Pittsburgh*	Car.-Mellon	SMU*
19	Virginia	Wisconsin	Washington*	Brown	Pittsburgh
20	Columbia	Northwestern	Texas	Maryland*	Rutgers*

*Denotes tie ranking with department listed immediately above.

Source: M. G. Baumann, G. J. Werden, and M. A. Williams, "Rankings of Economics Departments by Field," *American Economist* (Spring 1987): 56–61. An alternative ranking can be found in John Tschirhart, "Ranking Economics Departments in Areas of Expertise," *Journal of Economic Education* (Spring 1989): 199–222.

Ratings of MBA Programs

The table provides 1992 ratings of MBA programs compiled from surveys of graduates of 36 schools and 352 companies that recruit MBAs.

1992 Rank	University	Corporate Poll	Graduate Poll	Annual Tuition	Applicants Accepted
1	Northwestern	1	3	$18,780	23%
2	Chicago	4	10	19,250	34
3	Harvard	3	12	18,550	15
4	Pennsylvania (Wharton)	2	15	18,800	22
5	Michigan	6	9	18,600	32
6	Dartmouth (Amos Tuck)	12	1	18,750	20
7	Stanford	7	5	19,240	12
8	Indiana	8	6	12,318	35
9	Columbia	5	18	19,000	47
10	North Carolina	11	8	8,680	17
11	Virginia (Darden)	15	2	14,227	26
12	Duke (Fuqua)	14	7	18,500	30
13	MIT (Sloan)	10	14	19,500	20
14	Cornell (Johnson)	17	4	18,500	33
15	NYU (Stern)	13	16	18,030	40
16	UCLA (Anderson)	16	11	11,246	24
17	Carnegie-Mellon	9	23	18,600	34
18	UC—Berkeley (Haas)	19	13	7,700	24
19	Vanderbilt (Owen)	20	19	17,500	48
20	Washington—St. Louis (Olin)	18	24	16,750	42

APPENDIX 15

The Top
Economics Journals

Rank*	Journal	Impact-Adjusted Citations
1	*American Economic Review*	100.00
2	*Journal of Political Economy*	80.88
3	*Econometrica*	63.96
4	*Journal of Monetary Economics*	22.96
5	*Journal of Economic Theory*	22.58
6	*Review of Economic Studies*	22.52
7	*International Economic Review*	19.04
8	*Bell Journal of Economics*	17.43
9	*Journal of Finance*	17.42
10	*Journal of Econometrics*	15.99
11	*Scandinavian Journal of Economics*	15.13
12	*Brookings Papers on Economic Activity*	13.74
13	*Journal of Public Economics*	12.12
14	*Journal of Financial Economics*	11.57
15	*Review of Economics and Statistics*	11.45
16	*Journal of the American Statistical Association*	10.87
17	*Quarterly Journal of Economics*	10.70
18	*Journal of Human Resources*	9.93
19	*Journal of Economic Literature*	9.69
20	*Economic Journal*	9.59
21	*Journal of Law and Economics*	9.11
22	*Canadian Journal of Economics*	8.80
23	*Economic Inquiry*	8.70
24	*Journal of Mathematical Economics*	8.13
25	*Journal of International Economics*	7.96
26	*Southern Economic Journal*	7.67
27	*Journal of Money, Credit and Banking*	7.22
28	*Economica*	5.89
29	*National Tax Journal*	5.25
30	*American Journal of Agricultural Economics*	4.20

*Rankings based on "impact-adjusted citations" of articles published during 1975–79. Source: Liebowitz and Palmer, "Assessing the Relative Impacts of Economics Journals," *Journal of Economic Literature* (March 1984), table 1.

APPENDIX 16

American Recipients of the Nobel Prize in Economics

The Nobel Prize in economics is awared each year to one or more economists who have made significant contributions to economic analysis. The Nobel Prize in economics was first awarded in 1969. The Royal Academy of Science in Sweden picks the prizewinners each October, and they travel to Sweden for a presentation ceremony later in the year. In 1993 the Nobel Prize carried a cash award of $845,000, which is divided when there is more than one recipient.

Year of Prize	Name (year of birth)	Current Affiliation
1993	Douglass North (1920)	Washington Univ. (St. Louis)
	Robert W. Fogel (1926)	University of Chicago

For applying economic theory and quantitative methods to historical events.

| 1992 | Gary Becker (1930) | University of Chicago |

For analyzing household behavior and the economics of discrimination.

| 1991 | Ronald Coase (1910) | University of Chicago |

For pioneering work regarding the role of transaction costs and property rights.

1990	Merton Miller (1923)	University of Chicago
	Harry M. Markowitz (1927)	City University of New York
	William F. Sharpe (1934)	Stanford

For analysis of the risks, rewards, and pricing of various investments.

| 1987 | Robert M. Solow (1924) | MIT |

For contributions to the theory of economic growth.

| 1986 | James M. Buchanan (1919) | George Mason University |

For developing new methods of analyzing public sector decision making.

| 1985 | Franco Modigliani (1918) | MIT |

For analysis of household savings and financial markets.

| 1983 | Gerard Debreu (1921) | Univ. of California (Berkeley) |

For work on how prices operate to balance supply and demand.

| 1982 | George Stigler (1911) | University of Chicago |

For work on government regulation of markets and the functioning of industry.

| 1981 | James Tobin (1918) | Yale University |

For analysis of financial markets and their influence on spending and saving.

| 1980 | Lawrence R. Klein (1920) | University of Pennsylvania |

For developing econometric models to forecast economic trends.

| 1979 | Theodore W. Schultz (1902) | University of Chicago |

For work in development economics.

| 1978 | Herbert A. Simon (1916) | Carnegie-Mellon University |

For analysis of decision making within economic organizations.

| 1976 | Milton Friedman (1912) | Hoover Institution (Stanford) |

For work on consumption analysis, monetary theory and history, and stabilization policy.

| 1975 | Tjalling C. Koopmans (1910) | deceased |

Work on the theory of optimum resource allocation.

| 1973 | Wassily Leontief (1906) | New York University |

For developing the input-output method of economic analysis.

| 1972 | Kenneth Arrow (1921) | Stanford University |

For theories that help to assess government economic and welfare policies.

| 1971 | Simon Kuznets (1901) | deceased |

For developing the concept of the gross national product.

| 1970 | Paul Samuelson (1915) | MIT |

For raising the level of scientific analysis in economic theory.

APPENDIX 17

The Keynesians Return to Washington

David Warsh "The Keynesians Return to Washington," *The Margin* (Fall 1993): 8–9.

The Keynesians Return to Washington

The New Classical and Supply Side days are over; government activism is in.

In the weeks just after the 1992 presidential election, speculation about Bill Clinton's economics swirled around Little Rock. How much of a New Democrat was he? Would the relatively free market-oriented Progressive Policy Institute or the relatively *dirigiste* Economic Policy Institute prevail? Would he invite a moderate Republican into his government in an effort to steer a middle course, as his hero John Kennedy did 32 years before?

By the beginning of January, the matter was settled. There would be jobs for professed Democrats only—economists included.

As in any new administration, there was much uncertainty in this two-month period. Former Federal Reserve chairman Paul Volcker was spurned for the Treasury Secretary's job—too independent. The same was said of MIT's Lester Thurow as a potential chairman of the Council of Economic Advisers. Henry Aaron of the Brookings Institution was sidetracked after he disparaged the idea that the economy needs aggressive stimulus. Brandeis University's Stuart Altman—a University of Chicago economist whose first government job was as a price controller under Richard Nixon—was dismissed from the Health Care Task Force after he told the president that reform would produce no windfall savings.

Meanwhile, an informal economic transition team conducted a search among financial analysts for a "magic number" of deficit reduction that would permit the administration to talk interest rates down in the bond market. By the end of January the first appointments were beginning to fall into place.

Ordinarily the flagship of economic advice-giving is the Council of Economic Advisers, and President Clinton has nominated three very interesting persons to it. (Only the first, chairman Laura D'Andrea Tyson, had actually been confirmed by June 30.) It is said that they are typical of the can-do style and outlook of MIT, where each was trained. And each is in some sense viscerally opposed to the "New Classical" school of economics, with its deep pessimism about the extent to which deliberate policy can alter the outcomes of markets— except, of course, for the worse.

The appointment of Ms. Tyson came as something of a surprise in the economics community. She wrote her dissertation on central planning in Yugoslavia, not exactly a fast-track topic at macro-happy MIT. In the early 1980s she gravitated to the so-called "new" trade theory, whose exponents use models of high-tech industries with increasing returns to scale to question basic tenets of old trade theory—including the principle that government should encourage free trade in virtually any circumstance. (Ms. Tyson describes herself as a "cautious activist" in trade and industrial policy.) A few other economists openly questioned her suitability, saying she wasn't seasoned enough to hold her ground against opponents. But the University of California at Berkeley professor's basic skills are striking— she is forceful and very smart. And she was easily confirmed.

Next, Bill Clinton added Alan Blinder, a Princeton University professor whom many expected to be named chairman of the council. (It took a phone call from the president-elect to persuade him to serve.) Mr. Blinder is a veteran Keynesian macroeconomist, one to whom the IS-LM curve is second nature and whose quick wit and common sense endear him to readers of his once-a-month column in Business Week. He has written enough policy advice (his book *Hard Heads, Soft Hearts: Tough-minded Economics for a Just Society* is excellent and accessible) to be intuitively familiar with most of the macroeconomic issues that occupy the council's time. Professional economists welcomed his appointment.

The third appointment was perhaps the biggest surprise. Joseph Stiglitz has no experience in government but is one of the smartest economists of his generation. A Stanford University professor, Mr. Stiglitz is one of the leading theorists of the "new Keynesian" school, with its pervasive emphasis on imperfect competition in product, consumer, labor and capital markets. Indeed, only weeks before taking the job, Mr. Stiglitz rolled out a highly ambitious introductory text designed to teach the "New Keynesian" synthesis to college freshmen. His friends joke that since going to Washington, Mr. Stiglitz has not yet met a market whose performance he didn't think the government could improve through intervention. But his ebullience and lively intelligence have made him a popular figure in Washington. (A fine non-textbook introduction to New Keynesian views can be found in *Beyond Free Markets* by Marc Levinson.)

The Office of Management and Budget was staffed by some seasoned Washington hands, beginning with former House Budget Committee member Leon Panetta. His deputy is Alice Rivlin, a Brookings Institution macroeconomist who served successfully as chief of the Congressional Budget Office. Joseph Minarik, the CBO's chief economist, is a veteran Capitol Hill aide who, as an aide to Sen. Bill Bradley, wrote a good deal of the 1981 income tax bill.

But this is no ordinary administration. For one thing, Bill Clinton campaigned on a promise to create a national "economic security adviser," modelled on the office of the National Security Adviser. Once Mr. Clinton assumed office, however, his assertion that trade is war by other means

(which lurked behind this promise) seemed a little too bellicose. A National Economic Council was created instead. Robert Rubin, a lawyer-turned-investment banker who made a fortune as a paper entrepreneur at Goldman Sachs, was appointed chief. He was given a small but blue-chip staff, including campaign economic issues director Gene Sperling and Harvard economist David Cutler. Mr. Rubin's job is said to involve serving as an honest broker among the factions contending for the president's ear.

And factions there are. Perhaps the most important group to understand is the wide-spread network known as FOBs, or Friends of Bill. These persons have free access to the president. First in line are Robert Reich and Ira Magaziner, whose friendship with Clinton dates back to their days together as Rhodes Scholars at Oxford in 1968. Mr. Reich is a lawyer who writes widely on economic topics; Mr. Magaziner a business consultant. Though neither is an economist, each campaigned aggressively for the top economic policy jobs at the beginning of the new administration, until the professional establishment rode them off. Reich settled for a job as Secretary of Labor. Magaziner, as staff director of Hillary Rodham Clinton's Task Force on Health Care Reform, is seeking to reconfigure a sector that accounts for 14 percent of GDP. Both men are frequently at odds with professional economists.

What's more, there are persistent rumblings on trade. U.S. Trade Representative Mickey Kanter is a lawyer with little apparent commitment to principles of free trade. Commerce Secretary Ron Brown had his greatest success as Democratic party chairman. There are plenty of respectable economists working for them—none more so than Jack Triplett, a veteran statistician who is now the chief economist of the important Bureau of Economic Analysis in the Commerce Department. Mr. Kanter has stated his determination to pursue the two great negotiations brought near to completion by the Bush administration—the Uruguay round of the General Agreement on Tariffs and Trade and the North American Free Trade Act—but the atmosphere of Mr. Clinton's international trade activities is thunderous. Only in its support of aid to the former Soviet Union has the administration won the unqualified support of the international economics community.

Finally, there is the Treasury Department. Senate Finance chairman Lloyd Bentsen was prevailed upon to take the job. When he was a Texas Senator, Mr. Bentsen was sometimes known as "loophole Lloyd." But now that he has become the guardian of the U.S. tax code, Mr. Bentsen has put together a team widely regarded as the most forceful proponent of sophisticated economic advice in the government—period. In most economic debates in Washington, Treasury is the pole upholding mainstream views—cautious macro policy, free trade and limited intervention in industrial policy.

Harvard economist Lawrence Summers is the very model of a New Keynesian. He has gone through bitter battles over the difficulty of achieving successful government intervention, yet he is rooted enough in liberal values to have survived. (If you can believe it, Mr. Summers counts not one but two Nobel laureate economists among his uncles. They are Paul Samuelson and Kenneth Arrow.) Many thought he should have been chairman of the Council of Economic Advisers. But as the Treasury's point man on international economic coordination, Mr. Summers has a seat at nearly every important table. His counterpart for domestic economic policy, Alicia Munnell, is a highly effective advocate on issues ranging from Social Security to money and banking policy to health care. Both speak forcefully for deficit reduction.

Taken altogether, it is far from clear where the Clinton Administration will wind up, economically speaking. So far, when their goals collide with advice they are being given, Clinton people have shown a tendency to squeeze out economists and to proceed on a wing and a prayer. But certainly the government today is filled with remarkable people whose conviction is that markets need a lot of tending in order to function well. It is very different from the conservative public finance and University of Chicago traditions that characterized the government's outlook for the last 12 years.

BY DAVID WARSH

APPENDIX 18

Guidelines for Giving an Oral Report

By Professor John Hoftyzer
Economics Department, Southwest Missouri State University

1. **Delivery.** The delivery, or manner of presenting, material to your audience is obviously crucial. No matter how important or well-researched your report may be, all will be in vain if you cannot effectively convey the information. One might imagine a computer storage device containing a vast amount of information that simply cannot be accessed. Don't allow yourself to become such a device! Adopt the following suggestions:

   a. Stand when making your presentation. If possible stand in a place where everyone in the audience can see you clearly.

   b. Try to talk in a clear, resounding voice. Avoid rushing through the material. Talk at a reasonable pace.

   c. Do not read your report. Reading an oral report may seem to have several advantages—it is, for example, a way of guaranteeing that no essential points are left out. The disadvantages of reading, however, are that you have little or no eye contact with your audience (so the report becomes impersonal), you may talk too fast, and you may easily overlook inviting questions from the audience.

   d. Do not memorize your report. People tend to memorize in order to ensure that all major points are covered in an orderly fashion. Memorization may also help to avoid long pauses, perhaps due to nervousness. However, memorization takes too much time and effort, and (like reading the report) can result in a rigid delivery.

   e. A blend of (c) and (d) is appropriate. You should understand any technical remarks you will make, but do not memorize long, technical descriptions. Consider using note or index cards. Outline the main points of your talk on one or two cards and note any technical definitions. This will help you maintain the structure of your report but also permit you to maintain contact with your audience.

f. Practice your report once or twice to work out the "bugs" in the content or delivery of the report. Practicing will help build your confidence so that your report will be more relaxed.

g. Comply with any time frame imposed on the report. Using only two minutes for a scheduled five-minute report indicates lack of effort; taking 10 minutes for the same assignment indicates lack of concern for the audience and possibly an inability to distinguish between the important and the unimportant.

h. If you have constructed visual aids, such as graphs or charts, be sure to present them in a clear fashion and at the right time. Point out interesting aspects of the exhibit, such as notable trends or recent fluctuations. Explain the relationship between the subject of the report and the trends or fluctuations shown in the exhibits.

2.   Content. The purpose of giving a report is to provide information to an audience. *Information* tends to impart understanding of concepts and situations, and can lead to changes in the attitude of the audience. *Data* is not the same as information. Data must be "processed" by the human brain (possibly with the help of computers) to become useable as information.

The content level of a report is usually determined by both the topic and the amount of time allotted to the report. In structuring the report, make sure that essential information is included and less important information excluded. Reports involving technical economic concepts may well require the stating of definitions, numerical data and other relevant information. If necessary be sure to describe numerical data; what units of measurement (feet, thousands of dollars, etc.) are used? How have data been transformed (annual rates, seasonally adjusted, etc.)?

Many reports include graphs or statistical measures. Carefully build such information into the fabric of the report. Where should the information be discussed? What point does it illustrate or reinforce? Above all, avoid providing an excessive amount of technical detail or numerical data because your audience will get lost in specifics. Your job is to distinguish between the relevant and irrelevant rather than to tell your audience everything you know. You should not leave it to your audience to decide what is important.

3.   Organization. A good delivery of relevant material can still be ruined if the material is organized in a haphazard fashion. In structuring the report, include the following points:

a. An opening statement about what the report will cover. State in one or two sentences why the topic is interesting or relevant.

b. Define the key concept or idea you plan to discuss.

c. After (a) and (b), get down to business. Relate the essence of what you know about the subject, including a short historical overview if appropriate. If specific conclusions or recommendations are reached, state them explicitly so that your audience is not confused about your message. Back up your conclusions with graphs, data, historical observations, or other evidence.

d. After finishing the report, end by stating, "I would be happy to answer any questions you might have," or something to that effect. Avoid finishing by saying, "Gee, I guess that's all," or "Well, I think I'm running out of time, so I'll stop there."

    e. If your report is well organized, it will be easier to remember the major points you plan to make. Your delivery will thus be more fluid and natural.

4.   Attitude and preparation. Be well dressed on the day you give the report. Check out the operation of audio/visual equipment so that you will be familiar with it during your report. Show enthusiasm for your topic. If you consider it dull, so will your audience. If possible, give each member of the audience a handout with relevant graphs, data, technical information, or a list of your key points. This will make it easier to cover the material and will increase the comprehension of audience members. Aim the material and level of presentation at the specific audience you will address. Include information to make the subject more interesting to your audience.

APPENDIX 19

Statistical Tables

The tables on the following pages are used in conducting various tests of significance, which were discussed in Chapter 11. Additional statistical tables are available in most statistics textbooks.

t Distribution

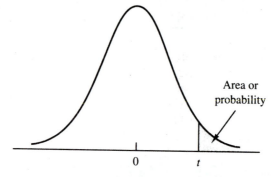

Area or
probability

0   *t*

Entries in the table give *t* values for an area or probability in the upper tail of the *t* distribution. For example, with 10 degrees of freedom and a .05 area in the upper tail, $t_{.05}1.812$.

Degrees of Freedom	Area in Upper Tail				
	.10	.05	.025	.01	.005
1	3.078	6.314	12.706	31.821	63.657
2	1.886	2.920	4.303	6.965	9.925
3	1.638	2.353	3.182	4.541	5.841
4	1.533	2.132	2.776	3.747	4.604
5	1.476	2.015	2.571	3.365	4.032
6	1.440	1.943	2.447	3.143	3.707
7	1.415	1.895	2.365	2.998	3.499
8	1.397	1.860	2.306	2.896	3.355
9	1.383	1.833	2.262	2.821	3.250
10	1.372	1.812	2.228	2.764	3.169
11	1.363	1.796	2.201	2.718	3.106
12	1.356	1.782	2.179	2.681	3.055
13	1.350	1.771	2.160	2.650	3.012
14	1.345	1.761	2.145	2.624	2.977
15	1.341	1.753	2.131	2.602	2.947
16	1.337	1.746	2.120	2.583	2.921
17	1.333	1.740	2.110	2.567	2.898
18	1.330	1.734	2.101	2.552	2.878
19	1.328	1.729	2.093	2.539	2.861
20	1.325	1.725	2.086	2.528	2.845
21	1.323	1.721	2.080	2.518	2.831
22	1.321	1.717	2.074	2.508	2.819
23	1.319	1.714	2.069	2.500	2.807
24	1.318	1.711	2.064	2.492	2.797
25	1.316	1.708	2.060	2.485	2.787
26	1.315	1.706	2.056	2.479	2.779
27	1.314	1.703	2.052	2.473	2.771
28	1.313	1.701	2.048	2.467	2.763
29	1.311	1.699	2.045	2.462	2.756
30	1.310	1.697	2.042	2.457	2.750
40	1.303	1.684	2.021	2.423	2.704
60	1.296	1.671	2.000	2.390	2.660
120	1.289	1.658	1.980	2.358	2.617
∞	1.282	1.645	1.960	2.326	2.576

F Distribution

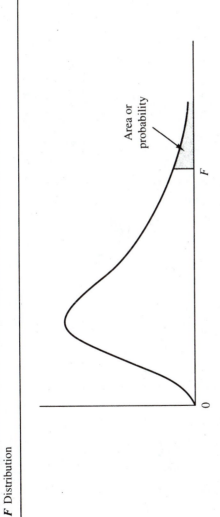

Area or probability

F

Entries in the table give F values, for an area or probability in the upper tail of the F distribution. For example, with 12 numerator degrees of freedom, 15 denominator degrees of freedom, and a .05 area in the upper tail, $F_{.05} 2.48$.

Table of $F_{.05}$ Values

Denominator Degrees of Freedom	Numerator Degrees of Freedom																		
	1	2	3	4	5	6	7	8	9	10	12	15	20	24	30	40	60	120	∞
1	161.4	199.5	215.7	224.6	230.2	234.0	236.8	238.9	240.5	241.9	243.9	245.9	248.0	249.1	250.1	251.1	252.2	253.3	254.3
2	18.51	19.00	19.16	19.25	19.30	19.33	19.35	19.37	19.38	19.40	19.41	19.43	19.45	19.45	19.46	19.47	19.48	19.49	19.50
3	10.13	9.55	9.28	9.12	9.01	8.94	8.89	8.85	8.81	8.79	8.74	8.70	8.66	8.64	8.62	8.59	8.57	8.55	8.53
4	7.71	6.94	6.59	6.39	6.26	6.16	6.09	6.04	6.00	5.96	5.91	5.86	5.80	5.77	5.75	5.72	5.69	5.66	5.63
5	6.61	5.79	5.41	5.19	5.05	4.95	4.88	4.82	4.77	4.74	4.68	4.62	4.56	4.53	4.50	4.46	4.43	4.40	4.36

(TABLE CONTINUES)

6	5.99	5.14	4.76	4.53	4.39	4.28	4.21	4.15	4.10	4.06	4.00	3.94	3.87	3.84	3.81	3.77	3.74	3.70	3.67
7	5.59	4.74	4.35	4.12	3.97	3.87	3.79	3.73	3.68	3.64	3.57	3.51	3.44	3.41	3.38	3.34	3.30	3.27	3.23
8	5.32	4.46	4.07	3.84	3.69	3.58	3.50	3.44	3.39	3.35	3.28	3.22	3.15	3.12	3.08	3.04	3.01	2.97	2.93
9	5.12	4.26	3.86	3.63	3.48	3.37	3.29	3.23	3.18	3.14	3.07	3.01	2.94	2.90	2.86	2.83	2.79	2.75	2.71
10	4.96	4.10	3.71	3.48	3.33	3.22	3.14	3.07	3.02	2.98	2.91	2.85	2.77	2.74	2.70	2.66	2.62	2.58	2.54
11	4.84	3.98	3.59	3.36	3.20	3.09	3.01	2.95	2.90	2.85	2.79	2.72	2.65	2.61	2.57	2.53	2.49	2.45	2.40
12	4.75	3.89	3.49	3.26	3.11	3.00	2.91	2.85	2.80	2.75	2.69	2.62	2.54	2.51	2.47	2.43	2.38	2.34	2.30
13	4.67	3.81	3.41	3.18	3.03	2.92	2.83	2.77	2.71	2.67	2.60	2.53	2.46	2.42	2.38	2.34	2.30	2.25	2.21
14	4.60	3.74	3.34	3.11	2.96	2.85	2.76	2.70	2.65	2.60	2.53	2.46	2.39	2.35	2.31	2.27	2.22	2.18	2.13
15	4.54	3.68	3.29	3.06	2.90	2.79	2.71	2.64	2.59	2.54	2.48	2.40	2.33	2.29	2.25	2.20	2.16	2.11	2.07
16	4.49	3.63	3.24	3.01	2.85	2.74	2.66	2.59	2.54	2.49	2.42	2.35	2.28	2.24	2.19	2.15	2.11	2.06	2.01
17	4.45	3.59	3.20	2.96	2.81	2.70	2.61	2.55	2.49	2.45	2.38	2.31	2.23	2.19	2.15	2.10	2.06	2.01	1.96
18	4.41	3.55	3.16	2.93	2.77	2.66	2.58	2.51	2.46	2.41	2.34	2.27	2.19	2.15	2.11	2.06	2.02	1.97	1.92
19	4.38	3.52	3.13	2.90	2.74	2.63	2.54	2.48	2.42	2.38	2.31	2.23	2.16	2.11	2.07	2.03	1.98	1.93	1.88
20	4.35	3.49	3.10	2.87	2.71	2.60	2.51	2.45	2.39	2.35	2.28	2.20	2.12	2.08	2.04	1.99	1.95	1.90	1.84
21	4.32	3.47	3.07	2.84	2.68	2.57	2.49	2.42	2.37	2.32	2.25	2.18	2.10	2.05	2.01	1.96	1.92	1.87	1.81
22	4.30	3.44	3.05	2.82	2.66	2.55	2.46	2.40	2.34	2.30	2.23	2.15	2.07	2.03	1.98	1.94	1.89	1.84	1.78
23	4.28	3.42	3.03	2.80	2.64	2.53	2.44	2.37	2.32	2.27	2.20	2.13	2.05	2.01	1.96	1.91	1.86	1.81	1.76
24	4.26	3.40	3.01	2.78	2.62	2.51	2.42	2.36	2.30	2.25	2.18	2.11	2.03	1.98	1.94	1.89	1.84	1.79	1.73
25	4.24	3.39	2.99	2.76	2.60	2.49	2.40	2.34	2.28	2.24	2.16	2.09	2.01	1.96	1.92	1.87	1.82	1.77	1.71
26	4.23	3.37	2.98	2.74	2.59	2.47	2.39	2.32	2.27	2.22	2.15	2.07	1.99	1.95	1.90	1.85	1.80	1.75	1.69
27	4.21	3.35	2.96	2.73	2.57	2.46	2.37	2.31	2.25	2.20	2.13	2.06	1.97	1.93	1.88	1.84	1.79	1.73	1.67
28	4.20	3.34	2.95	2.71	2.56	2.45	2.36	2.29	2.24	2.19	2.12	2.04	1.96	1.91	1.87	1.82	1.77	1.71	1.65
29	4.18	3.33	2.93	2.70	2.55	2.43	2.35	2.28	2.22	2.18	2.10	2.03	1.94	1.90	1.85	1.81	1.75	1.70	1.64
30	4.17	3.32	2.92	2.69	2.53	2.42	2.33	2.27	2.21	2.16	2.09	2.01	1.93	1.89	1.84	1.79	1.74	1.68	1.62
40	4.08	3.23	2.84	2.61	2.45	2.34	2.25	2.18	2.12	2.08	2.00	1.92	1.84	1.79	1.74	1.69	1.64	1.58	1.51
60	4.00	3.15	2.76	2.53	2.37	2.25	2.17	2.10	2.04	1.99	1.92	1.84	1.75	1.70	1.65	1.59	1.53	1.47	1.39
120	3.92	3.07	2.68	2.45	2.29	2.17	2.09	2.02	1.96	1.91	1.83	1.75	1.66	1.61	1.55	1.50	1.43	1.35	1.25
∞	3.84	3.00	2.60	2.37	2.21	2.10	2.01	1.94	1.88	1.83	1.75	1.67	1.57	1.52	1.46	1.39	1.32	1.22	1.00

(TABLE CONTINUES ON NEXT PAGE)

This table is reprinted by permission of the Biometrika Trustees from Table 18, Percentage Points of the *F* Distribution, by E. S. Pearson and H. O. Hartley, *Biometrika Tables for Statisticians*, Vol. I, 3rd Edition, 1966.

Table of $F_{.01}$ Values

(Continued)

Denominator Degrees of Freedom	Numerator Degrees of Freedom																		
	1	2	3	4	5	6	7	8	9	10	12	15	20	24	30	40	60	120	∞
1	4,052	4,999.5	5,403	5,625	5,764	5,859	5,928	5,982	6,022	6,056	6,106	6,157	6,209	6,235	6,261	6,287	6,313	6,339	6,366
2	98.50	99.00	99.17	99.25	99.30	99.33	99.36	99.37	99.39	99.40	99.42	99.43	99.45	99.46	99.47	99.47	99.48	99.49	99.50
3	34.12	30.82	29.46	28.71	28.24	27.91	27.67	27.49	27.35	27.23	27.05	26.87	26.69	26.60	26.50	26.41	26.32	26.22	26.13
4	21.20	18.00	16.69	15.98	15.52	15.21	14.98	14.80	14.66	14.55	14.37	14.20	14.02	13.93	13.84	13.75	13.65	13.56	13.46
5	16.26	13.27	12.06	11.39	10.97	10.67	10.46	10.29	10.16	10.05	9.89	9.72	9.55	9.47	9.38	9.29	9.20	9.11	9.06
6	13.75	10.92	9.78	9.15	8.75	8.47	8.26	8.10	7.98	7.87	7.72	7.56	7.40	7.31	7.23	7.14	7.06	6.97	6.88
7	12.25	9.55	8.45	7.85	7.46	7.19	6.99	6.84	6.72	6.62	6.47	6.31	6.16	6.07	5.99	5.91	5.82	5.74	5.65
8	11.26	8.65	7.59	7.01	6.63	6.37	6.18	6.03	5.91	5.81	5.67	5.52	5.36	5.28	5.20	5.12	5.03	4.95	4.86
9	10.56	8.02	6.99	6.42	6.06	5.80	5.61	5.47	5.35	5.26	5.11	4.96	4.81	4.73	4.65	4.57	4.48	4.40	4.31
10	10.04	7.56	6.55	5.99	5.64	5.39	5.20	5.06	4.94	4.85	4.71	4.56	4.41	4.33	4.25	4.17	4.08	4.00	3.91
11	9.65	7.21	6.22	5.67	5.32	5.07	4.89	4.74	4.63	4.54	4.40	4.25	4.10	4.02	3.94	3.86	3.78	3.69	3.60
12	9.33	6.93	5.95	5.41	5.06	4.82	4.64	4.50	4.39	4.30	4.16	4.01	3.86	3.78	3.70	3.62	3.54	3.45	3.36
13	9.07	6.70	5.74	5.21	4.86	4.62	4.44	4.30	4.19	4.10	3.96	3.82	3.66	3.59	3.51	3.43	3.34	3.25	3.17
14	8.86	6.51	5.56	5.04	4.69	4.46	4.28	4.14	4.03	3.94	3.80	3.66	3.51	3.43	3.35	3.27	3.18	3.09	3.00
15	8.68	6.36	5.42	4.89	4.56	4.32	4.14	4.00	3.89	3.80	3.67	3.52	3.37	3.29	3.21	3.13	3.05	2.96	2.87
16	8.53	6.23	5.29	4.77	4.44	4.20	4.03	3.89	3.78	3.69	3.55	3.41	3.26	3.18	3.10	3.02	2.93	2.84	2.75
17	8.40	6.11	5.18	4.67	4.34	4.10	3.93	3.79	3.68	3.59	3.46	3.31	3.16	3.08	3.00	2.92	2.83	2.75	2.65
18	8.29	6.01	5.09	4.58	4.25	4.01	3.84	3.71	3.60	3.51	3.37	3.23	3.08	3.00	2.92	2.84	2.75	2.66	2.57
19	8.18	5.93	5.01	4.50	4.17	3.94	3.77	3.63	3.52	3.43	3.30	3.15	3.00	2.92	2.84	2.76	2.67	2.58	2.49
20	8.10	5.85	4.94	4.43	4.10	3.87	3.70	3.56	3.46	3.37	3.23	3.09	2.94	2.86	2.78	2.69	2.61	2.52	2.42
21	8.02	5.78	4.87	4.37	4.04	3.81	3.64	3.51	3.40	3.31	3.17	3.03	2.88	2.80	2.72	2.64	2.55	2.46	2.36
22	7.95	5.72	4.82	4.31	3.99	3.76	3.59	3.45	3.35	3.26	3.12	2.98	2.83	2.75	2.67	2.58	2.50	2.40	2.31
23	7.88	5.66	4.76	4.26	3.94	3.71	3.54	3.41	3.30	3.21	3.07	2.93	2.78	2.70	2.62	2.54	2.45	2.35	2.26
24	7.82	5.61	4.72	4.22	3.90	3.67	3.50	3.36	3.26	3.17	3.03	2.89	2.74	2.66	2.58	2.49	2.40	2.31	2.21
25	7.77	5.57	4.68	4.18	3.85	3.63	3.46	3.32	3.22	3.13	2.99	2.85	2.70	2.62	2.54	2.45	2.36	2.27	2.17
26	7.72	5.53	4.64	4.14	3.82	3.59	3.42	3.29	3.18	3.09	2.96	2.81	2.66	2.58	2.50	2.42	2.33	2.23	2.13
27	7.68	5.49	4.60	4.11	3.78	3.56	3.39	3.26	3.15	3.06	2.93	2.78	2.63	2.55	2.47	2.38	2.29	2.20	2.10
28	7.64	5.45	4.57	4.07	3.75	3.53	3.36	3.23	3.12	3.03	2.90	2.75	2.60	2.52	2.44	2.35	2.26	2.17	2.06
29	7.60	5.42	4.54	4.04	3.73	3.50	3.33	3.20	3.09	3.00	2.87	2.73	2.57	2.49	2.41	2.33	2.23	2.14	2.03
30	7.56	5.39	4.51	4.02	3.70	3.47	3.30	3.17	3.07	2.98	2.84	2.70	2.55	2.47	2.39	2.30	2.21	2.11	2.01
40	7.31	5.18	4.31	3.83	3.51	3.29	3.12	2.99	2.89	2.80	2.66	2.52	2.37	2.29	2.20	2.11	2.02	1.92	1.80
60	7.08	4.98	4.13	3.65	3.34	3.12	2.95	2.82	2.72	2.63	2.50	2.35	2.20	2.12	2.03	1.94	1.84	1.73	1.60
120	6.85	4.79	3.95	3.48	3.17	2.96	2.79	2.66	2.56	2.47	2.34	2.19	2.03	1.95	1.86	1.76	1.66	1.53	1.38
∞	6.63	4.61	3.78	3.32	3.02	2.80	2.64	2.51	2.41	2.32	2.18	2.04	1.88	1.79	1.70	1.59	1.47	1.32	1.00

Table 13. *Percentage points for the distribution of the correlation coefficient, r, when ρ = 0*

ν	$Q=0.05$ $2Q=0.1$	0.025 0.05	0.01 0.02	0.005 0.01	0.0025 0.005	0.0005 0.001
1	0·9877	0·$9^2$692	0·$9^2$507	0·$9^3$877	0·$9^4$692	0·$9^5$877
2	·9000	·9500	·9800	·$9^4$000	·$9^3$500	·$9^5$000
3	·805	·878	·9343	·9587	·9740	·$9^4$114
4	·729	·811	·882	·9172	·9417	·9741
5	·669	·754	·833	·875	·9056	·9500
6	0·621	0·707	0·789	0·834	0·870	0·9249
7	·582	·666	·750	·798	·836	·898
8	·549	·632	·715	·765	·805	·872
9	·521	·602	·685	·735	·776	·847
10	·497	·576	·658	·708	·750	·823
11	0·476	0·553	0·634	0·684	0·726	0·801
12	·457	·532	·612	·661	·703	·780
13	·441	·514	·592	·641	·683	·760
14	·426	·497	·574	·623	·664	·742
15	·412	·482	·558	·606	·647	·725
16	0·400	0·468	0·543	0·590	0·631	0·708
17	·389	·456	·529	·575	·616	·693
18	·378	·444	·516	·561	·602	·679
19	·369	·433	·503	·549	·589	·665
20	·360	·423	·492	·537	·576	·652
25	0·323	0·381	0·445	0·487	0·524	0·597
30	·296	·349	·409	·449	·484	·554
35	·275	·325	·381	·418	·452	·519
40	·257	·304	·358	·393	·425	·490
45	·243	·288	·338	·372	·403	·465
50	0·231	0·273	0·322	0·354	0·384	0·443
60	·211	·250	·295	·325	·352	·408
70	·195	·232	·274	·302	·327	·380
80	·183	·217	·257	·283	·307	·357
90	·173	·205	·242	·267	·290	·338
100	·164	·195	·230	·254	·276	·321

$Q = 1 - P(r|\nu, \rho=0)$ is the upper-tail area of the distribution of *r* appropriate for use in a single-tail test. For a two-tail test, 2Q must be used. If *r* is calculated from *n* paired observations, enter the table with $\nu = n - 2$. For partial correlations enter with $\nu = n - k - 2$, where *k* is the number of variables held constant.

The columns for $2Q = 0.2$, 0.02 and 0.001 in Table 12 and $2Q = 0.02$ and 0.001 in Table 13 have been taken from *Statistical Tables for Biological, Agricultural and Medical Research*, Tables III and VI (Fisher & Yates, 1963) by permission of the authors and the publishers, Messrs Oliver and Boyd.

This table is reprinted by permission of Biometrika Trustees from Table 13, *Percentage points for the distribution of the correlation coefficient, r, when p=0*. E.S. Pearson and H.O. Hartley, *Biometrika Tables for Statisticians*, Vol. I.

Critical Values for the Durbin-Watson Test for Autocorrelation

Entries in the table give the *critical* values for a one-tailed Durbin-Watson test for autocorrelation. For a two-tailed test, the level of significance is doubled.

Significance Points of d_L and d_U: $\alpha = .05$
Number of Independent Variables

k	1		2		3		4		5	
n	d_L	d_U	d_L	d_U	d_L	d_U	d_L	d_U	d_L	d_U
15	1.08	1.36	0.95	1.54	0.82	1.75	0.69	1.97	0.56	2.21
16	1.10	1.37	0.98	1.54	0.86	1.73	0.74	1.93	0.62	2.15
17	1.13	1.38	1.02	1.54	0.90	1.71	0.78	1.90	0.67	2.10
18	1.16	1.39	1.05	1.53	0.93	1.69	0.82	1.87	0.71	2.06
19	1.18	1.40	1.08	1.53	0.97	1.68	0.86	1.85	0.75	2.02
20	1.20	1.41	1.10	1.54	1.00	1.68	0.90	1.83	0.79	1.99
21	1.22	1.42	1.13	1.54	1.03	1.67	0.93	1.81	0.83	1.96
22	1.24	1.43	1.15	1.54	1.05	1.66	0.96	1.80	0.86	1.94
23	1.26	1.44	1.17	1.54	1.08	1.66	0.99	1.79	0.90	1.92
24	1.27	1.45	1.19	1.55	1.10	1.66	1.01	1.78	0.93	1.90
25	1.29	1.45	1.21	1.55	1.12	1.66	1.04	1.77	0.95	1.89
26	1.30	1.46	1.22	1.55	1.14	1.65	1.06	1.76	0.98	1.88
27	1.32	1.47	1.24	1.56	1.16	1.65	1.08	1.76	1.01	1.86
28	1.33	1.48	1.26	1.56	1.18	1.65	1.10	1.75	1.03	1.85
29	1.34	1.48	1.27	1.56	1.20	1.65	1.12	1.74	1.05	1.84
30	1.35	1.49	1.28	1.57	1.21	1.65	1.14	1.74	1.07	1.83
31	1.36	1.50	1.30	1.57	1.23	1.65	1.16	1.74	1.09	1.83
32	1.37	1.50	1.31	1.57	1.24	1.65	1.18	1.73	1.11	1.82
33	1.38	1.51	1.32	1.58	1.26	1.65	1.19	1.73	1.13	1.81
34	1.39	1.51	1.33	1.58	1.27	1.65	1.21	1.73	1.15	1.81
35	1.40	1.52	1.34	1.58	1.28	1.65	1.22	1.73	1.16	1.80
36	1.41	1.52	1.35	1.59	1.29	1.65	1.24	1.73	1.18	1.80
37	1.42	1.53	1.36	1.59	1.31	1.66	1.25	1.72	1.19	1.80
38	1.43	1.54	1.37	1.59	1.32	1.66	1.26	1.72	1.21	1.79
39	1.43	1.54	1.38	1.60	1.33	1.66	1.27	1.72	1.22	1.79
40	1.44	1.54	1.39	1.60	1.34	1.66	1.29	1.72	1.23	1.79
45	1.48	1.57	1.43	1.62	1.38	1.67	1.34	1.72	1.29	1.78
50	1.50	1.59	1.46	1.63	1.42	1.67	1.38	1.72	1.34	1.77
55	1.53	1.60	1.49	1.64	1.45	1.68	1.41	1.72	1.38	1.77
60	1.55	1.62	1.51	1.65	1.48	1.69	1.44	1.73	1.41	1.77
65	1.57	1.63	1.54	1.66	1.50	1.70	1.47	1.73	1.44	1.77
70	1.58	1.64	1.55	1.67	1.52	1.70	1.49	1.74	1.46	1.77
75	1.60	1.65	1.57	1.68	1.54	1.71	1.51	1.74	1.49	1.77
80	1.61	1.66	1.59	1.69	1.56	1.72	1.53	1.74	1.51	1.77
85	1.62	1.67	1.60	1.70	1.57	1.72	1.55	1.75	1.52	1.77
90	1.63	1.68	1.61	1.70	1.59	1.73	1.57	1.75	1.54	1.78
95	1.64	1.69	1.62	1.71	1.60	1.73	1.58	1.75	1.56	1.78
100	1.65	1.69	1.63	1.72	1.61	1.74	1.59	1.76	1.57	1.78

This table comes from J. Durbin and G. S. Watson, "Testing for serial correlation in least square regression II," *Biometrika,* 38, 1951, 159–178.

APPENDIX 20

Glossary of Economic Terms

Adaptive expectations. A theory of expectation formation in which forecasts of a variable are a weighted average of past actual values of the variable, e.g., today's inflation forecast equals the average rate experienced during the past three years.

Administered prices. A term associated with "rigid" prices that change very slowly or not at all after changes in demand or costs. Usually said to occur in oligopolistic industries. The presence of administered prices is believed by some to make contractionary monetary and fiscal policies ineffective for fighting inflation.

Aggregate demand (AD). The total quantity of real goods and services demanded at different price levels. Sometimes measured by gross domestic product minus net additions to business inventories.

Antitrust policy. Legislation and the administration of laws that limit anticompetitive behavior such as cartel behavior and mergers between large competing firms. Also see "Sherman Act," "Clayton Act," or "F.T.C."

Appreciation. An increase in the market value of an asset. Often this term is applied to currency appreciation, in which the market value of a nation's currency rises relative to other currencies. A decrease in the currency's market value is known as depreciation. This is distinct from revaluation and devaluation of a currency, which occurs in a fixed exchange rate regime when policy makers make a semipermanent change in a currency's official value.

Autocorrelation. See "serial correlation."

Average total cost (ATC). Also called "unit cost". Total cost divided by quantity of output produced.

Balance of payments. The broadest measure of a nation's international financial transactions. Equal to a nation's current account plus its capital account (plus smaller entries for "official reserve accounts" that reflect transactions between national governments and the "statistical discrepancy" that contains unmonitored transactions). In a flexible exchange rate environment, the balance of payments must sum to zero so a surplus in the current account must be approximately offset by a deficit in the capital account, or vice versa.

Balance of trade. The value of a nation's merchandise (goods, not services) exports minus its merchandise imports. This account may be in surplus or deficit. Some economists interpret the balance of trade as an indicator of the nation's manufacturing productivity relative to other nations. See "deficit (international transactions)."

Bank. A business that accepts demand deposits and makes commercial (business) loans. Also see "money center bank" and "regional bank."

Basis point. A unit of measure applying to interest rates, equal to 1/100th of 1%. For example, the difference between 6.50% and 6.51% is one (1) basis point.

Benefit-cost analysis. A method for evaluating the payoff from investments. The costs of investments are typically incurred immediately while the returns are received over several years. Benefit-cost analysis reduces both parts of the investment to "present value" terms. According to the analysis, investments are worthwhile if the present value of returns equals or exceeds the present value of costs.

Blue Chip Economic Indicators. A monthly newsletter published in Sedona, Arizona, that reports economic forecasts by 50 economists and other analysts. The average ("consensus") forecast is considered a reliable indicator of future economic activity.

Board of Governors. The seven-member board that oversees monetary policy and other Federal Reserve operations. Members serve 14-year terms. Members of the Board are selected by the U.S. president but must be confirmed by the U.S. Senate. The president designates one board member to serve as chairman for a four-year period (as is subject to reappointment).

Bretton Woods. A city in New Hampshire where major nations met in 1944 to establish rules governing international financial arrangements that would be followed at the end of World War II. The meetings established a system of quasi-fixed exchange rates in which gold and the dollar served as international money. Following a series of monetary crises in the 1960s and early '70s, the exchange rate mechanism was replaced by flexible exchange rates in 1973. Also see "International Monetary Fund."

Burden of the debt. A concept that attempts to identify who will be harmed by government deficit spending. Some economists believe that the burden falls on the general public at the time the deficit is incurred. Others believe that the burden falls on taxpayers or the general public in future years—the so-called "future generation of taxpayers." Public choice economists argue that the willingness of elected officials to incur deficits is evidence that deficits do in fact postpone the burden of spending into the future. Also see "national debt."

Business cycle. A business cycle is a sequence of events of variable length. During one business cycle overall economic activity (1) expands, (2) reaches a peak, (3) contracts, and (4) reaches a trough (bottom). Business cycles typically last about 4–5 years but may be of any length.

Most macroeconomic theories were originally developed to "explain" the business cycle.

C.A.B. Civil Aeronautics Board. The federal agency that regulated air carrier ticket prices until deregulation of the airline industry in 1978.

Capacity utilization rate. The percent of productive capacity in use in the nation's factories, mines, and utilities. Utilization rates are also available for specific industries. "High" capacity utilization rates are sometimes believed to provide an early signal of inflation. Also see "industrial production."

Capital. The stock of produced goods that can be used to produce other goods. The term is often broadened to include "human capital"— education and work skills.

Capital account. The value of a nation's financial securities exported to foreign purchasers minus the value of financial securities imported from abroad. This account may be in surplus or deficit. Also see "deficit (international transactions)."

Capture theory of regulation. A theory of regulation which predicts that firms regulated by government will eventually gain influence over the regulator, at which point many regulations will favor the interests of the regulated firm—often, by restricting entry of new competitors into the market or by restricting supply by existing firms to increase price. Capture does not usually occur immediately, but over time as regulated firms become more adept at pleading their case, employ retired regulators, and provide campaign contributions to legislators.

Cartel. An agreement among competing firms to restrict market supplies and not to undercut each other's price. The world's best-known cartels include DeBeers, a central marketing organization for most of the world's diamonds, and OPEC, a group of petroleum exporting nations. Federal and state antitrust laws make most cartels illegal within the U.S. See "antitrust policy."

Chicago School. A group of economists linked to the economics department at the University of Chicago. In general this group includes current and former members of its faculty and former students. Theories developed by Chicago School economists typically assume flexible wages and prices and other competitive market conditions. They often explain market failures as the result of incomplete private property rights or high transaction costs, and remain critical of government programs designed to correct perceived microeconomic and macroeconomic problems. Chicago School members have won a disproportionate share of all Nobel Prizes awarded in economics.

Clayton Act. A law passed in 1914 that prohibits specific anticompetitive acts (mergers, interlocking directorates) and provides treble (triple) damages in private antitrust lawsuits. Also see "antitrust policy."

Cobb-Douglas production (or utility) function. A functional form in which output (utility) is the product of input (consumption) quantities raised to fractional powers that sum to one. For example, if Q equals output, L is units of labor, and K is units of capital, a Cobb-Douglas production function is: $Q = 2L^{0.7}K^{0.3}$. This functional form implies diminishing marginal productivity (utility) and is a fairly accurate description of certain empirically estimated production functions.

Coefficient of determination (R^2). A measure of the performance of a regression equation equal to the share of variation in a variable that is statistically linked to the explanatory variables in the regression. R^2 ranges from 0 to 1.

Coincident economic indicators, index of (CEI). The index of coincident indicators summarizes movements in four key economic indicators that typically rise and fall at the same time as the overall economy. Since these indicators are reported monthly, the CEI often provides a more timely picture of the economy's current situation than real GDP, which is reported quarterly and is subject to large revisions. The CEI is reported in the *Survey of Current Business* (yellow pages). Two CEI components are total nonagricultural employment and real personal income less transfer payments. Also see "leading economic indicators."

Common property. A setting in which property is owned jointly by members of a group (e.g., club members or all citizens). If the group is large, it is generally believed that members will exploit the property as quickly as possible in order to increase their own wealth at the expense of society at large. This is the "tragedy of the commons" which explains the disappearance of buffaloes, whales, clean water, and other natural resources. Also see "property rights" and "private property."

Comparable worth. A normative theory of wages which asserts that jobs should receive the same compensation if the work is of comparable worth. Plans to implement comparable worth usually call for a system that assigns "points" to each job on the basis of job attributes like risk and physical effort. Comparable worth proposals were common in the 1980s, but federal legislation was never adopted.

Compensation of workers. Money wages and salaries plus nonmonetary fringe benefits. In recent years, fringe benefits have grown more rapidly than wages; today fringes account for about 28% of total compensation.

Concentration ratio. The share of total sales by the domestic industry accounted for by the largest four (or sometimes eight or more) firms. This is the "market share" figure for a group of firms. An alternative measure of market concentration is the Herfindahl index (see below).

Consumer expectations index. Indexes of consumer expectations are prepared by the University of Michigan ("Index of Consumer Sentiment") and the Conference Board ("Consumer Confidence Index"). Both indexes are compiled by surveying the general public each month about their current situation and their expectations for the future. Since consumers are less likely to purchase expensive goods when they are pessimistic, the two indexes are often used to forecast consumer purchases of durable goods; they are also considered leading indicators for the overall economy, but in recent years researchers have questioned their usefulness for that purpose.

Consumer price index (CPI). The CPI is an index of the price of a basket of goods purchased by the typical urban household. The index equals 100 in the base year; a doubling of prices will cause the index to rise to 200. Also see "inflation rate."

Contestable market. A market that firms can enter or exit at zero cost. In a contestable market economic profits will equal zero. The theory of contestable markets suggests that entry costs may be a more important indicator of a market's competitiveness than the number of competing firms (which is stressed by traditional theories).

Contingent valuation. A method of valuing goods by surveying consumers or potential consumers about their worth. This is typically done for public goods and other goods that are not priced in the marketplace.

Convergence theory. A theory of economic growth which explains why nations that trade with each other will tend to converge toward similar per capita income levels. This implies that nations with below-average income levels will experience more rapid growth rates than nations with above-average incomes.

Cost-benefit analysis. A method of evaluating a capital investment in which the present value of the investment's future benefits (including revenues) are compared to the present value of its costs. The investment is justified if the present value of benefits exceeds the present value of costs. This analysis is sensitive to the selection of an interest rate used to reduce future dollars to present value. See "present value" below, and Appendix 9.

Cost-push inflation. A theory of inflation. In this theory a rising price level results from a decrease in aggregate supply. The latter could result from rising wages, rising oil prices, or other costs. Also see "inflation" and "demand-pull inflation."

Coupon interest rate. The interest rate stated on the face of a bond (or bank CD), paid annually to the bond (or CD) holder. If the coupon interest rate on a $1,000 bond (CD) is 8%, the investor would receive $80 in interest payments each year.

Credit controls. Regulations that can be invoked to direct credit toward certain uses or away from others (e.g., the stock market). The Federal Reserve administers some minor credit control policies and the president has the authority to invoke other controls in emergency situations.

Cross-price elasticity. An elasticity coefficient showing the percentage change in consumption of a good resulting from a 1% change in the price of another good. Substitute goods have a positive cross-price elasticity and complements have a negative cross-price elasticity.

Cross section data set. A series of data drawn from members of a population at a single point of time. Also see "time series data set."

Crowding out. A consequence of deficit-financed government spending. When government demand for credit causes interest rates to increase, it becomes more costly to finance private investment and consumption spending. Private spending is "crowded out" by government spending, and hence the stimulative impact of the fiscal policy is reduced.

Current account. A measure of international transactions. Net exports of goods and services plus net investment income, minus net unilateral transfers from Americans to foreigners. The current account includes the narrower "balance of trade" measure. The current account may be in surplus or deficit. See "deficit (international transactions)."

Cyclical. Relating to the business cycle, e.g., cyclical unemployment, cyclically adjusted budget.

Deduction. An approach to science in which a general law (combined with information about initial conditions) is used to deduce a prediction about a specific event or decision; these predictions are also known as hypotheses. Deduction is described as reasoning "from general to specific." Also see "induction."

Default risk. The risk that a borrower will not repay interest and/or the principal amount of a loan on schedule. Default risk causes lenders to add a risk premium to the interest rate they charge borrowers. U.S. Treasury securities are usually said to carry zero (or minimal) default risk. See also "interest risk."

Defensive open market operations. Monetary policy actions taken to offset changes in the money supply that originate elsewhere in the economy. Such policies are intended to stabilize monetary conditions rather than to initiate a new policy stance. See "dynamic open market operations."

Deficit (budget). A budget deficit exists when government expenditures, including transfer payments, exceed government taxes and other receipts for the year. A budget deficit requires the government to obtain additional financing for its outlays, which it does by issuing Treasury bonds and other securities. When government expenditures are less than receipts, the budget is in surplus. The most recent federal budget surplus occurred in fiscal year 1969. Also see "national debt."

Deficit (international transactions). A nation experiences a deficit in its international accounts when more funds (dollars) leave the nation than enter it during a given time period. Since funds leave a nation to pay for goods or financial securities, a deficit in a nation's monetary accounts implies that more goods or securities flow into the nation than out. The opposite of a deficit is a surplus.

Demand-pull inflation. A theory of inflation in which a rising price level is the result of an increase in aggregate demand and total spending (by households, business, or government). Also see "inflation" and "cost-push inflation."

Dependent variable. A concept or variable whose "behavior" is explained by theoretical analysis or empirical estimates. Changes in the dependent variable are explained by variations in one or more independent "explanatory" variables.

Diffusion index. An index number equal to the percent of a particular group of economic indicators signaling economic expansion. A diffusion index can be calculated for any group of economic indicators. To reduce the volatility of this business cycle indicator, many analysts use the percent of indicators signaling expansion over the most recent six months.

Discomfort index. See "misery index."

Discount rate. The interest rate the Fed charges banks for short-term credit, called discount loans or advances. The discount rate usually follows other interest rates up and down rather than leading them.

Disposable income. Personal income minus personal taxes. Disposable income is either spent for consumption goods or saved. Disposable income is also called personal disposable income.

Dow Jones Industrial Average (DJIA). An index of the prices of stocks issued by 30 major corporations such as AT&T, IBM, and GE. The Dow Jones index was first compiled for 11 stock prices in 1884; the index grew to include 30 companies by 1928. The DJIA bears no fixed relationship to the dollar prices of the stocks. Other widely used stock indexes include the Standard & Poor 500, the New York Stock Exchange composite index, and the Wilshire 5000.

Dummy variable. A variable that takes on the value of 1 if some condition is satisfied, and equals 0 otherwise. In regression analysis the coefficient on a dummy variable shows the shift in the regression line if the condition is present which makes the dummy equal one. Also called a qualitative, zero/one, or binary variable.

Dumping. A practice in which a good is sold for less in international markets than in the nation where production occurred. International agreements often limit dumping.

Durable good. A good whose expected life is three years or longer, e.g., a car or refrigerator. Durable good purchases can be delayed during periods of uncertainty, so durable goods industries go through more pronounced fluctuations than the overall economy.

Dynamic open market operations. Monetary policy actions that change the monetary base for the purpose of increasing or decreasing the money supply. Also see "defensive open market operations."

Economic rent. A "noncompensated transfer" of wealth, typically created by government policy. Transfer payments constitute a "pure" rent.

Economies of scale. A concept that relates average per unit production costs to firm output. If economies of scale are present, average costs decline as output is increased. Diseconomies of scale imply rising average costs when firm output is increased. Both apply in the "long run," when all inputs are variable.

Education vouchers. A proposal first advanced by Milton Friedman in the 1950s. Rather than being assigned a school to attend, students would be given a voucher (coupon) worth a certain amount which they could spend on tuition at the school of their choice (plus any additional cash required to meet the school's tuition charge). Governments would redeem these coupons from the schools at their face value. Because students could attend any of a number of schools, schools would have to compete on the basis of quality to remain in business.

Efficiency wage theory. A theory which states that employers will willingly pay their workers more than the market clearing wage in order to induce workers to be more efficient and remain in their jobs for a longer time (thereby lowering the employer's costs of training new workers).

Elasticity. A measure of the responsiveness of one (usually behavioral) variable to changes in another variable. Several elasticity measures are discussed by economists, including the price elasticity of demand. Economists calculate and use elasticity coefficients to predict the likely effects of changing policies or circumstances. See "price elasticity" and "cross-price elasticity."

Empirical evidence. Experience or experimental results used to "test" a conjecture (hypothesis).

Employment Act of 1946. An act in which Congress pledged to stabilize the macroeconomy, particularly employment conditions. This law reflected the concern of Americans with unemployment following the Depression of the 1930s. The act established the president's Council of Economic Advisers.

Eurodollars. Dollar-denominated deposits (usually time deposits) in banks outside the U.S. Such funds are frequently loaned to borrowers within the U.S.

Event analysis. A regression technique used to estimate the impact of some event on stock prices. The impact estimate equals the difference between a stock's actual performance during the event period and the performance predicted from a regression estimated for nonevent periods.

Exchange rate. The value of one currency in terms of another, e.g., 1.5 German marks per dollar. Because the dollar is an international currency, the common practice is to quote the number of units of a certain currency required to purchase one dollar. Because the British pound was an international currency before the dollar, the value of the pound is usually quoted as the number of dollars that exchange for the pound, e.g., $1.51 = £1. See "appreciation" and "purchasing power parity."

Exogenous. An "outside" shock to an economic unit (an individual, market, or national economy). For example, a newly imposed excise tax on tobacco imparts an exogenous shock to the tobacco market. Exogenous shocks also figure prominently in macroeconomic analysis. An exogenous shock is often the starting point in economic analysis; taking the shock as a given, the economist analyzes its effects on the economic unit of interest. The effects that occur internally (within the economic unit) are "endogenous."

Expectations hypothesis. A theory of long-term interest rates in which the long-term rate is an average of short-term interest rates people expect to prevail over the life of the loan.

Externality. A situation in which one person's consumption or production activities impose damages or confer benefits on others.

F.C.C. Federal Communications Commission. The federal agency that regulates companies in the communications industry (telephones, television, radio).

F.D.I.C. Federal Deposit Insurance Corporation. A federal agency that insures deposits in banks up to $100,000 per account. Nearly all banks have F.D.I.C. insurance. The F.S.L.I.C., which formerly insured deposits at savings and loans, exhausted its reserves during the late 1980s. Its successor is a division of the F.D.I.C.

F.T.C. Federal Trade Commission. A federal agency that enforces laws relating to false advertising and unfair competitive practices. Established in 1914.

Falsification. An approach to science which insists that theories are scientific only if their predictions are tested against empirical evidence; a falsified theory is one that is inconsistent with actual experience. Most scientists believe that numerous tests are required to reject (or refute) a theory.

Fannie Mae. A popular name for the Federal National Mortgage Association (FNMA). A federally sponsored credit agency that borrows funds in credit markets and uses the funds to purchase residential mortgages from banks and other financial institutions. This makes mortgages more liquid and lowers mortgage interest rates.

Federal funds rate. The interest rate banks charge each other on large, overnight, unsecured loans. Term Fed funds have longer maturities. In recent years savings and loan associations and some other financial institutions have gained access to the Fed funds market. Fed funds loans are sometimes secured by Treasury bills; these are also called repurchase agreements.

Federal Reserve. An agency that regulates banks, provides certain banking services (such as check clearing) and conducts monetary policy. Established by legislation passed in 1913, the Fed is legally owned by the "member" commercial banks who are its shareholders. Top Fed officials are appointed by the U.S. president with the approval of the Senate. The Fed is an "independent agency" of government. Fed profits in excess of the 6% dividend on stock held by member banks are paid to the U.S. Treasury. Hence the federal government receives most of the Fed's profits from creating money (seigniorage).

Fiat money. Money defined as legal tender by the government whose value in exchange is greater than its value as a commodity. Also called "token money." By contrast, full-bodied money has approximately the same value as money as it has as a commodity (e.g., a silver dollar).

Fiscal policy. Government taxing and spending policies. Keynesian economists emphasize the ability of fiscal policy to stabilize the macroeconomy.

Fiscal year. A 12-month period defined for accounting purposes. Many businesses and most governmental units do not use the calendar year as their fiscal year. The U.S. government's fiscal year is October 1–September 30. Fiscal year 1999 *ends* in 1999 (and begins in 1998).

Flow-of-funds table. A data series prepared by the Federal Reserve which reports the flow of funds in financial markets. The table has been called a "vast sources-and-uses accounting system for the U.S. capital [financial] market." See this table in the *Federal Reserve Bulletin.*

Future value. The number of dollars that would accumulate in an investment by a specific date in the future. The future value reflects the original amount invested, the interest rate (or rate of return) earned on the investment, and the length of the investment period. The future value is greater, the higher the interest rate. See Appendix 9.

G.A.T.T. The General Agreement on Tariffs and Trade. Ongoing talks between most nations designed to lower tariffs, quotas, subsidies, and other trade barriers.

Gross domestic product. GDP is a measure of final goods and services produced by workers and capital *located in the U.S.* during a single year. GDP is a measure of economic activity actually taking place within U.S. borders. Also see "gross national product."

Gross national product. GNP is the market value of all final goods and services produced by *U.S.-owned* resources, regardless of where they are located, during a single year. *Real* GNP is the value of currently produced goods and services, assessed at prices prevailing in the base year. Gross state product (GSP) is the counterpart to GNP, but applies to individual states. Also see "gross domestic product."

Herfindahl index. A measure of market concentration equal to the sum of squared market shares for all firms in an industry. Also see "concentration ratio."

Heteroskedasticity. A problem in regression analysis in which regression residuals have a nonconstant variance. This problem usually results in large standard errors in coefficient estimates. After detecting heteroskedasticity the problem is corrected by using "weighted least squares" techniques, in which regressions are estimated on weighted values of the original data.

High-powered money stock. See "monetary base."

Hypothesis. A statement that describes a relationship between variables ("concepts"), which can be tested against actual experience (at least conceptually, if not in practice).

I.C.C. Interstate Commerce Commission. The federal agency that regulates ground-based transportation companies (e.g., trains, trucks).

I.M.F. See "International Monetary Fund."

Implicit cost. A cost of taking some action that does not require the actual payment of money. For example, if the owner of a company paints the walls of the establishment for no pay, the value of the time is an implicit cost for the firm. Another implicit cost is the foregone interest on funds belonging to the firm's owner but used by the firm. The lost opportunity to receive this interest is one of the owner's implicit costs of doing business. Economic profits are calculated after deducting both implicit and explicit costs (dollar outlays) from firm revenues.

Implicit price deflator. A price index for all final goods and services. Equal to nominal GDP divided by real GDP, where the latter is currently produced goods valued at base year prices. Implicit price deflators are also calculated for components of GDP such as consumption goods, government purchases, automobiles, etc. The consumption deflator is sometimes used in place of the CPI to gauge changes in the prices of consumer goods.

Index number. A ratio of two values. The numerator of the ratio equals the current value of some economic indicator, while the denominator is the indicator's value in the "base year." The ratio is usually multiplied by 100 for scaling purposes. In this case the index number will equal 200 if the indicator doubles its base-year value.

Index of industrial production. An index of production at the nation's factories, mines and utilities. Only goods (not services) are included in the index. The index reflects real (not dollar) production levels.

Indexation. The act of formally (often contractually) linking wages, rents, interest rates, transfers or other payments to the general price level so their real purchasing power is maintained over time.

Indirect business taxes. Business taxes that are treated as a cost of doing business, e.g., sales and excise taxes, property taxes. Net national product minus i.b.t. equals national income.

Induction. An approach to science in which general laws are inferred from events or observations; reasoning "from specific to general." Also see "deduction."

Industrial production (index of). An index of real production in the nation's factories, mines and utilities. The index includes both final and intermediate production, and excludes services and other activities, so it cannot be compared to GDP. Nevertheless, economists monitor the industrial production index to track the broader economy. Published monthly in the *Federal Reserve Bulletin.*

Industrial policy. A name given to a broad range of policies that would encourage, organize, and subsidize businesses—presumably to increase their competitiveness in world markets. Critics believe business executives turn the policies to their own advantage so the policies produce very few of the promised efficiency gains. Japan, Germany, and many other nations have industrial policies but the U.S. does not have a formal, integrated policy.

Inflation rate. The percentage change in a price index over a one-year period. The December-to-December change is the best measure of inflation during a calendar year.

Input-output table. A table displayed in matrix form (rows and columns) which shows the relationships between all industries and the commodities they produce and use. Among other things, the input-output table can be used to estimate the impact of a $1 change in one industry's output on all other industries.

Interest rate. The ratio between annual income earned on an asset and the value of the asset. Also equal to the income received by a security holder per $1 invested for one year. Also see "time preference."

Interest risk. The decline in the present value of a bond that occurs when market interest rates rise. The inverse relationship between present value and interest rates also applies to certificates of deposit, mortgages, and other assets whose nominal future values are fixed in advance. The loss may not be immediately apparent for assets whose market prices are not published. Decreases in interest rates cause the present value fixed-income assets to increase. See also "default risk."

International Monetary Fund (I.M.F.). International monetary organization whose objective is to encourage the stable exchange of currencies and to promote balanced growth of international trade. It does so by providing technical assistance to nations that request it and by making temporary loans to countries experiencing balance of payments difficulties. Also see "Bretton Woods."

Investment spending. Business purchases of new structures and producers' durable equipment, the value of new residential construction, and inventory accumulation. Investment is an addition to the stock of capital goods.

Invisible hand. A proposition popularized by Adam Smith (in *The Wealth of Nations*) that in voluntary transactions (market settings) the self-interested behavior of an individual buyer or seller also benefits the other party to the transaction. The trader is "led by an invisible hand to promote an end which was no part of his intention."

J-Curve. A graph of a nation's international trade balance (in dollars) over time. Following the devaluation (depreciation) of a nation's currency, the nation's trade balance initially worsens and then improves. The downward-then-upward curve that traces the trade balance through time resembles the letter "J." The trade balance initially worsens because of relatively small short-run price elasticities of demand.

Keynesians/fiscalists. Economists who believe that fluctuations in private spending, particularly investment spending, are responsible for most swings in the business cycle. This group advocates government spending and tax policies to offset fluctuations in private spending and smooth the business cycle. They believe that the private economy is inherently unstable.

Labor productivity. Usually measured as output per hour of work. As such, it is a measure of average productivity.

Laffer curve. A curve that reflects the relationship between the marginal tax rate and total tax collections. Higher tax rates initially increase total collections, but eventually higher tax rates reduce the incentive to earn taxable income sufficiently to cause total tax collections to decline. The implication is that a 10% reduction in tax rates will cause total tax collections to decline by less than 10%, or may actually cause tax collections to increase.

Law of one price. An implication of supply and demand theory. If goods can be shifted between markets, then a price differential between two locations will cause sellers to withdraw supplies from the low-price market and move them to the high-price market. The relative supply shifts cause prices to move toward equality. In the absence of transportation costs, the prices will be equal.

Leading economic indicators, index of (LEI). The leading indicators index is an index number that summarizes movements in 11 key statistics that typically peak and turn down shortly before the national economy enters a recession, then bottom and turn up shortly before the national economy recovers from a recession. Three consecutive decreases in the index are often interpreted as a signal that a recession is imminent. See also "coincident economic indicators."

Limited dependent variable. A dependent variable whose value is constrained within a narrow range, e.g., a variable that ranges between 0% and 100%. Special methods must be used when limited dependent variables are used in regression analysis.

Liquidity. A characteristic of an asset. Liquidity refers to the ability of the asset holder to convert it into cash on short notice at low cost. A bank checking account is more liquid than real estate.

Loanable funds model. A theory of interest rates. In this theory the interest rate is the price of credit and is determined by the intersection of the demand and supply of loanable funds (or credit).

Lorenz curve. A graphical representation of the distribution of income among various income groups. The Gini coefficient is a numerical measure of income equality derived from the Lorenz curve. If Gini = 0, income is distributed equally among all groups; if Gini = 1, all income is held by the single richest group. In practice, the U.S. Gini coefficient is about 0.37 and that of France is about 0.42.

Luxury. A good for which the wealth (or income) elasticity of demand is greater than one.

Marginal cost. The cost incurred when producing one more unit of a good. When several units are produced simultaneously, MC equals the incremental costs or expanding output divided by the number of additional units produced. Assuming only one variable factor of production, MC equals the factor's price divided by its marginal productivity.

Marginal productivity theory of wages. A theory that explains why factor prices can be expected to equal the market value of the incremental output produced by the last unit of the factor hired.

Marginal propensity to consume. The MPC is the share (expressed in decimals) of an incremental dollar's worth of disposable income used to purchase goods Saving accounts for the remainder of the incremental income, so the marginal propensity to save (MPS) = 1 − MPC.

Marginal tax rate. The percentage share of an additional $1 of income that must be paid in taxes. For the federal income tax, the marginal rate on the top income earners was 91% in 1963 and declined in stages to 28% in the late 1980s. As a result of legislation passed in 1993, the top federal income tax rate rose to 39.6%.

Marketing policies. Activities undertaken to increase or decrease unit sales of some good. Marketing policies affect one or more of the "5 P's of Marketing": Price, Product (quality), Package, Promotion (advertising), and Place (location). Economists typically examine cases when only the first of these policies (price) is used to manage sales volume.

Mean. The "average" value of a series of data. If a series includes 3, 5, and 22, the mean equals 10.

Median. The middle value of a series of data. If a series includes 3, 5, and 22, the median equals 5.

Median price change. A method of measuring economywide inflationary forces. The U.S. Department of Labor reports an inflation rate for each major component of the CPI market basket (housing, food, transportation, medical care, apparel, entertainment, other). Some believe that the median of these rates is a more reliable indicator of inflationary pressures than an average of all seven, which includes one-time shocks unlikely to be repeated (caused by bad weather, wars, and microeconomic conditions).

Methodological individualism. An approach to economic analysis which insists that theoretical models should focus on individual behavior. Groups are comprised of individuals, so group activity is also understood by focusing on decisions by the group's individual members. Under this approach it is assumed that individual decision makers are motivated by self-interest.

Minimum wage. A mandated wage level below which workers may not be paid. Most attention is given to the federal minimum wage, which applies to companies engaged in interstate commerce. Many states also have minimum wage laws. The federal minimum wage was originally authorized by the Fair Labor Standards Act of 1938.

Misery index. A number equal to the inflation rate plus the unemployment rate, both expressed as whole numbers, e.g., the misery index is 10 if the inflation rate equals 4% and the unemployment rate equals 6%. Also called the "discomfort index."

Monetarists. A group of economists who believe that changes in money supply growth are responsible for swings in total spending and (therefore) major fluctuations in the business cycle and inflation rate.

Monetary base. Total bank reserves plus currency held by the public. The monetary base multiplied by the money multiplier equals the money supply. Also called the "high-powered money stock."

Monetize the debt. An action by the central bank to purchase government bonds from private holders to reduce the government's interest costs. This policy replaces government debt by money and is thought to contribute to inflation.

Money center bank. A major banking concern with approximately $50 billion or more in assets and operations extending into several states and countries. There are about a dozen U.S. banks in this group. Money center banks aggressively seek deposits from major customers and compete vigorously with other banks to make loans to large businesses and governments. See "bank" and "regional bank."

Money. Any good that is generally accepted in exchange for goods and services. This corresponds to the Fed's M-1 money supply. M-1 includes currency, traveler's checks, and checking accounts at banks and other depository institutions. Currently, M-1 is about $1,200 billion. Broader measures of the money supply (M-2 and M-3) include savings-type accounts, money market mutual fund balances, and other assets. Most economists have M-1 in mind when they say "money" or "money supply."

Money growth rule. A policy proposal supported by monetarist economists. This rule would require the money supply to grow at a constant percentage rate every year, e.g., 4%. See "monetarist."

Money multiplier. The ratio between the money supply and the monetary base; equal to the number of dollars of money supply resulting from a $1 increase in the monetary base. The multiplier is inversely related to the size of the required reserve ratio on checking deposits.

Monopoly. The only seller of a good or service with no close substitutes.

Monopsony. The only buyer of a good or service in a given market area. A "buyer's monopoly."

Moral hazard. When one party insures a second party against certain costs or unfavorable events, the second party has less incentive to avoid losses. The second party's reaction to the new set of incentives imposes costs on the insurance provider. This is the moral hazard problem. To minimize costs, the insurance provider may try to constrain the behavior of the insured party or provide incentives to the insured party to limit the risks taken.

Multicollinearity. A problem in regression analysis where two or more independent variables are correlated with each other. This makes individual coefficient estimates unreliable.

Multiplier. The Keynesian spending multiplier (k) equals one divided by the marginal propensity to *not* spend income on goods produced within the "home" economy. For a national economy without induced investment, imports, or taxes, $k = 1 \div MPS$, where MPS is the marginal propensity to save.

N.L.R.B. The National Labor Relations Board. The federal agency responsible for administering labor laws. Created by legislation passed in the 1930s.

National debt. The unpaid debt of the federal government, accumulated over all years up to the present. The outstanding national debt now exceeds $4 trillion. The national debt increases each year the federal budget is in deficit. See "deficit (budget)" and "burden of the debt."

National income. Income earned by owners of productive inputs. National income equals compensation of employees plus proprietors' income plus corporate profits plus rental income plus net interest income. Part of the national income and product accounts (NIPA).

Natural rate of unemployment. The minimum unemployment rate consistent with price stability; the unemployment rate when cyclical unemployment equals zero. Currently the natural rate of unemployment is believed to be about 5–6%. Economists believe that the natural rate of unemployment can be lowered through *micro*economic policies such as lowering the minimum wage and reducing economic regulation, but not through macroeconomic policies.

Neoclassical economics. The body of economic thought that began with Alfred Marshall's publication of his *Principles of Economics* (1890) and is the style of economic analysis used most often today.

Net interest margin. The difference between the average interest rate earned on bank assets and the average rate paid by banks to obtain funds. The net interest margin is a key measure of bank performance. In recent years the net interest margin has averaged 3.5–4%.

New Deal. A series of programs adopted in the 1930s. Proposed by President Franklin Roosevelt and legislated by Congress, these programs greatly increased the government's involvement in the economy. New Deal policies included Social Security, unemployment compensation, and public works projects.

Nondurable good. A good whose expected "life" is shorter than three years. Examples include food and clothing. See "durable good."

O.P.E.C. The Organization of Petroleum Exporting Countries. A group of nations that produce oil and sell it in international energy markets. Most of the nations are in the Middle East, but some are from other regions. See "cartel."

Occam's razor. A principle stated by William of Occam (or Ockham), a fourteenth-century British philosopher. According to Occam's razor, if there are multiple solutions to a problem one should choose the simplest one; if there are two explanations for a phenomenon one should prefer the simplest (least complicated) one.

Okun's Law. A rule of thumb that relates real GDP growth to changes in the unemployment rate. According to Arthur Okun, who served on President Johnson's Council of Economic Advisors, a 3% increase in real GDP corresponds to a 1% decrease in the unemployment rate.

Open market operations. Purchases and sales of government securities by the Federal Reserve. These transactions inject funds into or remove funds from official bank reserves. Typically, the national money supply changes in the same direction as bank reserves. Open market operations are the Fed's most commonly used policy to control the money supply.

P-star (P^*). A version of the Quantity Theory of Money used by some economists to forecast the inflation rate. P^* is the "equilibrium" price level for the economy. If the actual price level (P) differs from P^*, it is assumed that inflation will accelerate or decelerate until $P = P^*$. P-star is calculated from the quantity equation: $P^* = (M2 \times V_2) \div Q^*$, where $M2$ refers to the broadly defined money supply measure, V_2 is the long-term average velocity for $M2$ (about 1.65), and Q^* is potential real GDP.

Permanent income hypothesis. Milton Friedman's theory that consumption expenditures are a function of the long-term income of individual consumers. Long-term income may be only slightly affected by variation in current income, so a person whose income is temporarily below normal will continue to spend about the same amount as before. Franco Modigliani's life cycle hypothesis provides a similar theory of consumption patterns.

Personal income. Total income received by persons from all sources minus social security taxes and other "contributions" for social insurance. Personal income includes transfer payments and is calculated before the payment of personal income taxes. Personal income figures are also available for individual states and counties (in the *Survey of Current Business*).

Phillips curve. A curve that shows the trade-off that a nation's policy makers face between inflation and unemployment. To reduce unemployment, it may be necessary to tolerate higher levels of inflation (and vice versa). Some economists believe that the Phillips curve is vertical in the long run; stimulative policies create more inflation but do not permanently lower the unemployment rate.

Potential real GDP. A measure of the output the economy is capable of producing when all of its resources are fully employed. This measure is an estimate and grows at a rate that reflects growth in the labor force, changes in technology, and changes in other factors that shift the nation's production possibilities frontier outward. It is estimated that potential real GDP currently grows at a 2–2.5% annual rate, which is below the growth rate of earlier decades.

Present value. The number of dollars required today in order to accumulate a given sum by a defined future date. The higher the interest rate earned on funds, the lower the present value of the future amount (and vice versa). See Appendix 9.

Price elasticity of demand. A coefficient indicating the percentage change in consumption of a good resulting from a 1% change in the price of the good. The coefficient is negative for downward sloping demand curves. An elasticity coefficient whose absolute value is greater than one is "elastic" and a coefficient whose absolute value is less than one is "inelastic."

Principal-agent problem. A problem observed when one person (the principal) hires another person (the agent) to represent him or her. If the agent does not have adequate incentives to act in the principal's interest, he or she may seek private gain at the expense of the principal's wealth. For example, if a corporate manager (agent) prefers the easy life rather than working to cut expenses to the bone, this erodes the profits earned by shareholders (principals). See "moral hazard."

Private property. A setting in which property rights are owned by an individual who can deny others the right to use a particular asset, charge for its use, or sell it. Since the entire value of the asset belongs to the individual owner, that person has a personal incentive to maximize its value.

Producer price index (PPI). A price index of goods at intermediate stages of production, once referred to as the wholesale price index (WPI). The PPI is considered by many to be a leading indicator for the CPI, but the PPI market basket does not include services (as the CPI's does).

Production function. The relationship between the quantity of productive inputs employed and the quantity of output produced. See "Cobb-Douglas production function."

Productivity. Generally measured by the average output per unit of some resource, e.g., the value of production per hour of work. In contrast, most economic theories of productivity concentrate on the *marginal* productivity of resources.

Property rights. The rights held by humans over the ownership and use of property (assets). Owners may have the right to use property, to modify/change it, to charge for its use, or to sell it. These rights are distinct, so an owner may have some rights without possessing them all. See "private property" and "common property."

Public choice. A subdiscipline of economics that uses economic analysis to examine political behavior by voters, elected officials, and unelected government employees (bureaucrats).

Public good. The attribute that some goods have to provide simultaneous benefits to more than one consumer, e.g., national defense or mosquito extermination. Markets fail to provide an efficient quantity of nonexcludable public goods if consumers free ride rather than pay for the benefits they receive.

Purchasing power parity (PPP). A theory of exchange rates. According to the theory, exchange rates will adjust until a given basket of goods in one country costs the same as the basket in another country. For example, if a basket of goods costs $10 in the U.S. and £5 in Britain, then PPP predicts a dollar-pound exchange rate of $2 = £1. (See "exchange rates.")

Quantity theory of money. Pre-Keynesian macroeconomic theory. According to the theory, the economywide price level is proportional to the quantity of money in the economy. Adherents of this model assumed that price flexibility keeps the economy near full employment equilibrium at all times. The theory is formalized in the equation of exchange: $M \times V = P \times Q$.

Quota. A quantitative (numerical) limit on the quantity of goods that can be imported into a nation or sold in a particular market. Quotas are usually imposed to limit the supply of a good for the benefit of domestic producers. Marketing quotas limit the quantity of certain fruits sold in domestic markets by domestic growers. Quotas typically impose a far larger cost on consumers than the gain realized by protected producers.

R^2. See "coefficient of determination."

Random walk theory. A theory of the stock market. According to the theory, current stock prices reflect all of the good and bad news about a company currently held by all speculators. This implies that investors cannot earn above average returns over a series of investments. Economists have more faith in this theory than most noneconomists.

Rational expectations. A theory of inflation forecasts in which the individual considers all relevant information (variables). The information cost of forming rational expectations exceeds that of adaptive expectations, but rational expectations presumably yield more accurate forecasts. Among other things, the theory of rational expectations suggests that policy makers cannot easily "fool" workers, lenders, or other market participants about the consequences of macroeconomic policies.

Real balance effect. The increase in consumer spending that occurs as a result of a decrease in the overall price level. The price level decrease increases the real value of the money supply and therefore increases the wealth of consumers holding money balances. Also called the "Pigou effect."

Real business cycle theory. A theory of the business cycle which asserts that fluctuations in the real economy are the result of exogenous shocks in technology, tastes, and other factors that affect aggregate supply. In this theory aggregate demand is powerless to affect the real economy unless it affects the supply side of the economy.

Recession. A recession is a broad-based decline in the pace of national economic activity. An unofficial definition is a two-quarter decline in real GDP. The National Bureau of Economic Research (NBER) officially dates the beginning and end of recessions. Before World War II, recessions were called depressions.

Reductionism. A logical fallacy in which conclusions about individual behavior are based on observations of some unit of analysis other than individuals.

Regional bank. A medium-size banking company whose operations extend into several states. In recent years mergers between regional banks have created superregional banks that are nearly as large and often as aggressive as money center banks. The smallest banks, community banks, usually confine their operations to a single city or county. Community banks typically have only a few million dollars in assets. Many of these banks have been acquired or merged in recent years. Also see "bank" and "money center bank."

Regression analysis. A statistical technique that estimates the relationship between a dependent variable and one or more independent variables.

Regression coefficient. A (constant) numerical value estimated in regression analysis for each independent variable. The coefficients indicate the unit change in the dependent variable that occurs for each one-unit change in the corresponding explanatory (independent) variable. Coefficients are partial derivatives of the regression equation.

Regulation Q. A Federal Reserve rule that sets maximum levels on bank deposit interest rates. These maximums were far below market levels in the 1970s and early 1980s. By 1986, banks were permitted to pay market-determined interest rates on all accounts except demand deposits, which earn 0%.

Rent seeking. Actions taken to increase the probability of receiving a wealth transfer, usually by influencing government policy. Rent seeking includes hiring lobbyists, writing letters to legislators, and other acts. Transfer payments redistribute wealth rather than create it, so the costs of rent seeking reduce the total wealth of society. See "economic rent."

Replication. The act of duplicating the results of an empirical study. Beginning with the same data set, a researcher attempts to reproduce the statistical results of an earlier researcher.

Risk premium (interest rates). The additional interest charged on loans with greater default risk to compensate lenders for the greater likelihood of not being repaid. One measure is the yield on Baa corporation bonds minus the yield on corporate Aaa bonds. When lenders anticipate a recession they shift funds from more risky loans to less risky loans, causing the Baa-Aaa interest premium to increase. Therefore, some economists interpret an increase in the risk premium as a sign that lenders anticipate a recession. Also see "default risk."

Rule of 72. The Rule of 72 is a rule of thumb about the conditions under which an investment will double in value. The Rule of 72 is expressed by the formula: $72 = r \times t$. Here, r is the annual growth rate of earnings (or the annual interest rate), expressed as a whole number rather than a decimal (so $7\% = 7$ rather than 0.07), and t is the number of years required for the investment to double in value (assuming no interest or dividends are collected before that time). If $r = 6$, the investment will double in about $72 \div 6 = 12$ years. An investment that doubles in 18 years earns a $72 \div 18 = 4\%$ annual rate of return.

Sample selection error. An error committed in research when an improper sample is selected by the researcher; then, survey results do not reflect the behavior of the entire population.

Self-selection. A bias in statistical research which results when individuals select or recruit themselves into a group. Error may result if observations from that group are used to test theories about the behavior of a "typical" individual.

Serial correlation. A problem in time series regressions. The problem exists when residuals from the regression exhibit a "pattern." Serial correlation reflects a situation in which current observations are affected by past observations, e.g., through inertia. The problem is indicated by a "high" or "low" Durbin-Watson statistic. Statistically the problem may be indistinguishable from a case in which a key explanatory variable is excluded from the regression or in which a linear regression equation is fitted to a nonlinear relationship. Also called *autocorrelation*.

Shadow Open Market Committee. A group of academic and business economists that meet periodically to evaluate the Federal Reserve's conduct of monetary policy. The Committee tends to favor monetarist-type monetary policies (slow and steady money growth).

Sherman Act. A 1890 antitrust law that outlaws attempts to monopolize an industry or engage in a "restraint of trade." Also see "antitrust policy."

SIC code. The Standard Industry Classification code is a numbering system used by government bureaus and economists to identify industries. The system assigns a two-digit code to broad industries ("22

Household furniture"), then subdivides the industry into more narrowly defined industries ("22.03 Metal household furniture," "22.04 Mattresses and bedsprings"). In many cases the more narrowly defined industries are themselves subdivided, and additional digits are added to the SIC code to reflect the greater degree of specificity ("22.0103 Wood TV and radio cabinets"). Government agencies often release industry data grouped by SIC code.

Significance test. A statistical test that estimates the likelihood that one number is "significantly" different from another number. The specific test depends on the statistical exercise being carried out. Examples of significance tests are the t-test, F-test, and z-test. In general, the t-, F-, or z-statistic is the difference in two numbers divided by the standard error of estimate. If this ratio exceeds (about) 2.0, the analyst can be 95% certain that the difference between the two numbers is "significant."

Special interest legislation. Laws passed for the benefit of interest groups, usually by imposing small per capita costs on the general population.

Spreadsheet. A software program used to carry out numerical calculations with minimal effort. Most spreadsheet programs can graph data into pie, bar, and line charts.

Stock index. See "Dow Jones Industrial Average."

Supply-side economists. A group of economists who believe that major changes in real economic activity are mainly caused by changes in marginal tax rates and various government regulations that affect the costs of conducting business.

Surplus (federal budget). See "deficit (budget)."

Surplus (international transactions). See "deficit (international transactions)."

Takeover. A financial transaction that permits an investor (the "suitor" or "raider") to gain control of some company (the "target") by buying a controlling interest in its stock. Reasons for takeovers include management inefficiency at the target firm, a desire to achieve economies of scale, or the expectation of speculative profits when the target firm's market valuation dips below its perceived worth. When managers of target firms try to block takeovers, the suitor attempts a "hostile" takeover. Takeovers became common in the 1980s because of less aggressive antitrust policies and the easy availability of credit to suitors.

Tariff. A tax on imported goods and services. Tariffs can be levied on each unit of import or against the dollar value of imports. Tariffs are usually levied to protect domestic producers from competition by foreign producers. (The revenues raised by tariffs are comparatively small.)

Tax Freedom Day. Used to mark the share of annual income taken by government taxes. If taxes absorb 25% of income, those who calculate Tax Freedom Day assume that for the first 25% of the year people work for government rather than for their own benefit. Calculations include federal, state, and local taxes. Today, Tax Freedom Day is about May 10. In 1984, following the first round of Reagan tax cuts, Tax Freedom Day was April 29.

Time preference, rate of. The percentage amount by which goods today are preferred to the same goods one year from today. A 10% rate of time preference means that $1 today has the same present value as the certain promise of $1.10 to be received next year. Individuals will increase or decrease their share of income saved until, in equilibrium, their rate of time preference equals the interest rate earned on savings.

Time series data set. A series of data drawn from various points in time, usually separated by fixed interval (such as months, quarters or years). Time series data are assumed to provide useful experience that can be used in hypothesis testing. Also see "cross section data set."

Transaction cost. The cost of arranging a transaction. Includes the cost of locating a trading partner, conducting negotiations, and ensuring compliance with the agreement. If transaction costs exceed the net benefits from a proposed exchange, the exchange is prevented from taking place. Many economic institutions exist to lower transaction costs (e.g., money).

Transfer payments. A payment for which nothing is given in return. Examples include some or all of the funds distributed as farm subsidies, Social Security benefits, and Medicaid benefits. Also see "economic rent."

Underground economy. Unreported economic activity. A transaction is not reported because it is illegal or because parties to the transaction wish to avoid paying taxes on it.

VAT. Value-added tax. A type of sales tax applied at each stage of production in proportion to the value added by the producer. The tax can be collected at each stage of production or by the application of a sales tax imposed at the retail level. Most European nations have a VAT.

Wage differential. A difference in wages between different jobs, or between different workers performing the same job. In competitive labor markets the former wage difference is typically caused by differences in the supply of workers to various jobs, while the latter is typically caused by differences in the productivity of individual workers. Other wage differences may be the result of nonmarket considerations, including but not limited to discrimination.

Wage-price controls. A policy that outlaws changes in wages and prices. In less extreme cases, they outlaw changes greater than a certain percentage amount. Wage-price controls were last imposed by presidential order on August 15, 1971 (by President Nixon). The price "freeze" was gradually removed in several "Phases" extending over three years. Other presidents have attempted to "jawbone" the inflation rate down by asking/telling/threatening corporate managers and union leaders not to increase prices and wages. Studies have shown that controls have little long-run impact on the price level, but may temporarily lower the inflation rate.

Welfare programs. A term that includes several government transfer programs including aid to poor families (AFDC) and medical assistance (Medicaid). Government transfer payments to medium- and high-income Americans are not usually described as welfare, despite their functional equivalence.

Windfall profits tax (oil). The windfall profits tax (1970s–1980s) on oil was a charge on the price of domestically produced oil in excess of a target amount. For example, if the target price of oil is $10 per barrel and the actual price is $16, the tax would be levied on $6. As such, the tax was an excise (sales) tax rather than a profits tax.

X-efficiency. A theory of firm management. In the theory, corporate managers permit less than efficient operations to satisfy other goals such as personal leisure. Also see "principal-agent problem."

Yield curve. A curve formed by plotting bond yields on a graph that measures years to maturity along the horizontal axis and yield along the vertical axis. The yield curve typically slopes upward, indicating that higher yields are earned on longer-term securities. Some economists believe that a negatively sloped yield curve indicates that the economy is experiencing, or is about to experience, a recession.

INDEX